DRINKSTONE – SCHOOL AND VILLAGE

DRINKSTONE
SCHOOL AND VILLAGE
A Suffolk History

SHEILA WRIGHT

GREENRIDGES PRESS

ISBN
1 902019 08 3
Published November 2005

British Library Cataloguing in Publication Data.
A catalogue record for this book is
available from the British Library.

Published by
Greenridges Press
13 Vale Road, Hartford,
Northwich, Cheshire CW8 1PL
Great Britain

Websites: www.greenridgespress.co.uk
www.leoniepress.com

Printed and bound by Antony Rowe Ltd

CONTENTS

PREFACE

THIS HISTORY HAS been a pleasure to research, and I hope those who read it will enjoy what they find. It is longer than I had anticipated but I hope there is something to interest anyone who opens it. I've tried to give titles to the chapters that will help readers select the sections of most interest to them.

My initial intention was simply to write a history of the School. I had expected that the contents would derive mainly from Archive material – the Log Book, the three books of Managers' Minutes, the Admission Register and so on. However I began to talk with folk connected with the School and became fascinated by their personal stories. They were riveting, and everyone was so open and honest in what they told me. They told about their time at the School, but they told so much more: whole life-stories with details too engrossing to be left out.

I therefore decided to sandwich the basic historical facts of each era with "personal stories" relevant to that era of School history. The facts are not confined to School affairs. School affairs are the core of the book, but I have included general village events and changes as well. These are unique because they relate to a particular place and its people, but they are also typical of events and changes in thousands of other small schools and villages over the same period.

Because I was told entire life-stories, from the cradle to the grave, some personal accounts cover far longer periods of time than is covered by each chapter of archive facts. But I did not want to chop up people's stories, they are just too good, and carry us into the past – into country childhoods, classroom fun, sorrows and mischief, hard times, war experiences, and much more – all weathered with courage and humour. So there is an overlapping of time covered by each chapter. I have tried to present the School in its context of time and place.

Since I was aiming for a rounded picture of main players in the story, I have not shown them as angels. I have tried to show them as human beings, not perfect, but good in parts, as we all are! I hope readers will appreciate that a teacher's days in a small school are not always easy; teachers can be lonely, bored, grumpy, weary and uninspired some days, and may long for other adult company. Children are not angels either, and can be rude, lazy, rebellious and downright naughty! (In the interests of diplomacy, I didn't include all that was told me!) I sincerely hope that nothing written in this book will hurt or offend any reader.

Attitudes have changed radically over the centuries. In Victorian times, when the School was built, "spare the rod and spoil the child" was the approved view. Both at home and at school, corporal punishment was the norm. Children were told to respect and obey their "elders and betters" and were not surprised when asked to carry out all sorts of tasks both at home and at school, that are not the lot of today's children. So sometimes there is a touch of "Dotheboys Hall" in the recollections of older folk! But times have changed, and are still changing – that's the nature of our world.

I have never lived in Drinkstone. I don't know all the residents, or all the history. No doubt things that are important to some readers have been left out. For this I apologise.

Thank you to everyone who helped, to those who suggested folk to be interviewed, to those who took the trouble to write to me, and to those who lent me their precious old books and photos. Special thanks are due to Sheila Beswick of Drinkstone Local History Group for the generous loan of her fantastic collection of facts and photographs.

Thank you to my husband Ron, for encouraging me to press on and finish a project that kept me stuck at the computer for hours, and took me away from home time after time to talk with people he has never met, or to scribble notes in the Record Office. Thank you to Peter Davidson and Roy Arthey for being patient with me when they got an S.O.S. because I'm a computer simpleton. Sometimes my work chose to lurk in dark recesses of the computer under an assumed name and I needed help to find it!

Thank you to the people of Drinkstone and district, for your helpfulness, friendliness and hospitality, and for the cups of tea and tasty snacks that came my way! Please forgive me for not mentioning everybody who helped me by name.

Thank you to Anne and Jack Loader, friends and publishers, for their excellent work. Now read on!

Sheila Wright
March 2005

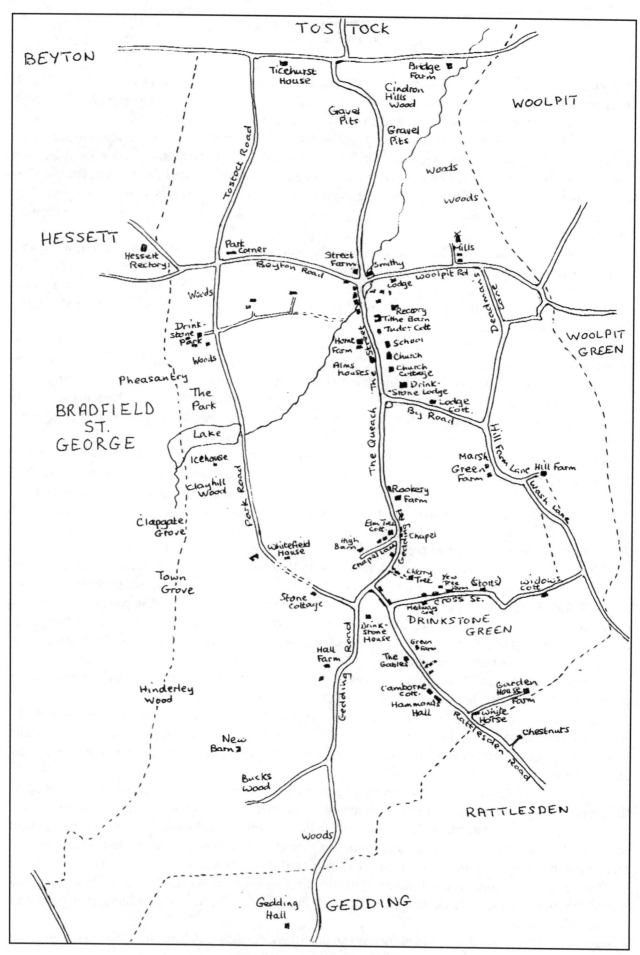

Drinkstone Parish circa 1900

Chapter One

MY FIRST VISIT TO DRINKSTONE

IN SEPTEMBER 1981 I was an unemployed teacher. I still had five children living at home, the eldest two boys being at university. My youngest daughter was approaching her eighth birthday. The time had come for me to find a job!

I had taught during the previous six months at Witnesham Primary, and for a year before that at Thomas Wolsely School in Ipswich. Both these had been temporary "Maternity Supply" posts. Witnesham had been a lovely experience, a spaciously designed village school in huge grounds with delightful staff and pupils, in which I particularly enjoyed taking music (the teacher I was standing in for was in charge of music, and I took over her duties). My classroom had its own door to the leafy grounds among the fields. Sometimes I would take my class of seven and eight year-olds outside to sit on the grass at story time. There was a sense of freedom in small village schools in those days, before the "National Curriculum".

My situation was that however much I enjoyed a "maternity" post, since these were temporary I just had to move on. The time had come to look again. I found an advertisement for a temporary teacher to take the infant class at Drinkstone School. I had never come across the name "Drinkstone" before, and the thought of becoming second teacher in a school of only 28 pupils immediately appealed!

Studying my map of West Suffolk, I discovered the village tucked away just south of the A45 road (now the A14), and sent off my application. A few weeks later, thrilled at being invited for interview, I set off towards Haughley Park, familiar with the first part of the route. What a shock when I reached the junction with the newly duelled A45 to find I couldn't access the westbound carriageway there! My heart sank to my boots as I turned the car around, had another look at the map, and set off towards Elmswell, where a roundabout and flyover enabled me to cross the A45 to Woolpit village, and find the winding lane to Drinkstone. I was thinking, I'll never get the job now, I must be late!

But when I found the School, parked my car in the shade of the churchyard trees and walked up the steep path to the Schoolhouse door, I immediately sensed that I had come to a special corner of the world, a place that would certainly be special for me. A squirrel scampered across my path; the softest of murmurings, like the sound of busy honey bees, came from the quaint red-brick building; all was serene and somehow timeless.

I knocked on the door in the tiny entrance porch with its graceful lancet windows, feeling my spirits lift and optimism return. I was greeted by Headteacher Mrs. Shirley Hall, and made to feel immediately at home. She led me into the large classroom, where twenty-eight small children sat pleasantly chatting over their dinners. At a word from their teacher, they all stopped talking and looked at her with total trust in their eyes – it felt just like a large family, everyone knowing everyone else and at ease together.

At my interview (a hazy memory now after twenty-four years) I believe a representative from the Education Office was present. But the folk I remember (besides Shirley Hall) were governors, Geoffrey Wilding and the Rev. Nicholas Cribb. They were thoughtful, kindly men, who made me feel I was among friends. Somehow we seemed to be on the same wave-length, and I was thrilled to be offered the job.

I was introduced to Mrs. Cathy Scott, the infant teacher currently expecting her first baby. Her classroom, with its beautiful arched window, pictures, sand and water play and home corner, felt like a friendly and stimulating place for children. I went home exhilarated, and started eager preparations for what lay ahead.

I started work in October. Cathy decided not to return after her baby was born, so the job became permanent. I was there for five years. Heads came and went – Shirley Hall took a post at Bacton School, and was replaced by Kevin Connolly. It was a new experience for the children to have a man as their teacher, and he had some exciting new ideas, such as our first (and last!) school camp – an adventure for the children but pretty exhausting for the staff! He went on to be Head of Woolpit School. On his departure, Mrs. Maggie Barber was sent by the Office to take over as temporary Head. The writing was well and truly on the wall by now and the School was definitely marked for closure. A later section of this book tells the story of the valiant efforts by parents, governors and others, who fought to save Drinkstone School. When Maggie Barber found a permanent post as Head elsewhere, after only one term at Drinkstone, I agreed to be Acting Head of Drinkstone for its final four terms.

During that last school year, 1985-6, the children did intensive research into the history of the village and School. Mrs. Sylvia Taylor, teacher of the junior class, was an enthusiastic and experienced history buff and knew how to go about this task, so between us all we produced a very creditable end-of-school exhibition (more is said of this later in the book). I studied the Log Book avidly in preparation for the exhibition; so when (many years later) Sheila Beswick asked me to give a talk to Drinkstone Local History Group about the School, I had some idea where to start. I dug out all my papers, records and photo albums again. Paddy Blackburn, who had in the past been a great friend and supporter of everything and everyone at the School, came with me to Bury St. Edmunds Records Office, and was an invaluable help to me, a research novice!

Preparing the talk was a marvellous experience for me. Good and bad times, happy and sad, came flooding back. I shook the cobwebs from my memories, and as the days went by I found that the names and individuality of those endearing little pupils came back to me as if it had all happened yesterday. I was not around to see these children grow and change and mature into adults, so to me they are frozen in time, never a day older than when I last saw them.

The revived memories, plus fresh discoveries, fascinated me, and I began to feel that this was a story worth telling – not only to the local history buffs, but more widely. How I regretted the time that had elapsed since the closure; years during which old folk who might have told stories of the School from before the 1900s, all passed on. Sadly, those three whom I best remember from my interview are all gone too. Geoffrey Wilding died in 2003, Shirley Hall and Nicholas Cribb even earlier. They had set the tone for a School in which children were listened to and valued. I am sure that children's early experience, and the way they are treated by those around them, has a huge impact on their lives for good or ill.

So, on with the story! I offer this history as an attempt to describe something important in the lives of many children and their families, something now definitely of the past, but hopefully never to be forgotten: just one small village school out of the thousands that educated Britain's children, together with a picture of its village.

Chapter Two

EARLY HISTORY OF THE REGION

THIS CHAPTER gives a brief history of East Anglia, Suffolk and Drinkstone up to the mid-19th century.

The earliest known settlers in East Anglia date from the Palaeolithic period. The areas we know as Breckland and Sandling were well populated by the Bronze Age, and settlement increased during the Iron Age. The countryside was lush and fertile, low undulating land with no large rocks to contend with, only flints. It was (and still is!) mostly chalky boulder clay, with loam and marshland forming river margins.

In the earliest recorded times, the land was inhabited by the Iceni people. Under Roman occupation, which began in the first century after Christ, Suffolk formed part of the province of Flavia. The Romans built numerous villas and, of course, roads, which were the foundation of a trade and communications system linking inhabited areas. The Romans introduced Christianity to the people.

After the collapse of the Roman Empire, during the fourth and fifth centuries invading Angles occupied the land, which became part of the Kingdom of East Anglia. Sigeberht, King of the East Angles, founded a monastery circa 630 where Bury St. Edmunds now stands. The township became known as Bedricesworth. In 654, Penda, King of Mercia, attacked the East Anglians and slew their King in a battle fought near Blytheburgh.

During the ninth century Danish invaders ravaged the coast, its low sandy cliffs and river inlets making it easy prey. In 871 (or a year or two earlier) they defeated and took prisoner Edmund, King of East Anglia, whom they put to death for refusing to renounce Christianity. His body was removed from Hoxne, where (according to gruesome legend!) he met his death, to Bedricesworth, hence re-named "Bury St. Edmunds". A later King Edmund gave the land surrounding the shrine of the martyred Edmund to the town.

The culture and architecture brought by the Angles is commonly known as "Saxon" or "Anglo-Saxon", despite the fact that it was the Angles who lived in this eastern county. There was a Church, probably built of wood, on the site of the present All Saints' Church in Drinkstone, before the Norman Conquest. The Norman conquerors brought French influences to our culture, although Latin remained for years the language of Church and law. Norman architectural features remain in countless local Churches and buildings, such as Moyse's Hall in Bury St. Edmunds. All Saints' Church in Drinkstone possesses a font of Purbeck marble which dates from the 12th century.

By medieval times the county boasted markets, towns, ports, churches, monasteries and castles, some of which heritage remains for us to enjoy today. The civil structure was based on ecclesiastical boundaries and groups. In medieval times, there were at least 500 ecclesiastical parishes. The first local Bishop was based at Dunwich. In the late 11th century Suffolk became part of the Diocese of Norwich. The Archdeaconry of Suffolk was sub-divided in 1125 into Eastern and Western parts. These were subdivided into Rural Deaneries, which more or less corresponded with the twenty secular "Hundreds". The Parish of Drinkstone lies in Thedwastre Hundred.

Agriculture locally focused on barley, flax, sheep and cattle; producing linen, malt for brewing, wool, leather, milk and meat. The woods south of Drinkstone belonged to the Abbey, and were a source of venison and other game, wood for fuel, fencing and building, and fish from the large farmed ponds which still survive amidst the ancient woodland. When I was teaching at the School we often took the children to these woods, where coppicing and other traditional skills are still practised. The woods shelter masses of bluebells and various species of orchid.

DOMESDAY RECORDS

It is fascinating to read about Drinkstone village in Domesday excerpts. The name "Drinkstone" is thought to have originally meant "Dremic's homestead". In the earliest written records it is variously written as Rengestuna, Drenkestuna, and Drincestona. Three entries for 1087 refer to lands in the Parish. Under King William, estates centred on Halls or Manorial houses were given to barons or abbots, who became "Lords of the Manor" and ruled over a demesne or estate. These Lords paid homage to the King and were expected to support him in battle, and they paid a "geld" or tax to the crown for their land holding.

The land was worked by ordinary folk who held allegiance to their local Lord. A bordar (or border) was a villein who held his cottage at his Lord's pleasure, serfs or thralls being subordinate workers. Villeins or bordars also held strips of land to farm for their own needs, and common land was there for all to use. "By commendation" means tenure for life, and "soc" (or soke) means the right of holding a local court. All disputes were settled in the manor court held in the Great Hall. This feudal system survives in part even today in the system of tied farm cottages.

In 1087 the land in Drinkstone parish was either held in the name of Saint Edmund for the Abbey of Bury St. Edmunds or for Saint Etheldreda for the Abbey of Ely, or by a noble tenant, Robert, Count of Mortain (or Earl of Moretaigne). There were 39 recorded inhabitants at this date. The term "carucate" means as much land as a team of eight oxen could plough in a season (on average, about 13 acres). An "oxgang" is one eighth of a carucate, being the share attributed to each ox in a team of eight. A "plough" means as much land as could be tilled with one plough, plus sufficient pasture for the ox. "Beasts" are cattle. There were three separate demesnes as follows:

"Lands of Robert Count of Mortain in Suffolk. Thedwastre Hundred – in Rengestuna, a freeman under Saint Etheldreda by commendation, in Saint Edmund's soke held 1 carucate of land. And 8 Bordars. Then 2 serfs, now 1. Then as now 1 ½ ploughs. And 4 acres of meadow. Worth 16s.

"Thedwastre Hundred – in Drenkestuna were 11 freemen with 1 carucate of land. And they had 6 bordars, and 3 ploughs, and 8 acres of meadow. In King Edward's time they could give and sell their lands. But so that the soke over the land remained in the Saint's possession. They were worth 10s and 8d.

"Thedwastre Hundred – At Drincestona Saint Etheldreda held in King Edward's time 2 carucates of land. A church with 12 acres. Then 15 Bordars, now 7. Then 6 serfs, now 4. Then as now 2 ploughs on the demesne. Then 3 ploughs belonging to the men, now 1. Woodland for 100 swine. And 6 acres of meadow. Then as now 2 horses at the Hall, 10 beasts, 32 swine, 30 sheep, 8 goats. Then worth 40s, now 60s: but it was rented at 100s and could not render so much. It is 8 furlongs long, and 7 broad. And pays 11d in geld."

When the children of Drinkstone School took part in a countrywide "Domesday Study" in 1985, the Rev. Nicholas Cribb brought us details of these three entries. The children were interested, as always, but I still find the lists highly confusing! I added up these men – Robert of Mortain, 12 freemen, 21 Bordars, and 5 serfs – and made 39 men, so it seems the count of "inhabitants" did not include women and children living in Drinkstone in 1087. The cultivated acreage of these three demesnes seems to be around 80 acres plus an unspecified amount of common grazing and strip-farmed land, and woodland. Since the acreage given for the Parish in the 19th century Suffolk Directories is usually 2,172 acres, it seems either that there was a great deal of common land and woodland, or that these manors did not take up the whole area of today's Parish.

MANORS AND "THE GENTRY"

I looked into "The Manors of Suffolk – Notes on their history and devolution", volume VI by Copinger, published 1910, and found the three excerpts from Domesday 1087 with several minor differences. I could not decide whether Robert of Moretaigne himself was listed as a freeman, or whether he had a freeman under him, working the land. I looked at the complicated later history of these manorial estates, and selected a few interesting snippets about the subsequent thousand or so years, as follows:

The Manor of Drinkstone Hall, otherwise known as Lovayne's Manor: at the time of Henry III the Lordship was held by Matthew de Lovaine (or Loveyne/ Lovayne), having links with neighbouring manorial lands in Felsham parish. On Lovaine's death in 1262, the Manor passed to his widow Muriel, who was in 1267 granted a market, pillory (stocks), ducking-stool, view of frankpledge, and a fair. As far as I can gather, this "frankpledge" meant, in feudal law, "a mutual suretyship by which the members of a tithing were made responsible for one another". It's good to discover that, even if women were ignored in some counts of inhabitants, they could rise to such heights of social status!

In the next couple of centuries the Manor passed, with Bildeston Manor, into the Bourchier family, who had links with Shelland and other manors. Henry, second Earl of Ewe, in Normandy, was in 1446 made Viscount Bourchier, and later became Treasurer of England, Knight of the Garter, and a Privy Councillor. He seems to have had a knack for both public and private acquisition since by his death in 1483 he owned six Suffolk Manors as well as titles elsewhere!

In 1538 a letter was found in the state papers of Henry Bourchier, First Earl of Essex and a favourite of Elizabeth I. In this letter, Bourchier complains that a certain Thomas Wrenn had "felled, stabbed and stocked 800 oaks" and had been indicted at the assize. This Thomas Wrenn had no right over the land, never having had any lease of the Earl's Manor of Drinkstone, although his deceased uncle John Wrenn had owned a rightful lease. This is particularly interesting since a certain John Wrenn, in 1564, founded Wrenn's Charity for poor householders of Drinkstone, giving 15 acres for their use. Maybe this was in recompense for his relative's misdemeanours! There is mention of a further 100 oaks felled at this time, so there must have been extensive ancient woodlands in the Parish long ago.

There were further dramas and troubles, "....Robert Devereux, 2nd Earl of Essex, married Frances, daughter and heir of Sir Francis Walsingham, and widow of Sir Philip Sidney, and losing his head on the scaffold 25th February 1600, the manor passed to his son and heir..." What famous names and events were linked to this little Suffolk village!

It is not easy to find any detail of the lives of ordinary villagers through these years. In accounts of inhabitants between 1500 and 1700, the terms bordar, villein, serf and thrall are no longer used. Instead we have husbandmen and yeomen, both implying working farmers a little above the rank of labourer. Tradesmen, shoemakers, millers, weavers, tailors, cordwainers (leather-workers) and clerk and rector are listed. In 1327, 24 taxpayers paid £2-18s-10d, increasing by 1524 to 42 taxpayers paying £8-3s-8d. In 1603 160 adults lived in the village, and in 1674 there were 60 households.

There are some surviving 16th and 17th century cottages and farms in Drinkstone (no doubt much altered, added to, repaired and patched up over the centuries). One of the oldest is Elm Tree Cottage, on the corner where Chapel Lane meets Gedding Road. This was built as a Suffolk Hall house, the first floor over the central Hall being added later. Another ancient home, Elm Green Cottage in Rattlesden Road, has roof timbers showing signs of being singed, suggesting this house also had a central Hall with a fire burning on the floor, until chimney stack, inglenook fireplace and first floor boarding were added at a later date. Kopsey Cottage (in Rattlesden Road, Grade II Listed) also began life as an open Hall house, chimney stack and first-floor boarding being later additions. These are oak-framed, thatched dwellings, probably built for Yeoman farmers. "Fyfers" (next door to Kopsey, in what was once Shop Lane) is also ancient, having a jettied upper storey, oak frame with wattle and daub in-fill, original elm boards to the first floor and diamond-paned mullion windows. Other cottages still thatched today are Camborne Cottage and The Gables (in Rattlesden Road), two homes in Cross Street, two in Chapel Lane, one in Beyton Road, and three cottages in The Street.

Some cottages of similar age have had their thatch replaced with tiles. One of these is Abbot's Lodge (formerly Tudor Cottage) just south of the School, which consists of at least three buildings all incorporated into one. Roof heights are uneven, and in 2004 a historian found vestiges of more than one oriel window. Parts of the house are thought to date from 1540. It is said that during the nineteenth century the gardener from The Rectory lived here, and his five children slept on sacks of straw arranged around the chimney stack on the first floor.

Like many Suffolk villages, Drinkstone started as two groups of housing, one around The Street, the other around The Green, plus scattered farms. Many of the farms date from Tudor times; these include Hill Farm, Burt's Farm, The Rookery, Whitefield House, Green Farm and Garden House Farm. Many of these have magnificent oak barns dating from the 16th century, the timber framework still extremely sound. Some of the cottages built to house workers, such as Marsh Green Cottage and Medway Cottage (now "Treaclebenders") are as old as these farms.

To return to the Lords of the Manor: Robert Devereux, 3rd Earl of Essex, disposed of the Manor, and in 1609 it was held by Sir James Skudamore, Knight. Later it was held by George Goodday of Fornham All Saints, then by Edward Diggs, and then by Richard Mosely (or Moseley). In 1760 the Rev. Richard Mosely, then Lord of the Manor and rector of the parish, built "a large and handsome house for his residence… called Rectory House, and occupied by the incumbent; but it did not belong to the living."

In 1804 he set up a charity to provide education for labouring families in the district. White's Directory says: "£700 was invested in funds for the support of day and Sunday Schools for teaching poor children of Drinkstone and Rattlesden to read and write, which legacy was laid out in the purchase of £1,091-3s-6d 3% consols, the dividends being employed in supporting Drinkstone and Rattlesden Schools."

In 1829 Drinkstone and Rattlesden Manors were offered for sale in London, together with the two farms of Rattlesden Hall and Drinkstone Hall and three other farms, land extending into the parishes of Gedding and Felsham, woods and plantations, in all around 1,070 acres.

All was for sale again in 1838. This sale included, as well as the Manor and the Hall Farms, Whitefield House Farm, cottages and gardens, with 373 acres, and High Town Green Farm of 102 acres. We can get some idea of prices at the time from the detail that High Town Green was "knocked down" at auction for £32-10-0. All were bought by John Mosely (presumably son or grandson of Richard). He had 2,000 acres producing just under £100 a year, and paid land tax of £22-9s a year.

Another Manor with lands extending into the Parish was Timperley's, owned in 1402 by John Hall, passing after disputes between Isaac Mootham and Thomas Wood, to the estate of Sir Henry Wood. White's Suffolk Directory for 1844 tells us that the lord of the Manor of Drinkstone Timperley was the Rev. Dr. Kilderbee. In 1844 farmer John Craske is listed as owner of a farm in Drinkstone parish then known as "Timperleys". I have not managed to find out exactly where Timperley's stood, though it was probably at the northern end of the parish. There are two definite remnants of moats, one near Home Farm in The Street, and the other, very clearly defined and beautiful with snowdrops and daffodils along its banks in springtime, in the gardens of Moat Farmhouse and Moat Cottages in the former Drinkstone Park lands. These Victorian brick cottages housed gardeners and farmworkers in former days (Nell Cocksedge lived in one of these as a child, when her father was horseman for Mr. Hargreaves). Drinkstone manor (Lovaine's) was at the south end of the parish, at The Green. The Hall stood where Hall Farmhouse now stands, the moat which surrounded the ancient building is still clearly visible around the newer building.

In 1760, the same year that benefactor Richard Moseley was building his Rectory House, Joshua Grigsby (or Grigby), town clerk of Bury St. Edmunds, was building an imposing mansion, "Drinkstone Park", in the west of the Parish, on wooded land of about 250 acres (a large part lying in adjoining Hessett parish). The beautiful park contained a large lake. The mansion was demolished in 1949, but features in many of the "Personal Stories" in this book. Captain Hargreaves, owner over several decades, was a generous and kindly "gentleman".

Other dwellings occupied by "gentlefolk" in the village include Drinkstone House "surrounded by lawns and evergreens", in Drinkstone Green (built around 1850 on the site of an earlier Eizabethan dwelling); and Drinkstone Lodge (once known as Bath House) in The Street, built circa 1650. Substantial farmhouses such as Whitefield House and Rookery Farm had tenant farmers, some of whom later bought their farms.

In the early 1920s a pair of cottages at the south end of the village became the subject of a study by

"The Society for the Preservation of Ancient Buildings", bringing fame to Drinkstone (see chapter ten). The village also has the distinction of owning both a post mill and a smock mill. Hundreds of years ago a horse-powered mill stood on the site, and in the late 18th century the smock mill was built onto the base of the horse mill. In 1896 the sails were removed, the stones henceforward driven by engine-power. The post mill was built in 1689 and was in continuous working order until 1972. The engine-powered mill was used when there was not enough wind to turn the sails of the post mill.

The people of East Anglia were proud of their history, as is apparent by the ancient "Exning Prayer" which may have been taught to Drinkstone schoolchildren –

"Give us, O Lord, the courage of Boadicea, the holiness of Etheldreda, the faithfulness of Edmund, King and Martyr. That we may, in our day and generation, Fight to right all wrong, be Pure and Holy in all our thoughts and ways. And serve Thee loyally all our days. Amen."

The next chapter is an attempt to describe how the move towards "education for all" came about.

Chapter Three

THE ADVENT OF "EDUCATION FOR ALL"

THIS IS THE STORY of one particular village school in one particular village context. The School and its village are unique; yet the School and its village are typical of many thousands all over England. All over the country, small village schools were established in the mid- to late 19th century. All over the country, they developed and thrived and played an important role in the lives of millions of country people.

From the middle years of the 20th century there was a gradual demise. All over the country, small village schools fell victim to inevitable change. They were a product of society and culture; as society and culture evolved over time, village schools had to evolve and adapt to changing circumstances and requirements. The rise and fall of Drinkstone School typifies the rise and fall of countless other small village schools. All were affected by the same changes and trends, summarised below.

Villages of the 19th century had a majority population of poor working families whose ancestors had also been farm labourers or domestic servants. During the 19th century the role of village schools gradually increased – first, education became compulsory, then the leaving age was raised bit by bit, until by the mid- 20th century all children had to stay at school until age fifteen.

The villages gradually became home to a mixed population who (like town-dwellers) adopted a wide range of occupations and professions. The coming of mechanisation meant that farmers employed only a fraction of their previous workforce. Rich families employing domestics became a rarity. Parents in villages (as in towns) wanted secondary and higher education for their children. Car ownership became the norm; people could work away from their home village, and experience an entirely different way of life.

Until the 1950s, most country children attended their village school right up to leaving age. As governments acknowledged that only large secondary schools could provide the resources and specialist subject teachers needed to educate children for the modern world, the role of village schools gradually diminished. All older pupils were required to attend secondary schools – a minority in Grammar Schools, the majority in large Secondary Modern Schools.

Then in the mid-1970s the Comprehensive System was introduced throughout Suffolk. In West Suffolk, the age range of pupils taught at village schools was further reduced as large Middle Schools for children aged 9-13 were built.

Hand in hand with the advent of these new schools, which were expensive to build and equip, came a reluctance on the part of Local Education Authorities to pour money into maintaining village schools, many being over a hundred years old by this time. Thus thousands of these small schools, each with its own proud history, and each a landmark in countless individual life stories, were allowed to become dilapidated and under-resourced. Many suffered closure.

Suffolk abounds with village schools built soundly and beautifully by the Victorians. Many are now private houses full of character. Of those that survive as schools, some have been extended and modernised out of all recognition. Others, with minimal change to the buildings, and low pupil numbers, linger on in constant dread of becoming the next to close.

It's easy for us today, having umpteen opportunities to continue learning in adulthood if we wish, to forget that "education for all" is a relatively recent concept. The "Main Education Act" of 1870 gave the State responsibility for providing schools where none existed – before the 1880s, not every town or vil-

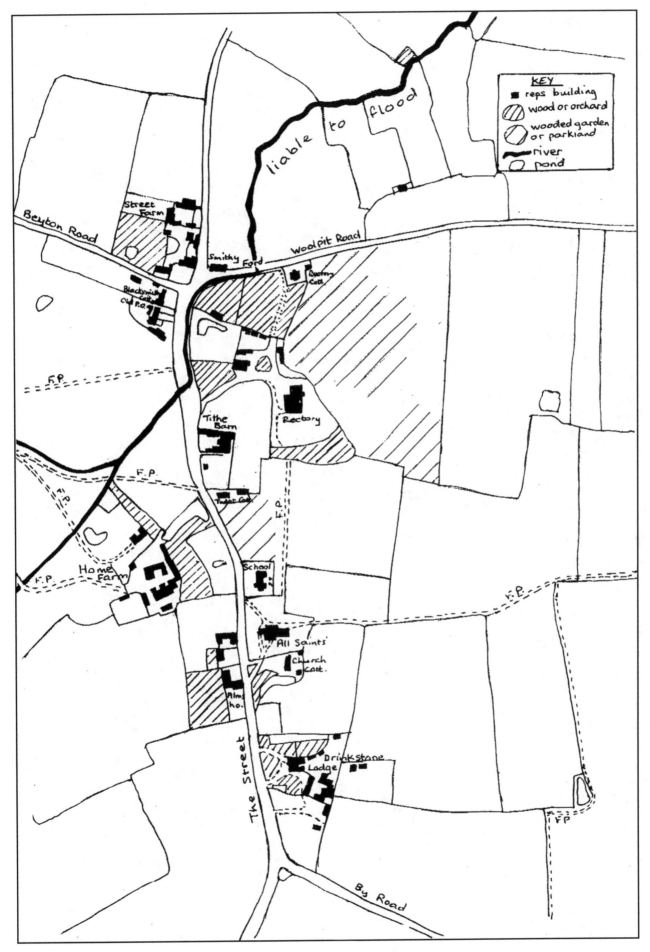

Drinkstone Street 1904

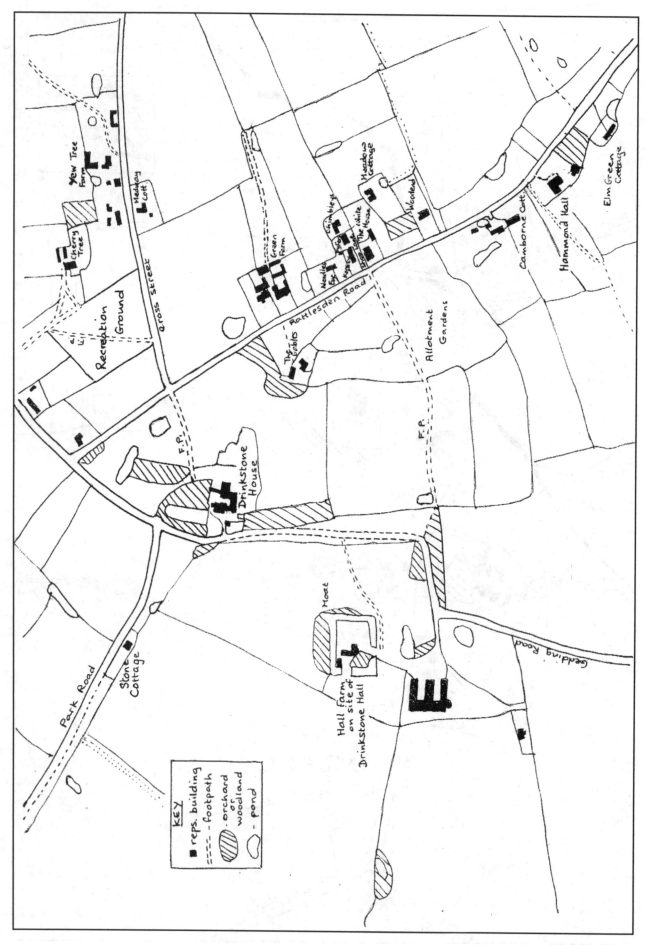

Drinkstone Green 1904

lage had a school. Education became compulsory in 1880, but only up to the age of ten years. In 1893, the school leaving age was raised to eleven years, and in 1899, to twelve years. Early in the 20th century the leaving age was raised to thirteen, then to fourteen years. In mid-century it became fifteen, and finally it was raised to the current statutory age, sixteen years.

So what happened before villages had schools? Where and how did "education" happen?

THE FIRST SCHOOLS

Going back through the centuries, in England (as in most of Europe) formal education involving book-learning and the arts was the privilege of the rich and ruling classes and those in religious orders (monks and nuns). Noble families (including royalty) educated both boys and girls, usually through private tutors, though boys might attend expensive Public Schools and proceed to Oxford or Cambridge. There were Grammar Schools: in Suffolk, William Wood founded one at Sudbury in 1491, and King Edward's Grammar School in Bury dates from 1550. In Boxford, Queen Elizabeth established a Grammar School in 1596. But in those early years, such schools were for boys only, and were small and elitist, certainly not for the "common poor". Many early schools had to close: for example, Sir Nicholas Bacon founded a Grammar School at Botesdale during the reign of Elizabeth I, but it was sold in 1883, the proceeds devoted to scholarships known as Bacon Exhibitions, open to boys from ten local parishes. Boxford Grammar School was similarly commuted to "exhibitions" for boys in four parishes.

A few Suffolk villages did have schools for poor young children, even before the 19th century. At Ampton in 1692 "James Calthorpe Esq. established at his own cost a charity school for the education of six poor boys". In Whepstead, Thomas Sparke left 24 acres of land "for the education of ten poor children in the parish". Again, not many of these early schools survived: for instance at Little Thurlow in 1618, Sir Stephen Soames left £30 a year "for the support of a free school for the parishes of Little and Great Thurlow", but by 1907 the school had become a private house and the annuity was used to endow scholarships. Only a lucky few early schools survived; at Tuddenham St. Mary, a school founded by John Cockerton in 1723 was endowed with "a dwelling-house for the schoolmaster, barn, and 90 acres of land". This was a generous endowment, sufficient to maintain the school into the future. Both school and master's house were re-built in 1840.

There were small day or boarding schools for boys or girls, usually run in private houses, for the" middle classes". Tiny "dame schools" for the children of better-off labourers existed in cottages and private houses. Pupils were taught reading, writing, basic numeracy and maybe drawing and sewing. These schools were entirely unregulated. Education was a matter for individual families to organise if they were able.

SURVIVING POVERTY

Working people did not learn from books. They learned the means of survival, usually joining their parents or other members of the family in some form of work at a very young age, and learning by experience. Craft and trade apprenticeships also existed through the centuries and were a thorough, exacting training, essentially practical. But it cost money to become an apprentice. (In Drinkstone, Camborne's Charity assisted boy apprentices).

For poor people, the priority was to survive. For young country folk this meant taking whatever was available, and handing your meagre earnings to Mum or Dad to keep food on the family table and clothes on the family's backs. Class attitudes were entrenched, the "humble poor" had no "rights", and were expected to know their place, which was of course, at the bottom of the pile, at the beck and call of their "betters". Formal education was not regarded as appropriate, or even desirable, for the "lower classes". They were meant to show respect throughout a life of hard graft, just scraping a living and getting by, while watching the rich enjoy leisure and luxury.

The lack of security poor families faced must have caused them huge anxiety. There are revealing comments accompanying the "Returns to the Population Act" for Suffolk. This Population Act is described as "An Act for taking an Account of the Population of Great Britain and the Increase or Diminution Thereof, passed in the 41st year of His Majesty King George III". Records for Suffolk began in 1800.

Many comments reveal desperation for employment and a place to live. For instance, in one village "the decrease of population is ascribed to the removal since 1841 of large families to other Parishes, some in consequence of their cottages having been taken down". There are overtones of criticism of "the poor" whatever they do - "the increase of population in Depden is attributed to the early marriages of the poor", and in Walsham, is "attributed to improvident marriages among farm servants".

Suffolk people of the 19th century were accustomed to re-locating in the search for work. In Glemsford "the establishment of a factory for weaving horse-hair has caused an increase of population". In Chelmondiston an increase is attributed to "labourers being temporarily employed in collecting stones from the bed of the river, for the manufacture of Roman cement" – by 1871 the population declined again, due to "the decline of the stone-dredging trade".

Drinkstone was always predominantly a farming community, lacking the small industries mentioned in other parts of Suffolk, such as silk manufacture and silk winding, or the weaving of wool, silk, horse-hair and even cocoa-nut fibre. In the Stowupland and Stowmarket area there were gun-cotton works, malt kilns, paper works and a "manure factory"! Elsewhere in the county, factories made tools, flax fabrics, and asphalt. There were coprolite diggings, race courses and racing stables, and from the mid-19th century steam railways were constructed. In 1851 Elmswell station opened, two miles away from Drinkstone. Within Drinkstone parish, options were limited to farm labour, or domestic work (either in cottage homes, such as laundry-work or dressmaking, or as servants in the homes of the rich).

Drinkstone had its share of craftsmen and tradesmen supporting local life. The list of (predominantly male) "occupations" for 1844 is as follows – butcher, corn miller, land steward, surgeon, wheelwright, two maltsters, two shopkeepers, school-mistress, blacksmith, beerhouse-keeper, and eleven farmers. The 1841 Census tells us there were 131 males under the age of twenty, and 130 aged over twenty. We can deduce that most males were agricultural labourers, and that life-expectancy was short!

Laws and restrictions made it hard for poor families to remedy their situation. In 1843 and 1844 there were "two cases of incendiarism due to agrarian unrest" in Drinkstone. Enclosure of common land was one of many blows to independence. In 1851 34 acres of common land in Drinkstone Great Green, "south of the stream", was "enclosed under the General Act 1848". Life for Suffolk country folk everywhere was hard. We read that in 1851 "the operation of the New Poor Law is said to have driven several large families to seek a settlement in other Parishes, causing a decrease of population in Wickham St. Paul"; and in Thetford in 1871, a decrease in population is partly due to "the cottagers being prohibited from taking lodgers". In Hartismere Hundred 1871, a decrease is due to "the lowness of wages and diminished demand for manual labour, in consequence of the introduction of steam machinery in agriculture". These factors, together with illness and accident, made life very hard.

RECORDING OF INHABITANTS

In the 19th-century Returns of numbers from towns and villages of Suffolk, inhabited and uninhabited houses are counted, and there are Returns for Hospitals, Gaols, Houses of Correction, Workhouses, Asylums, and Army Barracks. They managed to count persons living in barges, in tents, in barns, and even "in the open air"! There is mention of labourers emigrating to the colonies. The figures reveal gradual growth in Drinkstone. This is the summary for 1800:

61 inhabited houses accommodating 96 families. 106 employed in agriculture, 17 in trade, manufacture or handicraft. 246 are unemployed (this includes children and old people, and the "gentry" living on private incomes). There were 173 males, 196 females, total population 369 persons.

The population of Drinkstone was given as 344 in 1811, 456 in 1821 (a mysteriously sudden increase in only ten years!), 469 in 1831, 505 in 1841, 543 in 1851, 496 in 1861, 492 in 1871, 463 in 1881, and only 396 in 1891. So population peaked in mid-century. The number of houses gradually increased, there being 100 inhabited houses in 1851, and 6 uninhabited (were these not in a fit state to be lived in?). By 1871 there were a few more houses: 114 inhabited by 121 families or separate occupiers, although the population had decreased to 492.

In most villages, efforts were made to help those in need. Drinkstone had a good number of benign and generous benefactors among its professional and land-owning elite. There are figures for the Relief of the Poor (a legal requirement) - £107 in 1776, £209 in 1803, £472 in 1818, £464 in 1830, £460 in 1832, and £363 in 1834. Local benefactors had established Charities to alleviate poverty and improve quality of life. Some of these relate to education in the parish.

DRINKSTONE CHARITIES

1564 Wrenn's Charity. By deed of Feoffment by John Wrenn: 15 acres for use of poor householders. John Wrenn gave this land "to be ploughed, tilled and sown by poor householders of Drinkstone for their own profit". Presumably, later rectors decided to let the land and distribute proceeds. In 1840 the land was let at £17-10s p.a. and "rents laid out in bread corn, distributed to poor". By 1874 it was let for £30 p.a. which was "distributed in bread-corn by the rector and churchwardens".

1692 Camborne's Charity. By will of Thomas Camborne, rector of Drinkstone from 1679-1693: 27 acres 2R 26P plus house and outbuildings together with lands called Shortlands, "to be disposed of for setting and keeping to work the poor parishioners". The "house" was a block of labourers' cottages, already about a hundred years old. In 1840 the land was let at £46 p.a. and used for apprenticing poor children. By 1874 the Rent had risen to £58 p.a. Proceeds began to be spent on tools for young apprentices. The cottages and land are alongside the Rattlesden Road, in Drinkstone Green.

1804 Mosely's Charity. By will of Richard Mosely: Bequest of £700, dividends applied to support a Sunday School and weekly day school "to teach the poor children of Drinkstone and Rattlesden to read and write".

1814 Widows' Cottage. A block of two or three cottages, at least a hundred years old, was re-furbished for the use of "indigent widows of the parish". Cottage and land were let at £1-15s p.a. in 1840, with "rents applied to coals". In White's Directory for 1874 this property is described as "a cottage, garden and a piece of waste ground... ...appropriated by ancient usage to the relief of poor widows", and at this date was let for about £4 a year. The cottages were at the far end of Cross Street, and suffered several fires during subsequent years.

Gifted Glebe – Some time in early 19th century, some Church Glebe Land was given by the Reverend Spencer Woodfield Maul, patron of All Saints' Church. Initially some rental was used on Church repairs; in 1840 5 acres were let at £6-6s p.a. Later, rent was divided between Church and School for upkeep and repairs.

In 1859 the Rev. Maul gave the land on which School and Schoolhouse were built.

In 1870 the Rev. Frederick Horne (rector) bought an L-shaped block of old thatched cottages opposite the Church, for use as Almshouses for the poor.

There are several other local Charities, including "Perambulator and Footpath", "Drinkstone Allotments", and "Drinkstone Memorial Hall" (set up in the 1920s).

THE SCHOOLS IN DRINKSTONE

In 1804, the year during which Rev. Mosely's Endowment first supported a "day and Sunday School", there were between 44 – 60 pupils. The variation in numbers suggests that many did not attend on a regular basis. Those with means paid a few pence a week. I do not know exactly where this teaching took place.

In 1811 the "National Society of the Church of England" was established, to provide elementary education.

By 1833 the "school" had become two distinct schools, 34 attending the day School and 58 the Sunday

School (the "Mosely Schools"). These numbers include children from Rattlesden. The total population of Drinkstone parish at that date was probably around 480 persons. I don't know whether the rector did any teaching.

1834 the National Society gave the Mosely Schools a grant of £25.

In 1837 the parish of Drinkstone, which had been part of Norwich Diocese since the late 11th century, became part of the Diocese of Ely.

In 1844 Martha Manfield's name appears in White's Directory as "school mistress" in Drinkstone (she might have taught in the day School or the Sunday School, or possibly she ran a private school.)

In 1851 the Drinkstone teacher was paid £20-10s a year: this included the few pence paid weekly by some of the children.

CHILD EDUCATION IN DRINKSTONE 1851

The 1851 Census provides a useful overview of child education of all types in the village, ten years before the School had its own building.

Although the day and Sunday Schools were well established, not every child attended. Education was a matter of choice, affected by poor families' need to acquire more cash. This meant that many children were sent to work for tiny wages to eke out the family budget, rather than being sent to school. Attitudes to education of the poor were mixed. It was a new idea and many labourers saw school as a waste of time in comparison with earning money, however meagre the pay, while employers benefited from being able to pay tiny wages to children.

Slowly, attitudes to child labour were changing, for example 1840 saw a new law forbidding the sending of child sweeps up chimneys. However this law was initially ignored by employers; in 1864 the law was strengthened. Parliament finally outlawed child labour in 1869, but universal obedience to the law was a long time coming.

The 1851 Census in Drinkstone revealed that 65 children aged between five and thirteen years attended the day school: 60% of these were girls, 40% boys. One girl aged fourteen attended, possibly she was a monitress or pupil-teacher.

One nine-year-old boy, and six girls, only attended the Sunday School (no doubt they helped their parents during the week). One thirteen-year-old boy of a wealthy family, listed as a "scholar", probably attended a private school. One nine-year-old boy and thirteen girls from well-off families studied at home with governesses.

Eleven boys and eight girls aged five or over, were neither scholars nor employed.

Many more girls than boys attended school, because there was more paid work for boys. Of the girls, two were employed: a "nurse girl" aged twelve, and a servant aged thirteen. Eighteen boys were in paid work. Five boys – one aged ten, two aged eleven, one aged twelve, and one of thirteen – were agricultural labourers. Another twelve-year-old is described as "shepherd boy". Boys aged ten and eleven were "backhouse boys", cleaning cutlery, sharpening knives, polishing boots, chopping wood and so on. A thirteen-year-old farmer's son was "employed at home".

The largest category of employment for boys was "bird boy". This was the tedious task of scaring birds off crops – hours of lonely work done in all weathers.

As the old rhyme says:

"One for the rook, one for the crow,
One to rot, and one to grow"

Birds were a big problem for farmers. One boy aged only seven, three eight-year-olds, three ten-year-olds, one of thirteen and one of fourteen, were bird-boys. They must have become heartily sick of the work if employed this way year after year.

Most older girls went into domestic service, many living-in away from their homes. In 1851 Drinkstone, two boys were apprenticed, as shoemaker and carpenter. Teenage sons of the blacksmith, the miller, and several farmers, were "employed at home".

This 1851 Census gives place of birth of all inhabitants, showing that poor folk commonly moved away from the village of their birth, either on marriage, or in the quest for employment and a place to live. Of 113 households, only 16 consisted of a husband and wife both born in Drinkstone. In three households, only the wife was born in Drinkstone. In 39 households, only the husband was born in Drinkstone.

In 40 households, neither husband nor wife had been born in Drinkstone.

Although the majority of village residents had been born in Suffolk villages not far from Drinkstone, six came from Norfolk, three from Essex, and one came from each of the counties of Gloucestershire, Staffordshire, Kent, Wiltshire, and Sussex. One labourer's wife came from the Isle of Jersey! No doubt going into domestic service took many young people away from their home area, and in fact all thirty live-in servants listed in the Census were born elsewhere (one in London). Several "upper class" inhabitants were born elsewhere (including Chelsea and Sussex). Some labouring families had children born in several different parishes, illustrating the insecurity faced by those repeatedly seeking either new work or a new home.

The route of the Census enumerator can be traced on a map although many names have changed and cottages have disappeared – "The Street, The Rectory, the Cottage, the Mills, The Green right and left, Hall Farm, Whitefields House, Hammonds Hall, Jewer's Farms, Little Green, Cross Street, Saint Paul's Road, Wards Farm, The Malting, The Park, Hustler's Farm, Further Bucks and near Bucks, Bath House [later Drinkstone Lodge], Queach Farm, Old House Farm, White Horse Beer House and Marsh Greens" were visited.

Moving on from this Census year of 1851, White's Directory for 1855 lists two "teachers" living in Drinkstone, Mr. Robert B. French and Emma Maria Sidney. One or other of these might have taught in a private school, although it's possible both taught in the Mosely Schools. This is still four years before the school building we see today was erected. Education for the poor country children of Drinkstone Parish was available for over fifty years, before the School was built.

GIFT OF LAND FOR BUILDING DRINKSTONE SCHOOL

The Rev. S. W. Maul, patron of All Saints' Church in Drinkstone, gave land for the School. The Trust Deed in his name is dated 25th November 1859. It says:

"Conveyance of the Site of Drinkstone National School

"I The Reverend Spencer Woodfield Maul patron of the Rectory of Drinkstone in the County of Suffolk Clerk and also Rector of the same Rectory.... Do hereby freely and voluntarily .... grant and convey unto the Minister and Churchwardens of the Parish of Drinkstone aforesaid and their Successors All that piece of land situated at Drinkstone aforesaid (being part of a certain Enclosure of land called 'Churchpightle' numbered 131 on the Tithe Commutation Map of the aforesaid parish and which said Enclosure is part of the Glebe Lands of the said Rectory)....40 perches bounded by land belonging to William Whiten towards the North by the Highway leading from the Rectory of Drinkstone to Rattlesden towards the West and by the residue of the said Enclosure towards the East and South ....to be forever hereafter appropriated and used as and for a School for the education of Children and Adults or Children only of the labouring Manufacturing and other poorer classes in the Parish of Drinkstone and for no other purpose".

Another document of 1859 states the purpose of the new school as "the Education of the poor in the principles of the Established Church in England and Wales".

The building of the School was funded "by voluntary subscription" and by grants from the National Society. It was a substantial brick building set on high land north of All Saints' Church, consisting of one large schoolroom with a rear cloakroom or porch, adjoining a Schoolhouse with three rooms upstairs, three down. At the back were "offices": coalhouse, wash house and so on. Brick privies were built several yards away from the building (see plans and drawings overleaf). All was solidly constructed, with no stinting on bricks, with substantial chimneys and a slate roof, and must have been a source of great pride in the village.

The plot given for building, roughly square in shape, was one quarter of an acre. The plans drawn in

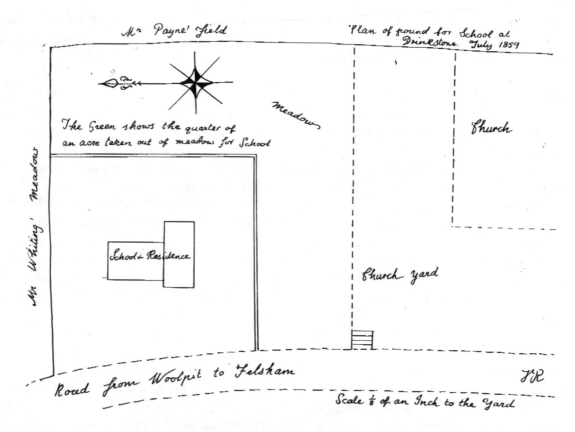

Plan of ground for School at Drinkstone, July 1859

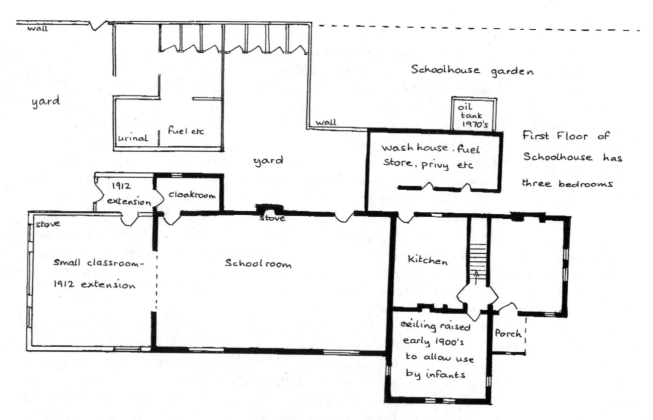

Ground floor plan of School and House

West front of School & Residence

Section

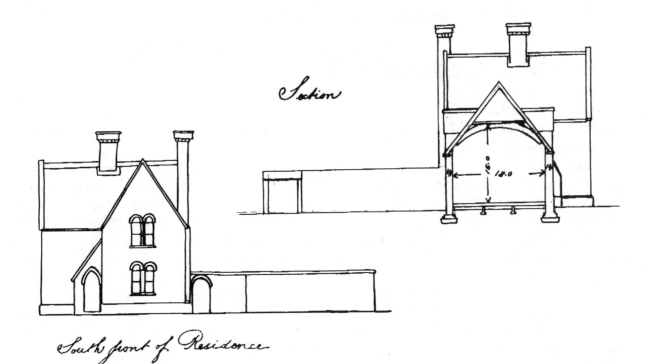

South front of Residence

*Mr Rednall's plans
for the School*

North End of School

1859 by builder John G. Rednall show an L-shaped corridor of land outside the School plot, on the east and south sides. This L-shaped section was part of Churchpightle meadow (the whole meadow had been about half an acre).

The Ordnance Survey Maps 1903-4 show that at this date a corridor of land still lay east of the playground wall (behind the earth closets), between playground and back meadow. A footpath ran along here, linking Rectory gardens and churchyard (handy for the rector!). On the south side of the Schoolhouse garden, by 1903 a long strip of Churchpightle meadow (one side of the L) had been added on to the churchyard.

At some date after 1903, and before 1946, the narrow strip of land to the east (back) of the building was incorporated into the School plot, as garden worked either by Headteacher, or by pupils. In 1977 this back garden area was grassed over for play. Thus when sold in the 1990s the School plot was about a third of an acre.

The original drawings of the proposed School show a brick wall extending to the rear and enclosing the earth closets. Another wall divides boys' and girls' closet yards. One delightful feature shown on the plan was never achieved (probably due to high cost). This was a kind of gothic bell-tower above the rear porch or cloakroom, with a narrow lancet window revealing the bell whose chimes would call the pupils to School. It's a charming detail. Mr. Rednall must have been sorry it was never built. However he and his men did a grand job and their work can still be admired today.

OTHER SUFFOLK VILLAGE SCHOOLS

This was an era when village schools were being built all over Suffolk. I was loaned an old book by Richard Lee of Rattlesden. The title is "West Suffolk, Illustrated". It was compiled by H. R.Barker, curator of Moyse's Hall Museum, Bury St. Edmunds, and was printed and published in 1907 by F.G. Pawsey and Co. Ltd of Bury St. Edmunds. One of the photographs in the section on Drinkstone village shows the blacksmith's building (now demolished) and several horse-drawn vehicles. A white post-and-rail fence marks the road verges. Although I did not learn anything new about Drinkstone from this book, it was a useful source of information on dates and funding of other Suffolk village schools.

Church Schools funded by "Voluntary Subscription" include Norton in 1835, Cockfield 1856, Cowlinge 1867 and Nowton 1880. The school at Cavendish, built 1863, was funded by "subscriptions and government grants". A good many schools built in the 19th century were erected "by rich benefactors" – either titled landowners, or rectors or vicars of a parish. Examples are Great Fakenham, 1814, Shimpling 1841, Hawstead 1847, Hopton 1855, Flempton 1866, and Cavenham 1871. The school at Aspall was "erected by a former vicar and his friends"! These were all designated "National" schools, the National Society helping with grants. Government grants were also received. After 1868 "Her Majesty's Inspectors" would call.

"The Main Education Act" of 1870 gave the state responsibility for providing schools in towns or villages which had none. Within two years, education was made free for every child, everywhere. An Act of 1880 made attendance compulsory for children aged five to ten years. In 1891 the small parental contribution asked of those able to pay was abolished. A high proportion of assistants were pupil-teachers or "uncertificated" teachers.

DRINKSTONE SCHOOL 1861-1905

Some early schools have Log Books dating from the 19th century. Drinkstone's only Log Book begins in 1927. The Admissions Register, a specialised ledger printed in 1891, has details of pupils born in 1880 and after. It seems that lists of pupils had been kept elsewhere until this date. When the new ledger was purchased (around 1892), names of all children attending the School at that time were copied in. (Admission number 19 was inadvertently left out, and added in on a later page. The birthdate of this nineteenth child is close to the birthdates of numbers 18 and 20). No dates of admission are given until entry number 66, a girl who started at the School in 1894. This suggests that the first 65 names were all written in at one session. During the ten years 1885 to 1895, ages suggest an average of nine or ten admissions a year.

The first Managers' Minute Book begins in 1903. Very little is known about how the school operated in its first decades, but we do know the first Headteacher of the School, Mr. John Knott, came all the way from Devon with his wife Charlotte and baby son. They travelled by steam train from Exeter to London, spending a night in London before travelling on to Elmswell. It must have been a mammoth undertaking; a two-day journey to a distant unknown village. Probably the new red-brick School-house with three rooms upstairs and three down, was enticing!

Soon after the new School opened, the Rev. Frederick Horne became patron and incumbent of All Saints' Church, living at the Rectory. His father, Captain William Horne, lived with his wife at Drinkstone Lodge, just south of the Church. Hornes were to live in the village, playing a major role and very faithful in their duties to the School, for around ninety years. Captain Michael Horne lived in Green Farm from 1951 to 1959.

White's Directory for 1874 lists Miss Maria Dixon as "National Schoolmistress", Roll 50. Kelly's Directory for 1875 gives "Mrs. Maria Willis" as mistress at the National School, so maybe Miss Maria Dixon had married and become Mrs. Willis.

In 1885 Mrs. Emily Annie Preston, Schoolmistress of Drinkstone, was living in the Schoolhouse. Kelly's Directory for 1888 gives average attendance 60, under Mrs. E. S. Pullin. Mrs. Pullin is still at the School in White's Directory 1892, which also mentions a Mr. John Thomas Clarke, who ran a (private) day and boarding school.

In 1895, Mrs. Emma Robinson took over as Headmistress of Drinkstone, remaining in post until 1905. Average attendance in 1900 was 60 pupils.

In 1902 the Board of Education ordered the appointment of "Foundation Managers" to oversee the running of schools such as Drinkstone. Possibly until this date the rector and churchwardens had fulfilled this role; there are no records. In September 1903 the first Meeting of Managers of Drinkstone School was held. The accepted view of the time was that only educated men of "upper class", who owned substantial houses or land in or near the parish, gave money regularly to maintain the School, and were practising members of the Church of England, might become managers. The "parish minister" was Ex-Officio manager, and usually acted as Chairman.

There are three books of "Managers' Minutes" of Drinkstone School. They are a wonderful source of information. At their meeting in October 1903, "Miss Nelly Robinson sent in her resignation as monitress for November 3rd being one month's notice". Nelly was the daughter of Headmistress Mrs. Emma Robinson, and it seems Nelly had been earning a little money by helping out at the School. The arrangements for staffing were quite flexible at this time, and the managers had considerable authority regarding who was appointed. At the same meeting, Mrs. Robinson asked for her husband and herself to be "taken together as master and assistant mistress (article 50)". She said the numbers of children (67) "will require a Headteacher and an article 50 assistant", and "her husband and she together would fulfil the requirement". Rev. Horne agreed to investigate this possibility but it did not happen. Not long after this meeting, Mrs. Robinson resigned, and Mrs. Gobbitt became Headmistress.

This all happened a hundred years ago, and at this distance of time it's hard to discover what life in Drinkstone schoolroom was like for the children. When the School closed in 1986, we heard from several ex-pupils who shared a few turn-of-the century memories with us. At the time, I was too pre-occupied with the business of teaching while preparing for the closure to listen to their memories – why didn't I realise that this was a once-only opportunity? They are all gone now! We did however absorb some basic facts: the children walked to School in all weathers, walking home for lunch and back for the afternoon session. They must often have arrived at School cold and tired. In photos they look stolid and plump, not particularly happy or animated, but no doubt obedient, they had to be! So many children in such a small place had to be controlled, in the classroom at least.

There were at least six "Standards" in the School, although there were never more than three teachers, generally only two. Pupil-teachers aged fourteen and over were employed. Headteachers had to take exacting examinations and were expected to teach the older children of several Standards. Depending on numbers, sometimes a room in the Schoolhouse was used for Infants (or "Babies" as they were then termed).

The children had lessons in poetry and verse, singing, drawing and painting, history and geography, reading, writing and arithmetic. Little ones used slates and chalks. They graduated to slate pencils, and by the turn of the century (if not earlier) older children used paper and ink. High on the curriculum were Scripture lessons given by the rector. Church services were held at Harvest, Christmas, Candlemas, Easter and Ascension Day. "Empire" seems to have been inextricably entwined with religion; on Empire Day in May, the rector would conduct a service. The boys learned gardening, the girls needlework and knitting, and older children walked to a Centre in Woolpit to learn cooking, woodwork and metalwork.

The Appendix to this history contains excerpts from Suffolk Directories and names from the Admissions Register.

Chapter Four

DRINKSTONE SCHOOL, 1905 - 1927

THESE TWENTY-TWO YEARS are the period during which Ruth Gobbitt was Headmistress of the School. During her headship the ordered, structured life of the community was disrupted by the turmoil of the First World War which inevitably brought changes in circumstances and attitude.

Mrs. Gobbitt lived in the Schoolhouse with her family. Attendance at the School peaked in the early years of the 20th century, with eighty-eight pupils on roll. Even for those times when tiny children were expected to sit still and quiet for hours, space was totally inadequate. So in 1912, fifty-two years after the School was built, it was extended, so skilfully that in later years this addition was very difficult to detect.

The managers of the era selected the cheapest tender for the work, from five ranging from £206 to £318! They chose Middleditch builders, who at £206 did a superb job.

The School end of the building originally consisted of one high classroom, eighteen feet wide, thirty-four feet long, fifteen feet from floor to ceiling, plus a small porch at the rear. There were two doors in the back wall of the classroom, one opening into the porch, the other to the outside courtyard. A large stove provided heating. At the south end of this classroom was the Schoolhouse, but there was no doorway between classroom and House. At the classroom's north gable end was a large window. According to the plans drawn in 1859, this north window would be rectangular, divided into eight panes, with a high

Wedding of Ruth Elizabeth Jane Minns to Henry Moyse Gobbitt in the late 1890s, or even 1900.

A school group pictured in 1909 – no names are known

narrow slit window set in the gable peak above (see plan, page 19). But the school photograph of 1909 clearly shows a window divided into three equal sections; this suggests that the graceful arched window which adorns the north gable wall today dates from 1859.

Tremendous care was taken to extend the School in consistent architectural style. The entire north wall was demolished. A new, equally high room, floor area eighteen by eighteen feet, was seamlessly built on to the original classroom. The new section of west wall had a sash window exactly matching those in the large classroom. The original tall arched window was reinstalled in the new north wall (no mean feat since it measures ten feet in height by six feet wide). New smaller sliding sash windows were installed on either side to let in maximum light.

The gap between old and new classrooms was partitioned off with high sliding doors, the upper section being of glazed panels. These doors could be moved to the sides to create one enormous long room.

A solid-fuel stove was installed in the north-east corner of the new classroom. The porch or cloakroom at the rear was extended. The new section had a door to the new classroom, and an outside door. These two distinct cloakroom areas were the only evidence of extension, since one had a pitched roof, and the other was lean-to. The work was completed by August 1913. The managers held a celebration for "all subscribers to the new building".

Two new hanging lamps were purchased. The cleaner asked for a rise due to the extension (granted November 1913), increasing her wage to 3s-6d a week!

It is quite difficult to discover exactly what staff members there were, besides Mrs. Gobbitt, during this period. Some years the managers only met formally two or three times, and often we read that a certain teacher has tendered her resignation, without her presence at the School having previously received a mention. Salaries were low, in 1908 "Supplementary" teachers received a salary of £30 per annum (about 12s a week). The managers had authority to hire and fire (subject to formal ratification by the Education Committee). In July 1912 we learn that "Mrs. Barker has applied for the post of Teacher in place of Miss Barker" (were these mother and daughter?) She must have been well qualified since her salary was £50 per annum, whereas in February 1913 Violet Hilders was appointed at only £30 per annum. Violet Hilders was "officially recognised" as a Supplementary Teacher in 1915. A great many teachers came and went during these years, but Ruth Gobbitt remained as Head.

Besides having power to hire and fire, the managers negotiated pay demands on behalf of the teachers (the Education Committee paid salaries). Thus in December 1913 Mrs. Gobbitt and Mrs. Barker requested "an increase in their salaries according to scale". But the Education Committee refused, saying Mrs. Gobbitt was receiving "the maximum of the grade" and Mrs. Barker "has not taken steps to improve her qualifications". Once again, in May 1917, Mrs. Gobbitt said she had been "£5 below the maximum for schools of a similar grade for several years." She asked for her salary to be the same as that paid to the Head of Beyton, a similar size school. The outcome of this is not recorded.

The autonomy of the managers extended to fixing term dates. In September 1914 the Education Committee wrote requesting that holidays should coincide with those of other local schools "which would be of great advantage to cookery and other classes arranged by the Education Committee". Managers negotiated Education Committee grants towards the cost of cleaning and spring-cleaning. In 1909 spring cleaning cost £8. There are complaints about standards of caretaking. In 1911 the managers wrote "cleaning should be done in day-time, and not at night with lights". In 1912 we read "Mrs. Catchpole does not clean Schools properly and the fires are not lighted sufficiently early during winter". So she was given a month's notice!

Whenever repairs – such as draught-proofing doors, repairing stoves, fixing leaks in the roof, repairing the pump or the harmonium, or mending walls and fences – were necessary, the managers asked the Education Committee to foot half the bill. There were small niggly exchanges, such as in 1914 when the managers wrote to the Committee to say the School had not been used for Sunday School for the last year, so they would not pay "the 10s…that is asked for". They made regular payments to the Committee for needlework materials.

The managers appear to have received no help with decoration, "distempering the Schoolhouse" and so on. The Headteacher paid a quarterly rent for the house.

Sanitary and Medical Inspectors called. In May 1907 the School was closed due to an outbreak of scarlet fever. In May 1916 they suggested "that earth pans in closets be emptied twice a week during summer months". In 1926 an H.M.I. said the temperature in the big classroom was too low and recommended asking the Education Committee to provide a more suitable stove. This heating problem dragged on and on through the decades, right up to the time of closure!

There are pleasant little snippets of information: in October 1906 fifteen children qualified for attendance prizes; in 1914 the managers proposed that the school bell be hung between two oak posts, six feet above ground, in the playground. (In 1986, Mrs. Austine, an ex-pupil, cycled to the School to talk to the

A school group pictured in 1912 – no names are known

children, showing us where this smart bell-stand stood.) The managers were kept in touch with the daily life and work of the School through the rector (who was Chairman of the Board of Managers) since he "gave the usual Scripture lesson" week by week, and also organised religious services for the children.

In 1918 Mrs. Gobbitt was joined by her sister Caroline Minns, infant teacher for the next twenty-two years. Miss Minns lived in a small bungalow, up the "By Road" just beyond the Church, with only Lodge Cottage for a neighbour. Her little home was constructed of corrugated iron lined with wood, hinting at a rather Spartan existence.

Mrs. Gobbitt's enthusiasm was wearing thin by the 1920s. Her husband had fought in the Great War, but had not returned to the family home when de-mobbed. She also had a sick daughter to care for. In 1920 she tendered her resignation, and the managers got as far as interviewing a Mrs. Sturgeon from Hadleigh. Then Ruth Gobbitt changed her mind and "Mrs. Sturgeon wrote offering to resign in favour of Mrs. Gobbitt". This scenario was repeated late in 1926, when she again resigned and then wrote to the Education Committee and was re-appointed. Her role as Headteacher came to an end in the summer of 1927 in unhappy circumstances.

Chapter Five

PUPILS' WORK FROM 1910 - 1912

WHEN WE WERE preparing to close the School we unearthed several dusty old tomes that had lain undisturbed for many a year. The best find of all was a small pile of mousy bookworm-nibbled school exercise books dated 1910-1912. These are now in Bury Record Office. They give a wonderful glimpse into the thoughts and experiences of children of those times and the work they achieved in School. The essays are so fresh and vivid, written by lively young boys enjoying life in the depth of the countryside, not recalled in old age like many memories in this book! The ancient exercise books are of "The Goliath" type, sold by E. J. Arnold and Son of Leeds.

The first is dated June 1st 1911, with the name "Lewis H. Coleby" written in beautiful neat copperplate, in ink (was Lewis the brother of Ruth Coleby, employed as pupil-teacher in 1908?). The Admissions Register tells us that there were at least two families with the surname Coleby living in Drinkstone in the early 19th century. Lewis's birthdate was 3rd June 1898, so he was approaching his thirteenth birthday when he began using this exercise book. The family had previously lived in Carlton Colville, and while Lewis was still of school age the family left Drinkstone parish. The father (also named Lewis) appears to have worked as grave-digger at All Saints' Church. It's interesting that young Lewis appears thoroughly integrated and at ease despite only living in Drinkstone since the age of eight. The Admissions Register (dates of birth and names are in Appendix Two) reveals that a large proportion of pupils were born elsewhere, Drinkstone being at least the second school they had attended. An equally large proportion "left the Parish" while still of school age. It seems Drinkstone was not a strongly insular village and young Lewis certainly felt at home in the community.

The book contains "Dictations", either passages from histories, or literary, such as one "In praise of Trees". There is work entitled "Along the Shore", beginning "if we were to go to the seaside today…" with descriptions of sea birds, and drawings of limpets and starfish. There are sections on Grammar, regular and irregular verbs. There is a delightful, lively account of pleasant boyhood days in the village, lovely to read:

"How I spent my last holiday.

"I had a very happy holiday. Nearly all the while I was riding horses from the Blacksmith's. Monday I went for a nice bicycle ride. Nearly every day my brother and me had our dinners down the meadows. We had a wade on Wednesday and had some fine sport. Some of the boys went to work but I did not.

"During our holidays there was a very sad thing took place. [Was this the sudden death of villager Mr. Constable, the subject of an earlier piece of writing?]

"Some of the time we were practising for the Coronation. Thursday we were fishing in the morning and playing quoits in the afternoon. Friday I cleaned my rabbits out and then I went down with Father; then in the evening I went to practise and had some hymns over. After we had finished I went up the green and saw Leonard Goodson's rabbits. Saturday I went to Woolpit after we were netting to line a grave. I was down the Blacksmith's all the rest of the morning. In the afternoon I played about. After I had my tea I done my work. I am glad to say that we had very nice weather, the heat was so intense that people were taken ill. This has been

so dry that there is a great deal of drought. We heard nearly everybody that we saw saying that
we wanted rain very badly. Plants and crops were nearly dried up."

Much of the work demonstrates the strength of patriotic pride inculcated into children of the time, including reverence for the Royal Family, pride of Empire, and (it has to be admitted) a rather suspicious and superior attitude to other nations! The country was preparing for the Coronation of George V, which may have been one reason why pupils were required to write out all four verses of the National Anthem – words that are seldom uttered today! These are verses two and five:

O Lord our God arise
Scatter his enemies,
And make them fall.
Confound their politics,
Frustrate their knavish tricks,
On thee our hopes we fix,
God save us all.

With England's crown today
We hail our King and pray
God save the King.
Guide him in happiness,
Guard him in storm and stress,
Then in thy kingdom bless
And crown our King.

There are several pieces of "history" all so structured as to glorify the part Britain played on the world stage, as in one short passage on Belgium which says "Belgium is known as the cockpit of Europe because so many pitched fights have been fought on its plains. The greatest battle of all was fought at Waterloo, twelve miles from Brussels…". (The word "cockpit" at this date, before aeroplanes were an accepted reality, refers to the cock pits in which hapless fighting cocks were set against one another.) A passage in similar vein celebrates Trafalgar:

"'England expects that every man this day will do his duty'. Just before the battle of
Trafalgar, these words were spoken by Lord Nelson. This saying made the sailors try very hard
to gain the victory. Lord Nelson was on the ship called the 'Victory'. At the end of the battle he
lost his life."

There are short passages describing the British attitude towards Russia, Germany and Switzerland. Patriotic feeling was particularly strong at the time, with war approaching, and the Coronation of George V imminent. Lewis wrote one essay on the eve of the Coronation, and one after the event:

"Tomorrow is the Coronation of George V and Queen Mary. I hope it will be a fine day and
that the King and Queen will have good health and reign over us justly. In our village there is
going to be a feed for adults and children as well. After this has taken place there will be sports
such as jumping, racing, pillow-fighting, and also a tug of war. The tug of war will be between
the married men and the single. Men can pay six pence and go in a ploughing match to see
which one can draw the straightest furrows. I am going in three races, these are 3-legged race,
sack race, and a race for boys under fourteen.

"At one o'clock there is going to be a service at the Church which will last about three quar-
ters of an hour. When we come out, the flag will be hoisted. We shall all march along the road
in pairs. This is going to take place at Mr. Taylor's. He has a very large barn for the occasion.
The young men have cleaned it out and the gardeners are going to trim it up. So altogether I
expect we shall have some fine sport. There are several prizes but no money prizes. The men
are allowed to have beer and the children minerals."

The next essay in Lewis's book is entitled "What I did on Coronation Day":

"At one o'clock I went to Church and sung some hymns and psalms. Then we went to the
flag to see it hoisted by Rev. F. E. Horne. After this took place we marched up to the meadow
in pairs. At 2.30 the adults had their dinner then at half past three the children had their din-
ner. After this was over the sports took place. Three balloons were sent up. I won two first
prizes, a shut knife and a fork."

A second exercise book, dated 19/5/1911 on the first page, contains the work of F. Sturgeon. He too wrote in a beautiful hand, an account of the Coronation villagers awaited with such pride and eagerness. He gives further detail of the ceremony:

"The Coronation of King George and Queen Mary will be performed at Westminster Abbey

on 22nd June. In most villages there will be a treat both for adults and children. The King and Queen will ride to be crowned in a state coach. On that day in the streets of London there will be a very large procession of people, regiments of soldiers, policemen etc. The Coronation Robes will be covered well with the tails of ermine. The streets of towns and cities will be illuminated by flags and other things to greet the King. It is suspected that it will be the greatest Coronation ever known. Nearly every person will wear something for the Coronation. The King will have some oil poured over his head and hands. Both the King and Queen had to wait a year before this great event took place because of the late King. This is so great a ceremony that it has to be rehearsed every day so that it should not go wrong on Coronation Day. The coach will be drawn by eight cream ponies. Some people will give a great deal of money to see the procession of the King and Queen. On that day I expect some people will be hurt and crushed by the throngs of people around them."

Elsewhere he adds:

"At our School we have had a flag pole put up and the national flag will be fixed upon it....we are allowed to take our football onto the meadows and play while the adults are having their dinner...and also we went on some swings."

Obviously these pupils had been most successfully taught by Ruth Gobbitt. I wonder how many young boys of today would be capable of listening so intently and producing such mature work, correct in spelling, (most) grammar, and punctuation. Pride of nationhood was encouraged day by day, and F. Sturgeon's book contains an article on Caernarvon Castle:

"Caernarvon Castle is one of the finest ruins in the kingdom. The walls which are from seven to nine feet thick, are surmounted by thirteen towers, and the space enclosed covers three acres. Edward I subdued Wales, but he wished to be on friendly terms with the people. When an infant son was born to him at Caernarvon in 1285 he called him Prince of Wales, and gave him Welsh servants so as to make him take an interest in Wales as he grew up."

The stories seem to have been told to these pupils in a way which really engaged their imagination. A passage on the Crusades tells us: "Edward I showed much bravery in fighting the wars of the cross", and goes on to describe Edward's attempts to take Nazareth and Jerusalem from the Turks, also, the story of a time when his knights had gone on a pilgrimage to Jerusalem, and there was an attempt to assassinate King Edward with a poisoned dagger as he lay in his tent; and his wife sucked the poison out of his arm.

These schoolchildren celebrated "Royal Oak Day" each year. F. Sturgeon's book tells us:

"Royal Oak Day comes on the 29th May. It was the day when Charles II hid up in an oak tree, out of the way of Cromwell's soldiers. It is said that he went to a house and changed his fine clothes to those of a woodman and took an axe in his hand ... he done this because he did not want Cromwell to know where he was. After a while he got to France in safety. Every boy and girl knows that they should wear a piece of oak on that day."

The subject of another piece of work is "Bad King John". Another describes the mix of peoples making up the British nation, and starts: "Saxon, Norman and Dane are we... when the Normans came they found a short dark people in Wales, like the Iberians in Spain."

Not all boys of the time could be quite as carefree in the holidays as Lewis! His classmate F. Sturgeon had to work, but does not seem to have minded this. After all, it was a mark of manhood and he earned money. This is his account of his Whitsun holiday:

"Last week I spent a very happy holiday. Four days I went to work at Mr. Lambert's, pulling carlicks with some more boys. On Thursday and Friday I helped my father to hoe the garden. On Tuesday night I went and saw a quoit match played with Drinkstone and Rattlesden on Mr. Bland's meadow. On Saturday I went to Rattlesden on my bicycle. It is printed in the paper that last week was the hottest Whitsuntide they have had for fifty years. On Friday I went after my money and I had two shillings to take. On Friday morning I cleaned boots and shoes and knives and forks."

Lewis's book has an account of harvest time:

"At harvest when the corn is ripe men take the reaper and binder into the fields to cut it down. Men work until it is very dark to get the corn up if they think it is going to rain. Harvest

time will soon be here again. At this time we break up and have a very long holiday and a great deal of enjoyment. Children go in the fields and often take their dinner with them, on purpose to catch the rabbits. Some of us like riding on the horses. Then the corn has to be tied up and carted and then it is made up into a stack. When the last load is being brought home there is a bough placed on the top to show that harvest is over. When all the corn is safely gathered in, the Church is decorated up, and we sing praises to thank God."

An account of Woolpit Flower Show (written July 13th, 1911) tells us:

"The prizes which were given away amounted to the value of over £64. Mr. A. Chriton's steam circus was in attendance... a field was lent for the men to have a drawing [ploughing] match on, by Mr. Robinson... in one tent was the drawings which had been done by some schoolchildren. There were many sports, such a shooting gallery, trying your strength etc. On the meadow was a quoit tournament. After four o'clock children were admitted to the grounds for 2d. The flying horses were driven by an engine, and at night they were lit up by electricity."

Two other exercise books, headed "The Colonial Drawing Book", contain some plain pages, and some covered in fine grid, like graph paper. These pages contain carefully measured and ruled geometric drawings. On the plain pages are pen and ink drawings and delicate water-colours, such as flowers, and a "goose girl" tending her flock. One book is the work of E. Gill, started June 14th 1910. The second belonged to Lewis Coleby, and contains maps, pen and ink drawings of fruit and flowers, and pencil sketches, including several of a weasel, seen from several angles as if a stuffed model was used.

I was impressed to see the range of subjects taught. There is work on wild flowers, spiders, the difference between spiders and insects, and detailed descriptions of fish species, all carefully illustrated. There is work on "evaporation" with drawings of an experiment to demonstrate this.

It was quite a moving experience for me to read the work of these young boys living nearly a hundred years ago. They had such zest for life. Their accounts of village life suggest a kind of age of innocence; young and old worked and played together, obeying the rules of a fixed class system, proud of their heritage and their nation. There was approval by great and small (and even by God!) of using war as a means of retaining power and control, whether against Llewellyn of Wales, or against Napoleon and the French, or against the "infidel" Turks in Jerusalem. There was tacit belief that the English were a race divinely destined to dominate and manage others; this belief was echoed in universal dominance of the wealthy educated classes over the poor.

How sad to reflect that only a few years later so many village men and boys experienced the horror and disillusion of World War I, which shattered lives and communities.

Chapter Six

PERSONAL STORIES
Major George Blake, Rebie Tidswell, Ada Lee,
Dorothy Lee, Nell Cocksedge, Nellie Bartram

THERE EXISTS NO School Log Book prior to Autumn 1927. It is obviously more difficult each year to find folk whose memories go back before that date. But as we prepared for the closure of the School in the 1980s we were delighted to receive letters from several ex-pupils. We heard from Major George W. Blake M.B.E., (brother of Nell Cocksedge) then living in Topsham, Devon. He wrote:

"It was in the Spring of 1925 that I left Drinkstone School at the age of fourteen years. The Headmistress at the time was Mrs. Ruth Gobbitt and her assistant was her sister Miss Caroline Minns. Up to that date four young Blakes had been pupils at the School.

"The fact that I only had a village school education appears to have had no ill effect on my progress in life. At one stage I even found myself doing a three-year stint as an instructor in the Regimental School of the County Regiment and my sympathy ever since has been with teachers. I shall always be grateful to Drinkstone School for all it taught me.

"In about 1925 an interesting event took place in Drinkstone Church next door to the School. It was the wedding of the late Dr. Malcolm Sargent and a good many pupils were allowed to attend – a great day for a small village school."

We heard from Audrey Hale of Thetford, daughter of Rebie Tidswell (née Squirrell) whose brother, also an ex-pupil, was living in Elmswell. Mrs. Hale told us that her mother, 87 next birthday (so born 1899 or 1900) was living in Norfolk and "often speaks of the slates and slate pencils they used at school." I regret to say we didn't find time to contact this lady for further details. We were only a few days away from the closure date when we heard from her.

We scouted around in July 1986, to find the oldest ex-pupil. Four of our pupils visited 91-year-old Ada Lee at her Elmswell home. She probably started at the School in the year 1900. She told us how she wrote with chalk on a little slate, books were few and far between, and a large brass bell summoned the youngsters to School.

The most exciting letter we received when preparing to close the School came from Dorothy Lee, one of Ruth Gobbitt's daughters. This delightful lady actually travelled up to see our closing exhibition and attended the end of school service at All Saints' Church. She first wrote to us in March 1984 from her home in Southsea, Hampshire, as follows:

"Dear Mr. Connolly,

"I am writing to you, on learning that Drinkstone School may be closed! My mother was Headmistress for several years (Ruth R.E.J. Gobbitt – 88 children on roll then!) myself and three other members of our family born in the Churchyard bedroom!! It grieves me very much that 'the School' may be closed and I do so hope and pray Sir Keith Joseph will rescind the decision of the Council.

"When I was a little girl (2 years) the dining room was used as an infant occupation, the ceiling having been raised! And that is why two steps are there, to main bedroom! Some happy

and very SAD memories are connected with 'The School' for us!! I do hope all concerned will be successful in saving Drinkstone School.

"Yours sincerely,

"(Mrs) Dorothy V. Lee (née Gobbitt)

"P.S. BEST OF LUCK! LET ME KNOW IF IT IS SAVED!"

We heard from Dorothy again in April 1986:

"Dear Mrs. Wright,

"I was so delighted to get your letter, a few days ago! And if I can, will let you have a few memories of C of E School, which it was very much so in the old days! ....Mr. Blamire, an Inspector from Bury St. Edmunds used to call and I always made him cups of tea and it was passed through a CUBBY HOLE FROM OUR KITCHEN!! I could write a book about it all, really!!

"My Mother was a teacher at nearby Norton before passing her exams for Headmistress-ship and my Brothers Henry and Richard born there! I was the first Daughter born at the 'School House' then another brother Herbert (Don), sisters Stephanie and Joyce followed (the latter an invalid, spastic).

"I am now 80 years YOUNG born 6-4-1906 and I am now the last of our immediate family! My eldest brother Henry (85) died three weeks ago at Felixstowe and so I must now keep the flag flying (I hope!)

"The Dining room, now your Office I believe, was the Infant School Room and I was in there at 2 years, having escaped our 'House Keeper'! (She always knew where to find me!) If you notice 2 steps go up into the front Bedroom! (the ceiling having been raised for regulations, no doubt!) My Mother taught up to Standard 7 and had an assistant and an Infant Teacher! Trained the Choir and played the Organ and organised most of the Festivities in and around! She had a wonderful singing voice, which I have inherited!! Her schoolchildren could be heard across the meadows and she was always in demand for Concerts and sang for Conservative do's!

"I left our school at 12 years old and cycled to Elmswell and was a pupil at Miss Boby's Private School! Such a Sweet, gentle Lady!! Henry (eldest) went to Woodbridge Grammar, Richard to Stowmarket Secondary, Don also, and Stephanie to the Suffolk County in Bury St. Edmunds (a long way to cycle!) and our garden at the School House was beautiful, especially in the Spring, and Roses and Clematis climbing up to Bedroom Windows and over FRONT PORCH!! My dear Mother is buried just over the wall! I came over last year to visit her grave and found the Churchyard in a devastating state. I wrote to the powers that be, and got a reply from the Canon at Woolpit, a nice letter, hoping it will be improved by my next visit! Which I hope may be one of your Functions, if I can arrange it!! (should like a Commemorative Mug!)!

"I'm upset the School is closing, of course!! It is very Victorian, and facilities not adequate in these modern times, for which I'm glad and thankful I do not belong and glad I was born in 1906. (What a state our people and world are getting into!!)

"I shall try to get over for one of the Functions during July, and will let you know later on and if I can put my memory to the Test, jot down more!! And Christian Love to you and Children,

"Sincerely, (Mrs) Dorothy V. Lee

"P.S. I have a Bury Free Press *Cutting with you all standing at the Gate! It was sent to me last year!"*

So, the past is not so far away after all.

Twenty-four years after meeting Dorothy, I was thrilled to discover other sources of information, through meeting Nell Cocksedge (younger sister of Major George Blake). Nell's personal memories appear in a later chapter; but she also "opened a door" for me to discover fascinating details of the years before she was born.

Nell lives in Gedding Road, Drinkstone. She is now in her eighties but is as lively in mind as ever, and is fascinated by local history. She gave me a copy of her article published in Drinkstone Parish Magazine in May 1998:

ONCE UPON A TIME.....by Nell Cocksedge.

I have been loaned an old book compiled from parish magazines of the Thedwastre Rural Deanery from January 1905 to December 1907. The book, once owned by Arthur Sturgeon, now belongs to Nellie Bartram, his sister of Woolpit. This is an excerpt from a report by Rev. F.E.Horne, Rector of Drinkstone, dated May 24, 1907:

"On Friday May 24, being Empire Day, the national flag was planted in the school grounds and at noon all the children and a good number of elders assembled round it for a ceremony known as 'Saluting the Flag'. A beautiful patriotic song was sung, the right hand being raised in salute, and the head bowed at the Holy Name in each verse.

"A stirring address from Major Duncan Webb, exhorting all to love and strive for the country, was followed by the singing of the National Anthem, after which there was a distribution of buns and the children and others dispersed. Our thanks are due to Major Duncan for his spirited address."

"In the same monthly report comes this announcement: 'On the 31st May a popular concert will be held in the schoolroom at eight o'clock (doors open at 7.30) when the following have kindly promised to perform: Major Duncan Webb; Mrs. Duncan Webb, guitar: Mrs. Gobbitt; Mrs. Radford, Norton; Mr. Wood, Ixworth; Miss Tayler, Rattlesden; Mr. Cook, Woolpit, flute; Mr. Bridwell, Beyton, violin; Mr. G. B. Horne, Beyton; Miss Pansy Phillips, Drinkstone, piano; Miss Jones, Hessett, recitation; Miss Violet Jones, Hessett; Mr. Ernest Allen, Drinkstone.

"Now [asks Nell Cocksedge] – who remembers Mrs. Pansy Mayes, née Phillips? She was my Sunday School teacher from 1924 until 1927 when I moved to Hessett. When I came back to Drinkstone in 1947, Pansy was still working for the Church. She was cleaner for umpteen years until it got too much for her. A regular worshipper, a stalwart in the village, one of her last duties (as the oldest resident) was to unveil the village sign to commemorate the Queen's Silver Jubilee in 1977.

"Born in 1896, Anna Elizabeth – Pansy as everyone knew her – must have been eleven years old when she played the piano in that concert of 1907. She died in 1979 aged eighty-three"

I was keen to borrow this ancient book and read it for myself. I was introduced to Nellie Bartram, (née Sturgeon), now aged 94 and living alone, in great independence of spirit, in her neat Woolpit bungalow. She told me her late husband Frederick Bartram had been born in Drinkstone, attended the school, and thought very highly of Ruth Gobbitt, the Headmistress. Nellie herself joined the Girl Guides (set up by Lady Baden Powell in 1910, because so many girls asked to become Scouts). Miss Hargreaves of Drinkstone Park was the local Guide Captain, and meetings were held in the ballroom of the mansion! Nellie says "I got to know a lot of Drinkstone girls through the Guides, and it was good to have space to run around. It's a great pity that mansion was pulled down, it was beautiful, very well built".

Nellie lived in Hessett as a child – just a short walk from Drinkstone village where her future husband was living. Communications between these two villages seem to have been friendly; girls met through Girl Guide meetings at the mansion. Nellie's father, a self-employed carrier who owned some land, grew wheat which he would take to Clover's Mill at Drinkstone to be made into flour for his wife to use. Nellie says:

"Mother never bought a cake, and she baked every week – a big day, baking in our house. So was wash day; we got our water from the village well opposite the Six Bells near Hessett Church. Even the farmers, when it was a dry spell, would cart water from there. Mum and my brothers would drop the bucket down – it wasn't a deep well – and would carry two buckets home. We wore white pinafores with frills to starch and iron. For Dad it was stiff collars with a front. He went twice a week to Bury with his horse and van. He took people, 6d return, wet or dry."

Interestingly, although these Hessett children were on good terms with the children of Drinkstone, relations with nearby Beyton were less friendly. Nellie says:

"If Beyton children came up to Hessett we showed 'em off home – they were foreigners! They'd come spoiling for a fight. We were hooligans really I suppose, but we weren't bad, we

never damaged anything. My Mother ruled us. If we did anything wrong, we 'went on the mat'. And Billy Kent, Headmaster at Hessett School, used to cane us. If I had the cane at school I didn't tell Mum, or I'd get it again!"

Nellie Bartram lives alone now. She has two grandsons. She and Frederick had two sons, one sadly killed at nineteen in the Air Force. The other died aged seventy-one. Nellie would have dearly loved a daughter, and always made a great fuss of Joyce, daughter of her cousin Mary Levett. Mary was cook for Rev. Horne in Drinkstone before her marriage, and daughter Joyce attended Drinkstone School. Joyce told me some of her memories of her years as a pupil there, and these are in a later chapter.

Chapter Seven

GLEANINGS FROM THE CHURCH MONTHLY
1905 - 1907

NELLIE KINDLY LOANED me the volume, "Church Monthly 1905–6–7", much treasured by her brother. It was printed at the "Church Monthly" Printing Office, Norwich. The book is a compilation of items selected from the monthly magazine, whose offices were at 30 & 31 New Bridge Street, Ludgate Circus, London EC. This high-minded and "improving" magazine contained an intriguing mix of history, Biblical exposition, moral tales (rather over-sentimental to most readers today), natural history, new hymns with accompanying music, lives of saints and notable churchmen, tales from the mission field and from British Colonies, and studies of particular churches and their architecture. The magazine was designed "for home reading" and has stories for women and children as well as articles for learned clerics. There are many finely detailed black and white drawings. The magazine seems to have been distributed to churches throughout the United Kingdom and its Colonies, and to missions overseas.

I was thrilled to discover that the last section of this book is made up of news from country parishes east of Bury St. Edmunds, comprising Thedwastre Rural Deanery. The main contributors were local vicars and rectors. The rector of Drinkstone, the Rev. Frederick E. Horne, was a dedicated priest and pastor who took his duties to the Parish and School most seriously. The extracts below (many of them written by Rev. Horne) give us a picture of life at the School and more generally in the Deanery, in the years 1905 –7.

January 1905 – *It seems wonderful to think, dear friends, that yet another Christmas Day has come and gone, the 39th that myself and Mrs. Horne have spent amongst you in Drinkstone, and, wonderful to relate, not once during those 39 years have either of us been prevented by illness or otherwise from occupying our accustomed places in the dear old Church.....some beautiful flowers and evergreens were sent by Mr. and Mrs. Hargreaves from the Park, and a most welcome selection of holly &c., from Major and Mrs. Webb, arriving just when they were wanted.*

February 1905 – *A very good performance was given by our excellent School Mistress, Mrs. Robinson, on January 5th at 7.30pm, when the children, many of them in fancy dress, sang action songs, recited pieces, and went through musical drill &c., in a most creditable manner. Some of the elder ones played piano duets very nicely indeed. The elder girls were dressed in brightly coloured Japanese costumes, and ten of the boys were in white and black dresses such as are worn by French clowns. Mary Robinson sang 'I've lost my child' very cleverly, and Nellie Robinson played most of the accompaniments.* [Mary and Nellie were the daughters of Headmistress Emma Robinson, and for some time Nellie worked in the School as "Monitress"]. *£2-1s-1d was taken altogether, and the room was quite full.*

On January 11th members of the Church Choir were entertained at supper at Drinkstone Lodge by the Rev. Fredk. and Mrs. Horne. Fourteen sat down to a substantial meal of meat, plum pudding, beer and dessert, in the saddle room, and afterwards played games and smoked.

On January 13th the Bell-ringers, Clerk, and others, 14 in number, were also invited to supper at Drinkstone Lodge, which they seemed much to enjoy.

The payments to the Choir Boys has now to be made. It amounts to £2-7s-6d, a sum calculated on the number of their attendances during the year. This and the washing of surplices (about 10s), wear and tear of books, &c, brings the Choir expenses to about £3-10s annually, but we hope in the summer to collect enough money to enable our boys to have an excursion somewhere. I think it would be a great encouragement.

We are extremely sorry to lose the services of Mrs. Robinson in our School, and hope that both she and her family will find a happy home at Troston, where they are going. Our best wishes will go with them all, I am quite sure.

March 1905 *– On February 10th a meeting was held in this School for the purpose of presenting Mrs. Robinson, our Head Mistress, with a testimonial on leaving us. The address was neatly illuminated in an album, and ran as follows - "Testimonial to Mrs. Robinson, Head Mistress of Drinkstone Voluntary School, on her resignation of the post after a period of 10 years, February 10th, 1905. We, the undersigned, beg you to accept this testimonial and clock in recognition of the faithful manner in which you have discharged your duties here, and in token of our respect and affection. With heartfelt wishes for your health and happiness." [Here follows a list of 62 names.]*

The presentation was followed by a capital tea given by Mrs. Robinson, to all the members of the School, numbering some 75 children. The tables were most liberally supplied with excellent cake, bread and butter, and jam. Tears somewhat interfered with the saying of grace, but nevertheless the day was much enjoyed by all the children, who, after tea, played various games, and dispersed later on with buns and oranges to take home. Mrs. Robinson leaves us for Troston early in March.

The next extract, dated May 1905, is mainly news of the Church, but the list of ladies who decorated the Church for Easter includes the name of Mrs. Gobbitt, who took up the post of Head Mistress left vacant by Mrs. Robinson's departure, remaining as Head for the next 22 years.

From an excerpt from Rattlesden news sent in by the Rev. E.J. Wild, we see that Drinkstone was one of sixteen local parishes who sent members of their choir and congregation on a mass outing to Yarmouth. Nearly 700 rode on the chartered train from Elmswell. Rev. Wild writes as follows:

August 1905 *– The full success of any such a venture depends so greatly upon the weather, that a slight cloudy morning naturally gave rise to a few anxious thoughts. No better weather, however, could possibly have been enjoyed than that with which we were favoured. The cool breeze from the North Sea was most refreshing after the sultry temperature we had so long, and if the paddlers found the dash and spray of the waves rather moistening and forcible, wet garments were but a slight price to pay for the exhilarating effects of the Yarmouth air.....The crowd at Elmswell, more especially on the return journey, whilst it would well have served a clever artist as a subject for a picture, with its ever shifting groups, restless horses, dim lights and passing trains, was, perhaps, a little confusing, and it may be a matter of satisfaction that no further damage resulted than the temporary exchange of a steed.*

(Tantalising! What mishap occurred at Elmswell Station that night, I wonder? And did gentlefolk of 1905 actually talk like this, or was it just their literary style?)

Rev. Horne of Drinkstone gave his own account of the day in the August magazine:

August 1905 *– On July 24th some of our parishioners joined a large excursion to Yarmouth. The Women's Help Society had been paying during the winter for their day at the sea, and only required the help of a van to take them to the station and back, and a few items in the way of buns, etc, to eat on the road. The Church Choir had their expenses entirely paid by kind subscriptions from Major Duncan Webb, Mr. Hargreaves, and the Rector, and others who enjoyed* *the excursion paid their own way themselves. A lovely day, not too hot, made it most enjoyable.*

August 4th, the Sunday School Treat was given by the Rector in the Lodge meadow. A light shower of rain made it necessary to take tea in the barn, but we were able to return to the meadow for the games. Thirty-seven children were present, and their happy little voices made pleasant music in our ears. Each received a pretty present and a piece of cake on leaving, and by the kindness of Mrs. Gobbitt a ride on her rocking horse, which was produced late in the afternoon, to their great delight.

August 11th, the Women's Help Society met in Church at 2 o'clock for a short service, followed by tea and games at the Lodge. Mr. and Mrs. Clement Bugg, and their son Reginald, were staying with Mrs. Bugg at the time, and gave us the pleasure of their company, he having been a choir boy of Drinkstone in former years, but now holding a responsible position in the cemetery at Upper Tooting. A photograph of the party was taken.

August 25th, a meeting of the Communicants of Drinkstone took place at Drinkstone Lodge. After a short service, croquet and other games prevailed till tea time, after which the Right Rev. Bishop Harrison kindly addressed us in Church...

November 1905 – *Our Harvest Festival this year was a great success....the following Tuesday the "fruits of the earth" offered in the Church were divided impartially amongst the aged and invalids of the parish.*

On October 2nd the Clothing Tickets were distributed as usual, and before long the Coal Tickets will also be given out. It should be remembered that a considerable sum of money is given by the gentry of the parish to provide the bonus, and when it is considered that this has been the case for the past 50 or 60 years, a certain amount of gratitude should be felt towards those who thus contribute to our winter comforts.

On Sunday, October 22nd, we celebrated the Centenary of Trafalgar. Special Psalms, Hymns, and Sermon graced the occasion, and our organist, Mr. Lanyon, dismissed us with "Rule Britannia" on the organ. The victory was a glorious one, and deserved a larger meeting of the congregation, but unluckily a heavy shower of rain deprived us of many of our usual worshippers.

On September 24th the Sunday School Bank was paid out with a bonus of one-fourth added. The payment is quite voluntary.

December 1905 – *The weather having turned cold, we are giving out the Coal Tickets to members of the Club tomorrow, December 1st, as they will be glad to have the coal now. Others who have not been so provident can only receive the smaller quantity which the bonus given by the subscribers affords. Our grateful thanks are due to Mr. Hargreaves and Major Webb, who have joined me in liberally subscribing to the funds of the Club.*

In the Magazine for this month, a painstaking pen and ink sketch of the 15th century chancel screen of All Saints' Church, drawn by Miss C. Townsend, is reproduced.

January 1906 – Speaking of the well-attended Christmas services at All Saints', Rev. Horne writes: *The Choir....sang sweetly, softly, and in tune, which, after all, is the great thing; and by their quiet, good behaviour they did not disgrace their snow-white surplices.* Did Mrs. Gobbitt's good work in School contribute to this achievement?

April 1906 – Fourteen young people of the village were among the candidates for confirmation in a service held in All Saints' Church, presided over by the Bishop of Ely. Rev. Horne writes: *The ages varied from 13 to 16....we have to thank Mr. Townsend for making an effort to come and help...on a very cold, snowy day, and Miss Townsend for kindly taking the organ for us. Her sweet, soft playing was remarked upon by several people present. The candidates were entertained at tea afterwards at the Drinkstone Schoolroom.*

May 1906 – as always, Rev. Horne lists by name all who have decorated any part of the Church for the Easter services, even Bertie and Fred Alderton (were they children?) who were very helpful in handing to the decorators. Gifts included *"a cart full of plants in pots for the altar from Mrs. Hargreaves.... and a quantity of beautiful narcissus, 'The Emperor', from Mrs. Webb, of Drinkstone House, were the greatest boon.*

July 1906 – *The summer seaside trip for the Women's Help Society is likely to be Felixstowe this year about the middle of July. All those wishing to join should send in their names at once to the Lodge as the railway tickets will have to be written for. The tickets will be 2s-6d, the dinner 1s, and tea 6d. If fine weather it should be a very enjoyable day.*
The School was re-opened on Monday, June 25th, and we greatly hope that all fear of a return of the fever is now over. The Sunday School has been open all along in the Church.
We should be glad to welcome any who would like to join the Sewing Meetings at the Lodge on Monday afternoons at 2.30 o'clock.

August 1906 – an excerpt from the news from neighbouring Hessett parish, contributed by the Rev. G. Jones, is as follows: *The fete held in the beautiful grounds of Drinkstone Park on July 12th in aid of the funds for the restoration of Hessett Church was a remarkable success .....the day, after a somewhat stormy morning, was fine, and from the time that the gates were opened, a constant stream of motor cars, carriages, bicycles and people on foot flowed steadily through the entrance gates. Over 1,000 tickets had been sold beforehand, and the total attendance must have numbered 3,000. The opening ceremony took place near the stall of fancy articles, over which Mrs. Hargreaves presided. The stallholders and their assistants, including the girls of the Hessett Sewing Guild, formed a circle, and the Rector, in a few words requested Viscountess Exmouth to open the fete. After the Viscountess had declared the fete open, a bouquet was presented to her by one of the children of the Guild, and a similar compliment was paid to Mrs. Hargreaves and Mrs. Harrison Topham. This ceremony over, the company dispersed in various directions, and visited those kinds of amusement which they most fancied. The switchback gondolas, Punch and Judy, and especially the motor gymkhana, which was held by members of the Bury and West Suffolk Automobile Club, attracting the greatest number of people. Mrs. Hargreaves' stall drew a large number of purchasers, and a great many sales were effected by the stall held by the Misses Hargreaves, and at that presided over by Miss Jones and the members of the Sewing Guild. The refreshments were under the able management of Major and Mrs. Harrison Topham, who were assisted by a band of willing helpers, who all worked with untiring energy to supply the wants of a multitude of hungry and thirsty folk. The band of the 3rd Battalion of the Suffolk Regiment, by kind permission of Colonel Scudamore and the officers, discoursed sweet music at intervals during the afternoon and evening, and to its strains a goodly number danced to their hearts' content. Many found great pleasure in the gardens, which were generously thrown open to the public......after deducting the expenses, there remained a net balance of £200, which has been paid into the bank. The parishioners feel that they owe a deep debt of gratitude to Mr. and Mrs. Hargreaves, and to all who kindly assisted to make the fete so great a success.*

September 1906 – *...how glad I am that the (Drinkstone) Summer Seaside Trip was such a success for the Women's Help Society and the Choir. The day was a perfect one, and the boating down to Felixstowe most enjoyable. An excellent dinner and tea was provided from the Beach Restaurant, and I am told by all the party that the food was the best we have ever had, well cooked, well served, and no hurry or confusion. We must not forget to thank Mr. Hargreaves, Major Webb and Major Prioleau for their kind subscriptions, which, added to my own contribution, made it possible to send the Choir entirely free, and to pay for the van and other small extra expenses for the W.H.S. who would otherwise pay for themselves.*
August 9th, the Sunday School children and younger members of the Choir, and some of our

old friends and neighbours, were invited to tea and games at the Lodge. Mrs. Gobbitt unfortu-nately was not well enough to join the party, but otherwise a very happy afternoon was spent, and the present which each child carried home seems to have given great satisfaction.

On August 17th, the members of the Women's Help Society and the Communicants gathered together for a social afternoon and tea, at the Lodge. Croquet, clock golf and other games were played, including "Mrs. Macquire", an unfailing source of amusement.

October 1906 – *I am sorry to have to record two fresh cases of scarlatina in the village, which I sincerely hope may prove the last. It has caused a vast amount of trouble, anxiety and expense since it first broke out in the early part of January to all concerned, and I trust that all parents will unite in taking every means of stopping the disease by keeping their children away from the invalids, and using disinfectants freely when attacked.*

Our Harvest Festival Services were well attended on Sunday, September 23rd...in the after-noon Mrs. Gobbitt kindly sang the solo of the anthem, and it went remarkably well. The beau-tiful fruit and vegetables were divided into ten portions the following day, and given away to our old friends.

December 1906 – In November, the Rev. Frank H. Horne of Beyton was married to Miss Coventry at Severn Stoke, near Worcester. Despite the marriage having taken place so far away, it was celebrated locally by the bridegroom providing substantial "meat teas" for all the parish-ioners of Beyton, in two sittings. This largesse was expected of Suffolk rectors, who were held in the same high esteem as local gentry. Frank (Francis) Horne succeeded his father as rector of Drinkstone in 1913.

December 1906 – the rector of Hessett includes in his report the fact that Mrs. Gobbitt sang at a concert to raise funds for the Restoration Fund of Hessett Church, and her songs "were much appreciated."

March 1907 – The Rev. Fred Horne reported the usual suppers given by him and his wife for Drinkstone Church Choir and Bell-ringers; also the progress of the Coal and Clothing Clubs. His report concludes with remarks about a School concert: *The children attending the Drinkstone School gave an entertainment on the 20th January, when each child gave either a recital or piece of some kind, and all distinguished themselves and did credit to Mrs. Gobbitt, our valued head-teacher, and her staff. A fortnight later a tea was given to the children by Mrs. Gobbitt, and the prizes (the result of the children's performance) given away.*

June 1907 – *A successful Jumble Sale was held in the School on Saturday, May 10th, in aid of Church expenses...the amount taken was £2-12s-6d, which was at once placed to the Churchwarden's Account. More buyers would have been better as many of the articles went unsold for want of purchasers, but these will be passed on to the Beyton sale, and another time, rather more notice will be given so as to attract people from a little distance.*

September 1907 – *With the kind assistance of Mr. Hargreaves, Major Duncan Webb, and Major Prioleau, I was able to send the elder School Children and the Church Choir to witness the Rehearsal of the Pageant at Bury St. Edmund's. The Carriers (Mr. Mothersole and Mr. G. Revens) conveyed them all safely and comfortably, and after partaking of a substantial tea, they found good places in the centre of the building, where they could both see and hear well the various stirring events represented, which they very much appreciated, and beg to thank warmly the contributors to the fund.*

Also I have to report the Members of M.H.S. chose Clacton-on-Sea for their seaside trip this year, and much enjoyed their day. They also were entertained at the Lodge on August 7th, and spent a pleasant afternoon. The Sunday School Treat was held the following day, when prizes for Good Attendance and Conduct were given.

The picture of life in Drinkstone revealed in these magazine extracts is of a paternalistic society revolving around Church, Gentry and School. Church and School are inextricably linked. All treats, special events and benefits to the villagers stemmed from these three sources, the same names recurring throughout. There is no anonymous giving – even the rector, in his reports, makes sure everyone knows that he himself has contributed to various "funds". No doubt he was a genuine and kindly man; however, everyone was constantly reminded that there were two distinct groups: those who gave, and must constantly be thanked and respected for having been born privileged; and those who received, and should know their place. This was so much a part of the status quo that possibly most villagers just accepted it as the way life was, and felt little resentment for their lot. Certainly the parish operated as a well-oiled machine, everyone playing their part at whatever level. I'm sure the various treats and excursions were thoroughly enjoyed.

Inextricably linked with Church and gentry, and fostered at school, was patriotism and pride in imperialism. In June 1907, Rev. Edward Burgess of Pakenham writes:

"Empire Day was kept imperially by us. Some of the coming men and women of the village assembled on the vicarage lawn, where the Union Jack flew most high. Kipling's stirring lines were sung; small boys raised tiny 'Jacks'; girls waved handkerchiefs, and we seniors gravely saluted the Ensign. And while we tunefully asserted that 'here in our village home, when Empire Day has come, in street, on fen alike, all men shall know that we are one', we felt the blood of Britannia coursing through our veins."

There are hints of an ulterior motive in the dedicated attempts to Christianise the Colonies, in remarks made by a representative of the Society for the Propagation of the Gospel, who came to speak in the Deanery about the work in India; he "felt convinced that in the future, the permanence of British imperial control would depend very much upon the Christianised natives and their loyalty"!

In Drinkstone, Empire Day was grandly celebrated in the grounds of Drinkstone School, faithful Rev. Horne present as always. I feel sympathy for the painstaking way he did his duty by everyone. He must have been "treading on eggshells" as he tried to record correctly exactly who had decorated each corner of the Church for festivals, who had given money, who had performed in concerts or played music, for many of his reports contain long detailed lists in an attempt to thank everyone for everything! The "gentry" of a village were expected by tradition to fulfil certain roles, as an excerpt from Ixworth Thorpe, (June 1907) makes clear. The bride of Mr. E. Johnson was welcomed into that parish with these public remarks from the rector:

"Everyone is pleased that Mr. Johnson has brought a lady to the parish, as for many years there has been no one to take the head in local matters, and no one to whom the people of the parish could apply in times of distress and trouble. We hope therefore that Mrs. Johnson will find time to take a personal interest in all that may be for the good of the village..."

Without support from Church, Church organisations and the well-to-do, life would have been well nigh impossible at anything but subsistence level for landless country folk. Rev. Wild of Rattlesden included an interesting run-down of typical weekly expenses taken from a Cambridgeshire village, presumably as an encouragement towards thrifty debt-free living, in his entry for October 1905, as follows:

"WIDOW AGE 73 – Goes out washing and earns a few shillings and has a small garden which a son digs for her. Weekly expenses – Rent 9½d, coal 8d, bread 5d, flour 1d, meat 4d, cheese 2d, butter 4d, sugar 2½d, milk ½d, tea 2d, soap etc ½d, oil 1d. Total 3s 4d a week.

"OLD COUPLE, BOTH 75 – The man earns 6s. Small garden. Weekly expenses – Rent 9½d, coal 1s, bread 1s 0½d, flour 4½d, pork and bacon 1s, suet 1½d, butter 6d, sugar 4d, milk 1d, tea 5d, soap etc ¾d, oil etc 1¼d, clothing club 2d. Total 6s a week."

Not much left over for extras! It seems to have been taken for granted that even elderly cottagers would still work, and still grow what vegetables they could. Allotments were available at tiny rents (sometimes even free as a result of Charities) and prizes were awarded for those best kept. The rector of Woolpit, in November 1905, confesses with disarming honesty, "The rector regrets he was unable this year to give his usual prizes for the three best cultivated plots on the Town Land owing to forgetfulness when the time came to have them judged"!

Drinkstone and all the other villages appear to have had Clothing and Coal clubs, of which the local vicar or rector took charge, regularly exhorting parishioners to keep up weekly payments. Thanks to contributions from the gentry folk could take out slightly more than they had put in, at the end of the year. Churches might hold concerts to raise a little more. Some villages also had Boot and Shoe clubs, and Charities which provided particular items for a lucky few, such as the Staniforth Charity at Norton which provided coats and gowns for the needy. Rev. Grimley reported that since dividends had fallen, in future he would select as recipients of the coats "those who still were constantly engaged in open-air work, and who had to face the pelting rain and the biting frost, rather than labourers who had ceased to toil, and who passed the days of wintry severity within the shelter of their homes." The names of twenty-five parishioners who had been given gowns or coats then follow.

Despite their own near penury, village women and girls were expected to join various worthy groups most of which either stitched altar linen or choirboys' surplices for the Church, or made items for the mission field. An entry from the rector of Woolpit, November 1905, invites girls aged ten and over to join the Girls' Friendly Society and "pass a profitable hour in making garments for....Central Africa". Another children's group raising funds for missions were the "King's Messengers". Likewise members of the "Guild of St. Etheldreda" made clothes, some for orphanages, and some to sell for their funds. When the time came for mission collecting boxes to be handed in, the amount each person had collected was publicly listed to the last farthing. I should think this acted as a deterrent to some families! But everyone could contribute to numerous flower services, when wild as well as garden flowers were brought to the Church and later taken to local hospitals, or even further afield, like the "full hamper of cowslips" sent to a poor London parish. Eggs and fruit were also donated for local orphanages and hospitals. The children of Drinkstone sometimes spent school afternoons picking and bunching flowers for giving.

Health problems were constant. Whole schools were decimated by epidemics of measles, whooping cough, and scarlet fever. The lists of parish burials are sobering, including many more babies, children and young adults than we would expect today. Occasionally even typhoid fever made an appearance. There were District Nurses, who in some villages worked anywhere they were needed, in others only where the family had paid full annual subscription (about 1s 6d). These were trained by the County Council, as were "Cottage Helps" (who had to be aged over twenty four), but the parish could decide how to pay their wages. Churches held concerts to boost the fund, and gentry made their contribution. In January 1905 Rev. Jones of Hessett announced, "We should like to draw the attention of our readers to the fact that we have an excellent district nurse for the parishes of Beyton, Hessett, and Rougham, who will be most glad to give her assistance in nursing any cases of sickness that are not infectious. No charge is made for her visits, but it is hoped that people availing themselves of her services will subscribe annually to the fund."

Wise old cures were still in vogue for some, and Rev. Burgess of Pakenham often offered his opinion on the subject, as in two entries from 1907. In April he wrote: "Last year there was a plentiful crop of what may suggestively be called 'spring blossoms', those painful skin eruptions which have left some ugly scars. Much of this might be avoided if a little precaution of the brimstone and treacle order is adopted"! In November he wrote: "There is much sickness of a low influenza type about. Added to this, little Teddy and Kitty have again been busy turning their 'innards' into a magazine for unripe fruit, with the usual results. When will those mothers throw powders to the pigs, and learn again to believe in the sovereign virtues of castor oil?"

However, in more modern manner, he also advocated milk as a food, not just a drink, and suggested that open windows and fresh air might dispel germs from cottages.

EDUCATION

The reports from parishes provide much information about the running of National Schools. There were regular visits from His Majesty's Inspectors, whose reports were extremely brief, very often only a

The Cherry Tree public house, circa 1885, with a fair in the grounds.

single sentence. Some typical examples from the Deanery are: "This little School maintains its excellent character", "This small school continues to be well taught", and "This little school continues to be very well taught and disciplined". An H.M.I. report on Norton School, from August 1905, baldly states, "The School continues to be carefully taught, but the Staff is at present unduly weak". The problem here seems to have been an inadequate number of Staff rather than poor teaching. Teenage pupil-teachers seem to have been rather arbitrarily placed in village schools by the County Council, to learn as they taught. They had to pass a series of exams in order to qualify as Supplementary Teachers. Further exams, including "The King's Scholarship Exam", were necessary if they were ever to attain Headship. A report in the Magazine from Pakenham, November 1905, complains, "The County Council has, in one swoop, carried off both our pupil teachers to educate in Bury, and has made no provision for filling up the vacancy here."

It is interesting to read that although most village schools were Church Schools, the managers tried hard to meet the needs of everyone, and at a Managers' Meeting of Rattlesden National School (village population just under 900 in 1905) it was decided to advertise specifically for a Free Church teacher. The advertisement asked for "a Baptist, Methodist, Congregational or Presbyterian" teacher. But no applications were received, and they had to settle for Church of England!

In 1905-7 the school leaving age was fourteen years, but certain attendance requirements had to be met before a child might leave. In June 1907 the Rattlesden rector called parents' attention to the ruling by the Education Authority that every child should make at least 350 attendances in each of 5 years before leaving school. "Cases have occurred where a child, attending 350 or more times for four years, and under 350 for each of the other years, has been called upon to go to school for an additional whole year." Nell Bartram told me that her brother-in-law William suffered from this ruling. Having joyfully left Drinkstone School to work on Squirrell's farm, Hessett, he was summoned back to remain as "scholar" for another year!

As an incentive, numerous prizes for good conduct and attendance were awarded annually by the Education Committee of the County Council, and winners' names were listed in the Magazine.

While most village children only ever attended their local village school, a tiny minority took up scholarships at "higher grade schools". Rev. Wild of Rattlesden's report in August 1905 begins "We congratulate Harold William Gardner on having secured first place in the list of candidates for the West Suffolk County Council Scholarships…. He is well ahead of the other 39 competitors". This boy was twelve. The Scholarship awarded was not a school place, but £20 p.a. for three years.

High on the curriculum were Scripture and Anglicanism. Diocesan Inspectors (who might be local rectors or vicars) made frequent visits and presented extremely detailed reports, almost always summing up the teaching in this area as "very good" or "excellent". A typical example comes from Pakenham School in 1906: "Standards II, III, IV: 26 slates, very accurate and careful work. Standard V: 13 papers, good work, but several of the papers are not independent of each other....Standards VI, VII: 16 papers, majority very praiseworthy.... Infants: Results very fair, about six children answered well, and some memory work was very nicely said. Very careful teaching...Standard I: Good work in Scripture and repetition." There was also a viva voce exam for higher grades: "Scripture Knowledge excellent, Prayer Book Work quite satisfactory". Classes were tested on knowledge of the Lord's Prayer, the Creed, and Baptism of Infants. Many pupils' names are mentioned in these reports, and individual work is often graded as being "correct /nearly /moderate /fair/ indifferent". The Inspector would take note of the "religious tone" of the school and assess the singing of hymns, usually as "tuneful and accurate".

At this time, the State was gradually taking over from the Church in oversight of village schools. Although the work of maintenance, and the bills for this, still fell mainly on the Church, the Education Committee was making more regulations, more demands. In February 1905 Rev. Harrison of Ixworth remarks, "My work in connection with Schools was always a great pleasure....notwithstanding the constant red tape worries connected with the new County Council management". The Board of Education required the thatched roof of Pakenham School to be replaced with tiles "for better ventilation". The Rector of Hessett, in October 1906, reports "a large sum has been spent this year upon the School, inside and out, and upon the School House, only a small part defrayed by the County Council, while for the Balance the Managers are responsible". Churches ran concerts, Magic Lantern shows and jumble sales in an attempt to raise funds for their schools. The Rev. Arthur Lee of Langham looked back nostalgically to humble un-regulated origins, writing in November 1905, "Langham schoolroom has a history of its own to tell, a record of development from the lowly Dame School to the full-blown Voluntary School under the Education Authority of today..... some were reminded of the far-off days when Dame Mrs. Tuck held sway, and taught the girls, if she learned them little else, how to sew, to fell and hem".

But worse was to come. During 1906 an Education Bill was proposed in Parliament which raised outcry in the villages. According to various public meetings and protests, it sought to "take away from the Managers of a School which has been built by Church people or others for the purpose of giving definite religious teaching of a particular kind, the right to have that teaching given in the School." The objections were listed at various public meetings, in town and village, as follows:

> "It affords no security for religious teaching in any form in elementary schools.
> "It violates religious liberty and equality.
> "It alienates property held in trust.
> "It confers exceptional and co-ercive administrative powers outside the control of the Courts of Law."

Petitions were signed and sent to both Houses. Everyone was up in arms, the rector of Rattlesden making several strong points in the Magazine:

> "Church Schools have been built and maintained at the cost of many millions of money in order to ensure Religious Education by Church teachers on Church lines in school hours....It is little short of an insult to say....that Trust deeds are to be set aside, and that Churchmen ought to be content at having a money compensation offered to them as atonement."

In opposing this Bill, Bishops circulated letters to be read out in Churches, and the Church Army got together some facts about schools in 1906:

> "For some 600 years almost all the education of this country was carried on by the Church. Up to 1870 the only public elementary education was given by Voluntary Schools. In 1902 Council Schools numbered 6,154 with 2,946,511 scholars; Voluntary Schools numbered 14,069 with 3,042,505 scholars (11,817 of these schools belonged to the Church of England). Since 1870 Church people have voluntarily given some £33 million for their schools, as well as paid their Education Rates....the cost of the buildings is all borne by Church people."

Also, out of 34 Teacher Training colleges, 31 were the property of the Church.

At a packed meeting in Rattlesden, attended by many local vicars and rectors including Rev. Horne of

Automobile Club Rally at Drinkstone Park circa 1915

Drinkstone, three strong points were emphasised:

First, children should be taught the religion of their parents.

Second, this teaching was to be in school hours.

Third, it would be taught by teachers "who believe what they teach."

The Bill was defeated.

Despite the existence of National Schools in most villages, a variety of private schools continued to spring up here and there, some large and prestigious, others tiny. Private schools were often started by young ladies such as the daughter of a Rougham rector whose boarding school was in the Rectory, and was called "Rougham Home School". There is an advertisement for another small private school in the Magazine, June 1907: "Miss French, School for Girls, Hessett, near Bury St. Edmunds. Boys received to 8 years of age. Terms on application". These private schools seem to have escaped regulation.

The curriculum of National Schools, apart from Scripture and the three R's, could still be quite individual, as suggested by an intriguing report from Pakenham in May 1907 which reads:

"The swing of the Educational pendulum! Such of our lads who are not likely to develop into great 'skollards', need not now waste all their precious life between the years of 12 and 14, sitting on school benches as idle as a painted ship on a painted ocean. Mr. Moore is well qualified to teach the young idea to shoot. It is pleasant to watch the lads busily and happily setting out to play the serious game of 'Back to the Land'!"

VILLAGE CLUBS AND CLASSES

For most villagers the land was still their source of employment. Second came domestic service. Most were housed by their employers, so it was not easy to change career. There were "continuing education" opportunities in most villages, some free, some requiring a small fee. Subjects included general studies, wood carving, dairying, poultry keeping, gardening, singing, nursing, first aid, ambulance classes, sewing and cooking. These were not always sufficiently well attended to keep running, and were widely scattered through the district – not every village would benefit.

Churches ran Sunday Schools and (separate) Bible Classes for girls, lads, men and women. There were Boys' clubs, Girls' Clubs, Men's Reading Rooms, Mothers' Meetings, and Mothers' Union. Some of the Clubs allowed bagatelle, dominoes and draughts, and in summer there were cricket, bowls and quoits,

Automobile Club Rally at Drinkstone Park circa 1915

even occasionally air-gun and rifle clubs. There were Friendly Societies, Foresters and Oddfellows, and Benefit Societies (Credit Unions). Glee clubs and theatrical groups were constantly busy preparing for concerts. At one time a drum and fife band was started (by the Revs. Horne, father and son). On rare occasions a dance was held. Then of course Church Groups – Choir, Bell Ringers, Communicants' Guilds and so on – had outings, and annual invitations to the Rectory. Children were so keen on Sunday School (plenty of treats and prizes!) that in Hessett it was necessary to restrict attendance to children aged over five years.

LIFESTYLES AND LEISURE

Drinkstone had some non-conformist residents and a thriving Wesleyan Chapel, built in 1866 in Gedding Road, attracted plenty of children and young people. Many older folk who shared their memories with me recall having attended both Church and Chapel sessions on long-ago Sundays. Around the year 1900, Glen Cottage in The Street (now known as Blacksmith's Cottage) was used as a temporary Chapel. The Wesleyan Nunn family (instrumental in building the Chapel in the 1860s), lived here. Further in the past, Quakers had a meeting-house and resting-house in Rattlesden Road. Quaker Cottage and Hazel Cottage, now incorporated into a single home, served as meeting room for Quakers and lodgings for visiting Quaker leaders. An area of the grounds was used for Quaker burials.

In the 19th and early 20th centuries, a variety of Christian groups all over the country campaigned vigorously for "Temperance" (abstinence from alcohol). In April 1907 Rev. Grimley of Norton asks ominously, "Are there any in the parish who are conscious that they have of late been yielding to the beguilements of intemperance?" If so, they were urged to attend special temperance meetings. For young ones, the "Band of Hope" held lessons on scripture and temperance, and these groups were inspected to ensure good teaching, and that recitations, singing and musical drill were up to scratch. The announcement of the Annual Temperance Meeting at Badwell Ash, to be held in the vicarage garden, says, "Recipes for temperance drinks, cool and refreshing in the harvest fields, will be distributed." I should think this hint went down like a lead balloon to men accustomed to traditional Suffolk ale and cider.

Drinkstone had a thriving public house, The Cherry Tree, in The Green, and a beer-house (White Horse Beerhouse) down the Rattlesden Road, both centres for much socialising. There is mention of White Horse Beerhouse (or beer retailing business) in Suffolk Directories between the years 1844-1916.

The Cherry Tree public house is first mentioned in White's Directory for 1874, and was in business for over 100 years.

Life was full, working hours were long, some farm work was skilled, some tedious. In Great Barton a regular feature was the judging of stacks at harvest time. The judge, Robert Edgar, writes:

"After carefully inspecting the different Stack Ricks in your Parish, I have come to the conclusion that those of Mr. Baldwin and Mr. Fyson are the best put up, but I give Mr. Baldwin the preference, because all his stacks save themselves, and have not been trimmed. The roofs of others are badly put on and stage holes very visible."

Individual life stories of the times are told in certain obituaries of older residents. For example, Caroline King, Church cleaner for twenty years, was buried at Rattlesden at the age of 92, when it was said of her: "So ended a long life of hard, honest work, 61 years of which were spent in one cottage on Bird's Green, under by no means luxurious conditions for the enjoyment of life".

At Pakenham in 1907, John Tipple died at the age of 85, having "spent the most part of an active life in and about the woods out Fakenham way, where his task of hurdle making was lightened by the presence of birds and beasts, and flowers, which he knew and loved so well."

Working country people had only a day or two of "holiday" a year. So it must have been tantalising to read in the Magazine of wealthy ladies going to the South of France to end their days in the warm sun; or this entry from Rev. Harrison of Ixworth, April 1905: "I spent a most pleasant month in Italy with Captain Cartwright …. nearly all the time we were able to sit out on the terrace in the sun till quite late in the evening, and the Riviera climate has quite spoilt me for England, for I have never felt really warm since I returned."

Some individuals and families made the big break. There are complaints in the Magazine of bell-ringing teams depleted by young men "taking the King's shilling" and joining up. And every so often, a family would leave for distant lands. The Magazine announces a gift of £40, sent to Rattlesden Church by a family who emigrated to America in 1634. In 1888, Mr. Hunt of Manor Farm, Pakenham, emigrated to Queensland. By 1906 he had prospered, having "200 acres, 16 cows, and prize-winning horses".

HISTORY AND CHANGE

Even the remotest corners of countryside are subject to change, excitement and new inventions. Thus in September 1907, the children from Norton who were taken to the historical pageant at Bury St. Edmunds were not transported in the usual horse-drawn wagons, carriages or vans, but in three trucks, one behind the other, drawn by "one of Mr. Downing's traction engines". The Bury St. Edmunds Automobile Association actually brought its motor-cars to the fete in Drinkstone Park. And during a Choir outing from Great Barton to Yarmouth in 1907 "an interesting thing happened when a great warship came and anchored near the shore, while five curious-looking submarines, like great whales, anchored just around her."

The various rectors and vicars, who shepherded so many aspects of parishioners' lives and regularly taught in the village schools, seized every chance to give the villagers a sense of history. On a trip to Castle Hill in Thetford, in 1907, one wrote that he was reminded of "two mighty mounds or barrows, in the village of Jelling, in Jutland, beneath which are the burial chambers of King Gorm and Queen Thyra who, nearly a thousand years ago, were there interred with pagan rites, and who were the last Danish King and Queen to be so interred".

The book abounds with snippets of history or legend relating to Suffolk and East Anglia, such as that Thomas Ratlisden (Rattlesden) was Abbot of Bury in 1479. On returning with the schoolchildren from a visit to the pageant at Bury St. Edmunds, one vicar took the opportunity to educate readers of the magazine, explaining that Gallio, a character in the pageant, was mentioned in Acts 18, and his brother Seneca's actions led to the revolt under Boadicea. Also, that in AD 960, Theodred, Bishop of Suffolk, bequeathed his lands at Pakenham to his cousin Osgot, who in turn granted it "to his kinsman Edmund" (that is, to the Abbey at Bury St. Edmunds). Since the Manors at Drinkstone, and many other local lands, were held under Saints Etheldreda and Edmund at the time of Domesday, these stories may well have been taught in the schools. St. Etheldreda was a favourite of these rectors:

> *"Etheldreda was born in Exning, Suffolk. She was the daughter of King Anna, King of the East Angles, and Queen Ereswitha. This queen was sister to St. Hilda, Abbess of Whitby. In 652 Etheldreda married Tonbert, Prince of the Girvii or Fen men, a tribe which inhabited the marshes of Cambridgeshire. In 660 Tonbert died, and Etheldreda married Egfrid, King of Northumbria, but at her wish he allowed her to withdraw into the convent of Coldingham, near York, being admitted by St. Wilfrid, Archbishop of York, in 672. Egfrid tried to draw his wife back by force. But she fled to Ely, where she founded a monastery admitting both men and women, married or single. She was the first Abbess, and on her death her sister Sexburga took her place.*
>
> *"In 870 the Isle of Ely was ravaged and the Church at Ely destroyed by hordes of Danish invaders. For a century the religious house lay desolate..."*

Certainly Etheldreda's name lived on in Suffolk villages, into the 20th century, as the women of her Guild met together to sew garments for the needy!

The Parish of Drinkstone was under the Diocese of Norwich until 1837, when it was transferred to Ely Diocese. Only in 1914 was the Diocese of Suffolk created. Then the Church of Saint James at Bury St. Edmunds became a Cathedral. Visits to the Cathedral, the Abbey gardens, and the historical pageants, were a constant feature for Drinkstone pupils. We were still organising such visits as closure approached in the 1980s.

Chapter Eight

DISCOVERING THE PAST IN ALL SAINTS' CHURCH

IN FEBRUARY 1913, Frederick Edward Horne "for 48 years Rector of this Parish" as his tombstone declares, died aged 77. For forty-eight years he had been a wonderful, faithful visitor and teacher at the School, Chairman of Managers, and friend to Ruth Gobbitt. He was succeeded in the Parish by his son the Rev. Francis Herbert Horne, who was to prove equally worthy of love and respect in the village. After 1914, oversight of Church and School came from the Bishop at Bury St. Edmunds, not from Ely.

At this time the population of the village was around 433 (the number at the 1911 census). What devastation to the whole working and social structure the 1914-18 War must have brought! I visited All Saints' to look for mementoes of this era, and found a Roll of Honour giving the names of "Parishioners on active service for their King and Country" in the first two years of the war. Forty-one men, most of whom would have been educated at the School! This is the list of names:

J. B. Hargreaves
Commander C.C. Horne R.N.
Major Duncan Webb
Lieutenant Vere Webb
Lieutenant G.B. Horne
Sergeant Major Gill
Sergeant Henry Gobbitt
James Cornish
James Gill
Henry Seeley
Ernest Smith
Alfred Stiff
Arthur Bland
Leopold Colson

Robert Buckle
Reginald Colson
George Cornish
Frank Harvey
Albert Edward Bennington
Reginald Barker
William Radford
Sydney Mayes
Stanley Mayes
Arthur Pryke
Walter Pryke
William Pryke
Christopher Revens
Cecil Colson

Nepland Revens
Percy Revens
Amos Rose
Cecil Rose
Sidney Rose
Philip Rose
Albert Smith
Reginald Smith
Sidney Smith
John Whiting
Walter G. Rose
Walter Rose
George Rose

Fifteen were killed in service. They were:

Thomas Barker, 7th Suffolks
James Cornish, Sergeant, 3rd Leicesters
William Edwards, Royal Engineers
James Gill, 2nd Suffolks
Alfred Harvey, 6th Yorkshires
Walter Halls, 8th Suffolks
Bertie Phillips, 25th Leicesters
Arthur Pryke, City of London

All Saints' Church, Drinkstone

George Rose, Sergeant M.M. 8th Suffolks
Cecil Rose, 8th Suffolks
Sydney Rose, 8th Suffolks
Harry Seeley, 2nd Suffolks
Albert Smith, 1st West Yorkshires
John Whiting, 8th Suffolks
Duncan Vere Webb, Captain M.C., 1st Leicesters

This is terrible enough, but it doesn't tell the whole story. There were those like Nell Cocksedge's father, Paul Blake – wounded or gassed – who continued to suffer when demobbed, and died a short while after returning home. There was no war widow's pension for Paul Blake's wife, because he died three years after war ended. William Edwards (father of Molly whose story is in a later chapter) died on his way home from war work in Italy, of a fever contracted on the continent. Johnny Smith, born in Drinkstone but living in Chelmsford at the time of his death, was killed in a bombing raid, aged 19 (Johnny was younger brother of Tom, whose story is in a later chapter).

All over Britain there were tragic stories like that of Clement Horne (son of the Rev. Frederick and brother of the Rev. Francis). After marriage, Clement lived at Park Corner (later known as The Meade). Clement returned after enduring who knows what horrors, only to have his wife Gertrude die in February 1919. His widowed mother (born Augusta Fanny Astley, daughter of Sir Astley Paston Cooper) died later that year, in August. Poor Clement shot himself on the stairs of Drinkstone Lodge in December 1919. The inscription on his tombstone reads: "Clement Cooper Horne, Captain R.N., C.B.E. died Dec. 18th 1919 aged 52 – 'Until the day break and the shadows flee away.'"

The Hornes were not the only family of a Drinkstone rector whose lives were touched by tragedy. When preparations to build Drinkstone School were underway, the Rev. George Peloquin Cosserat was the incumbent. Plaques in the Church reveal that no less than three Cosserat sons died in 1858-9. John Peloquin (his fourth son) "was shot in the mouth by a musket ball when commanding his Regiment the 1st Punjaub Cavalry against the rebels at Koorsee under Sir Hope Grant on the 23rd March 1858, and died of his wound at Lucknow on April 10th in the 34th year of his age". Later in 1858, on 18th September, the Rev. George himself died, leaving his unfortunate widow Jane to endure two further family deaths. On February 20th 1859, their third son Reginald Peloquin died aged 35. Then on April 12th, their second son, David Peloquin, died aged 41.

The village suffered much lighter losses in the Second World War – just three names appear on the Memorial plaque: Percy C. Bloomfield of the Royal Navy; Captain Michael Hargreaves (of Drinkstone Park), Grenadier Guards; and George E. Rose of the Royal Marines (George was brother of Walter, whose story appears in a later chapter). Others, such as Albert Horrex (known as "Doodles"), and Albert Brinkley, were prisoners of war so did not return to Drinkstone for some years. Albert Horrex's wife Mary tells her story later in this book.

The County Directories are a useful source of information on All Saints' and its history. Kelly's Directory for 1888 tells us, "The Church of All Saints is an old stone structure in the Perpendicular and Decorated styles, consisting of chancel, nave, aisles and brick western tower containing six bells, which have been recast." The new tower and bells were paid for from a £400 bequest of Thomas Camborne; the work was done in the 1690s. "In the year 1867 the Church was completely restored, with the exception of the south porch which was rebuilt in 1872, and is remarkable for its beautiful proportion and the uniformity of date displayed in the tracery of the windows, carving of the screen and finials: the east window was restored at the same time and filled with stained glass, in memory of William Horne, father of the present rector: the lancet window in the tower was presented by the late Henry le Heup Cocksedge Esq. in memory of a son lost at sea. The register dates from 1666."

The Le Heup Cocksedges (no relation of the Cocksedge families now living in Drinkstone) lived in Drinkstone House (formerly known as Drinkstone Place). Another interesting memorial in the Church relates to George Grigby (youngest son of Joshua Grigby or Grigsby who built Drinkstone Park mansion in the 1760s). George was "Captain of the 11th Regiment of Infantry on board a transport bound to Cadiz, he was run down by the franchise frigate, off Falmouth, February 21st 1811, and perished together with 233 souls, aged 39 years". (Was this a terrible accident, or deliberate?)

Other features are the 15th century carved oak rood screen and the 12th century marble font. The pupils of the School often went into the Church for study of history, or to draw, rub brasses, arrange flowers, or attend a service. The carved pew ends depicting griffons, angels, lions, a dove with olive twig, and various ambiguous hairy creatures that could be ox, horse, or monster, are fascinating to children. Generations of schoolchildren used the Church and churchyard as an extension of the School. This was so appropriate since without the Church, and the Reverends Mosely and Maul, Drinkstone School might have been built in a different location in a different decade and with a different ethos. Faithful rectors continued to mould the School's character and befriend the children over the decades.

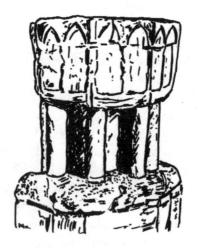

12th century font of Purbeck marble

Chapter Nine

RUNNING THE SCHOOL
The work of Charity Trustees and School Managers

MOSELY'S CHARITY

Charitable Trusts are complicated things inclined to lead to confusion, expense and involvement with solicitors. The Charity set up by Rev. Mosely in 1804 was certainly generous and beneficial, but over the years gave rise to many headaches and misunderstandings. Trustees are not immortal, nor are solicitors; and while some of these might have an excellent grasp of the business in their lifetime, what happens when they die and others are left floundering?

The Suffolk Records Office holds various documents relating to Rev. Mosely's Trust for the schools of Rattlesden and Drinkstone, and below are a few examples.

A Bill from 1859 from Solicitors French and Lawton relates to business regarding the Trustees of the "Drinkstone and Rattlesden Sunday School Endowment Fund" – "taking possession of it, and appointing new trustees". A Mr. Mosely (possibly son of Rev. Mosely) and Rev. James Oakes are named as the current surviving trustees. The Rev. S. M. Maul (Rector of Drinkstone who gave the land for the building of the School) was doing the "management".

The new Deed is dated 1st August 1859 and is headed "Appointment of new Trustees of a sum of £1,091-10s-6d Consols bequeathed by the will of the Rev. Richard Mosely deceased for the support of Schools at Drinkstone and Rattlesden, Suffolk". The solicitors' bill amounted to £9-3s-4d, a huge sum at that date.

A letter written (it is not clear to whom) on June 13th 1860, on behalf of French and Lawton, Solicitors at Eye, Suffolk, refers to the same transaction:

> "My dear Sir,
>
> "Mr. Mosely has written to the Bank of England and put the transfer of your Scole fund right – and it now stands in the names of Messrs. Mosely – Oakes – W. Parker and yourself. The enclosed power of attorney for the receipt of the dividends upon it – will you be so good as to execute it yourself and get it executed by Mr. Oakes and Mr. Parker. There must be two witnesses to each signature who must sign their names where the letters A.B.C.D. are pencilled – and must add their residences and occupations in life. When this is done we will have the power, signed by Mr. Mosely – and the dividends will then in future be receivable at Messrs Oakes, Bury St. Edmunds.
>
> "We enclosed the stock note date – the Commission will be charged to the account at the Bank. Yours sincerely, J. Warnes, for French and Lawton."

The Deed of Appointment is on a square of parchment, size about three by three feet. It is signed in ornate script, by solicitors in Lincoln's Inn, and also by various worthies of the Drinkstone district, each signature being duly witnessed:

> "Duncan Parker, in the presence of Joseph Russell Olorenshaw, Clerk in Holy Orders, Rattlesden;

"Ernest John Wild, Albert John Bolders, William Isaac Clark, and Henry Plummer, in the presence of J. R. Olorenshaw;

"Edward Montague Le Heup Cocksedge, in the presence of Julian G. Puck, Clerk in Holy Orders, at Tostock Rectory;

"Ernest Robert Le Heup Cocksedge, in the presence of Frank H. Horne, Gentleman, of Drinkstone Rectory;

"Frederick Edward Horne and Francis Herbert Horne, in the presence of Mary Ann Wilson, servant (spinster), Drinkstone Rectory;

"Signed, sealed and delivered by Thomas Harcourt Powell, in the presence of Fredreic Causswell, Gardener, Drinkstone Rectory;

"Windsor Parker, in the presence of James Buckle, Butler to Major Parker;

"Henry Le Heup Cocksedge, in the presence of John Jewers, Farmer, Drinkstone;

"John Boldero, in the presence of J.C.Warnes;

"William Windsor Parker, in the presence of James Buckle, Butler to Major Parker;

"James Oakes, in the presence of William Aylward, Butler to Rev. J.W.Oakes."

There follow eleven signatures, each with a stamped blob of red sealing wax between the person's Christian name and their surname, as follows:

"Jn Mosely, Jme Oakes, Thos. Harcourt Powell, Windsor Parker, Spencer Woodfield Maul, H.L. Cocksedge, John Bolders, John Jackson, James Sparke, William Windsor Parker".

In 1895, most Trustees having died, the whole business started again. A Declaration of Trust was sent to Duncan Parker, Esq. and the Revd. Ernest Wild. Proof of the deaths of the trustees had to be provided. The details are given on small cards each bearing a penny stamp. These are some of the details:

"Henry Le Heup Cocksedge, died August 14 1868 aged 52 years, buried at Drinkstone by Frank Horne.

"Thomas Harcourt Powell, died September 8th 1892 aged 73, buried at Drinkstone by Ernest J. Wild."

The following were all buried at Rattlesden by Rector Ernest J. Wild:

"William Windsor Parker, died July 22nd 1873 aged 42 years

"John Bolders, died January 4th 1886 aged 79 years

"Windsor Parker, died at Clopton Hall February 3rd 1892 aged 90 years.

"Died and buried at Risby – James Sparke, January 24th 1884, age 77."

What a business it all was! No wonder Wild and Wild, Solicitors, charged a total of £12-15s-4d for services during 1894-5. Additionally, Messrs Woodrooffe and Burgess charged £2-7s-6d following the death of J. Harcourt Powell, the last surviving Trustee at the time.

Another charge "Re Mosely's Charity" arose in 1895, relating to costs paid when arranging "the Transfer of securities upon the appointment of new Trustees". It appears costs were paid out of capital rather than from dividends, and the Charity Commissioners complained. Rather peevishly, one of the Trustees writes "we did not see what the Charity Commissioners had to do with the matter!"

Maybe as a result of this error, a document of 1899 is headed "Declaration of Trust as to Charity Schools at Rattlesden and Drinkstone (in) pursuance of the Will of Revd. Richard Mosely of Drinkstone, dated 3rd August 1829". This document goes on to say:

"All persons who should become Trustees are hereby directed to apply and dispose of the Clear Dividends for the support of a Sunday School and a weekly Day School in the Parishes of Drinkstone and Rattlesden. Signed F. Horne, on behalf of the Trustees, Mosely Charity".

The annual income from dividends at this time was £13, of which "£1 was claimed by C.C." [the Charity Commissioners?] leaving £12 to be disposed of. The "suggested division" was £5 for the Sunday School, £4-10s for the School building and £2-10s for the Schoolhouse… "Trustees, Rector and Churchwardens" were involved in this decision.

There was a meeting on 10th March 1905, once again to decide where the income should go (possibly a re-think due to the recent advent of Foundation Managers):

"Mosely's Charity for the Schools of Drinkstone and Rattlesden – at a meeting held on the above date (pursuant to due Notice) of the Trustees of the above Charity at Rattlesden Rectory.

Present, Revd. E. J. Wild, Revd. F. E. Horne, Revd. F. H. Horne, Mr. A. J. Bolders, Mr. W. J. Clarke, Mr. H. Plummer.

"The following resolution proposed by F. H. Horne and seconded by H. Plummer was carried unanimously –

"'That the yearly Income to be divided thus –

"Seven Pounds to each Sunday School.

"Four Pounds ten shillings to the Foundation Managers of each School for the up-keep of the School House and Offices.

"Ten shillings to the Trustees of each School Buildings for the upkeep of the School Dwelling House and Offices.

"One pound to Education Committee for each School.

"Total £13 for each School.'

"Windsor Parker Esqre. Was unanimously elected one of the Trustees of the above Charity.

"Signed, Frederick Horne, Chairman."

Things never seemed to run smoothly for many years at a time, and in 1925 the Bank of England, London EC2, wrote to say they were "now able to trace the stock, after a fruitless search"! It seems that the Charity Commissioners had suggested that the endowment of the Charity should be transferred to the Board of Education. There is correspondence between the Rev. J. R. Olorenshaw of Rattlesden Rectory with the Bank, on this subject. This transfer did not take place.

A subsequent document came from Greene and Greene, Solicitors of 80, Guildhall Street, Bury St. Edmunds. It was written on 8th July 1940 to the Rev. H. F. Wilson, D.C.L. of The Rectory, Rattlesden This is the letter:

"Dear Sir,

"Drinkstone and Rattlesden Schools

"As no doubt you are aware, a sum of £1,091-10s-6d Consols stands in the name of the Rev. F. Horne, late of Drinkstone, as the surviving trustee of the Mosely Charity, and the income is divided between the Church Schools at Drinkstone and Rattlesden.

"Owing to Mr. Horne's retirement we have been consulted by Major Fowler as to what should be done, and the Board of Education, with whom we have been in correspondence, suggest that the money should be transferred into the names of the official Trustees of Charitable Funds and that new administrative trustees should be appointed.

"It is suggested that these should be the two rectors and one or more Foundation Managers from each parish.

"Perhaps you would be good enough to let us know whether you would like to proceed on these lines and, if so, let us have the names of one or two Foundation Managers from your parish who would act as administrative trustees.

"The appropriate changes would be made at the same time with regard to the money at the Post Office Savings Bank and the current banking account.

"We are not quite sure how the Rattlesden half of the income is received and applied and whether you would like the existing arrangements to continue. Perhaps you would kindly let me know about this.

"We are, dear Sir, yours faithfully,

"Greene and Greene"

This is the latest document on the subject held in the Records Office. I don't know exactly what decisions were made. The clues may be in the Minutes of the Board of Managers of the School!

Years later, in October 1981, the Managers' Minutes record that "Mr. John Gibbs had handed over a cheque for £54.18, which was the total sum in the Bank of the "Old Trustees of Drinkstone Schoolhouse" (Lloyds Bank in Bury St. Edmunds) "...this account was therefore concluded". The money went into the School Fund and helped make the last years of the School more enjoyable for both pupils and parents.

The rest of this chapter describes some of the other difficulties these volunteer managers coped with over the decades.

THE WORK OF THE MANAGERS

The earliest reference to "Managers" that I have found is in the title pages of the first Admissions Register of Drinkstone School. This large hard-backed "No. 1 Durham Register" contains extracts from "the Revised Instructions issued to H. M. Inspectors, 6th February 1891". The requirements are quite stringent, and include the following:

> *"The Code requires that managers of schools shall provide suitable records – registers, log book and cash book (Article 8). In every school or department there should be 'a register of admission, progress and withdrawal' written in ink, with 'no erasures, no insertions.'"*

The first entries consist of a simple list with no home addresses apart from the name of the village, no details of progress, and under "Reason for leaving" the usual entry is simply "left", or sometimes "gone home"! As the years went by, entries become more explicit, including details of house name or number and Street name, and the names of villages or schools to which children moved on.

The earliest of the three Managers' Minutes Books currently held at the West Suffolk Archive commences with record of a meeting held in July 1903. Probably before this date, the rector, churchwardens and Headteacher together had "managed" the School. The incumbent acted as Chairman. He and three others were "Foundation Managers". A fifth manager (by 1903) was appointed by the County Council, and a sixth represented Drinkstone Parish Council.

The managers (all of them male) were of high standing in the community. In 1902 the Board of Education had issued an Order that all Church Schools must be run by a Board of Managers. The Order stipulated three necessary qualifications. Every manager must own property in or near the Parish, contribute regularly to funds, and be a practising member of the Church of England. So these first managers were all wealthy "gentlemen", or wealthy farmers. In 1903 they were the Rev. Fred Horne, rector of Drinkstone since 1865 (ex-officio Chairman); John Hargreaves of Drinkstone Park; John Chadwick Lomax of Drinkstone House; Arthur Constable of Rookery farm and John Jewers, farmer, of Whitefield House (son of John Jewers senior who is listed as "maltster" as far back as White's 1844 Directory). The sixth man (not a Foundation Manager, but representing the Parish Council and therefore not bound by the three qualifications above) was Charles Bland, shoemaker (listed in Morris's Directory of 1888 and member of a family which consistently achieved standing in the community through their own efforts and abilities).

So these were men of substance and influence, and they took their responsibilities as School managers seriously. When one of them had to resign, a similar gentleman would take his place; for many years Mr. Townsend of Hammonds Hall served, also Mr. Wicks of Ticehurst, and various members of the Bland family. In some cases it almost seems that being on the Board of Managers goes with certain houses! Drinkstone House (a substantial residence until an unfortunate fire burned most of it down) produced first Mr. Lomax, then Major Webb (killed in the 1914-18 War), then Major Fowler, all in succession serving as managers of the School.

The Rev. Christopher Blencowe M.A. of The Meade (formerly known as Park Corner) replaced faithful John Hargreaves who served right up until his death in 1935. John Hargreaves was a veteran of the First World War, and sadly, his son Michael died in the Second World War while serving in the Grenadier Guards. The Rev. Frederick Horne chaired meetings until his death in 1913, and was succeeded by his son Francis, the new rector. But most astounding of all was John Jewers. I don't know when he became a manager, but he was farming (with his father) at Whitefield House in 1888. In 1892 he had acquired Green Farm as well, and in 1916 he was farming both Whitefield and Green Farm. He eventually gave up Whitefield, staying at Green Farm where he ended his days in 1951 aged over one hundred! (When John Jewers died, Captain Michael Horne bought Green Farm and lived there until 1959).

John Jewers was still serving as manager of the School in 1946, at the age of ninety-six! The Rev. Blencowe gently suggested that it might be wise for him to step down. Major Fowler, in August 1946, records this event in the Minute Book, remarking on "the great interest of Mr. Jewers' letter…to be preserved in the Minute Book…an old gentleman 96 years of age!"

Today his letter of resignation can still be seen, stuck into the front of the Book. John wrote a humble letter in beautiful ornate hand, dated July 23rd 1946:

> *"Dear Mr. Blencoe, Thanks for your letter received yesterday: it is perhaps best for me to*

give up and let someone else younger take my place. I do not know that I have been much good as a school manager but I think I have always attended when meetings were held. I am yours truly, John Jewers."

(It can't have been too difficult finding someone younger!)

The first lady manager, Mrs. Mary Wilson then living at the Rectory, joined the Board in May 1946. She replaced Major Fowler, who after the burning down of his home, Drinkstone House, moved to Thurston "after many years of devoted work in the interests of the School". A second lady manager, Mrs. Ramsay, joined in July, as replacement for the faithful John Jewers.

Another manager for many years was Daniel Clover of the Mills. The Clover family had been continuous owners there since 1760! Daniel Clover also served the School right up to his death, in 1947. The then rector, Rev. D. Lilley, wrote a letter to his sisters Wyn and Eleanor Clover (who were still living at the Mills when I taught at the School in the 1980s!) expressing the managers' "great regret at the death of Mr. D. Clover, for many years a Foundation Manager and latterly the School Correspondent, and their deep appreciation of his services to the School". Captain Wilson of the Rectory took Mr. Clover's place on the Board.

The duties of these managers were to keep the teaching posts filled, and deal with repairs and refurbishment, problems with caretaking and so on. In the early 1900s, the managers had power to hire teachers and other staff such as pupil-teachers, and negotiated their salaries (paid by the Education Committee, which became in time the Local Education Authority or L.E.A., and had final say over appointments). The managers, in these early years decided on term dates. The local authorities were gradually getting all these factors standardised and more subject to central control. Managers retained the power to hire or fire caretakers and cleaners. Grants were made by the Education Committee towards these costs, and at Drinkstone the difference was made up from the Mosely fund. There was never enough money for everything the managers would have liked to do.

Drinkstone School, like other village Church Schools, was very much regarded as the property and responsibility of the village and the Church. So when in 1906 a proposed Education Bill seemed set to give the Government total control over the curriculum, managers everywhere were up in arms. There were huge fears that the specifically Anglican teaching by vicars and rectors might not receive priority, and that the local and Church ethos of these little schools might disappear. The managers were determined to preserve the spirit of the original trusts under which the schools were established. Bishops stepped in to heighten the protests! The Bill was defeated.

In 1936 the managers wrote to the Education Committee for support when a handful of parents transferred their children to Rattlesden School. The Committee had the pupils returned to Drinkstone. In 1939 the managers consulted with the Rural Dean over suggestions that in the near future Drinkstone School might take only infant and primary pupils. In the Autumn Term 1939 they wrote indignantly, with "grave concern", to the L.E.A. complaining about the disruption caused at the School by the arrival of evacuees and the flood of changes of routine imposed by the L.E.A. They persuaded the L.E.A. to equip the Village Hall as a classroom for the evacuees (although later when numbers decreased, the two groups were easily combined). During wartime, manager Major Fowler took responsibility for fitting and checking gas masks for the pupils.

In 1946 there were serious shortages of funds and materials, and the building was becoming seriously dilapidated. There was pressure to change the status of the School from "Voluntary" to "Controlled", and the managers strongly resisted this change. They feared losing control and wanted to be faithful to the intentions of those who had founded and funded it 140 years earlier. They took steps to ensure that money from the charity would not fall into L.E.A. hands, but would remain in the charge of rector and churchwardens for the Schoolhouse and Sunday School. The Diocese also stepped in to try to delay the inevitable – but neither managers nor Diocese came up with the extra cash which would have ensured "Voluntary" status! There is an extract from a letter sent by the managers to the L.E.A in 1946 which reads "the managers... do not consider themselves pledged to any cost" in connection with "the continuing existence of a School in Drinkstone".

Sometimes diplomacy was called for! One unfortunate teacher was asked to attend a meeting at which the managers "suggested to her, in the kindest possible way, that while they appreciated her seven years' work, and the very difficult times the School had experienced during the war years, yet they felt the time had come when a change would be a good thing both for herself as well as the School. The relations between her and the Headmistress had not been of the happiest and the long journey, since she had met with an accident, made it very difficult for her to be punctual. They asked her to think the matter over carefully herself, and suggested that vacancies existed at Norton, Woolpit and Pakenham". The lady resigned gracefully!

Sometimes there were puzzles to ponder. In 1946 the School, Schoolhouse and Garden were "discovered to stand on 60 poles of land, that being 20 poles more than the land specified in the Deed", and somehow "included the strip of Glebe land ascribed in the Deed, and shown on the Deed plan, as being between the School and the Churchyard. This should be borne in mind in the event of the School or School House being 'appropriated' by the Minister of Education at any future time."

I think the managers were half right here. Yes, there were 20 more poles of land than that specified in the Deed. But "the strip of land…between the School and the churchyard" had been added into the churchyard at some date before 1903. The 20 poles of "extra" land were the strip that ran behind the School closets, which had become School garden some time between 1904 and 1946.

In November 1949 the managers had to bow to the inevitable, and the School became "Controlled", meaning responsibility lay more with the LEA than with Church and village. However the long delays in repairs, and anxious waits for equipment, were just as frequent under L.E.A control. One reason for this was the possibility that Drinkstone School might be closed. There must have been a lot of anxious times for these managers. Staff came and went, sometimes in rapid succession, and there were periods when the Education Authority, debating possible closure of the School, would not allow any permanent appointment to be made. Rumours of closure recurred throughout the last fifty years of the School's existence. There were three main reasons for these ominous rumblings – firstly, the cost of maintainance; secondly, the frequently low numbers on roll (only 25 pupils in 1938); and thirdly, the various re-organisations which successively reduced the age-range of Drinkstone pupils.

Worries about the state of the School and the cost of upkeep were never-ending over the decades. Those "gentry" managers in 1902 were committed to funding the School in part from their own pockets. As the years went by, maintenance became more and more expensive, and with the L.E.A now bearing major responsibility the managers seem to have become out of touch with general costs. They were amazed, in 1959, to learn that Headteacher Mrs. Collins had herself funded prizes and parties for the children out of her own pocket. It seems they had assumed there was a "School Fund" for such things. Admirably, they set to work helping establish and maintain a fund (the "Managers' Fund for Prizes"), holding jumble sales, coffee mornings and so on. This brought teachers, parents and managers closer together, and the managers even supported the Headteacher in her running battle with the milkman and his failings!

In 1968, the managers all agreed to add to this School Fund from their own pockets.

Over the years, obtaining improvements – telephone, hot water, fire extinguishers, cycle shelter and so on – had necessitated many letters from managers to L.E.A. They several times tried to improve the sanitary arrangements, and pleaded for sewers and up-to-date flush toilets in vain. These deficiencies were always cited as contributing to rumours of closure. These fears were heightened in 1969 when the building was over-run with muttering L.E.A. officials, and again in 1972 when rumours of closure arrived from the Office.

The zoning of Hessett children to Drinkstone when Hessett School was closed, gave Drinkstone a temporary reprieve. But in Summer 1982 the L.E.A. withdrew transport, saying Hessett was in Thurston catchment area. So the final death knell, when it came a year later, was no great surprise.

In Summer 1980 the "Managers" had been ordered to change their title to "Governors… for reasons of uniformity". Members now had to attend stringent training sessions. In the summer of 1984 the committee were asked to get in touch with the L E.A. about "the new constitution of the Governing Board"! "Instruments of Governors No. B5031" came into operation in January 1985, the Board of Managers was disbanded, and new Governors were elected by secret ballot. In fact there was minimal change of personel, but ironically, new rules about the number of years any Governor could remain in office were received, decreeing that some should serve until 1988! They would have loved to do so!

Chapter Ten

AN OLD COTTAGE RESTORED

THE AFTERMATH OF the First World War, with its depressions, and the parlous state of agriculture with many farmers becoming bankrupt, made the search for employment and security in the countryside ever more desperate. Poverty was rife. I found a small book in the Suffolk Archive which was quite enlightening on the state of village life in Drinkstone, after the war. The book is entitled "An old cottage restored", and gives a glimpse of the dire struggle against poverty and poor living conditions, of one elderly labourer and his wife. These two were probably among the very first pupils at Drinkstone School and were in their seventies when the book "An old cottage restored", was researched and written.

The majority of Drinkstone families in the early twentieth century were still living in tied cottages, the tenancy linked to their work. These homes were not always well-maintained, and the tenant would have neither the time, nor the money, nor the motivation, to keep them in good repair. The owners, usually farmers, were having to struggle against rising costs and falling prices, and many neglected their workers' homes. Today, such cottages have either been demolished, or restored, modernised, and often extended, beyond recognition. So it is wonderful to have this detailed description of a Drinkstone cottage, both before and after restoration. The book was published in 1921, and was produced by "The Society for the Protection of Ancient Buildings" (one of the fore-runners of today's National Trust).

This Society wanted to educate the public regarding possibilities of restoration, hoping to inspire others to follow their example. In 1919, the Committee started searching for a suitable derelict cottage to serve as an illustration of what could be done. They chose a pair of Drinkstone cottages, giving three reasons for their choice:

The excellent workmanship evident in their construction.

The badness of their condition.

The very small cost of purchasing them.

Sir Philip Sidney Stott of Gloucestershire undertook to pay £600 for the work so that the Society could restore the homes "in the most appropriate manner". The work was supervised by Mr. William Weir, and Mr. J. G. Cowell of Soham, Suffolk, advised on thatching. The book that resulted from this enterprise contains "before" and "after" photographs. The left-hand cottage had three storeys, the right-hand one only two, the different levels of the thatched roof adding to the charm of the building.

The "before" photo shows the cottages in semi-derelict condition, with huge holes in the thatch, plaster fallen from the walls revealing damaged and missing lathes beneath, and broken glass in the windows. It is therefore quite disturbing to learn that at the time of purchase one of the cottages was still inhabited, by an elderly couple who lived and slept in the one and only useable downstairs room. Maybe this was not an unusual situation at that date. Certainly poor cottagers (especially the elderly) were very much at the mercy of their landlords.

The Society regarded restoration of the homes of the poor as a "national responsibility", believing country folk deserved help because they "have little outlook beyond their common surroundings", also that cottages should be revered as each marking an ancient hearth "from whence came the men and women who have borne on their backs the greatness of England by sea and land". So some "gentlefolk" were well aware of the lack of social justice in the community.

South front of Stott's Cottage after repairs, circa 1920

In the preface to the book, written by Alfred H. Powell, there is an account of an interview he conducted with the resident cottager. He writes:

"The labourer……is typical. He told me the story of his life……from the time when he began by scaring rooks at ten years old, until at last after a full seventy years, he had become familiar with every kind of work belonging to farm life…..his tale was the epic tale of many thousands that have lived only to labour on and on for the land that bore them."

Probably this old couple had been born circa 1850. As children they may have attended Rev. Mosely's "Day and Sunday School". They may have been pupils at the new National School (although school attendance was not compulsory at that time). One hopes that while at school these children had a chance to read books and listen to stories (most homes possessing only a Bible), thus having at least a glimpse of wider horizons beyond the life of a labourer on a Suffolk farm.

The little book "An old cottage saved" contains a photograph of the old couple in their all-purpose single room. They sit, upright and serious, epitomising resigned endurance, one each side of an inglenook fireplace. A frill of cloth is nailed along the mantelshelf, on which stand a few important objects such as tea-caddy and pipe.

The book contains a wealth of fascinating detail about the cottage and its construction. The general description begins "The cottages are approached by a grass grown lane and stand in the middle of a garden 23 yards N – S and 67 yards E – W. They are separated from the heart of Drinkstone by one or two fields, and are built on rather low ground."

There is a list of items to be dealt with:

Thatch fallen in, battens decayed. Ends of rafters, and some other timbers, rotting, but were so large originally that sufficient remained.

Both gables leaning out.

Walls of heavy oak timbers set on a brick base. Spaces between the upright posts (studs) filled in with pounded clay, straw, and lime applied to a reinforcement of upright hazel sticks. This filling then plastered on both sides. Later (in 18th century?) oak lathe and plaster was added to the outside.

No damp course. On top of brick base lies oak timbering.

Passages etc. at back of house in very poor condition, timber rotted and filling gone. The stairs in this area were too steep and dangerous. Larders here.

Back view of Stott's Cottage after repairs, circa 1920

Bedroom floors – boarded with tongue and groove oak. Crooked floor because main timbers sinking.
Ground floor – brick laid direct on earth, uneven. Level with ground outside.
There was no sink in either cottage. The east cottage had a copper beside the living room fireplace.
Attic reached by steep ladder-stair against chimney stack from first-floor landing.
Only one bedroom had a fireplace. Small windows.
Brick ovens of historic interest. Can use coal or wood.
No water supply – a well outside.
One privy for the two cottages.

There was no restriction on what might be done since there were "no building by-laws in force in the district" in 1919. As far as possible, restoration was achieved using traditional methods and materials. A massive amount of work was completed at a total cost of £722. The lean-to at the rear was given new roof timbers. Wheat straw was used for the new thatching, which was a good two feet thick. The writer comments that the thatcher insisted on doing the work "his own way." When half done, he asked for some payments –"some bread and cheese money to go on with". This work cost £63.

The leaning gables were "tied in to the chimney", which is described as "a great central chimney-stack of fine brickwork" with wide flues and large ovens.

New stud walls were constructed at the rear. The remains of the old filling was mixed with freshly-burned lump lime, and water. Plaster was mixed using three parts sand to one of lime putty. For the external plasterwork, they used one part slaked lime to three parts sand, with one pound of hair added to each cubic foot of material. This was applied with a trowel, then washed over with lime wash made from lump lime slaked with boiling water and sieved. A lump of tallow the size of a hen's egg was added to the lime in the pail, for added weather resistance. Mr. Weir was "puzzled as to what pigment could have been used to produce the delicate pink which he found on the cottage" (might it have been ox blood?). He settled for "Venetian Red" supplied by a local shop. The lime wash was to be renewed every five years.

A damp course was created, slate in cement being added length by length to the foundation walls. The brick base was dug out and re-pointed, and new concrete floors laid onto hardcore. In the large rooms six-inch square tiles were laid on the concrete. The lean-to at the rear was divided into two with a new brick wall, and new staircases were built, less steep, and nearly three feet wide. Within this lean-to area was a new scullery for each house. These each had doors to the garden, and a new glazed stoneware sink. A drain led from each sink to a soak-away at the end of the garden, with over-flow pipes leading to the ditch. Each scullery was given a galvanised-iron copper set in brick, with flues connected to the main central chimney flue. "Summer fireplaces" for cooking were built against the outside walls of the sculleries. For the first time, each cottage was given its own garden privy, with pantile roof. Luxury!

The living rooms were of excellent size, one cottage having a square room, its walls measuring sixteen and a half feet, while the other cottage had two smaller rooms. New cottage ranges were fitted. One ancient window was re-opened, and twelve new window-frames fitted. New doors with cottage fittings were installed.

The bedrooms and attic were repaired and made habitable, and new fireplaces built. A new attic stair-ladder was put in. When the bedroom ceiling plaster was removed, fine beams, joists and studs were exposed. Similar discoveries were made downstairs, the old beams having "nicely carved stops to the chamferings" in the form of decorated leaf shapes. Everywhere in the cottage were signs of fine traditional craftsmanship and quality work. The restorers deduced that this had once been a single homestead with servants' quarters. At the east end, brick paving was discovered directly on the earth, six inches below ground, meaning that the original ceiling height had been eight feet. Carved crosses were discovered on the beams, and four doorways with framed Tudor arched heads opened from the rear passageways to the house (two on each floor). Two of these had "interesting carving in the spandrils" and two bore the sign of the cross cut above the apex of the arch. The restorers uncovered three original oak mullion windows which had never been glazed. They estimated that the house had been built circa.1500, and noted that there was another small farmhouse in Drinkstone very similar in plan.

What a delight this transformation must have been to the tenants! Yet the gulf between today's comforts and the best cottage homes of the 1920s, a life-style still within living memory, is amazing. No piped water supply, not one tap, no mains drains, no electricity, fires for all heating and cooking. Mothers must have had a daily struggle to bring up children warm, clean and well-fed.

However it is grand to imagine the increased comfort this old couple enjoyed in their last years of life, and they must have felt such pride in their "new" home. I doubt whether many farmers followed the example of the Society and restored their tenants' and labourers' cottages to this high standard, since cottages at the time were bought and sold for between £30 - £100, and farming was in recession. They probably preferred to sell or demolish vacant cottages, or just let them self-destruct! The sum of £722 for restoration was a huge outlay by 1920s standards.

At some date after this restoration, Tom Smith and his father Albert lived in the right-hand cottage of the pair, Albert remaining there until his death. Cora Munford and her parents lived in the left-hand cottage, Cora now lives here on her own. After Albert's death, Margaret and William Plummer and their children lived in the right-hand cottage. Memories of Tom, Cora, Margaret and William are in this book.

A newspaper article from the *East Anglian Daily Times*, September 14th, 1954, has a photograph of these same delightful cottages, looking in fine condition, with a caption explaining that they had been offered as a free gift to Thedwastre Rural District Council by Sir George Stott. I suppose this baronet was a son of Sir Philip Sidney Stott who paid for the restoration in 1921.

Since 1954, this pair of cottages, which stands almost at the end of Cross Street (a cul-de-sac), has undergone further changes. At some time the District Council altered the charming thatched roof with its two levels; the lower side was raised, and (at different dates) both sides were roofed with slate.

The Council "modernised" the cottages, replacing the huge brick fire-places in the living rooms with smaller arched fire-places in brick. Some rotten windows were replaced with casements, and the only remaining original oak window frame is alongside the front door of No. 2 (filled in, not glazed). The Council offered to replace the Rayburn solid fuel cookers in the lean-to kitchens, and install central heating. This has been done in No. 1, but No. 2 retains its kitchen Rayburn, and this and the open fire provide the only heating. All oak beams remain impressive and sound. In Cora's cottage a carving resembling a bishop's mitre has given rise to a rumour that monks once inhabited the building.

Cora took the opportunity to buy her cottage (No. 2) in the 1990s. An extra bedroom was created at the back of her home, over the lean-to kitchen. This has a dormer window and ship-lap wooden walls. Both lean-to kitchen extensions, built eighty- five years ago, remain good and sound.

In the 1950s, this pair of cottages stood alone, half-way down the single track lane leading to isolated "Widows' Cottage", with no close neighbours. Cross Street today is a fascinating mix of every type of home. There are a few tiny thatched cottages, flint-faced cottages, brick cottages, and one plastered cottage with "fish-scale pargeting". These are the oldest homes, standing mainly at the top end of the lane near the Recreation Ground. Since then, all available space on the left-hand side of the lane has been filled with modern homes, some of them substantial buildings dwarfing the original dwellings. Together, these Cross Street homes present a comprehensive illustration of the range of homes now in Drinkstone.

During 1985-6, the last year of the life of the School, older pupils studied houses of differing age and construction around the village. There is wonderful variety, new and old, grand and tiny, each with its own story.

Chapter Eleven

PERSONAL STORIES

Tom Smith, Walter Rose, Nell Cocksedge, Molly Punchard, Moira Reeve

---

TOM SMITH

Tom was born in Essex, moving to Drinkstone at the age of seven. He has special reason to remember the School and its teachers with thankfulness, as his story reveals. Now a widower, after many happy years of marriage to Doris, he is pleased to talk about the old times, since almost all his contemporaries are gone and their names mean little to most Drinkstone residents in this twenty-first century. Once started, he found the memories came flooding back. Here is his story.

"I was born five miles this side of Chelmsford, in April 1913. My family's life was all upsets and downs really. My father Albert was a gamekeeper, so was his father, and his brother – all of them were gamekeepers. He was a soldier in the war. I can just remember him coming home on leave in his uniform. Then next thing we knew, he was wounded, and was in hospital at Lincoln. That was in 1918, and I remember him saying, 'If I'd been sent home three months earlier I wouldn't have got wounded!' After the war, his job was gone. There was no work, not much doing for a few years after the war. A lot of the lads went up to Yorkshire looking for work. Some of them even walked up; and a lot never came back no more. They made a new life and stopped up there. I don't know why it was worse in Suffolk, but they do call us 'Silly Suffolk', don't they?

"My father was under Captain Dunnett in the war, and the Captain bought farms and land in Drinkstone when he came out of the army. In 1920 he bought Rookery Farm, Burt's Farm, and the land behind the mills, where the gravel pits were. He offered my father a job as war-rener. That meant, keeping down the rabbits, caring for the game, and all the keepers' jobs he'd been brought up to do. So we moved to Drinkstone, everything came over here by horse-drawn wagon! We were living in Chapel Cottage, a double-dweller. I had two older brothers, Cecil and Victor, and Albert, he was eighteen months younger than me, and our sister Dorothy was younger than Albert. My youngest brother Johnny was born in Drinkstone. It was certainly different coming here, I was lost for a year or two until we got settled. I'd been used to a bigger school at Great Waltham, with a master and two other teachers. But Drinkstone was a good School, there was some good scholars turned out there. We had to do as we was told! The rector, the teacher, and the policeman, they made sure of that! We four brothers was all in the Church choir, and Mrs. Gobbitt the school-mistress sang in the choir with us, and if there was no organist she'd play the organ. The other teacher was her sister Caroline Minns.

"Misfortune came along when my little brother Johnny was about eighteen months old. Mother got pneumonia and died. I remember that day so well. It was a confirmation at the Church, all the children were down at Church to watch, it was 22nd March 1922. Mrs. Gobbitt the schoolmistress down the school, she just came to us and said 'Come on, you're coming

home with me'. So me and Albert slept above the Schoolhouse kitchen with her son 'Dondy'-he was a bit older than us, he looked after us. She kept our family going, as the saying was.

"My sister went to live with my father's older brother and his wife, in London. She was three then, and I didn't really know her until after we was grown up. Now she lives in Stowmarket. We're the only two of the family left. She's Dorothy Bray now, my son takes me to see her, and sometimes her daughter brings her over here.

"My little brother Johnny was taken to live with my father's twin sister in Chelmsford, and when he was nineteen he was killed in a bombing raid in the Second World War. Me and Albert stayed at the school two months. They were very good to us. Mrs. Gobbitt was down there on her own, her marriage went wrong. I remember Henry, the eldest son, and Dorothy. Joyce was the youngest girl, and she suffered with epilepsy. I used to sit with her in class to help look after her. She could learn like the rest of us; I'd call her mother when she got ill. She wasn't all that old when she died.

"When my father found a housekeeper, we went home again. She'd got a little daughter. But after three or four year, things went wrong – the bills hadn't been paid. My father didn't know until the butcher and grocer from Bury sent him a letter saying nothing had been paid for a few months. So she had to go. So then we had a local lady from the village. She came down daily from nine o'clock until twelve, and she cleaned up and did the cooking and the laundry. She was Emma Horrex. She'd got a son but the marriage went wrong and she'd come home to live with her mother up the Rattlesden Road. When you think, people like her, it was hard – they had to go out charring for three or four shillings a week, they had to.

"Dunnett went bankrupt in 1924, and he went off to Canada. John Taylor, who farmed at Drinkstone Hall, had given up and retired in 1920, and gone to live at Walsham. But when Dunnett went bankrupt, Taylor bought Rookery and came back to Drinkstone. Father was cow-man for him. When father was at Rookery I used to go up after school and clean the knives and spoons and forks on the old emery board for half a crown a week. And I used to go round with my youngest brother Albert, helping old ones in their gardens, and they'd say, 'Come along and have your tea.' They were very good to us. Everyone looked after us.

"We had to move to the other side of Chapel Cottage; then when my oldest brother got married, Burt's Farm was sold and they needed the cottage. So we had to move to Stott's Cottage in Cross Street (next door to Cora). Father lived there till he died.

"Our rector was Frank Horne. Nearly every week he used to come to school. He was good with us, he was a real village rector. The Reverend and his wife always took Sunday School, Sunday afternoons in the Church. There was three classes – poor old Pansy Phillips, she took one class. When we was boys we could never make out what happened, because Pansy and her father lived in one house, and her mother and sisters lived next door! Those were two old cottages at Cherry Tree Lane. It used to be one cottage, where P.C. Barrell the policeman, Pansy's grandfather, used to live. They had the other end built on for Pansy's father and mother. There's an iron memorial to P.C. Barrell in the churchyard. Later Pansy married Stanley Mayes.

"There was a lot of Hornes in Drinkstone. Before we came there, Clem Horne, son of the old rector Fred Horne, shot himself on the stairs at Drinkstone Lodge. They used to tell us boys all the bloodstains were still on the carpet there.

"When I was still going to School, Drinkstone Lodge caught fire one morning. There were a lot of pigs in old buildings round the back, a lot of them were burned and they were running around, squealing. It was a sight really; they were taken off to the bacon factory at Elmswell. I believe it was Dunlops still living there then, or was it Gores? Anyway the old fire-engine from Woolpit came, drawn by two horses. The men got a lot of us boys to help with the pumps. There was two big handles on the pump, we worked three each side. The old moat on the left-hand side of the drive, we pumped that dry. Then when the fire was out, we went on to School.

"The owners built new farm buildings around the back. Mr. Young who lived near the Church did their garden and looked after the pigs. Old Man Young, he came from London. He used to go round on his bicycle selling fish. Later on he had a pony and cart, and opened up a

little shop one end of his cottage, the end nearest the Church. When his son got married, they took over the shop, and they'd go around the villages with a little van. That was three cottages once. Mr. Young just bought one when he first came from London. His son had to go in the R.A.F. in World War Two, and his wife carried on the business. My wife Doris used to look after their two children.

"When I left School, at fourteen, I went to Drinkstone Hall and worked for Mann's in the fruit farm. I had a disagreement with them when I was nineteen. They called me lazy, but I wasn't going to be called lazy for getting half as much as the men for the same work. I was doing the same as the men, but getting a boy's wage. So I went down The Street and worked for John Bland at Bridge Farm, doing general labour. I got 28s a week. (The pay went up later, to 32s 6d a week, then it went down again, in '36, the year I got married, to 28s again!)

"Before I was married, I worked at Hill Farm for Mr. Snell. But at all the farms, we were set off from Christmas till April. They'd just say, I won't need you again till April. Three winters, I was unemployed, I never got a ha'penny. We'd poach a rabbit, or a pheasant maybe, and have a pie, sometimes. And we used to cut hedges – the farmer would give us a hedge, they didn't pay us for cutting it but we could sell the faggots. We'd sell some to the Church, some to School, some to the Village Hall – to anyone who wanted a score, or half a score, of faggots. We'd get half a crown a score but it would take us two or three days to do it. My brother Vic was at Burt's Farm then, he wasn't married, he lived at home, and he'd give me half a crown most weeks.

"We had to bike to Stowmarket to get our insurance card stamped. There used to be nine or ten of us, unemployed, cycling there every Tuesday. A lot of the roads were still stoned then, if anyone got a puncture half way we'd all stop and help mend it.

"I was still living at home, in Stott's Cottage, when I was courting Doris. She lived at Hessett, her name was Bullett, there were six families in Hessett with that name but she wasn't related to any of them! We were courting several year, she was parlour maid at Horne's Rectory. Then she went to be parlour maid at Tostock Old Hall, for Commander Harrington. She was helping at a dinner party there, and she heard one of the guests, Fred Hammond of Beyton, say he needed a tractor driver. She got her bike out and cycled down to Cross Street in the pitch dark to tell me. So next day I went to Beyton to ask about the job. Hammond was an old bachelor, his housekeeper came to the door and took me to him. That was in January 1931. A week later, he came round on his horse and told me I could take the job.

"Father married again around '34-'35. He married Nurse Harvey, a midwife who'd trained in London. When her mother died, she'd come back to Drinkstone to look after her father. She was a lovely step-mother to us. She was hard, as District Nurses were in those days, but she'd got a heart of gold.

"I married Doris in '36. For the first few months after the wedding we had to live at Hessett with her mother, but we were waiting to move into the first council house built in Drinkstone! I went down to see the council rep, Thompson, who was at the Rookery, and he put in a good word for me. We had no water or drains but we loved it. There was a wash house and earth closet side by side at the back. When they were building the council houses a pump was put in near where Field Bungalow is now – an old boy from Rattlesden put the pump in. We'd fetch two pails of water every evening, and that had to do us each day. There was a bucket under the sink, but you'd think twice before tipping any water away!

"We had our son Mike in '37, and Betty in '38. I worked for Fred Hammond until 1942, and he plagued me to stay, but I left in '42 because I was fed up with cycling there. The English '42nds' were at The Park before the Americans took over. When the Americans were there, there'd be a queue of U.S. army lorries all the way from The Park to Hessett every morning. I had to take my gas mask and my identity card every morning to show, or the Americans wouldn't let me through. So I left, and went to Hill Farm, Drinkstone, and I worked there till '54.

"All my life I worked on farms. A hard life, but I enjoyed it. I had five or six different masters at Hill Farm and Burt's Farm, they kept chopping and changing. I retired in 1978. We moved to this council bungalow in 1982, and Doris went blind in 1985. That was the hardest

thing of the lot because she always had bad hearing. I looked after her, Betty and Michael did what they could, and we had a home help, but it's a job to look after someone twenty-four hours a day, and then she scalded herself. She didn't want any doctors, she was always independent. It nearly broke my heart as well, because I couldn't look after her. Then I had a stroke and a heart attack and that finished me. The doctor sent her to hospital and the poor old dear finished up at Cedar Lodge, Culford. She died two year ago. We were the same age, just two days' different, she was born 18th April, and me 16th, in 1913.

"She was always doing something for the village – if there was a jumble sale or anything. She and Miss Clover, they always worked for the Church. She'd go every week, and our children were in the choir. Sometimes I'd go, or I'd stay home cooking the dinner. But it got so she couldn't see or hear, she didn't know what was going on. I don't go now, and they don't visit me from the Church. Years ago you used to know everybody. Now I go out and I don't know nobody. I'm in my ninety-second year and there's only half a dozen I know here now. But I see Ruby Bland once a week and she's been a friend of the family over fifty year.

"My children, grandchildren and great grandchildren all live out of the village, except my daughter in law Janet. She visits me. My son's at Elmswell, my daughter's at Great Barton. They both come a lot, they help me and do the cleaning, and help with my shopping and pension. I go to one or the other, alternate Sundays. I have a carer to help me wash, dress and undress, morning and evening, and meals on wheels come Tuesdays and Fridays. My next door neighbour cuts the grass, and I do the flower beds. I always loved gardening. Now I don't grow vegetables, just a few runner beans and tomatoes.

"I watch television. I'll be lost next week when Wimbledon and the football's over! I love all sports, I played football for the village until I was forty-two. I had my cataracts done, now I can read in bed every night, it's lovely."

WALTER AND EDITH ROSE

I met Walter and his wife Edith at their bungalow home in Stowmarket. Walter grew up in Drinkstone, Edith in Rattlesden, and they have been happily married for over sixty-two years.

This is what they told me, Walter beginning the story:

"I was born on 13th March 1917. My mother was Alice Mary (née Smith), whose family came from Walsham-le-Willows. My father was Philip Walter Rose, of Drinkstone. I was born in Drinkstone. There were three of us boys, I was the eldest, then there was George, and then Jim.

"My Dad was in the 4th Suffolks. He joined up in 1914 and he was going up the front towards the Somme, with a drug full of ammunition (a drug was a kind of trolley on four wheels), pulled by five mules. He got mortared. All the mules were killed, and Dad got his left arm all smashed up with shrapnel. They wanted to take his arm off but he refused. The arm was withered and all bent up after that, but he could still use it a bit. He'd been in the army about eighteen months, I think. He was discharged, and he came home and went back on the land, driving horses. He used to win ploughing matches.

"I used to go to work with my Dad sometimes when I was a boy, early in the morning, going to feed the horses. In summer-time they'd be in the meadow and Dad would have a brass whistle. He'd blow that whistle and the horses would gallop up to the gate to be let into the yard. When we used to open the gate, I just stood there one time and they all ran through towards Woolpit! So Father blew the whistle again to make them come back. Father would stand in the gateway with his whistle, and he'd whistle to make the horses wee before they went in the stable! He wanted them to do it in the field before coming in.

"When I started at Drinkstone School, we'd walk down in our big hob-nailed boots. The teachers then were Mrs. Gobbitt and Miss Minns, her sister. After Mrs. Gobbitt, Miss Hockley came, and she was a stingy one! If we done anything wrong she'd get us on the knuckles, with

her ruler edgewise, it really hurt. She used to give us the cane, and then we'd go and catch these little field mice to pay her back, put them in our pocket, then let them loose in School or put them in her desk!

"At School I liked writing and drawing. I used to draw old ships, and warships. I remember doing pictures of The Royal Oak, and H.M.S. Hood. Some of my work was put in Woolpit Fair; it was a map of England with the counties all coloured in. To be honest, it was just an average education, we done those few lessons and then when you got to be fourteen you were away! There was nothing to be educated for, there was no choice of work for village people, the girls went into service and the boys went on the farms. That's all there was for us.

"We had two places in Drinkstone. There's a thatched cottage on the right, on the corner of Chapel Lane – there used to be three cottages there, they're all knocked into one now. We lived in one of those cottages when I was little. That's where, later on, Jimmy and Teddy lived. They used to get drunk when they drew their quarter pension, we was only about twelve or thirteen then and we used to toss little pebbles through the window to tease them. Then we'd run away and they couldn't run after us because they'd had too much to drink! We never did real harm, it was only in fun.

"I used to go to dances at the Village Hall when I was only ten or eleven, because my mother was caretaker at the Village Hall. Once I went upstairs to my room to plaster my hair down ready for the dance, and the candle set fire to the net curtains and I nearly set the house on fire. I got a belting for that! The Hall used to be full up, especially New Year's Eve and Boxing Day. People came from all around.

"We spent most of our out-of-school time at my friend Les Bland's farm, that was Bridge Farm. We used to go in their yard, they had a long shed, and we'd go in there and play darts and cards. We had an old gramophone in there. Another boy I went to School with, was Cecil Taylor from Rookery Farm. When we came out of School, he'd go in his house and pinch his father's Woodbines, and we'd go in a ditch and smoke 'em. We enjoyed it until we got caught! We used to crush up dry leaves in the Autumn, and we used the stalks of Old Man's Beard as a pipe. We'd smoke the leaves, all rolled up in newspaper. It was a bit strong! We had more fun then than they do now. But I haven't smoked for fifty years.

"We used to have some good times. When we was cutting corn with the binder and horses, my mates and me, Percy Horrex and the others, we'd block up all the rabbit holes around the field. We'd shove grass down, the length of our arm. If we couldn't catch the rabbits when they were running, after everyone went we'd go and get them all out of the holes. Later on when I worked for Arthur Bland at Whitefield, he'd go rabbiting with us and we'd catch hundreds.

"There was a gamekeeper, Bob I think his name was, who used to lodge at Bland's. This gamekeeper used to go to the Cherry Tree for his drink. We boys would go in, buy a packet of crisps for about two pence, and look to see if he was in the bar. And if he was we'd be O.K. so we'd go and catch two or three of his pheasants with our catapults and take them home to Mother.

"We'd play tennis for the village, we went to Pakenham and Woolpit for matches. We played doubles, we practised behind the Village Hall. My regular tennis partner was Sheila Morley from Woolpit. She became a midwife – I saw her about eighteen months ago. When we were young we all used to walk for miles. We'd go for walks at night, a crowd of us, to Hessett Bells, and to Hitcham.

"When I was about fourteen we moved to a council house, number 1, near the Cherry Tree. I left School at fourteen and Father said to me, 'You're going up the farm with me.' I wanted to go with my mate Percy Horrex to a farm at Woolpit. But I had to go with my Dad, to Thompson's farm, looking after chickens with Eddie 'Headley' Brinkley. He was the boss. It was seven days a week, 7am till 5pm, for seven shillings a week. There were several thousand birds, Leghorns, Rhode Island Reds, and Light Sussex. They were for meat, they were in pens on the fields. They went in a hangar at night. There were seven or eight incubators in the incubator house and we used to have to take the trays out twice a day and turn the eggs.

"I met Edith when I was about fifteen. I was biking into Rattlesden one day, and I met her."
Edith takes up the story:

"I come from a family of thirteen (one died young). My father was Arthur Alfred King, he came from Wyverstone. My mother was Ellen Mary (née Sparkes), born in Rattlesden. When I was a girl, we lived on a hill in Rattlesden, and we could see over to Drinkstone. When Walter was going home on his bike after we'd meet, he'd turn his bike at the top of Drinkstone hill so I could see the dynamo light, and flash towards me. I'd wait at the bedroom window looking out to see he was getting safely home."

Walter says:

"When I was seventeen or eighteen I got a motor bike, an old AJS 350, second-hand. The chap in the village, Bennett, he fell off it and wouldn't ride it again. So I borrowed £6 off me mother to get it. I still signalled to Edith when I got to the top of the hill."

Edith describes her first experiences of work in service:

"I worked at Gedding Hall, for Gibson Jarvey, first. It was their holiday home, just for Easter, Summer, and Christmas, the rest of the time we were in London. Imagine it, in London, a little old kid of fourteen! But we were treated well, a nice bedroom, a carpet on the floor, a gas fire – our parents never could give us those things. I had as much food in a day as my family got in a week! Then I decided to find a job looking after children, so I went to work for Lord Belstead, in Ipswich, at Stoke Park (I came home to Rattlesden Sundays). They were lovely people. Very kind. I would have stayed there if it hadn't been for the war. But you were obliged, if you weren't in essential work, to join up or do war work, so that was when I moved back to Rattlesden to work on the airfield."

Walter goes on to describe his work experiences:

"They stood you off at the farm if they hadn't any work for you. So I found a job with some plasterers at Mildenhall. I used to bike forty miles a day, there and back. It was better money, £3 - £4 a week, That was a lot of money in those days. I got lodgings at Soham.

"In the late '30's I went to Wattisham to help build the hangars, because they knew war was coming. Me and my brothers all joined up. George got sunk on HMS Southampton, he was in the water seven hours before he was fished out. He was on the cross-turret up the top of the ship with the guns, and he saw these Italian planes coming right out of the sun, and they dropped four bombs on the ship. It was a place called 'Hell's Gate' in the Med. They couldn't get George home because of the fighting, so he ended up convalescing two years in Durban, South Africa. He had a shattered left arm (same arm as my Dad's), and just like Dad's arm it was bent, the fingers all jammed up. George contracted T.B. and died three years later. His name's on a plaque in All Saints' Church. Some of the men spent the whole war abroad and never saw their children.

"My other brother, Jim, was in the Royal Artillery. He come through all right, but he died a few years ago, I'm the only one left now.

"I joined the Marines, but I never went on active service because I got bronchial asthma. I think it was the dust and gas in Portsmouth that did it."

Edith says:

"They never should have passed him as fit really because he was asthmatic as a child."

Walter continues:

"So I came home and we were married in September '42 at Rattlesden. We lived with my mother a month or two. We were both working at the aerodrome at Rattlesden at the time. I went up there to see the foreman and he said 'Can you drive this truck?' and of course I said yes. But I couldn't get it started! It was one that started on petrol, then you had to switch it over to diesel, and I didn't know that! But I got the job, working with excavators and drag lines. I did some work at Cockfield, I used to bike over. Then I was sent to Ilminster in Devon – you had to go where the contractors sent you.

Edith adds:

"I was pregnant by then so I had to stay in Stowmarket, Violet Hill, where we'd moved to –

an old house, nothing new was built in war-time."

Walter continues:

> *"Then I went to Manston in Kent, and after that I got a transfer to Mendlesham.*
>
> *"After the war I went driving for CWS Creamery in Stowmarket. I drove tankers, collecting milk from farms. In winter I used to drive up to a hundred miles at a time. There were fifteen to twenty tankers and we used to shift 50,000 gallons a night. You never saw your children open their Christmas presents for years, you worked all through those holidays."*

A wonderful array of family photos adorns the bungalow, and Edith and Walter told me a little about their two children, five grandchildren, and four great-grandchildren. One grand-daughter is shown in regalia from Bath University. Their grandchildren all did well at school, and have had opportunities that were never available to their grandparents. One grandson is in the police drug squad as a dog-handler, based in Haverhill. He works in plain clothes, and his dog will detect any person who smells of drugs and sit in front of them waiting to be stroked; then the police move in! Another grandson now works in the prison service at Highpoint, after several years in Northern Ireland with the army.

Their son Nigel recently moved to a bungalow in Drinkstone, and has created a beautiful garden, in which Edith and Walter were treated to a Diamond Wedding party in 2002. A photograph of the celebration is displayed in their living room. Also on the walls, testimony to the couple's love of the Suffolk countryside, are paintings by a local artist which, as Edith remarks are reminiscent of Constable. As we admire them, Edith says: "Don't you just feel you could go splashing through those puddles? If this bungalow was on fire, there's just two lots of things we'd try to save – first, photos of the family, and second, these lovely paintings of Suffolk."

NELL COCKSEDGE

Ellen Cocksedge (Nell) was born on Christmas Day in 1919 – as she says, "a de-mob baby". The family was living in "The Black House" at Hessett, a little two-bedroom cottage tucked behind the old Hessett school (the cottage was later demolished so that a neighbour could build a garage on the site). Nell's father Paul Blake was horseman for Captain Hargreaves at Drinkstone Park. The Captain also owned Elm Farm at Hessett. Nell told me her story as we sat in her home in Gedding Road, Drinkstone, opposite the now desolate Cherry Tree pub site. She knows this site will soon sprout new dwellings with new neighbours – nine houses are planned. But she says, "Why should I mind? Why deny to others what I have myself, a lovely home in Drinkstone?"

Nell has seen so many changes. This is her story:

> *"The day before I was born, my mother was doing the usual weekly baking, with extra for Christmas. She'd bake bread and cakes in the side oven with the faggots to heat it. Early the next morning I was born, about four o'clock in the morning. My sister Olive was ten then, and Father gave me to her to look after, while he went to fetch my grandmother to help out. Olive said it was lovely having a baby to nurse, because the flannelette blanket I was wrapped in went right down around her legs and kept her warm. But when grandmother came she was strict. She believed girls should work. So she insisted Olive must help wash the nappies as well, and she didn't think much of that!*
>
> *"My Father borrowed a horse and cart from Mills the grocer, to go and fetch grandmother. She lived in a little cottage at the bottom of Hitchcock's Hill in Rattlesden. They went for her about six in the morning. It was Christmas Day and my father used to sing in (Hessett) Church choir. So when they got back, he went off to the Church and he sang as a tenor solo the first verse of 'Unto us a boy is born'. Mills the grocer and Herbert Bruce who kept the Post Office and the others in the choir, all grinned at him when he started singing.*
>
> *"At Michaelmas in 1920, when I was nine months old, we moved to a cottage at Drinkstone – along The Park road. You go left into The Park; we lived down a little lane further on, to the right. There was three brick cottages, the chauffeur Cornish lived next door [his daughter Stella still lives in Woolpit]. Behind us was the gardener's cottage [known as Moat Farmhouse*

Drinkstone Park

today]. *We had three bedrooms, it was a good cottage.*

" *My father was always singing. I remember he'd sing one song:*

The sunlight's up the morning sky,
And swift the clouds before him fly.
Then rise, for time is fleeting fast...

"*And my brother Frank, he was two years older than me, he'd get it wrong and sing 'The Sunlight Soap the morning sky....' He thought it was all about the bars of Sunlight Soap we used then.*

"*There were six of us children. Olive was the oldest, then George, then Harry, Frank, me, and Dorothy. My parents were married in 1908. Before the war, Father was a coachman at Occold. We had a photo of him once, sitting up there with his carriage and horses. Then they took his horses for the war, and he said, 'Well, they've took my horses, I might as well go too!' He didn't join up until 1916 but the men were dying like flies, so he soon got promoted. Stanley Mayes from Drinkstone was with him. (You know in those days children had to look after their old parents, and Stanley and his wife Pansy Phillips, who used to clean Drinkstone Church, were courting for years and years, because they both had to stay at home looking after the old ones. Then when they had all died, Stan and Pansy just went quietly down to the Church one Thursday or Friday morning and got married).*

"*Well, Stan was a sergeant, and Father was a Regimental or Company Sergeant Major. And Stan said of my Father 'he would never send his men where he daren't go himself'. This is the letter from his commanding officer in France when he was wounded –*

"*'BEF*

"*'April 29th 1917*

"*'Dear Mrs. Blake,*

"*'I am writing to inform you that your husband, 20226 Cpl. Blake S.P., was wounded on April 23rd last. I believe his wounds are not of a serious nature. I hope that you will shortly hear a good account of satisfactory progress.*

"'I would like to take the opportunity of letting you know of the very high esteem I have of your husband. I have known him for but a few months out here but I can assure that from the first time he was with me in Mons this last January till the time he was wounded I had an NCO in my Company on whom I felt I could rely very thoroughly then on Cpl. Blake.

"'He has on many occasions done most useful work for me scouting and was out scouting on the night of 22nd-23rd, prior to the battle bringing in most necessary information.

"'In the attack where he was wounded he showed most gallant conduct leading a "party of bombs" down the enemy trench.

"'You have every reason to be extremely proud of him.

"'Yours very sincerely, Harold Ashley Cooper,

"'O/C A Coy, 4th Suffolk Regt.'

"Worse than that time, was when he was gassed. He got the Distinguished Conduct Medal. He used to tell us how one time he went down into a cellar, and found some Germans down there playing the piano! And he managed to take them all prisoner. After the war, after he came home, he was always ill from the gas, and he had TB.

"Farm labourers got about 28 shillings a week then. Captain Hargreaves used to say my Father cared more about his horses than for his wife! He'd sit up all night with a horse, if it was sick. He loved those horses.

"When my Father got really ill he went into Addenbrooks Hospital, and my brother Henry was in the sanatorium at Bury St. Edmunds, he got TB as well. We'd all be waiting at home for Mother to come back on the bus, when she visited them. When my Father was dying Captain Hargreaves let us all go and see him, we went in the van, driven by his chauffeur. I remember my Father told me to be a good girl. It was on a dreary Spring day, I can remember looking out of the van, there was no leaves on the trees yet. After my Father died we had to move out of the cottage, into an old thatched cottage further down the lane. Captain Hargreaves owned that one and it happened to be empty, so we moved down there so the new horseman could live in the brick cottage, which was better built. My Mother couldn't get a war-widow's pension from the government because Father died so long after. She got about two shillings and six-pence a week for each of us. I remember after he died, she went stone-picking in the fields, and we'd go and help her. My Father wouldn't let her work on the land while he was alive. I was about seven or eight then.

"All these sad things happened, but when I was little in Drinkstone, they always seemed happy times. I seem to remember the sun always shining when we walked to the school. It was just a mud lane, but I remember great big sprays of wild roses hanging down from the hedges. We learned our letters before we went to school. I remember sitting at the front by the fire in Miss Minns' room, with the little ones. Miss Minns was lovely, I can remember her clanging the bell in the mornings. As you got older, you had to move nearer the back. We had slates and pencils, squeaky pencils they were. And we had counting beads on frames.

"I can remember the special days, like at the start of the holidays the boys would clang and clang that bell! I remember Oak Apple Day. We'd all have to come wearing an oak leaf, to cel-ebrate King Charles hiding in the oak tree. We'd have a history lesson about that. I think it was on May 29th. I can still remember a lot, some of the poems we had, there's one that goes:

> A dear little girl sat under a tree,
> Sewing as long as her eyes could see...
> A number of rooks flew over her head
> Crying 'Caw! Caw!' on their way to bed.
> And she smoothed her work and folded it right,
> And she said to her work 'Goodnight! Goodnight!'

"We did a lot of sewing at Drinkstone. We made shoe bags out of unbleached calico, with a drawstring. When we'd stitched them up, we had to embroider our names on the side. We wore heavy high boots and a white pinafore over our dresses. Mother made our clothes, she was a good seamstress. She'd go to the jumble sales, get a coat, unpick it, and make clothes for us. There was a women's club at Hessett, a clothing club, and she'd pay sixpence a week or what she could afford. Then she'd buy unbleached sheeting. It always used to go on the boys' bed first! My Grannie in Rattlesden, she always made all Grandad's shirts too.

"At school, I never went in Mrs. Gobbitt's class because we were waiting to move back to Hessett. I was old enough to go up, but they said, you're moving at Michaelmas, so you must stay in the infants' class for September and October, and someone else can have your place in the big class. But I liked Mrs. Gobbitt, I knew her because we used to have assembly all together every morning. We'd have the big panel doors open and we had songs and prayers. We all went to the Church on special days, like Ascension Day. My brother George admired Mrs. Gobbitt, and he was well in with her daughters. I've still got a school photo somewhere with all of us on it, George, Harry, Frank and me.

"I wasn't there long but it was a good education, we really learned things. Back in 1989 I took part in a TV quiz called 'Bull's Eye'. Sue and I made up the team and we competed against two pairs of male contestants. Sue had to score at darts, while I answered the questions. It all depended on the last round. Sue scored higher than the lads – now came the vital question:

"'Who went to Africa to find David Livingstone?' Answer 'Stanley!' So we won! One of my neighbours said to me 'However did you know that?' Why had it stuck in my mind? Because our rector at Hessett had been E. Morton Bartlett, and Henry Morton was Stanley's Christian names.

"We had some books in our cottage, and I remember a set of about ten, from a book club, all with red covers. One of them was 'Coral Island' and I enjoyed that. I remember a story called 'Teddy's Button', all about a boy who had a button off his father's army coat to remember him by. And this boy got into a fight, and the precious keepsake button rolled away into the ditch – the stories were all geared to the Bible, they were all moral tales.

"My Father liked reading, and when my sister Olive was in the Girl Guides, the meetings were in The Park, and once she went into Captain Hargreave's library to look for something for Father to read. Mr. Hargreaves' daughter asked what she was looking for, and she told her. So after that, Captain Hargreaves used to send us things for him, like the magazine 'Horse and Hound', after the family finished with them. He was stern, but fair. I remember we used to climb on the low branches of the trees in the Park, and swing them up and down. He'd tell us off for that.

"When we lived at Drinkstone, we still went to Church at Hessett. We would walk through the Park, along 'The Pickles' footpath, which came out into Hessett churchyard. We were scared stiff of the cows when we went through the Park! If it was wet and slushy we had to go the long way round, on the road. There was two fir trees on the left, standing alone, and my Father used to say 'If you get to the second fir tree before the bell tolls, you're in time to get to Church and put your surplice on.' Because Olive, George, Henry and Frank all sang in the choir.

"When we were walking to Church, Dorothy used to say 'My back hurts'. Dorothy was the youngest, she was so tiny when she was born that we called her Midge. Anyway, Mother took her to the doctor and he sent her to the hospital. There was something wrong with her back, and she had to lay on her back in a steel jacket, with leather straps over her shoulders and round her ankles, to keep her straight. When they sent her home, we got a long wicker pram on wheels to move her around in. She wore that long steel jacket from when she was six, until she was ten. The nurse used to come in most mornings and rub her skin with methylated spirit to stop bed-sores. And she would exercise her arms and legs for her, and rub her feet, moving them to keep the muscles good. We'd have to carry her upstairs at bed-time. After Father died, I used to sleep in the big bed with my Mother and Dorothy, and if your foot caught in one of those buckles it really hurt!

"My brother George joined the army in 1931 (later he was awarded the MBE). When he came home on leave he'd say 'Poor little thing!' and lift her across his knees and make a fuss of her. I used to keep asking my Mother 'Can I push Dorothy outside? Let me take her for a walk!' and she'd say 'No, you'll be tipping her out.' Then when I was about twelve she let me take her. It was grand the first time, and the second time, then on the third day I got a bit bored with it. And my Mother said to me 'No, you've crazed me enough all this time, so now you will take her out!' So long as Dorothy was by the roadside while we were playing, or in a gateway, or in someone's garden, it was all right and she could watch and talk to us as we played. It would be marbles, skipping, and ball games like 'Catch'.

"When she was ten, Dorothy was allowed to sit and stand, and then she learned to walk again. She still had to wear a steel support, like a kind of corset, for a few years. Then she could leave that off as well and she got completely better.

"It wasn't only Dorothy who was ill. Henry had TB for years and years. He came home from hospital, but his leg was open at the hip for about six years. My Mother had to dress it, and she had a leather bag made from an old cushion, and she'd go to the doctor's and get it all filled up with cotton wool and gauze for him. She was a brick. But after a while her health suffered, so Henry went into St. Mary's (that was a bit like the workhouse; now, it's for old people) and he was well looked after there. Then penicillin came in, and there was a German doctor at St. Mary's, who said 'Let's put him on penicillin', and it completely cured the infection. But Henry always had a limp, one leg was left shorter than the other. He went to Papworth, to a sheltered workshop where they made leather goods, and the doctors could keep an eye on him. He stayed there all his life. He died in his seventies.

"I still remember my childhood as happy, despite the troubles. We'd go to our Grandparents at Rattlesden sometimes, and meet our cousins on the Blake side of the family. The Blake Grandparents were George William, and Ellen. They were firm and strict, we had to behave, but we had fun. The cousins lived in Woodbridge. At Christmas it was lovely. They were all musical. One played the violin – she became a teacher, at Mendlesham. And Auntie Babs played the concertina. We'd play charades. Aunt Kathy was good fun, she'd make us Indian head-dresses with feathers, and we'd pretend we were sitting round a camp-fire. We had good imaginations!

"We had to move back to Hessett some time after my Father died. We were in a thatched house, four dwellings in a row. The cottages belonged to Mr. Austin, and he didn't do a lot about the state of them. It was 3s 3d a week for the rent, but we were warm, we always had enough coal and enough to eat. My Mother worked at Mills' shop, he was baker and butcher, she'd be out the back scrubbing up the scullery, and where they cut up the meat.

"Church was very important in our lives. After I was confirmed, when I was thirteen, we went to Holy Communion at 8am, then Sunday School at 10.30 (that was in the Village Hall, with the rector), then into the Church at 11 for Matins. Then we went to the children's service at 3pm, and to 6.30 Evensong. I had to stay even after that, for Frankie to finish choir practice so we could walk home together. At times like Harvest or Easter that was a long practice. Look at all the shoe-leather we wasted going backwards and forwards! It's nearly a mile from Hessett Heath to the Church.

"We all found jobs after school. There was a Drinkstone Charity set up to help, they gave money for boys to buy tools for farming or other work, and to buy uniforms for the girls so they could go into service. Olive's first job was for the Gore family down at Drinkstone Lodge. She went as Nanny to the children. Then she was Nanny for the Haygate family at Thurston. Then she decided she'd get more money as a general servant in London. Dorothy joined her in London in 1939 and got a job as a maid.

"Dorothy applied for the ATS when war broke out. She didn't say a word about ever being ill, and she passed the Medical A1! She was put on aircraft-spotting watch on the East coast. A few years ago I was on holiday in Hunstanton, and there's a War Museum there. We saw a photograph in the museum of Dorothy and two other ATS girls, all in uniform and smiling, sit-

ting at the top of the cliff-side steps. Later Dorothy married and had two children. She died in her seventies, I'm the only one left now.

"My first job was as scullery maid at Beyton House. I started when I was fourteen and I had to look after the stove. It heated all the water in the house. Every morning I had to clean out the clinker, make up the fire, and light it. Then it was made up again in the evening. One morning I looked in and it didn't look too bad so I didn't bother. I just shoved the sticks in with coke on top, and I went upstairs to do the beds – I had to do my bed, and cook's. Then I was reprimanded! The mistress used to come in and talk to the cook every morning at ten, and I was to the carpet! It was 'Nellie! Come down here!' There was people from London down to Newmarket races, and there wasn't any hot water for their morning baths! 'Don't let it occur again,' they said. The next time I was to the carpet it was Sunday dinner, and there was a great big meat dish with the joint of beef, and I had to take it to the larder. Well, I should have put the dish down to open the door, but I just rested it on my knee while I opened it, and it slipped. I saved the joint, but I couldn't save the dish!

"I stayed in Suffolk and I married Sindal John Cocksedge (brother of Jim, Vi's husband). We had seven children – Brian in '36, Michael in '38, Judy in '39, Patricia Jean in '40, Valerie in '41, David in '47 and Sandra in '48 (it's a good job my John joined up or there'd have been more!). We lived in Hessett until 1946, then we moved here, to Drinkstone, into one of the new council houses which were built as 'Homes for Heroes'! We still had oil lamps, there was no electricity, and no main drains. We had a 'front room', we never went in there. We'd all sit round the big table in this room, the children all doing their homework. I bought a piano for £10, and my daughter Jean had piano lessons from Mrs. Rodgers, who lived between Hessett and Beyton. Mrs. Rodgers was organist at Bradfield Baptist, and Jean would stay with my mother in Hessett at week-ends, to have the lessons.

"All my children went to Drinkstone School and they all liked it, except Patricia Jean. For some reason she always felt she was picked on at Drinkstone. When she went on to Beyton she thrived, she even became Head Girl. So perhaps it was good that she didn't pass the 11-plus. All my children took that exam but none of them passed. They were clever children – Michael was doing at eleven, the same work as the children of fifteen. Mrs. Collins the Headteacher let him sit the exam two years running because the first time he was ill with a bad chest. But he still didn't pass.

"At the school in those days, the boys did plenty of gardening, while the girls did needlework. They all did singing and country dancing, boys and girls. Mrs. Collins was all for music and dancing.

"I used to do work on the farms when my children were growing up. I used to fling bales and single beet, and my Mother used to say 'You'll regret that work one day'. And now, my knees are that stiff, I can hardly bend them some days.

"Well, the years have gone by and I'm still here in Drinkstone, and I love my home. In 1960 'Monks Hoot' near the Church was for sale for £800. It's built of corrugated iron lined with wood. We wondered whether we should borrow some money and buy it. But later on we were able to buy this house we were living in, from the Council. My daughter Judith, she took over the Cherry Tree, but now that's all closed and shut up. But I still enjoy my life. Last year I went to the Palace Garden Party and I thought, oh, how my Mother would have loved to know that! And I couldn't tell my sister even, they're all dead now."

I have the Parish Magazine for September 2003, which contains a sparkling account by Nell of her day in London at Buckingham Palace. She says, "At 3pm we were through the gates – the very gates I peered through in 1933 on a 2s/6d excursion from Thurston railway station." She had a wonderful day, chauffeured by a son-in-law and pushed in a wheelchair by daughter Sandra. No-one could have deserved it more.

Listening to these older people tell their stories, I am mystified by the phenomenon of the 11-plus and why so few of them and theirs passed. They are so capable, so articulate. Obviously, having only two classrooms and two teachers for an age range that might extend from four to fifteen years can't have helped, but the teachers were dedicated and (most!) of the children were attentive. I wonder just what was being tested. Certainly the system of the day seems to have reinforced the gap between the "Classes", as they were then called. "Class" difference was taken for granted in the village then. Passing for the grammar school in those days, undoubtedly presented new problems, as personal accounts in later chapters show.

MOLLY PUNCHARD AND MOIRA REEVE

Born Marjorie Helen Edwards in 1915, Molly was twice married, first to Philip Donaghy, father of her five children. Philip died in 1946 and in 1963 Molly married John Punchard (known as Jack). In 1985 Molly was widowed for a second time. She now lives in a neat bungalow among the fields on the outskirts of Walsham-le-Willows, one mile from the farmhouse where her daughter Moira and son-in-law Hugh live. From her bungalow Molly observes with a knowledgeable eye the progress of the crops. Molly is first cousin to Raymond Bland; his father was brother of Molly's mother. I visited Molly on a sultry summer afternoon when thunder threatened the ripening grain. Molly's daughter Moira added occasional memories of her own.

This is Molly's story:

"I was born in 1915 at Drinkstone, in a thatched cottage (now known as Kopsey Cottage) just off the Rattlesden Road. The cottage belonged to my mother Flo (Edith Florence Bland). She bought it from a cousin for about £50, some time before she married William Edwards, my father, who came from Hoxne near Eye. Father was a builder by trade, and he improved the cottage and made it more comfortable. He also helped build a fine large house across the opposite side of Rattlesden Road, in front of The Gables, a thatched cottage belonging to my grandparents. Grandfather Charles Bland lived at The Gables, he was a shoemaker, and my Grandmother's name was Abigail. Their son David, my uncle, had been supervising chef on the Queen Mary, a Cunard White Star liner. The new house they built was called Rolandia, a name made up from three names important to Uncle David – Kate Roden, Bland, and Aquitania. That house is now home to Victor and Meg Jack and has been re-named The Homestead. My father owned a horse and trap which were kept at The Gables.

"My mother bought a piano for me and my older sister Kathleen (who was born in 1914), and that cost her £40, almost as much as the cottage! My father William was in the Royal Engineers during the First World War. He was in Italy building bridges. Tragically, while coming home on leave, he contracted malaria, and was taken off the train in France, where he died. He was buried near Lyon in September 1918.

"In 1920 when I was five, I became a pupil at Drinkstone School, walking there with my sister and all the other children (about a mile). The roads were dusty then, our shoes would be full of dust. We'd take sandwiches and a bottle of orange or lemonade for lunch. There was a pump behind the schoolhouse, and if we wanted a drink, there'd be a pail full of water in the porch.

"I loved school. I was in Miss Minns' class at first, she took the infants. Miss Minns' mother lived with her in the bungalow up the By Road. Miss Minns and Mrs. Gobbitt were sisters. Mrs. Gobbitt took the big class and she was lovely. She sang very well, and she was a wonderful teacher, very good and kind. She was always friendly with my mother. We used to have a photograph of her in our house. Her daughter Dorothy gave me some piano lessons.

"We used to have an Attendance Officer come round – but I wouldn't have wanted to stay away! I loved all the lessons – drawing, books of all descriptions, maths – but I didn't like needlework. I had to do needlework, but after that lesson I always felt sick, I wanted to get outside. Maybe it was having to look so closely at the white material. We made little samplers of different stitches for the Show at Woolpit.

"On May Day we had a maypole set up in the playground. One Christmas, Mr. Hargreaves of Drinkstone Park gave all the schoolchildren a party in the Ballroom. There was a Christmas

tree with presents, and I had a needlework box made of wood, with a pincushion inside.

"*The rector used to come once a week and the Inspector used to come from Elmswell to test us, he was Mr. Sayers. We had to remember a lot by heart. We had a hymn and a prayer first thing in the morning, and a prayer before we went home. I remember once at School, Mrs. Gobbitt's daughter came in to see if we were all right, and she was telling us we all had to be christened or we wouldn't go to heaven. I always remembered that.*

"*Sometimes there was a School Play at the Village Hall, and a Show with all kinds of acts. I remember Tom Smith and the other boys were dressed as policemen one time, and they sang a song, it went something like this:*

> *We're members of the police force,*
> *A gallant, noble band.*
> *But oh, we are so worried*
> *When on our beat we stand!*
> *Some folks are always asking*
> *The nearest, quickest way,*
> *We are so tired of answering*
> *But cheerfully we say*
> *'Take first your right, and then your left,*
> *'To where the roadways cross;*
> *'Turn up to left and down to right*
> *'And down Befuddle Lane –*
> *'And then just ask again!'*

"*Once my sister Kathleen recited the poem 'Will you walk into my parlour? said the spider to the fly'. I did one called 'I must not tease my mother'. Irene Keeble, one of the girls, had a lovely singing voice.*

"*At playtime, the boys played football in Rectory Meadow. We girls played hopscotch, rounders, Oranges and Lemons, In and Out the Windows, and a game called 'Wolf, wolf, come home'. We'd say 'The wolf has gone to Devonshire, and won't be back for seven years, Sheep, sheep, come home!' And the sheep would say 'We're afraid!' and the game would end with a chase.*

"*After Mrs. Gobbitt, Miss Hockley was Headmistress. She was very good. We had a few Supply teachers as well.*

"*My family were Chapel people. Mother was a regular member of Rattlesden Baptist Church. But Mother got crossed off the list because she took us girls to dancing class at Drinkstone Village Hall! So then we changed to Church of England. I was baptised at All Saints Church, next to the School, with my sister Kathleen, when I was fifteen. Then we were confirmed at Bury St. Edmunds. My sister married Sidney Young, the local grocer who had his shop in the thatched cottage near the School. Miss Craske was the Postmistress and lived near Blacksmith's Corner.*

"*Later on, I met Philip Donaghy, he'd come over from Ireland to be foreman agent for a Public Works Contractor, Hayes of Warrington. Philip was a Roman Catholic. I remember one day Philip said to Mother 'Can Molly go to the convent?' and she answered 'Why? To be nun?' - but of course, he meant, to learn about the Roman Catholic religion. Mother didn't mind, she loved Philip, he was a lovely man. So I changed again! I remember when the Catholic priest was in our house once, I said to him 'I've been dodging the devil all my life!' and he laughed at that.*

"*So I became a Catholic, and I married Philip in August 1939, just before the start of the Second World War. We had five children – Neil in 1940, John in 1942, the twins Moira and Michael in 1943 and David in 1945. Philip was on the airfields laying ducts for telephones, he worked on airfields all over the country – Blackpool, Liverpool, Norfolk, Warwickshire – and sometimes we'd rent somewhere so I could go with him. But sometimes I'd stay with Mother, in Kopsey Cottage. Old Bert Halls lived opposite us, and I remember one night when a lot of planes were going over, he came and knocked on our door and said 'I had to come and see if you poor women with a baby are all right!' so Mother gave him a whiskey!*

"Later on, we bought 'Whitegates', a cottage opposite the Rectory. But in 1946 my Philip died of heart trouble. He'd had it all his life but he didn't tell me. I loved my kids, so it wasn't too hard. We had some fun and some mischief. I would fetch water from the pump, and it wasn't far, but I'd lock the children in the house for safety. They could see me out of the windows, they could see the pump..."

Here daughter Moira takes over the narrative, saying:

"I took Michael, my twin, opened the back window and helped him out, then I got out myself and danced up the path to meet her! I was the dominant one, Mother says I pushed poor Michael out of the pram once and he had to have two stitches in his head! When we were a bit older, we could all ride a bike except Michael, he wasn't very keen. So we decided to teach him! We put him on, just said 'Pedal!' and gave him a big push. But we didn't tell him about the brakes! Suddenly he fell off and landed among the potatoes. That was the end of that! So we all went to Rattlesden airfield, on the strips, to teach him.

"We had a good time. Mother would light the fire in the bedrooms, and she used to read to us a lot. When we were old enough, we went to Drinkstone School. Mrs. Collins was Headteacher then. But Michael and I only went there for about one term. Another Roman Catholic family took us to St. Edmunds R.C. School in Westgate Street. Later on, there was a school bus we could catch to get to Bury St. Edmunds, but we'd have to leave at seven in the morning to walk to Rattlesden to catch it, then we'd get home after six o'clock. David would fall asleep on the way home as he was so young. John and Neil went on from St. Edmunds to Beyton School because they wanted to do woodwork.

"I became a children's Nanny. I worked for Judge Butler Sloss in The Temple grounds, London, and for Ann Hayward the film star, in Kensington. Then I came home to Suffolk and married Hugh, and we've got four children.

"My brother Neil, the eldest, married Carol and has one daughter. He became a farmer but he's retired now. John and Michael never married, wise people! David married twice, and has two children from his first marriage. He's married to Hilary now and they live at The Rookery in Drinkstone. John's a plumber and Michael's a painter and decorator, Michael lives in Drinkstone as well. Neil, John, Mother and I all live around Walsham le Willows."

Molly showed me three wonderful old exercise books dating from the 1920s when she was a schoolgirl at Drinkstone. They are Nelson Exercise books, published by E.J. Arnold and Son, and the duck-egg blue covers show a drawing of Nelson's Column. Inside, Molly's beautiful, flowing cursive writing covers every page.

Here was an opportunity to discover what was taught in the School in those far-off days. These books are dated 1927-9 so they lead on perfectly to the next section of this history, which deals with the period 1927-1938.

Chapter Twelve

MOLLY EDWARDS' SCHOOL BOOKS, 1927 - 29

THE FIRST BOOK I opened contained Geography and History studies. To modern eyes these subjects seem to have been taught in rather arid mode (not surprisingly, in days with no television, and lessons taught from text books and blackboard to large classes with a huge range of age and ability). Lessons seem to have consisted of copying out facts, then learning them. There are lists of towns, sorted by industry or product or main feature, the same method being used for foreign countries.

Thus "GEOGRAPHY" starts with lists of towns of England:

PORTS – Hull, Portsmouth, Southampton, Plymouth, Bristol, Cardiff, Swansea, Liverpool, and Barrow.

WOOLLENS – Leeds, Bradford, Halifax, Wakefield, Huddersfield, Dewsbury

COTTON GOODS –Manchester, Bolton, Blackburn, Burnley, Oldham

IRON GOODS – Birmingham, Wolverhampton, West Bromwich

POTTERY – Hanley, Newcastle under Lyme, Stoke

BOOTS – Stafford, Leicester, Northampton

STRAW HATS – Bedford, Luton

FISHING – Grimsby, Boston

UNIVERSITIES – Oxford, Cambridge, Durham

PUBLIC SCHOOLS – Eton, Harrow

IRON – Newcastle, Middlesborough, Hartlepool, Sunderland, North and South Shields, Stockton

RAILWAY CENTRES – Carlisle, Crewe

WATERING PLACES – Whitby, Scarborough, Hunstanton, Wells, Cromer, Yarmouth, Lowestoft, Clacton, Eastbourne, Bournemouth, Torquay, Penzance, St. Ives, Ilfracombe, Llandudno, Blackpool

INLAND WATERING PLACES – Bath, Harrowgate, Leamington, Matlock, Buxton

PACKET STATIONS – Dover, Harwich

FRUIT – Hereford, Maidstone

Redditch = needles, Walsall = saddlery, Bromsgrove = nails, Kidderminster = carpets,

Coventry = bicycles, Nottingham = lace, Burton = beer, Sheffield = knives, Aylesbury = ducks, Norwich = mustard and starch, St. Helens = glass, Widnes = chemicals,

Keswick = pencils, Reading = biscuits and seeds, Rotherham = brass, Doncaster = railway stock, Colchester = oysters, Yarmouth = bloaters, Melton Mowbray = pork pies, Chatham = training sailors, Greenwich = time, Woolwich = arsenal, Clovelly = stair street, Salisbury = cathedral, Canterbury = archbishop, Winchester = ancient buildings, Ripon = agricultural centre.

PRODUCTS OF COUNTRIES

ENGLAND – Cotton goods, woollen goods, iron goods, ship building, coal mining

SCOTLAND – jam, ropes, tweed, cattle, horses, oats, barley

IRELAND – flax, linen, pigs, bacon, potatoes, poplin, peat

WALES – slate, coal

FRANCE – silk

SPAIN – oranges

ITALY – marble, macaroni
GREECE – currants
GERMANY – toys, musical instruments
RUSSIA – hides, furs
SWITZERLAND – watches, milk
HOLLAND – tulips, diamond cutting
BELGIUM – matches
DENMARK – bacon, butter
NORWAY – matches
ASIA – opium, tea, coffee, rice, gold, silver, copper
AFRICA – big game, timber, rubber, nuts, ivory, gum, gold, dates, coffee, cocoa, bananas
USA – tobacco, gold, maize, coal, petroleum, iron
SOUTH AMERICA – gold, pearls, iron, diamonds, salt, oats, tea, coffee, cocoa, dates, cocoanuts, rubber, bananas, sheep, rice.

There are similar summaries on colonial "ownership", physical features, latitude and longitude etc, of Africa, Australia, the West Indies, South America… I suspect there may have been sighs and yawns when these "subjects" were under study!

The HISTORY section, not unexpectedly, consists mainly of lists of dates, of kings, queens, battles and dramatic events, with brief summaries of various epochs. For example, the "Outline of British History from 1066 – 1837" takes up only five pages.

The second exercise book is a personal anthology of poems, and lists of books read. There are favourite poems, beautifully copied out, including works by Masefield, Henry Newbolt, Longfellow, Kipling and Shakespeare. There are religious and patriotic songs such as "Rule Britannia", "God bless the Prince of Wales" and "The British Grenadiers". I wonder how many were committed to memory?

The list of "Books I have read" has a familiar ring for a person such as myself, growing up in the 1940s and 1950s. It includes classics such as Alice in Wonderland, the Pilgrim's Progress, Little Women, Good Wives, Uncle Tom's Cabin, The Rivals of Maidenhurst; also various legends and folk tales, such as Hildred the Proud, the Seven Champions of Christendom, Sinbad the Sailor, and Robin Hood.

The "Grammar" section includes examples of "Parts of Speech" under the headings Interjections, Conjunctions, Prepositions, Proper Nouns, Common Nouns, Pronouns, Verbs, Adverbs, and Adjectives – a branch of knowledge that is a mystery to many of today's schoolchildren. Then there is spelling and handwriting practice; some consists of lists, such as names of fish species written over and over again. Occasionally passages of elegant prose or poems were used for handwriting practice.

There is an interesting list of "Notable Dates", including many that are not so well remembered today, as follows:

Jan. 1st, New Year's Day	Feb. 2nd, Candlemas Day
Feb 14th, St. Valentine's Day	March 1st, St. David's Day
March 17th, St. Patrick's Day	March 21st, Spring begins
March 25th, Lady Day	April 1st, All Fools' Day
April 23rd, St. George's Day, Shakespeare	May 1st, May Day
May 24th, Empire Day	May 29th, Royal Oak Day
June 3rd, King's Birthday 1865	June 21st, Summer begins
June 24th, Midsummer Day	July 15th, St. Swithin's Day
August 1st, Lammas Day	August 4th, War started 1914
Sept. 23rd, Autumn begins	Sept. 29th, Michaelmas Day
Oct. 18th, St. Luke's Day	Oct. 21st, Trafalgar Day
Nov. 1st, All Saints' Day	Nov. 2nd, All Souls' Day
Nov. 5th, Guy Fawkes Day	Nov. 11th, Armistice Day
Nov. 30th, St. Andrew's Day	Dec. 21st, Shortest Day
Dec. 25th, Christmas Day	Dec. 26th, Boxing Day
Dec. 27th, St. John's Day	Dec. 28th, Holy Innocents' Day

The third exercise book was for the subject "COOKERY". I found this interesting as it presumably gives a picture of the ideal housewife and home-maker of the period. But I wonder how many local housewives had the time, the money, or the energy to keep their families in the way the notes suggest! After all, farm labourers' wages were abysmally low in the 1920s, families were large, and most women supplemented their housekeeping allowance by seasonal work on the farms or domestic work. There would have been mounds of washing (no protective plastic pants for their babies!), not to mention ironing, mending, darning, knitting and sewing. The instruction was undoubtedly good, but seems more appropriate to a middle-class household with at least one maid-of-all-work. Four cooked meals a day are suggested, with no short cuts in the preparation or presentation. This to be achieved by busy women using coal or wood stoves, with small children underfoot ("Baby bottles must be kept clean, and feeds must be regular in time and quantity"!)

However the school work provides rich social documentary material – not to mention marvellous cooking hints! These are some examples:

PLANNING MEALS – POINTS TO REMEMBER
Amount of money to spend
Time of year
Number in family
Time to prepare and cook
Whether adults or children
If any invalids

INVALID COOKERY – Diet depends upon:
Nature of illness
State of patient
Doctor's orders
Light diet – Beef tea, custards, invalid fruit tart
Convalescent diet – Dishes suitable –
Meat – mutton chop or lamb chop
Fish – whiting or sole, steamed
Jellies (milk, orange, etc), egg, egg custard, blackcurrant tea, chicken broth, junket, arrowroot pudding, lemon sago

MAIN MEALS
Breakfast Dishes
Amount necessary – a good meal is needed, because we have a day's work to do and we have fasted during the night.
Time taken in preparing and cooking. Food is needed which can be cooked quickly.
Suitable dishes – eggs and bacon, oxo, fish, bread and milk, porridge, liver and bacon.

MEAT – choice of meat depends upon –
If it is fresh
If it will keep
If the family like it.

BRAISING is a slow method of cooking meat. Braised meat is cooked by the steam from the vegetables upon which it is placed.
Method – Wipe meat, and tie into neat shape. Clean vegetables and cut into dice or slices. Place vegetables in stewpan with herbs and spices. Nearly cover with water. Place meat on top and cover tightly with lid. Cook gently for three to four hours according to size. If large joint is used, put slices of bacon on the top to keep it moist. If small joint, baste frequently.

GRILLING.
Grilling is cooking by a radiant heat.
Rules –1. Fire must be red hot and glowing
2. Grid iron must be well greased
Food must be turned.

SUPPER DISHES – Food must be easy to digest. Food must be nourishing. Food may be re-heated dishes, or cheese dishes.

Suitable dishes – Welsh rarebit, macaroni cheese, potato and cheese balls, cheese rissoles, savoury cheese, cheese pudding, cheese custard, cheese eggs, savoury rice and cheese, cheese straws, gruel, bread and milk, porridge."

(Obviously these folk did not agree with the old wives' belief that eating cheese before bed-time causes nightmares!)

There are numerous complicated recipes and cooking instructions on bread making, cakes, scones, gingerbread, flaky pastry, short crust pastry, mincemeat, Christmas cake, and so on. Also some intriguing comments on vegetarianism –

VEGETARIAN COOKERY

Vegetarians are people who live mainly on vegetables for –

Reasons of health

Sense of duty

Poverty

Molly must have been in her last year of school when she diligently wrote down all the above. I take my hat off to the housewives of yesteryear!

Also in these exercise books are various jottings of a later date. Molly had enjoyed play acting and school performances of all kinds, and leaving school was not the end of these occasions for her. She says:

"We had a lot of fun. We dressed up as Adam and Eve once, that was me and Nell Cocksedge, and we had long skeins of wool for hair, and tight all-over pinkish clothes on. Later, Nell and I were 'Bunny Girls' at the Village Fete. Sometimes I was in comic sketches, there was one called 'Buying a Haddock', and at the end we sang a version of 'Daisy, Daisy' that we made up. It went like this:

Daisy, Daisy, buy my fine 'addock do!
I'm just crazy to sell my fine fish to you.
But my old man's a rebel,
He'll tell me to go to the devil,
Is it good to eat?
Yes, and very cheap,
And you get your fine fashions too.
Fishman, fishman, cuddle me closer, do,
Kiss me quickly, but don't let my Alf see you.
Yes sure 'tis the greatest pleasure,
And I'll give you right good measure.
Let's make it a date
And I won't be late,
(both) For I've fallen in love with you!

The comedy sketch is in the exercise book. It is certainly extremely funny and must have had the audience rolling in the aisles. But I was struck by the subject matter, which is wife-battering! I thought how outlooks have changed over the years – not always for the better, but in this case definitely so. For the sketch presents wife-battering as a normal daily occurrence, the wife having ended up in every hospital around London, except, so far, the Middlesex. It ends with the fishman watching the assault and saying "'e's 'ad a couple all right!" (Piercing shriek off stage) – "There's one for the other side o' her head! And never a 'arsh word! Hi, Ma! I 'opes yer gets to the Middlesex this time!"

Sadly, domestic violence is not a thing of the past. But hopefully the fact that it is no longer regarded as acceptable is a step towards better things. I was amazed when I discovered that well into the 20th century, "correction" of a wife by her husband was not a crime unless the result was mutilation or permanent disfigurement!

It's interesting to reflect on changing attitudes to physical punishment in schools. So many of the men and women whose memories are included in this history have referred to canings, or children being "given a thump" by the teacher (even, being banged on the head with a big Bible!) When the School opened, "spare the rod and spoil the child" was a popular dictum, and physical punishment was the accepted norm at school, and in most homes. We know all too well that even in this 21st century, maltreatment of children occurs behind closed doors in many homes. But at least it is not accepted as an appropriate way for teachers to deal with pupils. So perhaps attitudes are gradually changing for the better.

Chapter Thirteen

SCHOOL AND VILLAGE, 1927 - 38

THE SCHOOL

Dorothea Victoria Hockley proudly wrote her name on the first page of the School Log Book, announcing that she "took charge" as Headmistress of Drinkstone on October 4th 1927. Her infrequent entries in the Log Book suggest pleasant seasonal routines at a well-run school. Miss Minns remained as infant teacher. This is a sample of entries for the period:

11th November 1927 – Armistice Day. The children attended Church at 10.45am.

24th May 1928 – Empire Day. The children sang Empire songs to the rector, and had a lesson on the Empire.

> "BOARD OF EDUCATION REPORT – Inspected on April 8th 1929
>
> "Report by H.M.I. Mr. J.B. Russell
>
> "The Headmistress who was appointed in October 1927 has worked hard and in some ways successfully to improve the general efficiency.
>
> "Class 1 consists of five distinct grades. The older children take commendable interest in their lessons and are making fair all-round progress.
>
> "The Reading is good whilst some of the written English is above average for this type of School. The Handwork in various media is a valuable feature of the curriculum: it is providing good training in form and colour although some of the work at present is lacking in neatness and finish.
>
> "In oral questioning it is somewhat difficult to win the ready response of the children. Suitable training in oral expression would, no doubt, overcome much of their reticence and caution.
>
> "The chief points discussed with the Headmistress concerned the written Arithmetic, Drawing and Geography.
>
> "The teacher of the Infants is kindly and painstaking. The work reaches a fair standard. Suggestions were made with regard to the choice of Songs and Verse and the teaching of Reading.
>
> "Headmistress – Miss Hockley, Standards II-VI (to age 14)
>
> "Infant Teacher – Miss Minns, Standard I"

The Log continues:

2nd November 1929 – School chimney swept.

5th November 1929 – Standards 4-7 had a History Lesson on Gunpowder Plot instead of the usual Handwork Lesson.

20th December 1929 – Painting Christmas cards has been done by all scholars during the drawing lessons this week.

28th April 1930 – Diocesan Report received, on Religious Knowledge inspected March 31st 1930 –

> "I inspected the school and found the Religious Instruction well given. The children in each section

Drinkstone School 1929-30 (left to right):
Back row – Donald Sparkes, Albert Brinkley, George Rose, George Mayes, Douglas Harvey,
George Dykes, ? ? ?, (last two on lower level). Third row – Doulas Bland, Winnie Revens, ?
Maggie Brinkley, ?, Lily Mayes, Cathy Edwards, Elsie Leach, ? ?, Geoffrey Dykes, Wilfred Bland,
Lesley Bland, Walter Rose. Second row – Kathy Revens, Ruby Rogers, ?, Phylis Robinson, ? ? ?
?, Molly Edwards, Susan Bloomfield, Gladys Bloomfield, ?, Percy Bloomfield. Front row – James
Rose, Victor Sturgeon, Kenneth Sturgeon, Francisn"Nippy" Brinkley, John Bloomfield, Wiliam
Leach, Victor Sparkes.

are interested in their lessons and answer brightly."

23rd May 1930 – As Empire Day fell on a Saturday, the children celebrated the occasion on Friday 23rd. They were given lessons on the British Empire and on the Union Jack. They also marched round the school building singing suitable songs.

16th July 1930 – Result of Exhibition of Work at the Woolpit Flower Show. Prizes awarded to Drinkstone School 8 in number together with 2 Highly Commended.

Prizes – Maps of England and Wales showing products. Painting, Cushion Cover, Child's Socks, Pillow Case, Kettle Holder.

That is one of the last of Miss Hockley's entries in the Log Book, since she resigned and in October 1930 the Managers were searching for another Headmistress, with little success. Maybe the village was too remote. They interviewed a Mrs. Cowings and a Mrs. Peart, appointed the former who then changed her mind; so they wrote hopefully to Mrs. Peart – but neither lady appeared in the School. For almost a year, members of the County "Unattached Staff" came and went; in quick succession the children were taught by Anne Barnes, Frank Kerridge, L.C. Newton and Frank Nicholson.

THE VILLAGE

In April 1931 *Suffolk Chronicle and Mercury* published a special feature on Drinkstone village, in a series written by "Yeoman". There is a lot of detail about All Saints' Church, and the careers of notable residents from medieval times onwards. Drinkstone Park was described as "having many fine plantations and a pleasant lake, whilst the rich colouring of its trees gives a real charm to the district and makes the road a picture of sylvan delight in the scented days of spring and early summer". Drinkstone House (before the disastrous fire) is described as "an imposing and attractive residence" with "delightful gardens and shrubberies".

A photograph of Rookery Farm bears the caption "A farmhouse which possesses many fine chimneys". A photo of Shop Lane, off Rattlesden Road, shows Kopsey Cottage, Fyfers, and Chimbleys (all then thatched) with the caption "Unspoilt Old-World Cottages". The shop which gave this short lane its name was at White House, and supplied groceries and bread (baked on the premises). The shopkeeper also repaired boots and shoes.

The article concludes with the words: "A really delightful little place, set amidst acres of rolling woodland and gently sloping fields… Drinkstone village… with its strange variations in roofing styles which include the rural thatch, red tiles, and even, in places, corrugated iron! (At the time, Blacksmith's Cottage had an ancient thatched roof covered over with corrugated iron, and the bungalow in the By Road where teacher Miss Minns lived had both roof and walls of corrugated iron.)

Above: Rookery Farmhouse
Below: Kopsey, Fyfers and Chimbleys in the 1930s

Very few new houses were built in Drinkstone during the first thirty-five years of the 20th century. Rattlesden Road gained a few houses. Members of the Bland family had built the imposing double-front-ed white brick house known now as "The Homestead", in 1912. There was also a handful of pleasant cottages, mostly semi-detached brick and tile dwellings, built in 1913-14. One of these, "Threeways", was owned and occupied by the Wells family for many years, having been built by the grandfather of Mrs. Wells (who was living there in 2000 at the time of the village Millennium Survey), using Woolpit white bricks which were brought from Woolpit Brickyard by horse and cart. Others of this group are "Draycott", "Firside", and "Bramble Cottage", which was built and owned by the Cooper family who ran a village shop there until 1975. Firside, which is now known as Honeypot Cottage, was owned by Major E. F. Fowler of Gunton Old Hall, Lowestoft, from 1913 until 1948.

Apart from these brick homes in Rattlesden Road, new building was non-existent. First came the Great War, then the Depression. Farmers could not afford to maintain tied cottages, some of which simply crumbled. The Ordnance Survey map produced just after the turn of the century shows a few cottages just north of the Almhouses, in The Street opposite the Church, of which there are no remains. That area later became part of Mr. Thurlow's meadow. The Almshouses (at that time comprising six small cottages) were slowly becoming dilapidated, as were the row of cottages opposite Widow's Cottage, and Widow's Cottage itself was in a poor state. It was a stroke of unusual luck that gave Stott's Cottage a new lease of life (story in Chapter Ten).

Those cottages that were reasonably well-maintained, such as Kopsey's, Fyfer's and Chimbleys, were at times divided into "tenements", each cottage housing two or three families. Similarly, Garden House Farm (where Daniel Clover lived at the start of the new century) lists a surprising number of inhabitants.

Some time in the Thirties, another brick and tile dwelling was built in Rattlesden Road. This had oak panelling and an oak staircase, and was the property of Mr. Barker, a funeral director who continued living there for about fifty years.

THE SCHOOL

At the School, by September 1931, a new Headmistress had been appointed. She was Mrs. B. M. Williams. Somehow the children's education had continued; no doubt they benefited from the continued presence of Miss Minns in the infant room, and the weekly lessons given by the Rev. Frank Horne. At this time the total population of the village was only 377, and pupil numbers were in the thirties. Days were made more interesting for the older children by practical lessons at Woolpit; on 7th April 1932 we read "4 girls commence Cooking Class at Woolpit (Thursdays)."

In April 1935 the Diocesan Inspector called. Mrs. Williams copied his Report into the Log Book:

"I examined this school in Religious Instruction and found teachers and children working happily together. The Infants are well taught and answer nicely. In the Upper School, the children know their work in both Old and New Testament – memory work, singing and written work all good. J.D. Sayer, Diocesan Inspector."

Another regular monthly visitor was the Needlework Inspector. Presumably she was on the L.E.A. Staff, since money was sent to them in payment for needlework materials. She would inspect the work, which included cushion covers, pillow cases, table runners, socks, petticoats, nightdresses, aprons, and of course kettle holders!

(As a schoolgirl in Leicester in the 1940s, I too made kettle holders, and knitted miserable-looking dish-cloths out of stringy grey wool! We made skirts and dresses, all the seams hand-stitched, out of stiff blue serge. I don't remember ever wearing these clothes however!)

No doubt the ability to make and mend was essential to families in the Twenties, Thirties and Forties. Certainly no other subject except Scripture, and possibly gardening, came under such scrutiny. It seems that while the boys were out of doors working on the garden, the girls were busy indoors knitting and sewing. When an Exhibition of Work was imminent, all other lessons for the girls were suspended so the needlework would be ready. This was a sexist era when roles were prescribed. The boys entered maps of England showing products, compositions on "The Empire", and paintings.

Mrs. Williams resigned from her post in Spring 1936. By May, another procession of Supply and Unattached Staff began to arrive – J. M. Smith, S. L. Bond…. Meanwhile nothing of great note occurred; Rev. Horne would give "the usual Scripture lesson"; while there were small excitements such as on September 21st 1936, when the Log Book reads: "A very wet morning. 8 out of 32 present. Only one child present in the Infants' Classroom!" There were no comfortable cars in those days!

Nothing disturbed certain traditions; on 11th November 1936 the Teacher in charge wrote "Armistice Day. The two minutes silence was observed, the National Anthem sung, and the Head Teacher gave a short talk on 'The Benefits we are still receiving through the Sacrifices of the Great War.'"

Changes were taking place in the village in 1936; Camborne Cottage was sold to Major Ernest George Fowler. The Charity Trustees include many familiar names – the Rev. Francis Horne, Major Fowler, Daniel Clover, John Jewers and Sidney Snell. The money from the sale was invested and the work of the Charity continued. In 1938 the Cottage was sold again, this time to Mrs. Edith Summers of Hammond Hall (the property next door to Camborne). Mrs. Summers also bought the Old Almshouses block of cottages opposite the School, and let them out privately.

On December 1st 1936 a new Headmistress took charge of the little School. She was Miss Barbara Allen. The number on roll was only 30 by April 1937. A few parents had doubts about the quality of education the School offered, since some pupils were withdrawn and registered at Rattlesden School. The managers recorded with feeling "Great indignation was felt at the removal of the children without the managers' consent". They wrote to the Education Committee for support. The authorities sent the children back to Drinkstone School, promising to ensure that no child changed schools without good reason (so much for Parental Choice!).

The managers now included Rev. Blencowe, gentleman, of The Meade, who took the place of Mr. Hargreaves of Drinkstone Park who died in 1935. In Autumn 1938 another great change came with the

The Clover family of Drinkstone Mill, c1925. Back row: Lucy, Reginald, Ida, Daniel (father), Wilfred; John (left, sitting); Front row: Wyn, Eleanor, May (mother, née Sangster), Thelma, Olive and Katherine.

retirement of the Rev. Frank Horne. Major Fowler, current owner of Drinkstone House, stood in as temporary Chairman while a new rector was awaited. Then a terrible fire destroyed most of Major Fowler's home and he and his wife moved to Thurston – "only the kitchen quarters were saved, thanks to Stowmarket Fire Brigade". Ruby Bland was employed there as housemaid and in her memories (Chapter Fourteen) recalls the terrible day when the elegant house (for many years the pride of the aristocratic LeHeup Cocksedge family) was destroyed.

The managers worked faithfully on; their Minutes of December 1938 record that cash balances for their School account and Schoolhouse account were £3-6s-3d and £3-13s-8d respectively, and that these monies have been entrusted to Lloyd's Bank at Bury St. Edmunds.

In 1937, 1938 and 1939 some children sat the Scholarship Examination for Grammar School Entrance. Whether Headteachers simply omitted to record this most years, or whether it was a rare event, I don't know. But at least in these three years the exam was taken by some if not all of the eligible pupils. There were only about thirty pupils in total during these years, so there would not be many eleven-year-olds in a five-to-fourteen school. We are not told whether any passed. These are the entries:

19th March 1937 – 3 children attended Scholarship Exam at Woolpit Centre this a.m.

18th March 1938 – Joyce Leach attended Woolpit School for Scholarship examination.

16th March 1939 – Two children went to Woolpit School for Scholarship Test.

The shadow of war once again hung over the land, but I think the schooldays of these small children were not greatly affected.

When closing the School in 1986, we found on high neglected shelves several heavy tomes full of "new" ideas for work with young children. There were action songs and singing games, and imaginative ideas for art and craft and model making. Many of the themes were based on the natural world (such as leaf-rubbing, and printing with shaped potatoes). There were instructions for Easter gardens, Christmas cards and presents, cutting and sticking – all the things young children of any generation have enjoyed. I was surprised to see that many of the poems, stories and craft ideas came from that immensely popular "educator" and moulder of young minds of the era, Miss Enid Blyton!

Miss Allen set to work with a will. The managers congratulated her for wonderful work on the School Garden. No doubt Miss Minns, now elderly, was still usually "kindly and painstaking" in her infant classroom. So with 30 children on roll, ranging in age from five to fourteen, the months rolled forward inevitably towards war.

The next chapter contains the stories of folk who were pupils at Drinkstone between 1927 and 1938.

Chapter Fourteen

PERSONAL STORIES
Donald Sparkes, Ruby Bland, Mary Horrex and Ken Sturgeon

DONALD SPARKES

Don was born on 22nd May, 1919, in one of a row of three cottages in Cross Street. I talked with him in his bungalow home in Elmswell, where he lives with his wife Mary, in good health and "going for the telegram from the Queen!" Memories from the past are stronger than ever now, he says, and life has taught him far more than school ever could. These are some of his recollections.

"We lived in one of the tiled cottages, with Joe Rivens' family one side of us, and Mrs. Neville the other. One of the cottages was thatched. The two tiled ones belonged to Blands of Bridge Farm. Those two were sold later, and knocked into one to make a bigger cottage, for Joe Scrooby.

"I had an older brother who died when he was two from falling into a bath of scalding water. I never knew him. My older sister Lilian died from TB when she was twenty-one. I had two younger brothers, Victor and Frank. I'm the only one left now.

"My father was a very clever man. He worked on farms, that was the only work there was then, but he could turn his hand to anything. He could work with horses, milk cows, castrate animals, and do thatching – anything on the farms, he could do. He died at fifty from throat cancer, and my mother was left with three children to bring up, she was forty-two then.

"I started School when I was five, I remember walking there, about a mile. But everybody walked then, there wasn't the traffic, and we had fun on the way with spinning tops and hoops. Mrs. Gobbitt was Headteacher, and her sister Miss Minns took the infants, she lived in the old galvanised place up the By-Road. After Mrs. Gobbitt died (I think that was some kind of accident), Miss Hockley came. I think the teachers were fair. To be honest, I think they just taught you enough to work on the farms. We learned more after we left than we learned at School. I liked the sport, I was sport mad, so I liked playtimes. But we never had the facilities they've got now. For cricket we had to make our own bats out of a piece of willow, and our wicket would be sticks stuck in the ground. One day some gentleman saw us playing (I don't know who he was) and later he brought us a full set of cricket gear!

"They'd have football and cricket teams in Drinkstone every so often, they'd keep going a season or two, then it would all fall apart, the kit would disappear and the team would disband. I think the problem was Drinkstone's a very scattered village, there's the Queach, that long lane between the Green and the Church and School, about a mile with no houses. I heard there was some ruling that you can't build there, I think there's a covenant on it or something. So how was it they could build the electricity sub-station along there? A few houses joining up the village would have made Drinkstone a better village, it's difficult as it is to get a feeling that it's all one community. All our teams went to the wall after a bit, so I ended up playing for teams at Rattlesden and Felsham. But at least we did have steel quoits and tennis at the Village Hall

in Drinkstone.

"*I was fourteen when I left School, and I went to work for Barretts, at Valley Farm, Felsham. Working hours in winter were 7am till 5pm, and in summer we started at 6.30 in the morning. I had a bit of an argument with Barrett about the times, so I left there and went to work for John Jewers of Green Farm in Rattlesden Road. He was a marvellous old boy, he was about a hundred when he died! Then by coincidence Barretts who I worked for at Felsham hired Green Farm so I was back at square one! I didn't ask for that job. Barrett did a milk round and this particular Sunday morning he asked me if I'd come back and work with him. I was very good with the horses; I loved horses, and horses loved me. When I was about twenty I was in charge of his horses. Walter Orris, from a gamekeeping family, worked with me then. That didn't stop me shooting a pheasant now and again! There was a lot of poverty, there wasn't much money about, there wasn't much food about. We needed the odd pheasant.*

"*Well, I was in the age group which had to go in the forces. I got a letter to report at the Army Driving School at Herne Bay. But I was in Felsham football team and our chairman was Sir John Tilley of Felsham Hall. He said to 'me, 'You don't want to go there – join the Grenadier Guards!' So I went to Chelsea Barracks and joined up on 24th November 1939. I was in the Guards for six years and ninety-nine days.*

"*I went from Infantry to tank driving in the Guards Armoured Division. We went to Normandy. I stayed in the ranks, it was safer. A lot of chaps got killed because they had stripes! They'd be in dirty overalls, with bright white stripes on their shoulder, and the snipers could pick them out in the darkness. They got wise in the end, and they'd put the stripes on a band of elastic, so when it was dark they could pull the elastic round and have the stripes under their arm. It was every man for hisself to a degree, but then, you relied on each other as well.*

"*War changed everybody. When I was stationed in London, we'd go down the East End where they were friendly, to the pubs. I remember once we were in a pub and there was an air-raid warning, and the police came in and said 'If you want to leave, leave quietly', and one old cockney at the back he shouted out 'Stuff Hitler!' Those old cockneys, you couldn't get them down, they laughed at everything.*

"*My Tank Commander was Captain Berry, his father was Lord Kemsley, the* Daily Sketch *editor. There was a lot of trivial rules, they called it discipline! You had to keep your head down. But those officers would have died of hunger and thirst if it hadn't been for us Guardsmen! Because they were rich, they'd always been looked after, they hadn't a clue. We were camped near some woods once, and the Tank Sergeant, he was Joe Hunt from Birmingham, he said to me one night, 'Come on, we're going to get ourselves something good.' So we went in these woods, and we came to a smallholding. We looked over the fence, and there was a pig. Joe said, 'We're having that pig!' So he shot it, then he got his jack-knife and slit it top to bottom. Then we got it out and carried it back to the tank. I didn't know, but Joe was a butcher by trade.*

"*But that pig had been noticed by the powers that be! Two days later, the Squadron Leader was livid, he'd wanted it for the officers. He was saying 'There was a pig in these woods we were going to get, and someone's had it!' We'd all been eating pork chops for two days! So Joe said 'Keep yer mouth shut!' and we had a good laugh. If you can't laugh you'd be lost.*

"*We saw some bad things. Those tanks were petrol driven, and every time one was hit it flew into fire. The Germans called our tanks 'Ronson Lighters'. You'd be speaking to your mates in the morning and they'd be dead by night. We saw some horrors. But the thing is, I was lucky, I wasn't affected mentally by it.*

"*Those Germans, they were obsessed with Hitler. I saw one German taken prisoner and he was daft enough to do the Nazi salute and shout 'Heil Hitler!' when he was brought in. That's not going to help you when you're a prisoner, is it? But when it all finished, we were on the Luxembourg border. They'd always been neutral, so after being in darkness every night, suddenly we could see all these bright lights over there!*

"*I was de-mobbed on April 1st 1946. It was worse at the finish, in a way, because you'd got used to a lot of fellows around you, and suddenly you're on your own. In the Army, if there was a job needing to be done there was ten fellows to do it. Now, suddenly, you've got to do it on your own.*

"There was a big gap between officers and men, but when we got overseas in action, that seemed a bit different. They depended on us men, there was more respect for us. I remember once, the Sergeant Major actually called me by my first name! We were walking along, and he just called me 'Don'. I nearly fell over from the shock! I said to him 'Are you sure you're feeling all right, Sir?'

"It's funny, I believe the day I was born, my life was all mapped out. There was a Territorial Hall in Finborough Road, Stowmarket, and a lot of my mates signed on there. I didn't. They all ended up as prisoners of war in Japan. The ones that came back were so thin. There was one, Albert Horrex, we called him 'Doodles', he was a thin fella, and when he came home he was no thinner than when he left! He was tall, too, and they'd say to him 'You must have been all right, you were too tall for the Japs to clip you round the ear!' but he said, 'Don't you believe that, I got a double dose. They'd kick me in the shins first, then when I was down they'd have a go at me!' Albert was a great character. When those POW's came home, they were told 'It's not safe for you to drink alcohol yet,' but he went straight to the Cherry Tree and drank two or three pints and he was still the fittest one there! That was a good pub when we were teenagers, Walter Steggalls and his wife ran it and she'd make these lovely crispy rolls. We'd have cheese and rolls in the pub.

"Anyway, when I came home from the war, I got a job as tractor driver at Little Waldringfield. I was married by then, Pearl came from Somersham, we had two daughters, Wendy and Carole. We moved to Felsham and I was driving tractors for Billy Land at Felsham Hall. Later I worked at I.C.I. in Stowmarket. That's where I met John Scuffins. [This was interesting to me because my own home for thirty-five years, in Wickham Skeith, used to be known as "Scuffins House. The Scuffins family were smallholders there, and that's where John grew up]. *John was real steady, everyone respected him, but he was so slow! You used to have to look at John twice to see if he was walking, and he weren't no faster on his bike! We'd look, and line him up with something, to see if he was moving, then look again! And yet, when the foreman Bob Paddy came in, he'd walk straight over to John, and he'd talk to him about fifteen minutes. We'd laugh about that.*

"My second wife, Mary, she comes from Nottingham. She had two sons, Jim and Dougie. Jim lives just up the road from us, we see him every day, he was in the army for twenty-two years. Dougie, the youngest, was in the army thirty-three years, he became a Major and went to the Palace to be given the MBE. And Dougie, Mary's youngest, married Carole, my youngest. They have two daughters, one's a policewoman, and she trained as a physiotherapist, the other one lives at Cockfield. My daughter Wendy lives at Onehouse. We've got six lovely grandchildren, they're all doing well. We have a good life and I'm heading for the hundred now!"

RUBY BLAND

I visited Ruby Bland several times in her delightful home, "Field Bungalow", and every time I visited she had friends coming or going, just popping in unexpectedly, or (like Patsy the Post Lady, who says she only got the job because of her name!) regular daily visitors to this hospitable lady. Ruby takes a friendly interest in everyone she meets and is always ready for callers with drinks and biscuits on offer. So it was at Ruby's house that I met Mary Horrex, whose childhood experiences were so different from Ruby's. The two have been friends for many a long year. Both ladies had grandchildren at the School in the 1980s while I was teaching there. James Bland, a little fair-haired chap, started in my infants' class, while twins Tracey and John Foster were in the juniors when I first taught at Drinkstone.

Ruby Bland (née Rogers) was born June 18th 1922, in Great Barton. Her father Frank was a Hessett man. Her mother, Agnes, came from Rede. The family moved to Corner Farm in Rattlesden when Ruby was four years old, so her first brief experience of school was at Rattlesden. The family moved again, to Yew Tree Farm up Cross Street, Drinkstone, when she was five. Her father owned all the meadows around Ruby's present home. The bungalow she now lives in was built on his land, and Ruby still owns two meadows in the village. Some new houses in Cross Street were built on land previously part of Yew Tree Farm. One of these, Furlong House, has nine acres with stables, and between 1970-1987 was home to Mr. and Mrs. Hargreaves, distantly related to the Hargreaves family who owned Drinkstone Park mansion.

These are Ruby's memories:

"We had to walk through the fields to school, at Rattlesden, then at Drinkstone, and it was a long way for a child. My little legs, they used to ache! And in summer it was so hot. But we didn't know much different, we didn't mind so much as they would now, because everybody walked.

"We had a good School at Drinkstone. Miss Minns was my teacher in the infants, then Mrs. Williams in the big class. I didn't like arithmetic, but I enjoyed everything else. Every Wednesday we walked across the fields to Woolpit, to a Village Hall that stood opposite the Church (where the car park is now). The boys did woodwork, and we did cooking, and I loved that.

"What I remember most about School, was knitting! I was always good at knitting, my mother taught me to knit when I was quite young. At School I was always knitting, and I used to knit for Mrs. Williams, I made skirts and jumpers for her! I remember a pattern that went 'knit six plain then four purl' and the teacher loved my knitting. I'd knit on curved needles for her. Even at playtimes and lunch break I'd still be knitting. I used to go through into the Schoolhouse kitchen while the teacher got her lunch, and sit there knitting, and she'd give me some lunch as well! I did take sandwiches to school, but I'd eat those before time usually.

"The Rev. Horne used to talk to us two or three times a week in the mornings, and while I was listening I still had to keep knitting. I didn't mind, I loved it, I'd knit jumpers and shawls and babies' jackets for shows, and I got prizes and medals for my work.

"Now I've got rheumatism in my hands, but I can still knit scarves, in moss stitch, and my daughter puts tassels on the ends for me. Now I'm knitting for the Church, to raise money for the new window. The wool was much cheaper when I was a child. During the war, we knitted with darning wool, using all the different coloured skeins and making lovely patterns. We had to knit balaclavas then. It's hard to knit now. When it's hot, my hands get sticky and my rheumatism plays up, but I still love it.

"My husband Wilfred was at School with me, we've always been together really. When we were children, he lived across the meadow at Bridge Farm, and although that was quite near the School he was always late in the mornings. So to get him there on time, the teacher gave him the job of ringing the bell. He had to ring it first at ten to nine, then again at nine o'clock, and after he was given that job he was never late!

"When I left School I went to work at Drinkstone House as housemaid for Major and Mrs. Fowler. But that ended when the house burned down. We had to get out in a hurry, we lost all our things. It was a good thing that fire didn't start at night. The upstairs was nothing but a shell afterwards. The Major and his wife hired a house at Thurston for a while, but then it was war-time and he went off to war. When war started, I had two choices – I could either work at the sugar-beet factory, or on a farm. I didn't join the Land Army because I could work on my father's farm. I used to go around the village with him on the milk round. Wilfred joined the Home Guard, and they would go up to the Mill and go on watch there.

"Wilfred's family and mine were always at the Chapel. Our families ran it really, we had a lovely Sunday School, and the Honington Band would come and play for special days. The Chapel wasn't licensed to do marriages, so Wilfred and I were married at All Saints' Church when I was twenty-one. Our first home was The Gables, Rattlesden Road (Wilfred was first cousin to Raymond Bland). We had two children, Valerie was born in 1944 and Anthony in 1948. Valerie lives at Wisbech now, and Anthony's at Stowlangtoft. He works for Opalworks, at

Stanton. He's really busy at the moment clearing out Bridge Farm ready to sell up. Douglas Bland lived at Bridge Farm for years, that farmhouse was built from brick and flint, built into the south end of the Tithe Barn. My son Anthony is building a new house behind the old cart shed, south of the Tithe Barn, between that building and Abbot's Lodge.

Both my children went to Drinkstone School, although Anthony missed a whole term through meningitis. He was in Bury Hospital for six weeks, it was a terrible time, I almost daren't visit him. My son and daughter are both very good to me, people are very good and kind."

The reason for the kindness Ruby finds surrounding her is clear, since she is so thoughtful of others and interested in other people. She and Mary Horrex have a long-standing friendship, as I discovered when looking at newspaper cuttings in Bury Archive. I read there about the Chapel Centenary Celebrations in 1966, in an article from the Bury Free Press dated 01/07/66:

"One hundred years ago, a Methodist Chapel was founded at Drinkstone by Mr. William Nunn, a blacksmith. On June 19th a direct descendant, Mr. Arthur Nunn (now living at Elmswell), aged 85, was in the centenary service there. When the Chapel opened in 1866, the tiny grey brick chapel was 'crowded to excess, many being unable to gain admittance' at every service".

Another cutting from the same paper, only a few years after the grand centenary, is headed "Rise and Fall of Village Chapel". The chapel had to close down due to lack of local support, and was sold by Lacy Scott and Sons for conversion to a house.

The accompanying photo shows "Mrs. Ruby Bland and Mrs. Mary Horrex, who used to do the cleaning at the Chapel".

MARY HORREX

Mary, who was helping Ruby look back in time and remember details, now told me of her earliest years. They had not been without sadness, although she is admirably philosophical about her childhood. She told me her story:

"I was born Mary Brinkley, on 22nd August 1924. We lived in one of the little thatched cottages opposite Chapel Lane, near the bridge. Those cottages are gone now, there's two big new houses in their place. My mother died when I was two. I had one older brother, and a sister who was just a baby. I was sent to live down at the Almshouse cottages with Mrs. Buckle. I started at Drinkstone School, but I wasn't there long. I remember Miss Minns, she was a funny little woman, and when she got a bit riled with us, she'd say 'I'm leaving!' and she'd put on her hat and coat and walk out, up to her cottage! Once she thumped me on the head with a big Bible, I suppose I must have done something wrong! At dinner time, I used to have to take her her milk, before I was allowed to have my dinner. I'd have to walk to Blands' with a can to get it, and carry it up that By Road where Miss Minns' cottage was, a long walk for a five-year-old. I don't know why I had to do that. Albert Horrex (who became my husband) had to walk to the School all the way from Barcock's where he was living then. That's a long way to walk for a five-year-old too.

"When I was six, I was sent to live in Yorkshire with my father's brother and his wife (my uncle and aunt). My brother and sister stayed in Drinkstone, living with my grandmother in one of that row of old cottages, near my father's cottage where I was born. I was kind of pushed out, and I lost contact with my own family for a few years.

"In Yorkshire, there was a Workhouse right opposite the school I went to, and it was a bit scary at first, seeing these poor people coming in and out. You'll never guess where I always spent Christmas Day in Yorkshire – it was in the Workhouse! Because my aunt and her daughter used to cook on Christmas Day, for all the tramps and all sorts! We had a good time, we'd go round singing carols and have some fun.

"When I was fourteen, I left school, and I came home to Drinkstone to look for work. But my father had married again, and I couldn't get on with my stepmother. So I went back up to

Yorkshire and joined the NAAFI there, looking after the men in the Forces. After the war, when I came out of the army, I came back to Drinkstone. My poor old man, Albert, he'd joined up too, we were a military family. He was a prisoner of war in a Japanese camp. Albert Brinkley (who had two nicknames, 'Nanniker', and 'Sonny') was a Prisoner in the same camp, and my Albert nursed him through a time when he was very seriously ill. Everybody helped each other out in those terrible times. They both came home – they were luckier than some.

"My Albert's been dead eight years now, but before he died, that experience all came back to him like it was happening again, like a nightmare. I think war is a dreadful thing, it achieves nothing. The way I think, war's there just to thin the population.

"It's all different for children today. They're not babies for long. Ours were still in a shawl at six months. Today they seem to be sitting up in a push-chair the minute they're out of hospital. And I think they start school too early, too young, too much sitting at desks when they should be out playing. They don't get any childhood today, there's too much pressure on them and they try to cram too much in.

"I had a funny childhood, but if you're brought up hard, you learn to fend for yourself, and you do appreciate what people do for you. I always say to children, 'Look after your mother, because you'll only ever have one.'

"Albert and I had one son and two daughters. All our children went to Drinkstone School. One of my daughters lives in Woolpit now, not far away. Two of my grandchildren, John and Tracey Foster, went to Drinkstone School. They were living in Hessett at the time."

I remember the twins John and Tracey, grandchildren of Mary and Albert, from my time at Drinkstone School in the 1980s. They were a pleasant, helpful pair.

I was able to tell Mary I had seen mention of her husband Albert, in a press cutting at the Records Office, taken from the *East Anglian Daily Times* of 29th July 1995. The article was headed "Plaque to Two World Wars" and explains the history of Drinkstone Village Hall:

"A former POW of the Japanese and the longest serving Royal British Legion member in his village, has unveiled a plaque commemorating both World Wars.

"Albert Horrex, 84, of Gedding Road, Drinkstone, carried out the ceremony at the Village Hall. It was an Officers' Mess at Great Ashfield airfield during the First World War. In the 1920s it was presented to Drinkstone as a War Memorial, taken there in sections by horse and farm cart.

"The Plaque is the Drinkstone Royal British Legion's way of commemorating both VE and VJ Days. Mr. Horrex, who served with the 5th Suffolk Regiment, was taken prisoner two weeks after landing in Singapore."

Mary and her husband Albert lived in various Drinkstone cottages before moving into their comfortable Council House home in 1949. One of their previous homes was Elm Tree Cottage, then (late 1940s) a pair of cottages, the other side being occupied by "the twins", Jimmy and Teddy, bachelor brothers who enjoyed a drink! Elm Tree Cottage is now a single dwelling, and is home to Tony and Jean Conyers, who have a keen interest in the past life of the village (both buildings and people). Jean tells me she talked a lot with Albert before his death in the late Nineties, and learned from him that when "the twins" returned home in a particularly riotous state, Albert and Mary would listen until all went quiet next door. When the two old boys were dead to the world, Albert would quietly walk round to their side of the cottage, to make sure they had not accidentally knocked the oil lamp to the floor. He'd set things straight, and extinguish the lamp which he feared might set fire to the old thatched building.

KENNETH STURGEON

I talked with Ken Sturgeon in his comfortable Stowmarket home, where he lives with his wife Barbara and their tabby cat Ziggy. He and his nine brothers and sisters all went to Drinkstone School. Ken is grateful that he and Barbara are still together and able to get out and about. This is his story:

"I was born in Drinkstone on 17th December 1926. My father was Charles Thomas

Sturgeon. He worked on Mr. Mann's farm, Hall Farm on the Gedding Road, right at the south end of Drinkstone parish. We lived in Orchard Cottage, a tied cottage in the farmyard. My mother was Mary Howlett, she was the daughter of Rev. Howlett, the parson at Woolpit. I had three brothers and six sisters. I was number ten, the youngest of the lot. The others are all gone now. There were a lot of Sturgeons. I had some uncles; Uncle Thomas lived at Hessett. There were lots more Sturgeons at Hessett and at Rougham, but they were no relation to our family.

"When I was old enough, I walked down to the School with the others, it was at least a mile. I stayed at the School until I was fourteen. I can't say I liked School, I didn't like reading and I didn't really learn much. I sometimes wish now that I'd learned a bit more. The things I liked were sport, playtimes and gardening – a chap came down to teach us gardening about once a week.

"I started with Miss Minns, she was tall, a biggish lady. I played around a lot and I remember her poking the cane in my face when I wasn't working properly! Her brother used to come down for a week or two and stay with her, and when he was visiting, he'd walk to School with her in the mornings. One time I was a bit late, and I ran to School, and he was standing outside and he gave me a penny for running to School like that. He was a nice man.

"When I was older I moved up to the big room with Miss Allen. I didn't like work, but at playtimes, because we hadn't got a School field, we were allowed to go over the road to Thurlow's meadow. There were apple and pear trees, and some of the pears would fall in the ditch. We'd climb up the trees to get more pears, and we played football together. I loved me sport. I played for the Drinkstone, Rattlesden and Woolpit teams at one time or another. My mates from School, the Sparkes brothers Don, Victor and Frank, all played for Felsham. I was friends with some boys down the Rattlesden Road, John Malone and James Hovells, but they went to Rattlesden School for some reason. Cora Munford from Cross Street, she'd cycle down to Woolpit School. Maybe it was because those were bigger schools.

"I was friends with Harry and Freddy Robinson who lived near the Village Hall. Their sister Betty was just one day younger than me. Their father bought an old cottage at Tostock, opposite the Church, and Betty lived there after her parents died. All those Robinsons went to Drinkstone School with me.

"My brothers stayed local, but my sisters mostly ended up in London. They went as living-in domestics. Two of my brothers were in the army. When I left School, first of all I worked with my father at Mann's, then after a couple of years I went to work for Douglas Bland at Bridge Farm, opposite Thurlow's. I was lorry driver's mate, carting sugar beet, and I'd help with the harvest. I wanted to join up like my brothers, I volunteered and passed the medical all right. Then the army sent a letter to Bland's, saying they wouldn't take me because I was doing farm work, and in the war producing the food was as important as fighting. I don't know why they didn't send that letter to me!

"After the war I got a job at Suffolk Lawnmowers, and I worked there twenty-six years. First I used to cycle over, then I got a moped, then I got my motorcycle licence, then in the end I got a car. I volunteered for redundancy and worked my last sixteen years at Elmswell bacon factory.

"I married Barbara in 1954, and we lived in Badwell Ash for eighteen months, then we moved to Stowmarket. Barbara came from Bury St. Edmunds. We had three children, and now we've got five grandchildren.

"It's been a good life. We've got our little cat for company, she was a stray. We put food out but she wouldn't even come in the house for the first few months. Now she loves it here, she always wants to sit on my lap."

Chapter Fifteen

SCHOOL AND VILLAGE, 1939 - 1948

IN JANUARY 1939 there were 29 pupils on roll (the previous January the number was only 25!), Miss Barbara Allen was Headmistress and the faithful Miss Minns was still with the infants. The first months of 1939 saw the familiar seasonal events of Suffolk village life. In the Log Book for 24th May 1939 we read:

> *"Empire Day. A Flag and Flag Staff presented to the school by Major Fowler. The managers attended a short service, when the flag was hoisted by the Senior Scholar. Organised Games were held on the playing field during the afternoon".*

Major Fowler, who lived at Drinkstone House until the fire, was Acting Chairman of managers while the parish was without a rector.

I have included the years 1946-48 in this section because the effects of war hung on well after 1945, with food rationing, coal shortages, and German and Italian prisoners of war still in Suffolk. Many local men were abroad, either enduring hardship as prisoners of war in distant lands, or serving as part of the Occupying Forces on the continent. Then in 1947 the worst winter for a hundred years added to the hardships.

During the late 1930s, Thedwastre Council began building Council Houses in Gedding Road. Eventually there were fourteen sturdy semi-detached houses (some near The Cherry Tree, some near the Village Hall). These homes provided welcome comfort and security for local families, and greater freedom of employment since tenants were not limited by the tied-cottage tradition.

War years are inevitably terrible, bringing much disruption and tragedy. But for these country children, with their faith in the power of adults to make their world safe, the war brought mainly excitement and adventure. The parents, who knew all too well the devastation that war brings, must have done an excellent job, remaining unruffled and positive.

Drinkstone Park mansion was requisitioned by the War Department, first as Divisional Headquarters for the Army, and later as barracks for American black troops. Finally it was used to house German prisoners of war. The Rectory was requisitioned to house British Army troops. Suffolk being a flattish County near to the East Coast resulted in airfields being constructed all over the district. Drinkstone village was virtually surrounded by airfields.

THE SCHOOL

In June 1939 the Managers' Minutes mention a consultation with the Rural Dean over the possibility that in future Drinkstone School might take only infants and juniors, while older children would be catered for elsewhere. Maybe, if war had not intervened, this might have happened in the 1940s. In the event, it was a case of battening down the hatches and trying to keep some semblance of normality.

Soon after the declaration of war, life at the School was disrupted by the arrival of evacuees from London. On 11th September 1939, Miss Allen wrote: "School opened for the Autumn Term. Owing to numbers of evacuated children, School is working in double shifts according to Education Authorities' instructions. Drinkstone children attend from 8.30-11.30am. Afternoons given to gardening and games."

A week later, everything had changed. On 18th September she wrote: "Working in School changed to three whole days per week, Monday, Wednesday and Friday according to circular received from office. On Tuesdays and Thursdays children meet in the Village Institute for oral work and handwork." This plan was equally short-lived, so that by 27th October she was writing "…programme to be commenced on Monday 2nd October. Drinkstone children to work in School each morning and in the Institute each afternoon."

The managers were incensed by all this chopping and changing and disregard for local children's education. Their Minutes for October record that they sent a letter to the L. E. A. saying:

"The managers view with grave concern the present arrangements for the education of the children in this Parish. They desire to know if there is a possibility of equipment being provided for separate accommodation for the evacuated children, as they believe such accommodation would be available."

At the same meeting they agreed to cover all School windows with wire-netting as a precaution against injuries from broken glass in the event of bombing raids.

The London County Council had sent teachers as well as children to Drinkstone, so in these first months the two groups of children were taught separately, although the visitors lived with local families. Following the managers' complaint, evacuees were taught in the Village Hall, leaving the School for the sole use of local children.

In 1940-41 the School Log Book shows how important food production was in those times, with the School Garden producing vegetables, and local farmers employing schoolchildren in order to harvest crops while most able-bodied workers were away at the war. These are some excerpts from the Log for these months:

3rd May 1940 – This week chiefly devoted to gardening as the school garden has been neglected owing to inclement weather and severe illness among children.

14th May – School re-opened according to instructions received on wireless, cancelling all Whitsun Holiday.

3rd June – Major Fowler visited School to change the respirators of two children.

13th June – Major Fowler visited School and fitted new gas-mask to one child.

26th September – Building inspected after Anti-Blast treatment to glass."

By this date, Rev. Lilley, the new rector, had joined the Board of Managers as Chairman. The managers were Rev. Blencowe, Mr. Daniel Clover of the Mills, Mr. John Jewers of Green Farm, Mr. J. Bland, and Major Fowler.

Another momentous change came in the Autumn of 1940. Miss Minns, infant teacher for twenty-two years, retired. The Managers' Minutes record "the managers accepted her resignation with much regret and expressed their appreciation of her long service to the School, and wished her all happiness in her retirement." When the post was advertised in October 1940, there was only one applicant! A Supply teacher filled the gap for a few weeks, until Miss Stiff, an "uncertificated" teacher, was appointed in December. The entire School numbered 29 children. The usual visits by Dentist and School Nurse continued. Teeth would be extracted on the premises, and the Nurse spent most of her time searching for nits! (During the war, the unfortunate evacuees were blamed for any nits, lice or fleas discovered!)

Some Log entries for 1941 –

10th February – Mr. Thompson A.R.P. Warden, tested gas masks of Class 1.

11th February – Gas masks of Class 2 tested 11-11.45am.

20th March – Two sand bags delivered at school for A.R.P.

21st March – Lessons not kept to time-table owing to fine spell. Gardening has been taken each day of the week. Herbaceous border re-set and work commenced on vegetable garden.

In April 1941 Miss Allen had two days leave for her marriage to Mr. Clay (probably he was a serviceman with only two days' compassionate leave – no honeymoon!)

The Managers' Minutes tell us "Hours during Summer Term will be 10am–5pm", presumably because of the introduction of "Double Summer Time".

Food production became more and more important. The Log Book tells us: "16th October – Six children absent. Potato picking for Mr. Blencowe. Report to Office. 20th October: Eight children absent. Potato picking for Mr. Renson." Major Fowler visited the school and checked registers, and on 27th October Mr. Groves, Enquiry Officer, visited the School with Mr. Jefferies, L.E.A. Solicitor "re children employed by farmers." There seems to have been a new decision, accepting war-time priorities. On November 14th we read: "Instructions received from Mr. Carter to cancel all marks of children over 12 years for the fortnight 10th November – 21st November re employment of children for potato lifting on Mr. Thompson's farm."

The large group of evacuees who had originally arrived in the village slowly began to drift back to London. By the end of 1941 the two groups of children merged into one, all working together in the School:

17th November – Miss Carlton commenced here this a.m. 14 children admitted from L.C.C. Party. 7 tables, 14 chairs, 1 easel, 1 towel roll, 1 drinking can, transferred from the Institute to Drinkstone School. 18th November – H.M.I. Miss Barton called re amalgamation of L.C.C. children.

27th November – Three children employed by Mr. Thompson this p.m. for potato lifting.

28th November – 2 children admitted from L.C.C. Party this week. Miss Carlton returned to London.

In January 1942, boosted by the evacuees, numbers on books were 38 children. However during February Mrs. Clay wrote: "Low attendance all week owing to deep snow". Average attendance for the week was 24 children. Rev. Lilley was a regular weekly visitor at this time, giving "the usual Scripture lesson" to Class 1.

In October 1942 we read: "School closed for gathering fruits of National Importance". Were these potatoes? At the end of October 1942 Mrs. Clay left the School, and Mrs. Brand of County Unattached Staff filled the gap for a few weeks until the new Headteacher, Mrs. Winsall, took up her post on 30th November. The Managers' Minutes record that the rent for her use of the Schoolhouse was £13 per annum, payable quarterly in advance (5s a week).

In January 1943 School opened with 38 on roll. Miss Stiff was frequently absent; she had to cycle to School and the weather must sometimes have made this hard. But on 17th February Mrs. Winsall wrote in the Log, "As weather was very favourable the garden boys spent most of the day on the garden which was in a very bad condition. Separate plots were measured out. The boys spent their time in digging and ditching."

On May 3rd 1943 she wrote: "43 on roll but only 15 present owing to an epidemic of measles." The health of the nation's children was high on the political agenda in these war-time years. Soon daily milk, and school dinners, would be provided in every village school (larger schools such as Woolpit provided school meals a few years earlier). On July 7th "Miss Burleigh visited the School regarding school dinners". These would be cooked at Woolpit and delivered to the School. First, plans had to be made: where and how to serve them, eat them, and wash up. New staff had to be employed. Crockery and other equipment arrived in January 1944. On February 21st 1944 we read: "Forms arrived for canteen. Dinners commence today."

The war-time difficulties and shortages are apparent in the next entry, on February 24th: "Letter sent asking for soap permit". On 27th March "Miss Horsefall visited the school during the dinner hour, to see the canteen dinners". Providing dinners created more paperwork, and on 4th April Mrs. Winsall recorded: "Money for Canteen dinners sent to Office, also Milk Forms etc."

Times were still volatile. On 17th July 1944 Mrs. Winsall wrote: "7 evacuees admitted this afternoon. 53 on roll." On 19th September the Log Book tells us "Headmistress absent owing to husband on leave from overseas."

January 1945 brought more harsh weather. On 29th, Mrs. Winsall wrote: "Only 16 children present owing to deep snow and slippery roads", and on the following day "only 12 children present"! It is not clear what the number on roll was at this date.

A few months later came the marvellous news – "9th May – Holidays owing to Victory Day in Europe".

In August 1946 Mrs. Winsall left the School. Once again, a member of the County Unattached Staff filled the gap; Christian Hilda Brimelow took charge, with 45 children on roll, until the arrival of the newly appointed Headmistress, Dorothy Jackson from Yorkshire, on October 1st.

The war might be over, but new problems loomed up for the managers to ponder. Costs were escalating, repairs were constantly needed, and it was difficult to keep up the standards required by the L.E.A. There was talk of school closures in some villages. The managers were proud of Drinkstone's "Voluntary" School, and strongly resisted suggestions that it was not viable. Nor did they want to see it become a "Controlled School" (under more rigorous L.E.A. control). They did not want their village school and its curriculum to be at the mercy of outside decision makers.

In May 1946 they wrote a letter to the Diocesan Board of Education saying: "The managers of Drinkstone School desire the retention of a school in their village, but do not consider themselves pledged to any cost in connection therewith. They consider that the population of Drinkstone is more likely to increase than the population of the village of Hessett."

The managers were simply unable to raise the funds to maintain the land and buildings. At their August meeting they discussed the dangerous state of the playground, and the need to distemper the Schoolhouse. They wrote: "The managers were distressed by the untidy state of the School and the quite deplorable condition of the canteen equipment. A Rota was fixed, each manager to be School Visitor for two months of the year." On a happier note, "the Secretary was asked to thank Mr. Thurlow for allowing the children to play on the meadow opposite the School."

Their difficulties were compounded by several factors – sheer expense, the difficulty of obtaining materials in post-war Britain (this was the reason why the playground was left un-levelled), and poor work on the part of caretakers and cleaners. In October 1946, new problems arose – a new copper was needed in the Schoolhouse, the playground wall needed repair, and the stove in the infants' room "has one side burned through and appears dangerous".

Reluctantly the managers had to face the fact that maintaining the School as "Voluntary" was becoming impossible. They began to worry that money left in trust for their School might fall into L.E.A. hands! They decided to close the Post Office Account and pay the balance to the rector and churchwardens. They asked Lloyd's Bank to pay future dividends of the two-and-a-half percent Consolidated Stock, held under the Mosley Trust, to the rector and churchwardens "for the use of the School (until it becomes a Controlled School), the Sunday School, or any other scheme for the benefit of the children of Drinkstone which they may deem to be advisable." They chose to "defer" the question of the handing over of the School.

At a later meeting the managers recorded that it had been found "impracticable" to put the School Fund in the Churchwardens' Bank Account, so the money had been returned to the Post Office Account. They did their best to improve matters at the School, and the Cleaning Grant was raised to £14-0s-3d a quarter. But the odds were against them. In November 1947 a letter from the Medical Officer complained of "the disrepair of the closets, lack of washing basins, and the condition of the playground". The managers were in despair. Mrs. Ramsay advised that county authorities be requested to take over the School as a Controlled School. After a "thoughtful discussion" the following motion was passed:

"The Managers feel regretfully constrained to request that their School should be accepted as a 'Controlled School." However on hearing of their decision, the Diocesan authorities wrote to each of the managers individually, asking them to defer making a decision "until the Development Plans are finalised."

THE VILLAGE

While all this sombre discussion was going on in the background, life for the pupils appears to have been quite jolly. Miss Jackson wrote in the Log, on 5th May 1947, "We paid a visit to Mr. Clover's old windmill and spent a most delightful hour there".

The post mill, which bears the date "1689 S.S." was still in working condition, making it the oldest workable mill in Suffolk. The smock mill (of which only the octagonal top section or cap, bearing the sails, was turned to face the wind) was built in 1780. Since it had been converted to run by oil-fuelled engine in the 1890s, its sails were long gone. It was painted or tarred on the outside, and plastered on the inside, in an attempt to keep out rain. At this time the Clover family still ground corn with the wind-powered postmill when the wind obliged! They owned these two mills for over two centuries.

Over the years many alterations and improvements were made to the mills. The round house was added to the post mill around 1830, to give protection to the trestle timbers and provide extra storage space. This mill had the earliest type of sail, that is, wooden frames with a cloth covering. This covering had to be threaded over the windward face of the frames and furled according to the strength of the wind. Drinkstone post mill was unusual in having two such sails right into the twentieth century, the other two sails being of the later, more easily managed "spring sail" type.

Of course almost every small village had at least one mill (the earliest of all being water mills) in the 19th century when Drinkstone School came into existence. In 1900, from the top of Bradfield St. George smock mill, eight working mills could be seen – at Gedding, Great Welnetham, Woolpit, Cockfield, Rattlesden and Drinkstone (also the derelict Rougham mill). Very few of these mills exist today, yet Drinkstone still has two!

Nellie Bartrum (born 1910) recalls how her father would take his wheat by horse and cart, from his smallholding in Hessett to Drinkstone mill. The flour was for home use, a year's supply for his wife's baking of cakes and bread for the family.

Probably most children of that era knew the riddle:

I'm round yet I'm flat, I travel with speed.
I go on a good pace the hungry to feed.
I've been in use for a number of years,
I have a good eye, but I never shed tears.
My back it is broad, my face is the same,
And I guess there's not many can tell you my name!
(Answer – a mill stone).

As well as the lovely 1925 photo of the Clover family shown in this book, there is one from 1938, showing Daniel Clover and his son Wilfred at their mill. Daniel was a manager of Drinkstone School right up until his death in 1947.

Through the years many Drinkstone teachers have taken their pupils to see and enjoy these mills, sometimes to draw them, sometimes trying to fathom the fantastic mechanism, such as the wind-powered sack hoist, and sometimes seeing the millstones in action. We continued the tradition in the 1980s.

In 1947, with the war only just behind them, Thedwastre Council built eight attractive new Council Houses in Gedding Road (today they are all odd numbers, 9 to 23). Despite having no electricity and no sewerage connection, these houses were far more comfortable and easy to run than the old cottages. Families were proud to move into these smart new homes, with wash-house, privy, and gardens of excellent size.

THE SCHOOL

Returning to the Log Book record, on November 20th we read: "Holiday for Royal Wedding of Princess Elizabeth".

In March 1948 Miss Jackson resigned, due to "domestic difficulties". In April she returned to her Sheffield home. In May, Miss Stiff also resigned, her place being taken by Miss Pearson.

The managers decided to raise the rent for use of the Schoolhouse to 15s a week, an enormous increase. The managers would continue to pay the rates. In May 1948 they were still discussing unsatisfactory work by caretakers, and the need for dustbins and disinfectant. The same month, a new Headmistress was appointed. She was Mrs. Constance Collins of Hawkenden. Until she was able to commence work in September, I. J. Gibbs filled the gap.

The Log Book reports some cheerful happenings during this Summer Term in 1948. On 18th June we read: "Miss Hampshire spent most of the morning and part of the afternoon with the boys in the School garden. She left a list of the work to be completed by July 2nd when she hopes to come again." Around the same time, an adviser came to assess a boy finding schoolwork hard, and advised "child to be given as many outdoor tasks as possible". So sometimes School wasn't a bad place to be! He wasn't the only one set to work outside, for on 21st June "Rev. Lilley called and brought a dustbin. Bricks were stacked away from the rubbish dump in readiness for this to be cleared". So the children spent time moving and stacking bricks! Many of the children, especially older boys, seem to have found being in the schoolroom for so many years frustrating and boring. I think it was asking a lot of teachers to provide relevant learning for children of such a wide age range, in the older class. The leaving age had been raised, but resources had not been provided to help teachers make the long years of education more appropriate or interesting to older children.

In September 1948 a new era began. Mrs. Collins, the new Headteacher, arrived on duty. She was to stay in post until October 1972! Presumably thinking the rent for the Schoolhouse rather high, she immediately asked for various improvements. She asked for a bath to be installed, but in December the managers wrote "an excessive estimate for fixing a bath in the Schoolhouse was rejected". She also wanted electric lights in the School, a rare luxury! In December 1948 the Log Book tells us: "School was closed at 3.30pm. We were unable to see either to read or write".

So ended the years dominated by the Second World War at Drinkstone's little School.

Chapter Sixteen

PERSONAL STORIES

Ernest Rivens, Raymond Bland, Gerald Mayes, Cora Munford, Mary Hovells, Rene Hall, Freddy Robinson, Derek Cross and Joyce Rouse

---

ERNEST RIVENS

"I was born on 20th June 1928, youngest in the family, with three older sisters. We lived down Chapel Lane. We had fun together, my parents never seemed to get very cross with us. One day we were playing in my sisters' bedroom because it was raining, and we got the old wind-up gramophone, and my sisters stood me on the turn-table to see if I'd go round! The turn-table just smashed in two. On fine days we'd play outside in the lane, it was just a narrow stoned lane then, there wasn't much traffic. We'd get an old bicycle wheel and we'd get all the spokes out and make a hoop. One afternoon I was playing with my sisters with one of them hoops and we were throwing the hoop up so it would come back to us. I was bending down and it came back and cut me across the nose. See, I've still got the scar! Going to school, there wasn't much traffic, and we'd take our hoops and a stick and bowl the hoops along all the way to school.

"There was two thatched cottages next to our bungalow. Percy Smith lived there with his father. There was a hedge and a ditch between us and they had a gooseberry bush just by the hedge. They was rare gooseberries! We'd lay in the ditch and put our hand through and get the gooseberries. My sister Kathleen married Percy.

"The bungalow was small, and us children's bedrooms were at the back, beyond the brick pantry. The Council said it was overcrowded and they wanted us to move into one of the new Council houses. They were being built on an old orchard just across the meadow from us. So my father sold the bungalow to someone in the family. We carted all the furniture across the meadow, my sisters all had to carry something. I was still quite small, and I was walking behind my mother who was carrying a big bundle of faggots. Just as we got to the plank bridge over the ditch, she turned round suddenly to see where my sisters were, and she knocked me into a ditch full of nettles! So that was when I came here, and I've lived here ever since.

"I remember at Easter, we'd have a little party at Drinkstone Lodge, and all of us got a chocolate Easter egg in an Easter cup. We had that several years.

"At school, my first teacher was Miss Minns. I think she sometimes had her sister living with her, because she'd say to us, 'Be really quiet and you'll all hear my sister drop a pin!' Miss Clay had the top class. Every morning she'd put the milk near the tortoise stove, and it was lovely to drink, just right! We'd go home for dinner, and back for the afternoon. We'd run with our hoops to make it more fun.

"There was a boy we called 'Clickie' because he used to stutter, I'm afraid we used to torment him. His father used to do the milking over the road at Thurlow's, so he'd go running after his father. We'd scatter over the fields, and Miss Clay would say she'd get the Parson to come

and get us back into school. It was just a bit of fun really. The Parson was Frank Horne from the Rectory and he'd give us a little sermon about it!

"One time we were having a play at the Village Hall and we was all in it. It was the last day of the summer term. There was a meadow opposite with a tall tree. Us boys ran across the meadow and hid behind this tree, and made silly noises. And when Miss Clay came along with all the girls, she said, 'I know who you all are in there, I know your names, and when you come back to school you'll all get the cane!' And we said to each other, 'It's all right, she'll forget!' But she didn't!

We used to go for nature walks and pick flowers and find out all the names, and they had a garden round the back. We even went down to the big Rectory – that had a big wall around it – and we'd help Mr. Boreham the gardener, who lived in Rectory Cottage (his daughter was at the school), and he'd teach us all about gardening. A man used to come once a week and help us, show us what to do. It's more healthy to have stuff out of your own garden. I still spend hours in the garden and I keep busy with my vegetables. My father had a little allotment behind the Village Hall, and he had one of those old harrows that a horse would draw, and he'd pull it himself! He lost a leg through diabetes, but he said, 'I'll have a wooden leg, then I can still do the garden!' He worked at Mr. Thompson's farm, and every Saturday morning he'd go up to the shop (Mrs. Cooper's then, I was very friendly with Peter, her son) and buy 7oz bacca, boxes of matches, and a box of chocolates for my mother. He'd smoke an ounce a day in his briar pipe. We used to have three shops in the village then. The Post Office was right down the bottom, opposite the Church.

"I was still at the School when the war started. We had British soldiers at the Rectory, and black Americans at Drinkstone Park. I left School when I was fourteen; I left on Friday, and started work on Monday. I worked for Mr. Mann at Drinkstone Hall. There used to be three horsemen, and I took over one horse. The others would feed 'em and get 'em ready, then I'd lead one with the harrow or the plough. During the war, all the planes used to take off and circle, ready to set off together for a raid. Gerald's father was yardman at Drinkstone Hall, and there were sheds with cattle in, and I'd have to get the hay and straw for them, and take it down in the tumbril. One day I sat on top of the tumbril and looked up, and I saw two of these planes smash together and blow up in mid air. The horses had blinkers on so it didn't worry them.

"Another time, a pair of twin-bodied American planes were circling around, having a practice dog-fight, and they crashed. One pilot landed next to Ray's field, and it made a tidy old dent in the ground where he'd hit. The plane went on and landed in Town Wood, there was bits of metal all along the lane, and we found the pilot's shoes. Those planes had taken off at Ashfield, and they crashed over Drinkstone; bits of crashed planes are still turning up today, I heard some bits were found in the river at Needham Market.

"I was big friends with Raymond, and if I wanted to go to Bury he'd take me in his father's car. Mr. and Mrs. Bland would take me with them to Felixstowe on a Sunday, and treat me to my dinner. Raymond, and Ronnie his cousin, they had guns, and I had a ferret. I'd go with them and I'd put my ferret down the holes and they'd shoot the rabbits as they came out. We'd take them to Addison's the butcher at Woolpit and get money for fish and chips. Ronnie lived at Bridge Farm. We'd collect firewood in Town Wood, and Arthur Bland'd let me have a tractor and trailer to bring the wood home winter time. He was very generous.

"The Americans used to have a dance up the Village Hall every Saturday. They'd go around the villages and pick the girls up. We'd stand inside the door and watch them. They had dozens of jam puffs, and they'd give us some too. The music was good; that band leader, the one who crashed, Glenn Miller, half his band were up here playing!

"My father was in the first World War. He remembers how the Village Hall was brought here from Ashfield, on a horse and wagon! My father put some money towards that, it was put there as a Memorial Hall. That was a gift, it was given as a Memorial, so that name shouldn't be changed.

"I was in the Air Training Corps, we went to Rattlesden twice a week for lectures. We got so *we could go up the Rattlesden Air Base and the Americans would give us a meal. You'd have all the food on one plate – gravy and potatoes and vegetables and meat, then on the other half of the same plate you might have jam pud and custard! But you'd never tasted anything like it, it was gorgeous! We'd try to get there every Sunday. We got to know those pilots. We'd sit in the Suit Room, they'd come in and get their suits. We'd say, 'Hiya, mates!' and they'd say, 'Hi, want to come for a ride?'*

"....'Where're you going?'.... 'We're off to Lincoln to pick up some crew!'

"We'd all go in their Flying Fortresses with them. We'd all have parachutes on when we went up. Jimmy Hovells was over there one time, and they were testing this bomber out, he was with them and the plane more or less caught fire. They were ready to bail out, but then they somehow managed to put out the fire. Jimmy was a bit happy when they landed!

"Just before D-Day all the tanks and army vehicles were parked along this road, they were all camouflaged and half in the hedges. The soldiers was all writing letters ready to go, and they asked my mother to post them. And next morning when we got up they were all gone.

"At the end of the war Drinkstone Park and Rattlesden Air Base were used for prisoners of war. That was when I was working at Thompson's at Rookery Farm. Mr. Thompson wanted a tractor driver and my father asked if I could do it, and I was there eleven year. They'd bring these POWs round on a lorry and if the farmer wanted any workers, they'd drop 'em off for the day. The two we had were good workers, they were Josef and Karl. Mrs. Thompson used to feed them, they used to love coming up there. They was very nice people. They made me a ship in a bottle but I broke that. But I've got two carved photo stands they made me, all carved with a knife. [He shows me a pair of beautifully crafted wooden stands holding family snaps.] They didn't want to fight no more than we did – they were just like yourselves. The whole trouble is – like now – there's somebody got to be better than somebody else – people ain't satisfied. There's poor people who try to get on the property ladder and they can't; and there's others who've got money and they buy all the houses up to let. And that's why the houses are so expensive. All anybody needs is one house, and then live in it! I'm happy with this house. Father died in '74, and my mother took it over. When she died in '84 I went to the Council, they let me have it. I've just got one sister left now, she lives in Bury. I never got married, I had a few girl friends, but the way I looked at it was, after me father died, I thought, my mother and father always looked after me, and it was my turn to look after them.

"It's all different on the farms these days. When I went to Drinkstone Hall, there was fourteen men. And those farms across the fields [in front of his home] Hill Farm and Burt's Farm, they each had twelve or thirteen workers. When I went to Rookery, there was five of us. Then Thompson's son came out of the Navy and took over from his father, and I worked for him. I used to love working with horses. But then the cars and tractors started coming in. Francis Thompson had a great old car. It stood in the barn, and we'd pile old sacks and any old rubbish on it. Later, he did it up and got it going – it was one of those with a cloth hood you could pull up, and all things on the steering wheel, like 'more petrol/ less petrol' and that. Then he fixed long metal spines on the front and when we'd be in the hay field making big stacks he'd drive up and push all the loose hay over to us at the stack.

"Thompson sold Rookery Farm and moved right over west of Duxford, and he wanted me to go and work for him there. He took me over there once, to help him check all the numbers of the cattle; they were marked in their ears, you know. Well, after that one time he took me, he asked me to drive his old tractor and trailer over – it was an old Fergie. So we piled up all the tools and stuff he wanted on the trailer, and I set off at six one morning along the lanes. I wasn't sure of the way. I kept thinking, 'Is this right?' They was all little lanes then, they all seemed the same. I'd think, 'Yes, I remember that pub, and that farm', so I carried on. I couldn't go fast, it's a good thing the roads were so empty then! I was meant to carry on until I met Thompson and his wife in their car, they'd set off from the new farm to meet me. But we could have missed each other, going different ways, and I'd still be lost today! Was I glad to see their car coming towards me! His wife drove me back here, and we got home four o'clock. Thompson

took the tractor on to the new place. I'll never forget that day!

" I didn't want to leave this village to work near Duxford. So I went and worked for Mr. Renson right down the bottom on Tostock Lane corner, at Street Farm. I had an argument with him because he said I bent some bit of machinery. I didn't, it was like that, and he knew it because when I first picked it up to use it he said, 'It's bent but we'll never straighten it, so use it as it is!' He'd borrowed it from a farm at Woolpit, and then he put the blame on me. So I went to Stow mowers and I worked there thirty-two year – ended up as a fork-lift driver. Before that I was doing boring piece-work. I was more happier with the fork-lift because I had the run of the factory and I got to know everybody. It was very enjoyable. When I left the boss wanted me to carry on until I was seventy. I got on very well with him."

Ernest proudly showed me a large reproduction wall-clock in dark wood, with pendulum, given pride of place in his neat living room. This clock was presented to him on retirement. Beneath it on the polished sideboard are the photograph stands carved for him by those German Prisoners, treasured mementoes of the past.

RAYMOND BLAND

I talked to Raymond and his wife Vera in their pleasant lounge looking out onto wonderful gardens surrounding the new house they built for their retirement. This is Raymond's story :

"I was born in 1929 at The Gables, a cottage up the Rattlesden Road, Drinkstone – opposite Green Farm. My father was the blacksmith, at the forge down near the crossroads (at the School end of the village). He had worked for Hargreaves of Drinkstone Park, shoeing the horses, and trimming the cows' feet in wintertime when they became overgrown during the months spent under cover in the barns.

"In 1933 Captain Hargreaves offered my father the tenancy of Whitefield House, one of the estate farms. It was the time of the Depression, and the previous tenant was asked to leave because 'he couldn't pay his bills'. That's what people would say in those days, when a man went bankrupt. No-one actually used the word 'bankrupt'. He wasn't the only farmer who 'couldn't pay his bills' in those days!

"So we moved into that big Tudor farmhouse in Park Road. It was mixed farming then, we grew mangolds, oats and beans, and sugar beet which was a new crop on Suffolk farms then. We reared cattle and pigs. We had a few house cows and made butter to sell, the separated milk went to the pigs. We'd buy in more calves from Bill Morley at Woolpit. The cattle were on grass in summer, in winter we'd feed them on hay, roots, beans and oats that were all grown on the farm. The only thing we bought in was a little nitrogen fertiliser which came from abroad. We'd grind that up and spread it on the land.

"Our blacksmith's forge was just left; all the gear and the anvil and tools were left in the shop, and father would keep the door locked until anything needed making or mending, then we'd go down and do it all ourselves. The fire was sparking hot, they'd put one bit of metal on the anvil and hammer it to shape, then the next bit and hammer it together, for the farm machinery. My father would repair all the harrows. He'd take all the teeth out, and he might lay a bit on the teeth if they were a bit short, and weld it on firm. Then he'd sharpen all the teeth up. There were still horses to shoe, and he used to make the metal rims for the wooden wagon wheels. We called it 'shoeing wheels' and we'd need a really hot fire. The rim was carried outside with tongs while it was red hot, to go on the wheel. I'd be ready with a couple of full watering cans, out of the river opposite the forge shop, to pour on and cool the metal. The rim would contract and get good and tight as it cooled, and we'd hammer in some iron pegs to keep the spokes firm. There was a lot of skill to it, and it's sad to think that forge was just left. Over the years we stopped using it and eventually I think it fell down.

"I always had to help on the farm. We had a big open-hearth fire in the backhouse or scullery, with bricks around it and bars across. I wasn't allowed to go out until I'd split enough

logs for my mother to use all day!"

(His wife Vera laughs and says, if he was late courting me, that was always the excuse: "I had to chop the wood for Mother!" Raymond takes up the tale again....)

"There were two big dutch ovens where the bread was baked and the cooking done, and a copper. We needed boiling water for the calves' mix and it was all heated by wood. I'd help with cleaning out the pigs as well, and at harvest time we'd be leading the horses, all the wagons and tumbrils were drawn by horses.

"Well, I'd better tell you about the School. I started there in January 1935. We had to walk across the fields, so wellingtons were a must, we had to have a pair. Geoff Bennett took me the first day, he was about four years older than me. After Easter I'd go on my own. All the fields had names then, I'd cross Home Meadow, Church Field, and The Joys, then I'd be at the road (near where the electricity sub-station is now). We called that road The Queach – I don't know where that name came from! So I'd walk along The Queach to the School. We'd take lunch with us, sandwiches and a bottle of drink (usually water), there were no school dinners."

(Vera joins in to explain that she attended Woolpit School at the same date, a larger school where school dinners were brought in big metal trays each day).

"We did have milk at School. One of the oldest children would have to fetch it, before morning playtime, just cooled, and straight from the dairy. There was a half-pint scoop in the can, and the milk was poured into glasses for us. In winter time someone would run down to the farm early so the milk could stand on the stove for a while and get warm.

"My first teacher was Miss Carrie Minns. She was a strict old girl! She soon put a book round your ear or a ruler across your knuckles if you misbehaved! Miss Allen, the teacher who took the older children, married a sergeant in 1939, after that she was called Mrs. Clay. There were about fifty children in the school, fifteen or twenty would be in the infants class, all the rest in the big room. In that big room there was the big tortoise stove in the middle and a blackboard each side. We'd all go in there first thing in the morning to have a prayer and sing a hymn.

"When I was eight I got a bicycle and I went to School by the road. Not many had a bike. Those who lived within a mile of School all walked. We left the bikes out in the yard, no bikeshed then. Very few cars were on the road. There were occasional steam vehicles – Ruby Steam Wagons – taking goods around. By '38 – '39 they had lorries. My uncle bought three lorries, for taking corn to the barley merchants and corn mills, cattle to the weekly markets at Stow and Bury, and beet to the factory.

"When you were about nine you'd leave the infants and go in the big classroom. At first you'd sit on the left, near the partition. Then as you got older you'd move further to the right, nearer to the Schoolhouse end, and you'd leave School at fourteen. The work was mostly enjoyable. We used to do plays in the Village Hall. Before the war there'd be socials, they'd all meet up, the women would bring food, the men would bring beer. Then the men would take turns getting up on the stage to sing songs.

"At playtime, we never had anything to play with, like footballs or cricket balls. If we got hold of an old football and the inner went, there was no rubber, so we'd stuff the outer case with paper. We played stool ball. There was a square board on a stand, and you had a little wooden bat – it might be like a table-tennis bat, or like a rounders bat. We played conkers in season, and we had hoops.

"When all the refugees were in the village, we had a new Headteacher, Mrs. Winsall. We had a boy living with us, named David Harbour. He's still in Shoreditch, the Bethnal Green area. His two sisters lived with my Auntie Florrie. When they left, we all corresponded for two or three years, then of course the letters got less and less.

"When the war was on, we had to work in the school garden when the weather was fine. We'd dig it over in the winter, and we'd sow onions, carrots, potatoes and beans. 'Last Brothers' used to give us a load of muck over the back hedge, and we'd use wheelbarrows to get it to the land, then dig it in. We didn't get any vegetables to take home. They were given away, I think. Once a week, on a Friday, the top class would walk up into the village, to a field

opposite Thompson's. We'd have to bash up tins for the war effort. If anyone had any old iron, we'd have to go and fetch it.

"We had no air-raid shelter at the School. Every now and again the teacher would say, 'Some time today we're going to have a practice air-raid warning.' Then she'd suddenly say, 'Air raid – get under the desks!' It was a bit of fun for us, we weren't scared, and we'd get hit round the ear if we giggled. I don't know what good it would be, getting under the desks...."

(Vera laughs as she remembers air-raid practices at Woolpit School, when inexplicably the children were instructed to run out into the playground and stand against the wall!)

"The Park, Captain Hargreave's place, was full of soldiers, and army vehicles and bombs. There were soldiers everywhere, there'd be manoeuvres and searchlights going, they used to feed the airfields from here with ammunition that was stored at The Park. There were airfields all around our village. Hundreds of RAF Lancasters went up every evening. When planes came over, you'd listen and if the engine cut out before it got to you, you'd get in the ditch. Doodlebugs came over, we'd listen to the sound of them, but we weren't scared. It was like a game to us. All us boys would congregate together and we used to play soldiers.

"After '42, The Park was full of black American soldiers. If a Gerry came over, they'd fire at it with rifles. We'd never seen a black person until they came. They used to give the children Christmas parties. They'd collect all the children up in lorries and jeeps, give you gum and candy, and have a bit of music for us and play games. We liked the Americans, we liked to do things for them. We'd make fish hooks out of wire, tie up with wire on a cork, point 'em up sharp and fix on a little bit of shiny tin (a 'twizzler' we called it) like a propeller type that would turn and attract the fish. We'd go down to the lake, catch the pike and take 'em to the cook at Park House, and in exchange we'd get a ride in their Command Cars. Some of the bigger boys got to drive the vehicles in the Park. The soldiers would say, 'Take it for a ride, boy! Don't bash the bloody thing up before you bring it back!' A dozen or so of us would crowd in where there should have been only four or five!

"When I was fourteen, in 1944, I left School to work on the farm with my father. Captain Michael Hargreaves who owned the farm was a Tank Commander with a squadron of tanks under him. He was killed in Egypt. The whole estate was sold after that, to the tenants. My father bought Whitefield House in 1949, with 165 acres at about £36 an acre. My father died just before I was twenty-one, so it was just my mother and me. Then I married Vera, and we had our three daughters, Christine, Vanessa and Susan. Later on, in 1957, we bought another 64 acres from Thompson's.

"We built this house where we are now (at the end of Chapel Lane) sixteen years ago. This was the meadow where we used to keep our Landrace pedigree pigs. I'm retired now but I still get up early. I take my dogs picking up after the guns at winter shoots, they're all good working dogs, they're all friendly when people come here.

"Of course, our daughters all went to Drinkstone School. Mrs. Collins was Headteacher then. She was one of the old brand of schoolmistress, very strict. Our daughters laugh now when they tell how she used to put her dog in the sink to bathe it – the same sink where the cups and plates were washed! And some of the children were chosen to be 'dog runners'. Christine was one that did this dog running job. That meant, if an inspector called, Christine had to run up the road and put the dog in Mrs. Collin's car so the inspector didn't know it was ever in the School! Christine went on to the East Anglian School in Bury (that's at Culford now). Vanessa and Susan preferred their horses to studying. They went on to Beyton, then Thurston."

Obviously Raymond has lived a fulfilling life and leaving school at fourteen never held him back!

GERALD MAYES

My next visit was to Gerald, dapper and smiling as he invited me inside his brick-and-flint cottage, aptly named "Stone Cottage". The cottage is in Park Road, with no near neighbours. I noticed a photograph on the living room wall showing two very smart young ladies on fine horses. Gerald explained that these two were Raymond's daughters Vanessa and Susan, who were members of the Suffolk Side-Saddle Team. The two were star members of a display team which performed in London, and Susan was a national champion.

Gerald has remained a bachelor. He loves his cottage home, and another favourite picture shows the countryside around. This idyllic scene of woodland and fields was painted by Rosemary Hazell (daughter of Margaret of Chapel Lane). Standing in front of his cottage, Gerald tells how when he was a boy, this end of the village (Drinkstone Green) had far fewer houses. In those days Park Road had wide grass verges either side on which his family tethered their goats on long chains. It was Gerald's job to move the tethers, lead the goats out, and bring them in for his parents to milk.

He shows me the long narrow garden alongside the lane on both sides of the cottage, where once neat rows of vegetables grew. These days his health is poor and he can tend only a small area around the cottage. He uses only the downstairs rooms now, so everything he needs is close at hand. This is his story:

"My father Reginald was born in Drinkstone, up the Gedding Road, nearly at the parish boundary. He worked as stockman for Mr. Mann at Drinkstone Hall Farm. Drinkstone Hall stands on the site of the old Drinkstone Manor – it had to be built in the same place because there's a moat most of the way around the site. There was a manager or foreman living at the Hall. The owner, Mr. Mann, lived somewhere in the Fens, Soham I think, and he owned other farms too, one was at Tostock. Every now and again Mr. Mann and his wife would arrive by car, to look over his land, and there'd be a pony and cart waiting ready to take them around the farm.

"When my father married Violet, my mother, they couldn't find a cottage in Drinkstone. So at first they had to live in Buxhall. I was born there, in 1930. In 1933, when Mr. Bland (Raymond's father) took over the tenancy of Whitefield House, we got the tenancy of this cottage. Originally this cottage was for Whitefield workers but it wasn't needed. So we moved in only a day or two after Raymond Bland's family moved into Whitefield. Captain Hargreaves of Drinkstone Park owned Whitefield House and farm then, and this cottage was his (now it belongs to Raymond). Captain Hargreaves also owned Home Farm opposite the school, and at least one farm in Hessett. But Rookery Farm belonged to Mr. Taylor, and then to Mr. Thompson.

"I was an only child. It was quiet in them days. It may have been hard but we didn't know any different. Our water came from a well near the kitchen door, and it's never been dry the whole time I've lived here. That chain, about forty yards long, doesn't even reach the bottom. The Blands used to come here for drinking water until they got a bore hole. It was good water, it never did us no harm. I remember Raymond used to cycle up with a bucket, and so did his father. Then when he got a car, he got clever and carried it that way! We got the mains water in 1972.

"About the School – I don't really remember my first day, so it can't have been that bad! My mother took me at first. I used to walk, later I got a bike. I remember sunny days – it weren't quite so good if it was wet or snowing. Quite often if the weather was bad and not many got there, we'd all sit round the fire and get nice and warm.

"My first teacher was Miss Minns, I got on all right with her most of the time. Miss Allen was my teacher in the big class. She became Mrs. Clay later. I liked playtime best. When we got in the big class, at playtime we could go in the meadow opposite the School. I don't remember suffering over the work. There was lots of copying off the board, you soon got told off if your writing wasn't neat. I didn't mind mental arithmetic and spelling. Reverend Horne used to come in regularly to give a talk, he used to walk up and down in front of the class. He died before the war, I think.

"One morning while I was at School, just before the war, part of Drinkstone House burned down. That was a big house on the Gedding Road, on the opposite side from Drinkstone Hall Farm. My father and some of his workmates saw what was going on and ran over to help. They saved some of the furniture. That house stood derelict through the war, and was rebuilt later,

but on a smaller scale.

"At wartime we had two evacuees, an aunt of mine and her daughter came to stay. So then we hadn't got enough room. Neither of them evacuees stayed long. At first the evacuee children had a separate school to us, in the Village Hall. There was a Headteacher from London with them. As their numbers got smaller they amalgamated with us, with just our teachers. We'd get half days off to go potato picking, at The Meade and at Thurlow's. We were surrounded by air-fields, at Rattlesden, Rougham, and Ashfield – all round us really. The planes went off in the early hours of the morning and bombed in daylight, and came back late afternoon. The U.S. soldiers were living in The Park, and British troops were at The Rectory, they were transport forces. Most of the Americans were coloured, and they seemed pretty nice. The officers all lived at Tostock.

"I left school at fourteen and went down to Barcocks, a free-range poultry Farm on the Rattlesden Road. It was past Hammond Hall, down a long drive on the left-hand side. Then when I was eighteen, in 1949, I started two years' National Service. It seems strange to start with but you soon get used to it. I went to Malaya. I wouldn't ever have got there otherwise! I was in the Suffolk Regiment, at Kuala Lumpur, the capital. It was the time of the rebels and ter-rorists. I was doing guards, escorts, general fatigues about camp. It seemed hot to start with but compared with the rest of the Regiment who were in tents, we were lucky. We were in a mas-sive great Nissen hut.

"After the war, in the 1960s, Barcock's changed from poultry to a plant nursery. The plants are better, you can work nine to five! Now it's a private house, Barcock's closed down. But one field is still a Nursery, under another name. When it closed in 1989, I went round jobbing gar-dening on my own. I cycled to work, never bought a car. I did start learning to drive early on, but then petrol rationing came in."

Gerald has some family photographs on show, and I asked about these. His mother is shown in All Saints' Church, where she was a stalwart member of the congregation. Gerald followed in her footsteps, serving on the Parochial Church Council, and as churchwarden for many years. While I was teaching at the School, he was a most tolerant and helpful churchwarden and cared for the graveyard. He remains a faithful Church-goer so has a circle of friends keeping an eye on him now he lives alone.

Another photograph shows his father Reginald, standing with his pony and cart on the Gedding Road. Gerald says:

"Father and I always had our own pony and cart, we kept the pony in a stable in the gar-den. We had a pony into the '60's. We'd go to Stow or Bury St. Edmunds. We had two ponies, they each lived with us a long time, until they had to be put down. At first we had a Governess cart, with two huge wheels, a door at the back, and seats along each side. Later we had a High Cart with two wheels and a seat across the front. You got up into it from the front. We sold those carts in the end".

Gerald was very helpful to me as I researched this history, writing to me more than once with infor-mation and names of residents of this village he loves.

CORA MUNFORD

Cora kindly wrote down for me some of her memories. Since her girlhood, she has lived in Stotts Cottage (the left-hand cottage of the pair) in Cross Street. Some of the war-time detail she recalls is par-ticularly fascinating. This is her story:

"I was born at Wortham, a village on the Norfolk/ Suffolk border. I walked the three-plus miles to School from the farm at the other end of the village. Wortham School was lovely, with its arched façade of 'Faith, Hope and Charity'.

"As quite a small child I remember my Saturday chore was to turn the handle of the butter churn, for which I received 6d. I loved to watch my mother make the butter up with the wood-en butter pats. I would like to put the wooden roller across the made-up pats, this made a dec-

orative pattern on top. Another of my Saturday chores during the summer was to help out in the strawberry fields. After the main crop had been picked, the small fruits were sent to a well-known jam factory, but first of all they had to be hulled (removing the green calyx). They were then put into large wooden barrels and collected once a week by the jam factory. You can imagine in hot weather how the fruit would ferment! I had to stand on a wooden box to reach the top of the barrel, and leaning over once, I was overcome (or maybe drunk!) by the fermenting fruit! One of the fruit pickers found me sound asleep beside the barrel. I don't even remember getting my 6d for that day!

"We came to live in Drinkstone in August 1939, initially temporarily, but war broke out four weeks later and changed my parents' plans. My father was an Air-Raid Warden, but thankfully we didn't have much action around here. We saw a lot of the American 'Flying Fortress' planes, which were stationed at Rattlesden, limp home after a mission. On one occasion a plane came over very low making a struggling noise, and shortly after there was a terrific explosion – it had crashed! We had a row of tomato plants near the house and the force of the explosion had blown all the fruit off the plants. My father was a great gardener, every piece of ground was cropped, even the verges in the lane produced lettuce, radish, onions and potatoes. We always had plenty of fresh vegetables and fruit. We also kept chickens, ducks and geese, we used to boil up scraps of vegetables etc. to mix with the meal which we would get from Clover's Mill. I was always fascinated to see Mr. Wilfred Clover grind the corn.

"The Clovers were a great family. Miss Olive Clover was the distributor for the W.V.S. of wool for knitters to make socks, gloves, scarves and so on for the soldiers and airmen. My mother received a certificate for knitting the most garments in the village. Miss Wyn Clover was voluntary organist at All Saints' Church for a great number of years and played a part in the Church flower festivals, and making the posies for Mothering Sunday. My mother also collected National Savings each week. I recall her saying one lady (who was evacuated from London) 'invested' 6d one week, and wanted it back the following week with Interest! Her 6d was returned (out of my mother's own pocket) needless to say without Interest! When 15s had accrued the money was taken to the organiser, Mrs. Phyllis Thurlow of Home Farm, and a Certificate was issued. Drinkstone was awarded a Certificate of Honour which still hangs in the Village Hall:

"'This Certificate of Honour is awarded to Drinkstone Village Savings Group in recognition of Special Achievement during the Wings for Victory National Savings Campaign 1943. I extend my thanks to all concerned in this important National Service. (signed)

"'Archibald Sinclair, Secretary of State for Air'

"During the war years, my mother (Mrs. May Munford) who was a member of the W.V.S., together with Mrs. Violet Mayes (Gerald's mother), also a W.V.S. member, collected salvage. They would tie large hessian sacks to the handlebars and across to the seat of their cycles, pushing them through the village collecting tins (there were not so many tins as there are now), paper packaging and blue sugar bags. They took everything to Mrs. Gore's at Drinkstone Lodge, where they would be sorted, and the tins squashed by a large piece of wood attached to a broom handle. The salvage would periodically be collected for the War Effort.

"I don't remember much about the war, I was never allowed to venture further than the end of the lane. I would visit Ruby and Daisy Rogers at Yew Tree Farm, we would go blackberry-ing in their father's meadows. We'd go to Chapel on a Sunday as there was no Sunday School at the Church. Once a year the Chapel held the Sunday School Anniversary, when we sang choruses and recited verses. John Oxborrow was Sunday School teacher and his sister Joyce played the organ. We always had a new straw hat for the Anniversary. It was a sad day when the Chapel closed, as it held many happy memories.

"I was confirmed at Beyton Church in May 1945, and was a member of All Saints' Church choir (Drinkstone) for several years. We had a very good choir in those days, some of the names I can recall are the Smith brothers, Vic, Tom, and Cecil, also Loll, Bob and Arthur Stiff, Gerald Mayes, Rosa Fisher, Ruby Stiff, Maud Bullett and many more. Since the early 1940s I

have seen nine incumbents of All Saints' Church. I have served on the Parochial Church Council for over fifty years.

"In the 1950s we had a Brownie Pack in the village. I also helped with the Beyton Girl Guides which was run by Mrs. Lavender Parker who was Captain. I was her Lieutenant. The Company was disbanded when Beyton Secondary Modern School was built, as the School then started a Guide Company (which sadly folded up). Lavender re-married and moved to Drinkstone with her husband Captain Michael Horne, they lived at Green Farm. We decided to start up the First Drinkstone Brownie Pack, we had great fun with the Brownies at Green Farm. Christmas parties were held in the Village Hall, when the District Commissioner, and Girl Guides and Brownies from neighbouring companies – Rougham, Stanton, and the American Guides from Shepherds' Grove – were invited. They were so pleased to be invited. When they disbanded they presented me (Mrs. Horne had moved from the village by then) with the American Girl Guide Badge of Friendship. Party food was not very plentiful in those days but we always managed a few extras. Mrs. Violet Mayes and my mother made lovely trifles, which were quite a treat in those days. My father was Santa Claus and each Guide and Brownie had to go on to the stage where they were given an apple, an orange, and some nuts, which he produced out of a hessian sack. No presents – we couldn't afford any – but they were such happy days!

"In the 1950s there was a Ploughing Match (some folk called them a Drawing Match) using either horses or a tractor. This was held in a field off Cross Street. It was a competition to see who could draw the straightest furrow. The winner overall was Arthur Munford, my father. He was presented with a copper kettle. This was usually the overall prize in those days. It was particularly special as it was hand-made by Mr. Minns, a blacksmith from Bedford, who used to visit his sister Miss Carrie Minns who was school teacher at Drinkstone School. He also made several flower containers for the Church.

"Drinkstone had a Quoits Team: a heavy iron ring was thrown onto an iron peg which was knocked into a bed of clay. The Cherry Tree Public House had two good Darts Teams. Two silver trophies were presented each year, one for the Ladies' Team and one for the Men's Team. Drinkstone's first Women's Institute was started by Mrs. Amy Ramsay who lived at The Lodge. She was a very enthusiastic lady with the Produce Guild, W.I. Choir, and various other classes. Together with Mrs. Gabrielle Thompson from the Rookery, she produced several award-winning plays. The W.I. ceased for a while, but it was re-started by Mrs. Edna Gunnett who was president for many years until it once again folded.

"In the late 1940s Drinkstone had a Concert Party and held several good concerts in the Village Hall. For many years the Over-Sixties attracted a lot of members. It was founded by Mrs. Phyllis Thurlow. It was later re-named The Windmill Club, and was well known throughout the County for winning trophies at the County Biennial 'Age Concern' Handicraft competitions. To name but a few prize-winners, there were Ruby Bland, for her exquisite knitting, Nell Cocksedge for rugs and wall hangings, Margaret Hazell for her patchwork cushions and bedspreads, Violet Mayes for fine crochet lace (which can be seen on the Church altar cloth), Molly Punchard for dressed dolls, and John Gibbs for woodwork. John Gibbs also designed and made the village sign. Sadly the Club closed owing to small membership.

"There were in those days several 'village characters' whom I'm sure you have been told about. Freddie and Ollie Read who lived in Rattlesden Road – Freddie was a great hedge-and-ditch man. He would cut the hedges and make them into faggots. The sticks would be made into bundles and held together with a withy. The withy was a straight stick that would bend, usually hazel or willow, with the thin end turned over and twisted to make a loop for the other end to go through, and twisted under the other end. Faggots were then sold by the score (20), and most cottages and back yards had a supply each year, ready to be chopped into sticks for firelighting the following winter. I could go on and on about past times in the village really!"

MARY HOVELLS

Mary (née Brinkley) was just seven years old at the start of the Second World War. Then as now, she took troubles in her stride and maintained a sunny philosophical outlook on life. Today she lives just a couple of miles south of Drinkstone, in Gedding village, her three children and five grandchildren within easy visiting distance. She has kept well in touch with a number of childhood friends and acquaintances through her work for the weekly Luncheon Club attended by elderly folk from several villages. This is held in Felsham Village Hall (Felsham and Gedding villages being only a short walk apart). Mary is chief cook and takes great pride in ordering good supplies and providing a tasty nourishing meal for the old ones.

It seems she has given a lifetime to looking after others and it was a pleasure to talk with her and share her memories of her childhood. This is Mary's story:

"I was born on 10th June 1932, in the Old Almshouses opposite Drinkstone School. I was brought up there by my grandparents, Annie Elizabeth (Lizzie) and Robert James (Bob) Buckle. I hardly ever saw my real mother, so I called my grandparents Mum and Dad. They had a foster son, Arthur Cornish. He was about five years older than me and was like a brother to me. I had a good time with my Mum and Dad. I remember my Dad taught me to knit, that was even before I started at the School.

"We had great times down there as children. We played on Thurlows' Farm (Home Farm). They had two sons we'd play with. A lady from Hammond's Hall in Rattlesden Road owned the Almshouse Cottages at that time. She was a funny little woman and we'd laugh about her. We pretended she was a witch. When we came out of School we'd go up to the orchard next to the Almshouse cottages. We'd go there partly to get apples, but it was mostly just to be naughty for that little woman. We'd hide among the trees and she'd try and chase us – we'd wait till she got close, then we'd run like heck! It was only in fun, she was a tiny woman, she had a car and she'd sit on a cushion to drive it, otherwise she couldn't see over the steering wheel.

"Well, about the School. On my first day I hated it, it was horrible. I cried and the boys kept laughing at me. But after a bit, I liked it. We lived so near the School I'd never go out of the house in the morning until I heard them ringing the bell. Then I'd just run across the road, and

Hammond Hall

111

in I'd go. It was quick for me to go home at dinner time, too. Although I was happy there, I used to get into a bit of trouble, the boys egged me on and I kept getting into fights. They teased me because I was a bit plump, they'd say I bounced like a ball when I skipped! So I had to stand up for myself. I got on all right with the girls, only once there was this girl I didn't like sitting in front of me and I remember I used to dip the end of her pigtails in the inkwell on my desk!

"I got on all right with the teachers. Sometimes when the boys were naughty they had to come and get the cane out of the cupboard, they'd have to walk past us and we'd watch them being caned. I liked the lessons, I was good at composition, we'd have to write about the stories they read us. I was good at art too. We used to sit out in the summer and have our lessons outside. We used to go to Church on Ascension Day, and then we got the rest of the day off. We thought that was lovely!

"The Headteacher was Mrs. Winsall, she lived in the Schoolhouse. I remember there was a cubby hole through from the classroom to her kitchen, and if she had to go into her house for anything, she'd peep through that cubby hole to see we was behaving ourselves! She had a daughter who was sometimes ill, and I had to spend quite a lot of time in the Schoolhouse with her daughter. I had to do school work with her, mostly reading books together. I missed quite a lot of lessons that way. At the time I thought, this is good! Now, I wonder what did I miss in education by being chosen to do that?

"At playtime we'd have little wooden spinning tops and whips to play with. You'd have an old leather bootlace on a stick for the whip, and you'd wind it round the top then pull to make it spin. We'd roll an old bicycle tyre for a hoop. And we did skipping. I remember one of the rhymes:

> Up in the North a long way off
> The donkey had the whooping cough.
> The only thing to make it better
> Was salt – vinegar – mustard – PEPPER!

"Once at playtime a tennis ball hit me in the eye. Another time, I had a bad graze all down my face from the playground wall. The teacher put iodine on – very painful!

"When the war started, we had evacuees in the village. One of them, Rene, became my friend. She's in New Zealand now but we keep in touch. We had to help the War Effort by picking rose hips during our school nature walks. Sometimes we had to go up to the Village Hall for our lessons while the evacuees were having their hair washed for nits. My Mum (my Gran really) would comb through my hair every day, so I never caught it.

"My Mum used to clean the School and House for Mrs. Winsall. Because Mrs. Winsall's husband was away in the forces, sometimes my Mum would sleep there. There were soldiers billeted in the Old Rectory. When the Sergeant Major's wife was on visits to her husband, they'd come to our cottage. He had an accordion and he'd play 'Kiss me Goodnight, Sergeant Major'. We'd sit on the floor and listen to him.

"In the war, I used to walk to Woolpit with my Mum to get the meat. It would sometimes be flooded down by the bridge in Drinkstone, so we'd have to walk through the grounds of the Old Rectory. The soldier on guard would walk behind us all the time with a fixed bayonet! It didn't scare me though. We didn't realise how serious the war was. My brother and I would go and sit in the army lorries of the British men when they were on manoeuvres. They'd be parked on the grass triangle near the cottage that was a shop, just up from the Church (where the phone box is now) while the neighbours made them cups of tea. Although it was war, it was safer in those days, the men were kind to us. At Christmas we'd be picked up in a big lorry to go to Tostock army camp for a party, and they'd give us toys and food. The American troops would throw out sweets to us as they went past in their lorries. But the husbands who were away fighting weren't too happy about U.S. troops giving the women and girls silk stockings!

"After the war, when I was about twelve, we moved to Drinkstone Green. I had a long walk

Home Farm – where Mary did domestic work

to School after that, and I remember walking all the way in snow. When we got there, we hung our wet clothes around the old tortoise stove and sat around it to get warm. The milk was heated on that stove too, I hated the taste of warm milk! So I used to take a bit of Bournvita or Ovaltine, to take away the taste. I had school dinners when I lived at The Green. I remember having sponge pudding and lumpy custard.

"I left School when I was fourteen. I was at school one day, and at work the next. I did domestic work down at Home Farm, where my Mum worked. I had to live in, and I got 2s 6d a week. I didn't like it, but we didn't have much choice of employment then. I had to clean all the house. We had a vacuum, but I still had to get down on all fours to scrub the floors. One good thing while I was there, one Springtime I brought up a little lamb. It was one of triplets and the ewe could only feed two. I fed him with a bottle and he'd follow me anywhere, even if I went up to Young's shop near the Church! You could come across the meadows to the shop then, you didn't have to go up the road. When my lamb was older I took it up to Drinkstone Park where Thurlow kept his sheep, to join the flock.

"Education's different now, it's better in some ways, my eldest grand-daughter's doing A-levels. In the old days, I remember my aunt paid for her two girls to go to a convent school and they were not happy. They were 'lower class' and they couldn't fit in. It's improved now, it's totally different, there's not much class distinction now. But it's a shame apprenticeships have gone, they were good. My son was trained as a carpenter, and the employer paid for him to go to college for three or four years.

"Well that's about all I've got to say. I had a lovely childhood really, they were good to me. We don't realise how much they gave up for us in the war."

RENE HILL

Mary has kept in touch with Rene (née Hill), one of the evacuees who attended the School during the war years. Rene, now far away in New Zealand, was kind enough to jot down a few of her own memories of those long ago days:

"Mrs. Winsall was our teacher and a very kind person she was. Her husband was a soldier and their young daughter was named Ann. When her husband came home on leave once, he helped serve up school dinners. He was so handsome, while Mrs. Winsall was a plain, homely body.

"One day at dinner time, we had macaroni cheese. We were all sitting at long tables, and one of the infants took a mouthful of her dinner and promptly brought it back up onto her plate. She obviously did not like macaroni cheese! The rest of us children all went out into the playground and no amount of friendly persuasion from Mrs. Winsall could get us back in to eat our dinner! If ever I am offered macaroni cheese, I still remember that incident over sixty years ago – each time I am given that stuff – Yuk!

"Another time, Billy Smith bumped into me coming away from the dinner line with a plate full of dinner and gravy. It went all down the front of my new gymslip and I had to wear it for the rest of that week. In those days, we had one on, and one in the wash.

"One day we lined up by the playground fence and was throwing stones onto the road below, and a stone hit the windscreen of a truck driver. He came into class with blood running down one side of his face. Donald Mackenzie said it was Joyce Whitmore that threw the stone, but truthfully it could have been any one of us in the row.

"In those days, a few of the children smelled of stale wee, so nobody wanted to play with them! I remember when we played families at playtime, if Kenny Bullock was 'Dad' he'd run around the playground with his hands up, pretending to drive, and he'd say 'Here go me, funny old doody in the moonlight!' In this 'families' game, 'Mum' stayed at home with one of the infants for our little boy or girl. This particular day, Freddy Robinson whom I secretly adored, but would die rather than let him know, was 'Dad'. Freddy chose another girl to be his 'wife' that playtime, and as I was standing behind him, I swiftly but very forcibly kicked Freddy up the bum! He spun round holding his backside and said 'Who did that?' and no-one answered. There were others behind with me, but no-one said a word. They knew Rene Hill might give them the same! I was quite a bully, but I had to stick up for myself as I was billeted out for some years with Mrs. Brinkley, her husband and daughter Kathrine, and their son (Francis, but we called him 'Nippy'). They really were a lovely family and looked after me well. Kathrine was so kind to me. Their daughter Mary was a nurse, I think in Ipswich Hospital, during the war.

"My remembering mostly involves Freddy. We were told to write about our family one day. Mrs. Winsall said that Freddy Robinson had written 'I live in a Coly holy house' instead of 'Council house', but it was all said in good humour, and Freddy was not embarrassed, he laughed too".

When I visited Freddy in 2005, I asked whether he remembered Rene who had such a crush on him in the 1940s!

FREDDY ROBINSON

I asked Freddy about Rene. He remembered her, and her sister Florrie. I asked if he knew she had a crush on him, and he said, "No – I think I might have been a bit shy back in those days!"

Fred and his wife Irene live in a cottage in Boxted, a tiny hamlet just south of Hartest. There is a wonderful view of willows and water-meadows behind their home. Irene told me the farmer who owns the land always used to graze a house cow there, but now it is rough and wild. Irene was born in a cottage near Boxted Church. She and Fred have one son, Graham, who lives with them.

Freddy is the seventh of eight children, although the oldest daughter died at birth and one of his brothers, Alan, died as a child. All the children attended Drinkstone School (some only briefly). They were Phyllis, Harry, Ethel Elizabeth (Betty), Lucy, Alan, Freddy and Joan. Now only Lucy, Freddy and Joan are left. (Betty's son Dennis Bradley tells his story in a later chapter.) Here is Freddy's story:

"My father, Frederick Charles Robinson, was from Elmswell. He was too young to serve in *the First World War. Around the year 1919, when he was about seventeen, jobs were few and far between in Suffolk, so like many other men, Frederick somehow got up to Yorkshire, to find work. He might have walked, or hitched, or even (knowing what he was like!) jumped up onto a goods train at Elmswell to get there! He found work on a farm at Hemsley, on the road between York and Scarborough. My mother Muriel (née Wright) was working as kitchen maid on the farm. She was an orphan girl. They married, and the family arrived, most of them were born in Yorkshire. I was the first to be born back in Suffolk. I was called Charles Frederick, but people started calling me 'young Freddy' and that's the name that stuck. My parents had rented Meadow Cottage (set a little way back from the Rattlesden Road in Drinkstone) behind Bert Hall's shop. That's where I was born, on December 21st 1933. My father went to work for West Suffolk County Council as a roadman. Each roadman had about five miles of road to look after – cutting the verge, edging it, looking after the drains and ditches (no-one looks after them these days). In summer time they'd get together in a gang, fifteen to twenty men working together, to do the tarring. They'd pump on hot tar, using a hand pump, and some would follow behind with barrows full of shingle to put on. In winter, they'd stand on the back of the lorries and throw handfuls of sand on the roads when it was icy.*

"No-one had much money in those days. We hardly ever had the doctor because you had to pay. My mother used to pay about 3s a month to Pansy Phillips, as a kind of Insurance for times when we might need the doctor or hospital. Pansy collected the money from everyone and paid it in. When I was about three, my brother Alan, who was six, got ill. My mother used to tell me he said, 'Don't jump on me please, Freddie, I've got tummy ache.' He died of pneumonia.

"In 1937 we moved to No. 3, Council Houses (the ones near the Village Hall). Those four houses were numbered 1,2,3,4 then. Later they were changed to 1,3,5,7, so the one we had is now number 5. I started at Drinkstone when I was old enough, I didn't mind School. Miss Minns (Carrie) never used the cane on us, but she'd walk around the room, smacking us on the ear if we misbehaved. But when we went up to the big class, we'd get the cane from Miss Jackson! She came from Yorkshire, she had a terrible temper! Her mother lived in the Schoolhouse with her. There used to be a little cubby hole between the classroom and the house, and when it was time for music, Miss Jackson would go and call to her mother through the hole, 'Come and play the piano for us!' I used to get sent out to do the garden when we had singing, because they said my voice had broken. I'd be out there cutting the grass and weeding. Sometimes Mrs. Jackson would come out and talk to me. I got on better with her, than with her daughter the teacher.

"At playtime we'd play 'Sticky Glue'. That was a chasing game, you had to touch everyone and when they were touched they had to stand still with their arms out. Someone else would be running about freeing them again. You had to try and catch everyone. We played 'Shove against the Corner' – you'd stand in a line and the last person would be in the corner between the wall and those big brick buttresses. We'd all push together, it was really just a way of getting warm. There was hopscotch too, and hoops, we'd even play that in the road because there was no traffic. I can remember when there were only three cars in the village. Cecil and May Cooper (at the shop) had a Vauxhall, PVS172. Arthur Bland had a Vauxhall, DLC517, and Toby Bennett had a little Austin 7, GV3.

"We'd skive off School some days. If the fox and hounds came along, that would be about eleven in the morning, three or four of us would go off following them, and we'd play truant for the rest of the day. Next morning it would be 'Where'd you go yesterday?' and we'd get the cane. One morning I got to School early and I broke the cane in half! Miss Jackson called me 'a nasty mean horrible sneak!' But she had some more canes!

"In the war we had evacuees in the village. We used to go and work on the farms, planting potatoes, and lifting them. We'd be allowed twenty half-days off for farm work (sometimes we'd do two half days together, three and a half hours in the morning and the same in the afternoon). When we'd done the twenty, we could apply for twenty more. We liked that, it was better than School and my mother was glad of the extra money. My father went off to the war, but he never talked much about it. My Mum used to have groceries from Hopgood's van, and at one time she owed them a lot of money (about £13) but they'd still leave her bread, although they knew she couldn't pay. The men on the van were Jack Baker from Rougham, and Jim Sutton. Bit by bit she scraped the money together (she had a pension because my father was away at the war) and when she finally managed to pay Jack Baker the last money he said, 'Thank you, Mrs. Robinson, I never thought I'd see that.' But he wasn't going to let us go hungry anyway.

"While I was still at School, I used to run errands for Walter Steggalls down at the Cherry Tree, and I used to cut fire-wood with him, using a cross-cut saw, each pulling one end in turn. He'd give me half a pint of mild, with a hot poker in it, and a few bob. I used to go up to the shop for Addy Fisher who lived at the Cherry Tree (I think she was a relative of Walter). She'd give us pies, she was a good cook – meat pies, and Cornish pasties. The newspapers were delivered to the Cherry Tree. I'd deliver about twenty of them before School each day. I earned more while I was at School, than after I left!

"I liked maths at School, I was very good at mental arithmetic. In maths I used to have to sit with a boy called Kenny who found maths hard, and try to help him and explain things. When Mrs. Collins came (I only had her for my last term in School) she said she wished she'd got me earlier because then she 'could have made something of me!' But when you're young, you don't concentrate much. I think I've learned a lot more since I left School than when I was there.

"When I left School, I went to Gedding Hall as an understudy groom. I wanted to be a jockey, at Newmarket. I was small then – I'd need an elephant to carry me now! I earned 45 shillings a week there. 2s 10d went on the Insurance Stamp each week, 25s went to mother for my keep, 10s a week went to my Dad, to repay the £26 my bike cost. He helped me get a bike to cycle to work, but he took every penny of it back from me! That was hard, because he didn't treat us all the same. He bought one of my sisters a bike and just gave it to her, but he wouldn't give me anything. Well, at the end of each week I had 7s 2d for myself and that went on beer and tobacco! I didn't manage to save any. But I gave up smoking years ago.

"Around 1949/ 1950 my father bought Meadow Cottage where we used to live. He bought it for sentimental reasons really, I think, it only cost him about £100 and he sold it again soon after. In 1954, when I was about twenty-one, he bought a cottage at Tostock and we moved there. He gave one or two hundred for it. A long time later, when he went into sheltered accommodation, he let my sister Betty have it for £300 and she stayed there for the rest of her life. Her husband still lives there. My mother died before my father, I wished it could have been the other way round, because I would have liked to make more fuss of her. My father was very tight, and right up until she died he treated her quite rough, not the way a wife should be treated. My father was a real bugger to my Mum. When I was little, I couldn't do much about it. But when I got to about fourteen I'd say to her, 'Why do you stay with him? Why don't you leave?' But she'd say, 'Oh, I'm not going now!' and she put up with it. She always made out things weren't too bad. But any small thing – like one day she boiled the kettle dry – Dad would fly into a rage. She stuck with him through thick and thin. People stayed together in those days. Today, it's just one argument and they're getting divorced!

"My father had a terrible temper. He used to get so riled and angry if he lost at cards – he was terrible! If they were playing rummy, my Mum would always let him win."

(Irene tells how their son, when only a small boy, beat his Grandad at cards and "he got in a dreadful rage! Graham didn't know that you had to let Grandad win!").

Freddy says:

"I can tell you, I used to have a temper, but since we've been married I've got a lot more patience. I would never do anything to hurt my wife, that just should not happen. I met Irene when I was driving Eastern Counties Buses. We married in 1965. We're coming up for our fortieth wedding anniversary now.

"Later on I worked as a driver for Glasswells Furniture Removers. Sometimes I'd drive right up to Scotland and it's beautiful up there. Our son works for Glasswells now.

"We had some right old characters in Drinkstone. Albert Horrex (he was a prisoner of war in Japan), we always called him 'Doodles', he was a joker. Once he was in his garden, smoking, and a lady walked past – she was a Jehovah's Witness, I think. As she went by she turned round to keep talking to him, so she was walking backwards. She said, 'If the Lord had intended you to smoke, he'd have put a chimney on your head!' So Doodles said, 'Yes, and if the Lord wanted you to walk backwards, he'd have put eyes in the back of your head!' We used to go up to the Cherry Tree with him, he was full of mischief. There was an old couple, Geoff and Millie Catchpole, living down the smithy end of the village, and they used to walk up to the Cherry Tree, she'd walk one side of the lane and he'd walk the other. That was because he'd be smoking and she couldn't stand it. She never let him smoke indoors. But when they got to the Cherry Tree, old Doodles'd get his pipe and sit right close to her, puffing all the smoke into her face – and she didn't say nothing!

"I'd like to go back to the old days really. I know what hard times are, and it was hard times – but people were happier then. You could trust people in those days. You could leave your house open and no-one would touch nothing. I think the television's the rudest thing there is, today. Everybody watches all the rubbish and if you go in most houses they'd rather keep watching than talk to you. If anyone comes in here, the first thing we do is turn it right off, because it's people that are important."

DEREK CROSS

Derek and his wife Heather live next to the Village Memorial Hall. Their home, number 1 Gedding Road, looks across open fields, and was a Council house. Like most of their neighbours, they chose to buy their home. Heather comes from Mendlesham Green (further east). The couple married in 1959. This is Derek's story:

"I was born on 5th April 1934 in one of the row of cottages opposite Clopton Green. That's a nice place [just east of Drinkstone parish, on the road between Woolpit and Rattlesden]. *My father was working for Windsor Parker of Clopton Hall.*

"My father was born around 1903 and he worked on several different farms, starting as assistant horseman. Until he was married, he'd give his mother a little help each week. He used to tell us how he once lost 12s wages out of his pocket, when he was ploughing for Mr. Snell at Hill Farm. The old boy must have paid him while he was at work, and the coins dropped out and were ploughed in! He never found a penny of it.

"My mother was a Hessett girl, her father kept the 'One Bell' Pub between Hessett and Gedding corner. She'd walk the one and a half miles to Hessett School. She used to say of her father, 'If he runn'd out of beer, he'd have a quick brew up!' My mother worked extremely hard all her life. She started in service at Horringer, and later she worked at Marks Tey, and that's where she learned to cook just about anything. She could do bread, home-made wines, anything. And she looked after her parents, and one sister who couldn't manage on her own.

"We moved when I was two or three years old because my father went to work for Hargreaves at The Park, and Thurlow at Home Farm in Drinkstone. We lived in a cottage set right back from the road that runs between Hessett and Drinkstone cross roads, it was one of a pair owned by Mr.Thurlow. Today it's all one house, very smart, called 'Parkfield House', and there's a made up drive going north to the road. When we lived there, it was a double dweller, and you had to walk up Park Lane and turn left along the grass lane leading to the brick cottages by the moat, belonging to Drinkstone Park. It was a long walk and just a kind of grassy track, in those days.

"After a while we moved up to Street Farmhouse near the crossroads. My mother's brother Percy Renson lived there, he was a tenant farmer then and Street Farm was owned by Mr. Pike of Elmswell. In 1932 when he went there, all he had was £100 he'd saved up. He bought a few horses and got started. He was like a beanpole but he lived to ninety-three! Arthur Sturgeon

worked for him then, and Arthur's sister Jessie married my uncle William Renson. Another brother, my Uncle Ted Renson, really did well in life. Like the others in the family he only ever went to the village school at Hessett, but it didn't hold him back, he worked his way up to becoming a Detective Sergeant at Scotland Yard.

"I remember on my first day at Drinkstone School I walked there with my brother Gilbert. He was eight years older than me. Miss Caroline Minns was the infant teacher, and her brother Jack was a great friend of our family. Jack Minns had a plumbing business near Bedford, and whenever he was staying with his sister up the By Road, he loved to come down to ours at Street Farm to play a game of crib. Jack used to make lovely copper kettles, so when they had a local ploughing match he supplied copper kettles as prizes for the straightest furrow.

"The Schools were a bit basic then but we had some treats. I remember we'd take a little old jar of Ovaltine with us to School in the winter, and put it in the milk that was warmed on the old tortoise stove. We liked to go out gardening, it was a way of getting out of the classroom. The first time the teacher asked me to cut the hedge she really praised me up, she said, 'You made a lovely job of that hedge.' I still love gardening today. At playtime we played football on Thurlow's land, opposite the school. There's houses there now and more being built today, 'five quality homes'.

"Daniel Clover from the Mills was a governor of the school then, I remember him visiting the school. Miss Stiff was the infant teacher after Miss Minns, she cycled over from Norton. My last Headteacher there was Miss Jackson. She came from Sheffield, she was a proper Yorkshire lassie. She lived in the Schoolhouse, with her mother. I went to Woolpit School in 1946 and did my last two years there – I don't remember why, maybe because it was a bigger school.

"There was a lot of characters in the village then. I remember Mr. Osborne from Cross Street, he had a pony and cart and he used to go to Elmswell Station for his coal. And if his pony got tired – this is the honest truth! – he'd tie the pony on the back of the cart, get between the shafts, and pull the cart himself! When we were in the playground we'd hear him coming along, he'd always be talking to himself, and us boys would shout, 'Here comes Ozzy!' and we'd run down and hang on the back of the trap, pushing it down, and we'd lift Ozzy right off his feet at the front and he'd swear at us! It was only our fun, we never did any real harm. Ozzy used to mow the verge up Gedding Road with his scythe, to get hay for his horse, and he'd mow it so close and smooth it was just like a machine had done it.

"There was some other rum old characters, like Reggie Wells who lived in those old cottages of Thurlow's, (where we once lived, now called Parkfield House). The cottages weren't needed for the farm any more, and they got a bit derelict. Reggie lived there, and he used to get on the roadside hoping for a lift. I'd pick him up and take him as far as Ticehurst Farm where he'd leave his bike. He was in the army for a while. He went off Norton way afterwards, and the cottages stood empty for years. Then Mr. Thurlow sold them and they were made into one house, real smart, with a good driveway across the field.

"There were two old boys living at Elm Tree Cottage (the thatched one at the top of Chapel Lane) and we called them The Twins. They were Jimmy and Teddy and they got away without doing much in the way of work – just a bit of thatching on the straw stacks occasionally, that's all they did. They'd get a few pounds and go for beer. One played the accordion, so when they were in the pub we'd ask him to get the old squeeze-box out because that always annoyed his brother!

"Ollie Alderton lived in an old bus opposite Chapel Lane for years. He used to be out in Canada taking the logs down the river, and that's how he lost a finger. When he first came here, in the 1950s I think, he'd work on the land on the sugar beet, then he went to Seaman's Builders at Stow (where my brother Gilbert worked). He didn't pack up every day. He'd just put a loaf of bread in his docker bag, and cut a slice or two each day, to eat with a bit of cheese or whatever he had. He was a nice old boy. He biked miles to work and back, and he lived to be ninety. There was a chap called Bill Lingwood, he lived in a bungalow down Chapel Lane. My wife Heather would do a bit of washing for him. Anyway, Bill, he'd like to talk to Ollie. One time

he said to me, 'Ollie had just stoked up when I got to the bus and I couldn't see him for smoke. There was more smoke coming out of that old tortoise stove than there was coming out of the chimney. I couldn't see if he was in there so I shouted, 'Are you in there, Ollie?' and he said 'Come in, bo'!' I'd always kick the old armchair before I sat down in case there was a rat in it!'

"There's a new house built there now, and they went really deep for the foundations because that's such a damp marshy spot. That new house was sold for £300,000! My old uncle bought Street Farm for about £3,000, and that had about a hundred acres with it! I remember one day, Mr. Pike from Elmswell who owned the farm cycled over for the rent, and my mother gave it to him, and Mr. Pike said 'now you can tell your brother that I'm selling the farm!' So that's when my uncle bought it. He also bought Blacksmith's Cottage and the Old Post Office, for £100 each, for his labourers to live in. Later on he sold the Old Post Office to Mr.Ivor-Jones. Mrs. Ivor-Jones still lives in the village, at Burt's Farm.

"Ollie who lived in the bus, he bought a couple of cottages. He bought 'Lane End Cottage' down Cross Street – it was known as 'Slugs Hole' in those days. There was an old tin reservoir down there, where they got the water. Ollie concreted the floors of the cottage. My brother laughed at him because he did them too high, so he couldn't open the doors! Then Ollie bought Meadow Cottage, down the Rattlesden Road, as well. Those cottages were in a bad state, and Ollie told me, 'That Wyatt, the Sanitary Inspector from Elmswell, he keeps on at me saying they're not up to living standards and he's going to condemn them!' so he got worried and sold them both. Lane End Cottage has had a big extension added since those days.

"There were some rum old places. The Old Almshouses, I can remember seven or eight families living there. It was L-shaped but most of the end nearest the road has been knocked down – you can still see the big chimney on the end wall. Before, the two end cottages were right near the ditch. If you came out of the door you had to be careful you didn't fall in! There was a narrow path and a plank bridge. I think that ditch is covered over now, and the Old Almshouses are all made into a single house. F.W. Mulley and Sons of Woolpit did the work, but they went bankrupt later.

"There were a lot of little houses. Chris Rivens, Ernie's uncle, had a little bungalow on the right, in Chapel Lane. You can't see the place now, it's behind a high hedge.

"Well, I'd better tell you what I did when I left School. I was fourteen when I went to work with father and my uncle, at Street Farm. At eighteen, I did two year's National Service. I was a cook with the Royal Army Ordnance Corps in Germany. I quite enjoyed it; there were a lot of Liverpool chaps, they were all comedians, it was good fun. We'd sail home on leave from the Hook of Holland, and those boats would creak and groan. I'd make sure I got a top bunk because some of the others got sea-sick bad!

"After National Service my uncle wanted me to go back on the farm, but I wanted a change. I worked for Mulleys; then I worked sixteen years at Thomas Stewart's at Bury, as a crane driver. Then I was made redundant. The last few years I was driver for a firm at Stanton, delivering wooden buildings like mobile classrooms. I still drive for them sometimes. We see a lot of family, we've three sons and some lovely grandchildren. My daughter-in-law Jo keeps horses over winter down Raymond Bland's, in his stables. We see a lot of the family. We both love the garden".

Derek was County Veteran Bowls Champion in 2002, but was too modest to mention it! It was through Derek that I was loaned a book (belonging to Richard Lee of Rattlesden). Named "West Suffolk Illustrated", published 1907, it was a useful source of information on 19th century village schools.

JOYCE ROUSE

Joyce was the eldest child of Mary and Jack Levett. Mary (née Cocksedge) came from Hessett, and Jack's family came from Rattlesden. Mary had worked as a kitchen maid after leaving school. Later she was cook for Rev. Horne at Drinkstone Rectory. In 1935, she and Jack married, and moved to live in Church Cottages, Drinkstone (now "The Old Almshouses"). Joyce was born in 1937.

Today Joyce and husband Len live in a neat bungalow in Woolpit, with Angus, their dear little West Highland terrier. This is Joyce's story:

"Although I can't remember my first day at School, my memories do go back to when I was quite tiny. I remember riding on a seat tied to the crossbar of my father's bicycle, and we were at Hessett, visiting my mother's parents. The bike was leaned up against the box hedge – I remember the smell of the leaves – and I was threading the little twigs through my fingers, stripping off the leaves. I liked the way they fell off so easily. Another early memory I have is seeing a funeral party arrive at the Church, across the road from our home. It was daytime. I think I must have been ill, maybe with measles, because I was looking out of the upstairs bedroom window. I saw all the men wearing black top hats and tails, and two black horses pulling the hearse. There was a frightening feel to them, I think it was all the black, and the formality.

"I can remember war-time too, I remember hearing the bombs when we were coming home from Hessett. The Old Rectory was used as a soldiers' billet, and we had the Americans at The Park. If the lorries were coming back to Base and the Americans saw us children, they'd stop and hand out sweets. Mum and Dad didn't like us having chewing-gum, but I did have it sometimes, unbeknown to them! We'd buy sweets at Mary Cooper's shop just up the Rattlesden Road. Mrs. Cooper lived there with her husband Percy and their son Peter. They had an annexe converted into a shop, you could buy cycle repair kits, and sweets. We'd take our coupons round for sweets after Chapel on a Sunday. We'd buy Sharpe's Toffees, I liked the green peppermint ones, not the blue ones which had Brazil nuts in. Mum liked dark chocolate, Fry's Cream.

"Mum lost two children before my sister was born, in 1943, so there's a big age gap between me and Cicely. In April 1944 we moved house. We moved by horse and tumbril, from down the bottom of Drinkstone to The Green. There were two council houses built, just before you get to Cherry Tree Lane. That got me more children to play with – there weren't many down near the Church – but I was too young to mind about that before we moved anyway. Then in 1945 my brother Ivor was born.

"I loved being with Dad. He worked for Hector Mann at Hall Farm. Mr. Mann had fruit orchards, he was based at Tostock, he'd drive through the village in his big car. He was quite an aloof man, I think. He had a daughter Susan, about my age. Mr. Fabb, the foreman, lived at Hall Farm. At Harvest season, we were allowed to go up in the harvest fields. We'd take 'the fourses' up to Dad, at four o'clock. We'd take him tea in a bottle and something to eat. They couldn't stop working until everyone was ready, then the men would all come and sit down. The tea might be half cold by then! We'd take sandwiches, and some of Mother's home-made lemonade. She made it using lemon-peel, quite simple but very refreshing, it was lovely. We'd be allowed to stay in the field until Dad came home, it was quite safe. There was only the binder, and a little grey Fergie tractor, and I do remember seeing horses there as well.

"After harvest, I remember being allowed to sit on the tractor and steer for the muck-spreading. Dad would walk along beside me. In the holidays, all the family helped with the fruit-picking. They didn't let children pick the apples, but we could climb the ladders and pick the plums, filling a wicker basket. That's how we got the money to buy clothes. I was obviously a help with the family budget, although we didn't earn much. All the families were there together.

"The children had a lot of fun together. Roads were safe then, we used to be able to play hopscotch on the road – but woe betide if they put gravel down, it spoiled our chalk markings! I never could learn to spin a top. Another game we liked to play in the road was 'Dead Man's Dark Scenery'. For that, we'd pick two teams. One team would cover their eyes. The other team would pick a person to lie down in the road, then they'd all take off their coats and cover her up, and go and hide. Then the first team would open their eyes and come over, and poke the one in the road, trying to find out who it was. Then we'd shout 'Dead Man's Dark Scenery!' People would be horrified if children played that now!

"One thing did scare us, when we played in the road, and that was if the policeman came. He was P.C. Sayle, a big man on a bicycle, and if he came along we'd drift off into the gardens until he'd gone. He was strict, and that wasn't a bad thing really.

"Families would go on walks together then, particularly on a Sunday afternoon or evening. One favourite walk was 'The Circle' – down the village, past the School, round The Park, and back home again. Another favourite was to go down past Barcock's Nursery, across the fields, out at Slugs Hole (that used to be Widows' Cottage) where an elderly lady lived. We called her 'Millie Hanton'. She took Sunday School down at the Chapel, and she had a couple of sons living with her, big men they seemed to me. Then we'd walk up Cross Street, and often we'd meet up with Ruby Bland and her family and the parents would stop and have a chat. Then we'd stop off at the Cherry Tree and have a packet of crisps and a bottle of pop. Children weren't allowed in the bar, but they'd smuggle us into the 'best room'. The bar was always full – that was in the days before people had cars and went out of the village. You lost a lot of the village life after that, people could go off anywhere.

"We'd play cards on a Sunday evening, 'Newmarket', games like that. Friends would pop in to play. Gosh, it used to be lovely, it was the highlight of the week-end, you weren't stuck in front of the box then. We're quite insular now. You drive through Drinkstone now and it seems dead, you don't see a soul.

It was a very safe time, people used to leave their doors open, with money out on the table to pay for food that was delivered. They'd know the tradesmen would leave the right amount of change. I remember Basil Bolton, butcher's boy from Addison's in Woolpit. He'd leave us a pound of sausages every week. By the time Mum got home from looking after Gran and Grandad at Hessett, my little sister would have eaten half of every sausage! She'd say, every time, 'It wasn't me!' She was often after the marge. and lard as well. Perhaps she needed it, she's taller than me now!

"I remember 'double summer time'. Mum would hang a blanket over the window so we could go to sleep. It was devastation for me, when I discovered Father Christmas was Dad! That was sad! We'd go to bed, each Christmas Eve, and the house would be just as usual. But in the morning when we woke all the decorations were up and it was so special! I thought I would re-live my childhood with my grandchildren; But now it's money that's important to people, it's not the same. I had a lovely childhood.

"Well, I'd better tell you about the School. I loved School, I loved reading. I think that came from my Dad; I can remember being very little, sitting on my Dad's lap with my head against his chest and I can still hear the resonance of his voice, reading to me. I just ate books! One Christmas, I remember getting a little book with glossy pages, all about a Scottie dog, and I just devoured it, it was finished in an hour!

"My infant teacher was Miss Stiff. She always had some knitting on the go and it was always grey. I think she knitted for the Forces. Miss Stiff would let me hear the little ones read. I remember I taught all the infants to say 'the Marquis of Cabbage', not 'Carabis', because I didn't know the word and I didn't want to ask the teacher!

"We used to have milk at School, one of the senior boys would fetch it from Thurlow's in a jug. It was warmed on the tortoise stove in winter, and we'd put in Bournvita. When it was wet, we'd dry our clothes on the metal guard around that big old coke stove. I remember the smell when we used to take off our lisle stockings and hang them all around – there's no smell quite like it! I suppose it's the combination, the smell of sweaty feet that have been in wellingtons, mixed with the smell of wet wool and the smell of the river! Some of us used to get deliberately wet – we'd walk in the stream on the way to School.

"We had the lisle stockings to keep us warm, and liberty bodices with suspenders to button on to the stockings, the sort of buttons all covered over with linen. We got those clothes at Mason's in Woolpit, we bought shoes there as well. You'd only go into Bury St. Edmunds once or twice a year in those days.

"In the top class, we had a lot of different teachers. Mrs. Clay was there during the war.

Then we had Mrs. Winsall, but when her husband came home from the war she left. Then we had a Miss Brownlow, she was only there a matter of weeks, but she used to bore me to tears! Every afternoon she'd read a story to us in the top class and I used to fall asleep! Then in 1946 or '47 Miss Jackson came, she was a very nice teacher. She took me under her wing for one reason or another, and she gave me homework. I used to love that. Miss Jackson had work cards, instead of all the work being put on the blackboard, the same for all the children, mixed in age and ability. I suppose that headed me towards the 11-plus. I wasn't asked whether I wanted to take it. Only two of us took it, me and Michael Smith. I didn't particularly want to pass, and I think I must have been borderline, because I had to go before a panel at Shire Hall. Anyway, I got a place at the County Grammar in Bury St. Edmunds.

"Well, the first day, there was Joyce in her black beret! I had black shoes, thick black stockings, stripey knitted-jersey tie (that got all stretched and twisted), white blouse, the dreaded gymslip and my brown leather satchel. I had to cycle to Rattlesden to go in a taxi. And that very first day I didn't know anyone, except Audrey Barcock from Barcock's Nursery. She was about three years older than me, she was a big girl, she seemed like a grown-up to me. She used to walk to Rattlesden and look after her brown-and-white skewbald pony who lived in a field half-way along, and she'd see to the pony again on her way home. I used to cycle past her right quick. I didn't know anyone else who had a pony – only old Ozzie who grazed his on the grass verges.

"At school, I was the only girl in black stockings! You'd still got the remnants of the summer uniform, and I felt like a fish out of water! I was the new girl among new girls. The Sixth Form, they seemed like grown-ups to me, the boys even wore suits.

"When you got in the class you realised it was a different world. The girls used to do ballet. Ballet classes – that was unheard of! Lots of them came from the town, and the ones from the surrounding countryside were farmers' daughters. I was in awe of them. But I soon had friends – Margaret Stebbings from Brandon was my friend. My Mum said, 'Ask her if her Mum's name is Gladys', so next day I asked, and yes, it was! It turned out she had been in service with my mother at Thurston! So it wasn't quite so bad, but still a bit of a challenge, because Margaret's parents ran the hotel at Brandon, and that sounded a bit grand. My other friend was Janet Lee from Rattlesden, her father had a smallholding rented from the Council. So that was our little gang.

"I loved Geography, I hated French, I didn't like Physics but I liked the Chemistry experiments with the crystals and things. I said I wanted to be a doctor, so they put me in the Science stream. But then I thought, a doctor has to cut people up, and that sent a funny feeling right through me. So after that I didn't have any particular ambition.

"My brother and sister had whooping-cough, and then I contracted it, and I had a whole term off school. I think they must have kept me in quarantine. After that, I was constantly 'playing catch-up' and it didn't work! I used to get away with lots of things. My Mother got lung cancer and she was only forty-two when she died. By this time, she was in and out of hospital, so I had a ready-made excuse if my homework wasn't presented on time. I didn't know how ill she was until the day before she died, when my Dad told me (that was after I left school).

"I left School early, in 1953. My Mum and Dad gave me a letter to take in, I didn't know what it said. I gave it to the Headmaster and he said, 'Oh, so you're leaving!'

"All the time I was at that School, at the back of my mind I felt I'd left my area, I was in the wrong place. It had taken me away from a School with forty-eight children, a place I knew and loved. One or two Drinkstone girls said to me, 'Oh, I suppose you'll be all snooty now, you won't want to talk to us!' So you were trying to please both camps. I never felt I belonged with the children at the Grammar School, I was really in awe of them. I think I would have been a lot happier if I'd stayed with the girls I knew. I suppose I could have done better at School but I didn't realise the importance of it all at the time.

"I met my husband Len when I was eleven. His sister married my uncle, and I was a bridesmaid…"

("She kicked me!" Len interjects, laughing).

"The very first words I heard Len say were, 'I could have caught another rabbit, Mum, but it got away!' We all used to go in the fields after rabbits! Then we didn't see each other for about four years, but when Mum died, on the day of the funeral, we all came back to stay with Vi and Jim for a few days, at Welnetham where Len was born. So we got together, and in 1957 we married. We had a tiny house, one up and one down, for 3s 6d a week rent, behind the 'Rushbrook Arms'. Later on we had a bungalow, and my brother came and lived with us when he came out of the Army (Dad was dead by then, he died of stomach cancer ten years after Mum). We had one daughter, Angela, and we had a three-bedroom house later on. Now we have two grandsons.

"Drinkstone was full of characters in the old days. There were the twins, Jimmy and Teddy, they used to walk about at night. You'd be out in the dark and suddenly they'd appear! They used to think a lot about the stars, they'd be star-gazing and they'd tell you the war was caused by the stars! Then there was Ma Summers from Hammonds Hall. She owned Church Cottages where I was born. She was a wizened little woman, she sat on about three cushions when she was in her car, one of those little box-like cars. That used to stand under the trees in her over-grown garden. Everything was green, even the brickwork, because there were creepers grow-ing all over it and trees everywhere. It was a really eerie place. She terrified my little brother and sister once. Mother had just told them they could go in the meadows to pick primroses, when she came to the gate and screeched out, 'I can see you! I can see you!' and they rushed back to Mother. We thought she was a witch. She always wore the same long dark clothes. We'd scrump green gooseberries from her old cottages opposite the Church, and she'd lay in wait for us. Those cottages got more and more derelict and in the end she sold them to Mulley's.

"After the war, Captain and Mrs. Wilson lived at The Old Rectory, and Mrs. Gore was in Drinkstone Lodge. There were still some of the Horne family living around the village, Rev. Horne's brother lived in 'Monk's Hoot' where Miss Minns and her mother used to live. Captain Michael Horne lived at Beyton, he married Lavender Ramsay. His sister Patience Horne mar-ried Brigadier Collet-White, and lived at Sicklesmere House. Their daughter was one of the last 'Debs', in 1958.

"We still go over to Drinkstone once a fortnight, to take Auntie Nell Cocksedge to Bingo at the Village Hall. It's nice to see everyone. There's about seven or eight from Drinkstone, and the others come from Woolpit, Rattlesden, Gedding and Felsham.

"I look back on my life now, and I think, 'Gosh, I was fortunate!' My Mum died at forty-two and my Father wasn't much older when he died, but at the time I thought they were quite eld-erly. When I was a child, grannies would be sitting in the corner, they weren't working grannies. Now I think, I've had twenty-five years longer than my mother had."

Chapter Seventeen

SCHOOL AND VILLAGE, 1948 - 1972

SCHOOL

Mrs. Constance Collins moved into the Schoolhouse and became Headmistress in September 1948. Miss Pearson was infant teacher. Mrs. Collins immediately asked for improvements: electric light in School and a bath in the House. Not unreasonable in the year1948! However the Council Houses built in Gedding Road at this time had neither electric lighting nor main drains.

Reading between the lines of Managers' Minutes and Log Book, relationships were uneasy during Mrs. Collins' first years at the School. As time went by she proved to be innovative and loyal. Gradually she and the managers began to work as a team.

One of her first entries in the Log Book was the remark (December 1948): "School was closed at 3.30pm. We were unable to see either to read or write." The hard-pressed managers were finding maintenance costs exorbitant. The first estimate for installing a bath in the House was "excessive". However by 1st January 1949 Mrs. Collins was writing: "Captain Wilson visited the School to inspect bath fitted into house." This bath was tucked under the stairs in the kitchen. It was not plumbed in, (although possibly it was linked to the drains for easy emptying), so it was not the height of luxury or convenience.

There was no tap anywhere in the School. Dinner plates and coffee cups had to be washed up. Maybe the children had warm water for hand-washing, for the Log Book, January 1949, tells us: "Marjorie Underwood accidentally walked into boy carrying kettle of water for washing, scald on leg – dressed with pad – return sent to Office."

In May 1949 Mrs. Collins "applied for a licence for decoration of Schoolhouse", and once again asked for electric light in the School. In June 1949 "Mr. Crease and Mr. Spall called re wiring of school for electric light".

Gardening was still an important subject. On 2nd March 1949 we read: "Mr. Foat gardened with senior boys. Gardening continued in the afternoon to complete planting." One week later "Mr. Foat took boys for gardening lesson 9.30-12.30". On June 17th 1949 produce was carried off to supply the schools' canteen: "Mr. Groves called – took 48 lettuces to canteen."

Mrs. Collins did her best to add interest to the children's days and widen their experience. On 15th July 1949 (her first summer term) we read: "School closed for the day – Educational visit to London – The Tower – Hampton Court Palace and Teddington Lock." She involved parents, managers and others in the life of the School: "A Harvest Festival Service was held in the School at 3.30pm. Managers, parents and friends were invited. Gifts of garden produce sent to St. Mary's Hospital at Bury for use of the aged poor. Five large boxes were taken in by Mrs. Young."

DRINKSTONE BECOMES A "CONTROLLED" SCHOOL

By 1949, the managers had reluctantly asked the L.E.A. to take over the School as one of the growing number of "Controlled Voluntary" Primary Schools. As an Aided Voluntary School, managers had been responsible for finding 20% of capital costs. Now the L.E.A. would be responsible for all costs. The downside was that Religious Education was no longer under Diocesan guidelines. The approved L.E.A. syllabus would be followed (although parents had the right to demand Anglican R.E., and worship must still meet the requirements of the trust deeds). Minutes for November 1949 say "The Proposed Instrument of Management for Drinkstone Voluntary Controlled Primary School was received and approved by the managers." This is the last entry in the earliest book of Minutes.

A new Minute Book was started at the first meeting of managers under the new structure, which took place on August 24th 1950. Rev. Lilley was chairman, and the managers were Messrs. Bland, Barcock and Thurlow, and two women, Mrs. Ramsay, and Mrs Wilson (wife of the Major). Before business commenced the managers were told the Rules for Managers of Controlled Schools. Possibly to comply with these Rules, Minutes of meetings from this date onwards are much more detailed and certain new items are regularly on the Agenda. One of these is a Head teacher's Report. From this we learn Miss Pearson (infant teacher) has transferred to Woolpit School. Attendance at School was good (90%) and 44 of the 52 pupils have the daily milk funded by Government. The boys have gardening instruction once a week, while 8 girls attend Cookery at Woolpit School. 4 boys are in Woolpit cricket team, and 4 in their football team. Special activities included a Concert, and a visit to London. A visit to the Railway is planned for the Autumn Term.

The managers must have felt great relief at seeing repairs carried out by the L.E.A. They requested a lock and key for the coalhouse. They reported no outstanding bills. The managers under the former "Voluntary" structure had paid the small balance of their repair fund into an account opened by the Trustees (rector and churchwardens) for maintenance of the Schoolhouse.

Miss Colclough would teach the infants from September 1950.

The managers set up a Rota for termly visits to the School during school hours. In practice, quite often the designated manager was "unable to visit the School". No doubt they were all busy folk! Rev. Lilley kept his part of the bargain, rarely failing to "take the usual Scripture lesson" and holding regular services in classroom or Church.

At their next meeting, the managers asked the L.E.A. for a new window sash cord, and a new cord and pulley for the flagstaff in the playground (but the L.E.A. had not yet provided the coalhouse lock and key!) Some new L.E.A. furniture was "a great improvement", but they reported "a lot of junk in the cloakroom"! This "junk" included the gardening tools. The managers sent a request for a cycle shed, large enough for storage of tools. Also, disaster! The school clock had stopped. They wrote a letter to the L.E.A. "handing over ownership of the clock to them". Despite this clever move, the clock was to prove a bone of contention for some time.

Mrs. Collins complained that "a few children have left". During her first years several boys found her a hard task-master and played truant. It was probably a case of adjusting to new ways and a new regime, but it seems she related more readily to older girls than to boys or very young pupils. Attendance had been poor owing to mumps and "fear of infection". Pupils were rehearsing for the Rural Schools Music Festival and Mrs. Ironside-Ward was training them in verse speaking.

The bucket toilets were causing problems. The School was cleaned on Friday evenings, yet the buckets were not emptied until Saturday morning! "Mr. Buckle will be asked to empty buckets on Fridays before cleaning"!

At the March 1951 meeting Mrs. Collins reported School numbers down to 44. There had been poor attendance due to illness among infants. "Parents were grumbling about the extra penny on school dinners" but the quality of meals was "very good". There had been sales of garden produce and needlework.

At this meeting there were ominous rumblings about possible closure of the School. Mr. Large, an H.M.I. "forecast that when the Secondary Modern School at Beyton was opened numbers at Drinkstone would probably fall to 30 and only one teacher would be allowed". Mrs. Ramsay assured the meeting that closure was unlikely (she seems to have been the manager representing the County Council). At this time a few more homes were being built in the village, including Council bungalows in Chapel Lane, which might increase pupil numbers.

The Log Book provides plenty of evidence that Mrs. Collins was a resourceful teacher. In January 1951 she wrote: "Miss Colclough absent from school – time-table re-arranged – instead of Art, senior children arranged bowls of evergreens". On May 3rd: "Normal time-table altered to listen to opening cer-emonials of the Festival of Britain". On June 5th: "Senior children enjoyed a nature ramble in search of wild flowers for a competition. Highest number in collection was 60 [different species]." On 8th June: "School closed for Suffolk Show."

On 18th and 19th June there are two fascinating entries: "Nature ramble. Habitat a marshy meadow – over 1,000 orchis maculata collected in 30 minutes for gifts to hospital". (How many orchids were not torn up that day, I wonder? At that date it seems no-one feared they would ever become a rarity). On the following day "the *Bury Free Press* called and took a photo of children and the rook they had reared".

On July 5th "12 senior boys and girls left Drinkstone School at 1.15pm to catch 1.33 bus at Tostock corner to visit the cinema to see "Red Shoes".

Constance Collins was a strict and demanding teacher seeking high standards in every area. After a visit from the School Nurse in June 1951 she sent a note to the mother of one boy "re-length of his hair, his eyes and ears"! She must have been quite alarming to some children and parents.

There were several changes among school staff. In May 1951, "Miss Best took up duty as clerical assistant – 2 afternoons per week…Tuesdays and Fridays (15 hours per month). Mrs. Bradley undertook work of office cleaner – Mr. Buckle retiring – ill health" ("offices" means toilet closets). In July Miss Colclough resigned.

A Managers' Meeting scheduled for July 2nd 1951 was cancelled since only Rev. Lilley and Mr. Thurlow turned up. At the next Managers' Meeting in November 1951, a letter from the Chief Education Officer was read out. He was sending Miss Hunt, a newly trained teacher, to take the infants' class. She was on the County Supply List during her first year of teaching. The managers were assured she would not be placed on the permanent staff of Drinkstone without consultation.

More new furniture arrived, a double desk for the top class, and a dozen table-desks for the infants. Mrs. Wilson, Correspondent, resigned (moving to Thurston). Mr. Clarke of Church Close (the former Almshouses) agreed to replace her.

Mrs. Collins reported 50 children on roll, attendance 90%. Her Reports and Log Book entries provide an interesting account of daily events. Children attended the film "Lorna Doone" in Bury St. Edmunds, and would soon visit the office of the *Bury Free Press*. On December 6th Mr. Groves, the Attendance Officer (formerly known as the Enquiry Officer), called at the School to talk to a boy who had been absent to help at a shoot, receiving 10s for his services! That was a lot of money, very tempting no doubt! Then on 11th "Judith Cocksedge ran splinter deep down finger nail – treated for shock – sent to Hospital by car – Accident form sent to Office". Ouch!

THE VILLAGE

Big changes were underway. Drinkstone Park was to be demolished. In 1949, the *East Anglian Daily Times* ran the headline "Another Suffolk Mansion Goes". The Auction was under Gaze & Son. Fixtures, fittings and fabric were sold for £1,582. The actual shell was sold for £760. An agreement of sale was, to demolish within six months. Items sold included oak panelling, sixty sash windows, sixty panelled and glazed doors, deal and pine floors, chimney pieces, magnificent sawn roof of pitch pine, oak and pine joists, lead, Welsh slates, and thousands of Woolpit bricks.

This must have been a sad day for many people: girls who had been members of the Brownie and Guide packs that met there, men and women who had worked as domestics or labourers, living in the mansion itself or on the estate; gardeners who had cherished the arboretum, greenhouses and fernery that featured in the *Gardeners' Chronicle* years earlier (1884). Many older villagers would remember the fan-tastic fetes and celebrations to which all were invited, the bands, the feasts, the games and races, the auto-mobile club gatherings, and all the flamboyant events of the halcyon days before the two terrible World Wars.

All was not lost; the painting of Park and mansion by Gainsborough would tell the story; and the coach house and stable blocks were left intact, both later converted to charming homes. Garden Cottage (built 1860 and so not as old as the other buildings) was purchased and extended into a gracious home. Two new houses were later built on the land. One had the mansion's potting shed in its garden. The garden of the other contained a remarkable feature – the mausoleum of Joshua Grigby who built the mansion in the 1760s!

At some time in the 1950s, a hapless grazing heifer disappeared down a deep hole in the Park farmlands. In this way, an 18th century Icehouse was re-discovered!

THE SCHOOL

Back at the little School, life went on regardless. By March 1952, 53 children were on roll, attendance was usually 90%, 40 children took milk and 26 had school dinners. The clock sent for repair months ago had not re-appeared. Managers were told "it must take its turn"! Two broken windows were also not repaired. Unfortunately, no managers had visited to see for themselves how the School was running. Mrs. Collins was absent through illness for several weeks in February and March, also in July. Some boys were still rather unsettled, and in May Michael Cocksedge and Gerald Emmett transferred to Rattlesden School. Anthony Lingwood and Alan Bradley both intended to transfer there in September. This all got too much for poor Mrs. Collins, so that on September 17th she wrote in the Log: "Mr. Groves called re transfer – at request of parents – of Michael Read to Rattlesden. I said that I was dead against his transfer from every point of view".

At the Managers' Meeting in July 1952, it was reported that the clock had finally been returned but "it is no good and won't go"! Poor attendance by two boys was reported to Mr. Groves. Mrs. Ramsay had visited the School and found all good except the attendance of some boys, and "the state of the lavatories". Mrs. Collins explained that she had obtained more supplies of disinfectant. Rev. Lilley said Mrs. Wilson would be missed for "her genial presence and sound judgement".

By December 1952, the L.E.A. had promised to supply a new clock. But where was the long-awaited cycle shed, and why were loose roof slates not yet dealt with? The managers agreed to have Miss Hunt on permanent staff. At this date, the managers appointed by County Council were Mr. W. Bland and Major Edward Gosling, while those representing the Parish Council were Messrs. Thurlow and Clarke.

Children took part in a Nativity Pageant at Bury St. Edmunds. There was a Christmas Party for the younger ones. The seniors would hold a dance in the Village Hall in the New Year! (Mrs. Collins certainly tried to make life interesting for her pupils).

Around this time the L.E.A. were considering transferring pupils aged 8 to 10-plus from Hessett School to Drinkstone, to economise on number of staff employed at Hessett while ensuring retention of Headteacher and one assistant at Drinkstone. In fact both Schools remained unchanged for the time being.

During Spring Term 1953 Mrs. Collins was off duty due to illness for some time, "Supply" teachers filling the gap. She reported to managers in February, roll 49, poor attendance due to influenza and measles, two children would sit the 11 plus (we learn later that one did not sit the exam, and the other did not pass). All the pupils took internal "examinations" which were the basis of reports sent to parents. Mrs. Collins took trouble to widen the curriculum and wrote that senior children would visit Wattisfield Potteries to "see pottery professionally made and glazed before their own work is sent there to be fired".

The managers did not agree with all her suggestions. This was Coronation year of Elizabeth II and the Minister of Education had granted 2s per child to all Schools for mementoes or celebrations. Mrs. Collins suggested part should be spent on a visit to the Odeon at Bury, to see the Coronation Film (not many homes had television), the rest spent on "three or four pictures to hang in School as a lasting commemoration". The managers rejected the idea of pictures, preferring to buy "mugs or beakers" for each child. (As a child, I was happy to be presented with a commemorative mug). Later both ideas were shelved in favour of a New Testament for each child (I'm not sure the children would have chosen this!)

In her absence, they rejected Mrs. Collins' proposed summer outing to the East Coast. She had planned to take the children to Oulton Broad, Lowestoft Lighthouse, the coastal defences and Yarmouth Harbour. According to the Log Book the only summer outing was to see the film at the Odeon, although some pupils took part as dancers in an "operatic" by Drinkstone W.I. in Bury St. Edmunds.

Heating was a problem. On 4th March 1953: "Both fires were out when we arrived this morning. Children had games in playground whilst fires were re-lit and rooms got warm." On March 26th: "No fires laid or lit – senior room very chill – children playing in yard until 10am. Senior room fire lit but 1 gallon paraffin bought for stove in infant room". Then on 23rd April: "Fires laid but not lit, rooms very cold. Lavatory buckets not emptied. Note left for cleaner re-fires and buckets".

In June 1953 there are three Log entries connected with the Coronation:

> "1st June – The managers came to school at 3pm and attended presentation of New Testaments to each child – Coronation gift from the L.E.A.
> "2nd June – School closed for the Coronation of Queen Elizabeth II.
> "8th June – 35 children taken to Odeon Theatre, Bury – 9am Coronation Film."

During 1953 the L.E.A. said they could not afford to supply any cycle shed "this year", and there was a worrying visit from Dr. Rae who inspected the school lavatories. He reported they were "the best built but dirtiest in Suffolk"! Mrs. Collins was indignant, though she acknowledged the seat of the infants' closet was "always wet" and there was "scribble on one wall". She wrote in the Log: "Have reported same to cleaner. I don't agree with the findings…. But the coke is somewhat scattered…and I did notice that drains could be cleared and area around dustbins cleaned up. Snow and frost had been prevalent for days".

DRINKSTONE BECOMES A 5–11 PRIMARY SCHOOL

In September 1953 Beyton Secondary Modern School opened. Children aged 13 years and over started in September. Those aged eleven or twelve would join them in Spring / Summer Terms 1954, when all the classrooms were built. The Ministry of Education required managers of schools in Beyton catchment area to pass a Resolution accepting this change. The wording was: "The Managers concur in the arrangements which are now in operation in regard to the senior pupils attending Beyton Secondary Modern School". Drinkstone numbers had been well into the fifties in recent years. Roll would now be much reduced.

I imagine Constance Collins sometimes felt she was ploughing a lonely furrow. There were many staff changes. Miss Hunt resigned in July, transferring to Hadleigh School. Mrs. Clayton, "Supply" teacher, took the infants in September 1953. In December, Mrs. Collins complained about extra washing-up incurred by children eating packed lunches and requested L.E.A. funding to cover this. At the time, there was still no tap in School. Washing up of dinner plates and cutlery was done in a low sink in the cloakroom, the water carried there in buckets and heated over a small paraffin stove. All very inconvenient and dangerous with young children present! There was no wash basin; and if children wanted a drink they had to dip a cup in a bucket near the sink. A visiting manager remarked: "Coke spreading all over yard. Paraffin stove smells objectionable". A letter was sent to the L.E.A.

By March 1954 there were three positive moves from the L.E.A. They hoped to provide "some protection for the children's bicycles and a store for the coke" in the next financial year. Provision for washing up, and replacing the paraffin stove, would be "dealt with in order of priority". A second letter suggested coal etc. could be stored against the wall opposite the girls' toilets if a door and roof were added (this explains the maze of crumbling brick walls behind the building in the 1980s!). Calor gas would replace the paraffin stove (a primus belonging to Mrs. Collins). Soon, wonder of wonders! Workers from the L.E.A. actually arrived to measure up for the coal shed and select a site for the cycle shelter!

The managers wrote to the L.E.A. saying "the dentist had not visited the School for four years". Mrs. Collins reported children had danced in a W.I. concert. She enjoyed teaching dancing; both boys and girls learned traditional country dances.

Mrs. Collins was frequently absent in the Summer Term. She may have been quite stressed by the problems and changes. There were 47 on roll, and the six oldest would transfer to Beyton in September. A calor gas stove had been provided, but no cycle shed or fuel store, and the L.E.A. wrote saying the School Dental Service was "seriously understaffed and it would not be possible to visit all Schools". The Head should therefore "forward requests for treatment to the Health Department in order that appointments may be made". Another job for the teachers!

There was good news on a Scripture Exam taken by five pupils. All passed, two with Credit. Further good news arrived in July: "Mr. Wyatt and the Building Inspector will meet managers on 24th August with regard to supply of piped water to the School". The work was done in November 1954. In March managers wrote: "Water has been laid on from the mains to a stand-pipe in the cloakroom".

Autumn Tern 1954 saw 43 children on roll. Mrs. Collins read the managers a letter from a Chapel Lane resident complaining that "children were paddling in the ditches when they should have been at school". A certain boy had been "very unruly". Worse still, his mother had been "very rude" to Mrs. Collins, and another parent had "a rude interview" with her on the same matter! West Suffolk Education Committee had been consulted, and had made an official visit to the families.

There are hardly any records of serious escapades in the Log or the Minutes. Occasionally a child got into trouble with the police, but generally, mischief such as "paddling in the ditches" was the worst that happened.

During Spring 1955 "attendance was affected by illness and bad weather". A proposed outing to a puppet show was "cancelled because of the railway strike".

Repairs were needed to the cloakroom, and the playground wall was dangerous. There were delays in repairing the wall because the County Architect "could not say who was the owner!" He referred Head and managers to Rev. Snell of Tattingstone for advice. Eventually this wall was mended. Managers met the Architect to consider "the maintenance programme for next year". At last the cycle shed was erected.

An Inspector called in June 1955. H.M.I. reports are confidential; the Copyright is vested in the Controller of H.M. Stationery Office. I obtained permission to reproduce this Report, since it was written fifty years ago and the School no longer exists! It is a commendable Report, on both teachers and pupils:

REPORT BY H.M. INSPECTORS – 6th JUNE 1955
– ON DRINKSTONE PRIMARY SCHOOL, SUFFOLK (WEST)

In September 1954 this became a Primary School and now has 19 children in the Infant and 22 in the Junior Class. The children all live within 2 miles from the school, but they come from a scattered area. There is little village community life for them to share. Their appearance gives the impression of much home care but the docility, especially of the younger children, suggests a lack of experience which is somewhat limiting. The two-roomed school has the usual small space for the Infants and the storage space is further reduced by the use made of it by the school cleaner. The school is due for redecoration, a new floor, a new stove and washing basins. Soft boarding for display in the Infants' room and some shelving would prove a great boon. Arrangements for the midday meal are satisfactory and some twenty children remain for it. The elder ones are responsible and helpful and it is made a pleasant occasion for all of them.

The County Library supplies books for home reading: it is desirable that the school should build up its own collection also.

The Mistress in charge of the Infants is sympathetic and gives the children confidence. She uses their interest in stories and nature to encourage them to draw pictures and to talk. There is a shop to help them with number and a fair supply of simple reading books. The children are making steady progress. It is difficult to get them to think for themselves or to show initiative. The more frequent acting of stories and the use of a greater variety of materials for handwork might encourage more lively and spontaneous effort.

The Head Mistress is in charge of the Juniors. The class contains children of varying ability as was evident when talking to them and looking at their work. The latter indicated systematic and steady progress in the various subjects. Many of the children did not find it easy to maintain a conversation, and it appeared that they, like the Head Mistress, had not yet become accustomed to being without the pupils of senior age. The Head Mistress is very clear about the particular needs and abilities of each child and she expects and obtains from them their best efforts. The pupils enjoy the lessons they all have together – story, singing, dancing and dramatic work. The singing and dancing were particularly well done. The acting needs to be built up from simple beginnings with a view to the children making it as much their own as possible. Language training is particularly needed and, although uphill work, the devices used to assist the children to appreciate words are clearly beneficial; for they enjoyed descriptive passages of story and poetry. The Head Mistress is still adjusting herself to the smaller and younger group of children but she is able and gifted and should have no difficulty in doing this.

In September 1955 the managers held a special meeting to discuss the H.M.I. Report. They commented on the need to run a library at School. There is no real praise for the achievement of the teachers in a changing situation. They passed a Resolution saying "whilst appreciating all the Headmistress is doing to adjust herself to the smaller and younger children yet she has more aptitude for those over eleven years of age".

None of the managers visited during school hours that Summer Term. Around this date, Mrs. Collins produced a kind of brochure, presumably to advertise the School and show that it was doing a good job. There are photographs of the children enjoying outdoor games, doing clay work, painting, sewing and knitting (boys as well!). They look cheerful and busy.

In December 1955 the County Architect agreed to replace the small stove, provide lavatory basins "as soon as possible" (which meant, never!), and do exterior painting and repairs at Easter. Mrs. Collins planned a Christmas party for the children, also dancing displays for Drinkstone Old Folks' Club and Rattlesden W.I.

In the icy February weather of 1956 there was fun, and danger, at playtimes: "Valerie Whiting slipped on a slide – broke small piece of bone from clavicle. Child taken to Dr. Jones. Sent to hospital for x-ray and setting". Afterwards, Mrs. Collins was pleased to receive "a note of grateful thanks from parent of child".

In three consecutive Februarys ('56, '57 and '58) Mrs. Collins mentions the 11-plus exam. In '56 and '57 the School closed on the day of the exam. The entry for 1958 says "Mrs. Wood called to tell me of Richard's ill health and discuss his missing the Grammar Schools' Entrance Exam this Friday". Most years there is no mention of this exam. I know from talking to parents and ex-pupils that in many years, children were entered for it. Vi and Nell Cocksedge between them had ten children, who all took the 11-plus in the years 1947 – 1964. Michael Cocksedge sat the exam two years running because he had been unwell during his first attempt. In these clever families, only one passed (Mary, in 1964). She went to the Grammar School, hated it, and pleaded with her parents until she was allowed to leave!

The Managers' Meeting in March 1956 was cancelled since only Rev. Lilley and Mr. Clark arrived. The meeting was re-arranged for 17th September, with exactly the same result – no quorum, only the rector and Mr. Clark present, meeting cancelled! They finally managed to meet on 23rd October 1956. Mrs. Clayton had resigned in July, and Mrs. Henley was teaching the infants. Captain Michael Horne (descendant of faithful rectors and benefactors) took Major Gosling's place on the Board.

The managers discussed the parlous state of various crumbling walls near the closets and around Mrs. Collins' garden. There were glowing reports of the first-ever individual school photographs of pupils. These and the group photos were thought "excellent". Once again, no managers had visited during Term.

In April 1957 Mrs. Henley resigned and once again an infant teacher was sought, with little success. Miss Bareham, Supply, came for the Summer Term only, replaced in September by Miss Jennifer Clayton, an untrained student wanting teaching experience before her College training. The Autumn Term saw a welcome increase in roll since Hessett School had closed and thirteen new pupils from Hessett arrived each morning by school bus. There were 44 on roll.

An entry in the Log Book for 4th November 1957 is one of my all-time favourites – the story of Mary and the counting bean. What a day of crisis!

"Mary Cocksedge inserted a counting bean in her nose at noon today and we could not dislodge it. Telephones were out of order so Miss Clayton set off to Woolpit on her motor cycle to bring the doctor but the road was flooded. Therefore she went to Beyton where she contacted Mr. Clayton, who allowed Mr. Williams to come and collect Mary and her sister and take them to West Suffolk Hospital with Miss Clayton. There the bean was removed and Mary was safely back in school by 1.45pm".

PE lesson in about 1956-57

1956-57 – Back row: David Cocksedge, Dennis "Sooty" Bradley, Edward Horrex, Mrs Venley, Mrs Collins, Peter Smith, Anthony Bland, Peter Bird. Third row: Richard Wood, Mary Scott, June Lingwood, Ann Clover, Shirley Lark, Sandra Cocksedge, Janet Sturgeon, Rosemary Bird, Robert Irving. Second row: Sylvia Sparkes, Elsie Bradley, Rosemary Horrex, (girl) Scott, Daughter of Mrs Henley, Gillian Sparkes, Linda Palmer. Front row: Nigel Haill, Richard Bradley, Clive Lark, Michael Haill, Jimmy Bird, (boy) Scott.

1958 began with complaints that school milk was not being delivered until 1.15pm or even 3.35pm each day. Then in February heavy snow caused havoc:

"25th February 1958 – Dinner van arrived at 1.30pm – delivery delayed by heavy snow. By 12.30 the children were getting very hungry. Phone out of order so no contact with office or kitchen could be made. Biscuits and cheese were therefore bought from village stores. School bus arrived 2.25pm to take Hessett children home. As it travelled via Drinkstone village all children were sent home".

26th February – "Heavy snow. One child present. Heavy snow falling so child sent home.

"27th February – School closed for one day."

The managers held a meeting in April 1958 at which they observed two minutes' silence in respect for Mrs. Dawson, one of their number who had died unexpectedly. Rev. Lilley said "she had been a very great help to the managers and to the School in many ways, very regular at our meetings. She would be greatly missed". Her husband Mr. Dawson took her place on the Board of Managers.

This Summer Term opened with 48 on roll, and Mrs. Lomax, "uncertificated untrained Supply teacher", in charge of the infants class. The only special event noted was a W. I. Concert at which the children sang. For some reason it was nearly a year before the managers met again, in March 1959, with Mrs. Cocksedge and Mrs. Neave now on the Board. By July Mrs. Lomax had resigned, and Miss Hunt was appointed from September. The children had a day-trip to London to see the Royal Military Tournament. There would be a Concert and Prize-giving at the Village Hall in July.

At the Managers' Meeting in December 1959, Rev. Darwin, the new Rector, was chairman, and the new County Council-appointed Manager was Mrs. Valentine of Lane Farm, Hessett. Mrs. Collins asked for a milk-cooler or fridge since the milk was still always late. Miss Hunt had married and become Mrs. Northeast.

At this meeting the managers were told in no uncertain terms by Mrs. Collins that there was "no such fund as the School Fund"! It seems the cost of prizes presented in July came up, and the managers were astounded to learn that Mrs. Collins had met the £5 deficit incurred out of her own pocket. Why hadn't she just taken the amount from the School Fund? Because there was no School Fund, they were told!

This meeting marks a turning-point in relationships between managers and Head-mistress. Managers had not been fully in touch with the workings of the School. After this date, they appear more appreciative of Mrs. Collins' work and more supportive. They said, next time ask the managers for help.

The L.E.A. were unable to provide a fridge. Fires were still a problem: on 25th February 1960 "Temperature of room 43 degrees. Fire hardly alight – doused in dust. Room smoky and very cold". No wonder Mrs. Collins was often absent with "a slight chill"! At the next meeting, March 1960, the managers offered to pay 13s 4d deficit from the Christmas party. At last, the hoped-for trip to Oulton Broad and Lowestoft was approved. The L.E.A. promised £3 towards the cost of this trip.

The Log Book, May 5th, records: "School closed till Monday – Princess Margaret's wedding May 6th." The milk problem saga continues, and on 31st May: "Milk repeatedly left at gate in spite of many requests for it to be put at back porch. Two bottles punctured by birds and undrinkable." 15th June: "Letter sent to Mr. Apperley re non-delivery of milk on June 1st, and delivery of milk on June 10th when school was closed, and non-collection of empties. Mr. Clarke read the note before it was despatched and will take action himself if no improvement is shown. Rev. Darwin visited school, commented on empty milk bottles and spoke to milkman re- same. Following Monday milk delivered to rear porch and empties gradually removed." It is good to see the mood changing, managers now involving themselves with the day-to-day trivia of school life, and doubtless their support meant a great deal to Mrs. Collins.

In 1960 Mrs. Collins and her children left the Schoolhouse, moving to a cottage in Hessett. She was probably glad to put distance between herself and the pupils and parents, and be less accessible outside School hours. Mr. and Mrs. Alan Bradley moved into the Schoolhouse, later taking over the caretaking and cleaning duties.

By the Summer Term, Mrs. Northeast was gone and Mrs. Lomax was back, as temporary infant teacher. Mr. Clarke, correspondent manager, resigned because he was leaving the district. Mrs. Neave took over as correspondent. The outing to Lowestoft was "successful". An open evening with displays of children's work was held. There was a prize-giving with refreshments, £4 spent on prizes.

In September 1960, there were 30 children on roll. Miss Raynham was in temporary charge of infants.

Managers paid tribute to Mr. Clarke for his "faithful and efficient work" during eight years as correspondent. Mrs. Land joined the Board. (I suspect the more frequent meetings of managers show the influence of the Rev. Maurice Darwin whom I knew personally as a most generous and dedicated priest and pastor.)

Mr. Dawson proposed formation of a "Managers' Fund for Prizes". He paid the deficit arising from the recent open evening and prize-giving. Managers organised a jumble sale to raise funds, and "Mrs Collins was thanked for her kindness in regard to prizes presented on previous occasions".

By the next Managers' Meeting in November 1960, Mr. Dawson had become Treasurer, with a balance of £20 from the jumble sale. £3 was given to Mrs. Collins to buy presents for the children's Christmas party in the Village Hall. In previous years, each child brought food for the party. This year, managers would buy and prepare the food, and pay for the hire of the Hall (£1-2s-6d). Mrs. Collins was ill and unable to attend this meeting.

1961 began with Mrs. Lomax again teaching the infants. The L.E.A. agreed to install an electric heater in the school porch (the cloakroom, where dinner washing-up was done). One child sat for the Grammar School Entrance Exam.

Mrs. Collins was away ill for long periods during Summer Term 1961. The juniors were taught first by Miss Raynham, then by Miss Hailwood. Mrs. Lomax resigned, the infants were taught by Miss Hazlewood. On 31st May the School closed so families could attend the Suffolk Show. On 12th June, "the day the Queen would visit Bury, children would be taken down the lane to watch Her Majesty pass by on the Ipswich Road". An outing to London Zoo took place on June 14th. The L.E.A. contributed £4. Parents were also asked to contribute. There was a Concert and Prize-giving in July. Managers gave £2 towards the cost of prizes. One child won a place at Culford (private) School; another, a place at King Edward's Grammar School in Bury.

No electric wall-heater for the cloakroom had arrived, but there was now a hand wash-basin (just one) in the cloakroom!

In September 1961 Mrs. Proctor was teaching the infants. Those poor infants had so many different teachers, no-one stayed long, and Mrs. Collins was often away ill. There were two new managers, Mrs. Frost and Mrs. Jenkins. For the Christmas party, managers gave Mrs. Collins £3 for presents, Mrs. Valentine gave crackers, and Mr. Dawson bought food with money from the Fund. Rev. Darwin visited regularly to talk to the children.

In Spring Term 1962, both Mrs. Proctor and Mrs. Collins were frequently away ill. A new "supply" teacher, Mrs. Lewis, often took charge. Mrs. Neave resigned as manager because she was leaving the village. No longer did managers remain on the Board for decades, as in John Jewers' time! Mrs. Le Roux was now Correspondent. There was a Summer Open Day for parents. Managers paid for prizes as usual. In June 1962 (too late for winter!) a wall-heater was fitted in the chilly cloakroom.

In September 1962 there were complaints about milk crates of empties left at school, also complaints about "the conditions of the school meals". It's not clear what was wrong, but letters were sent to the L.E.A. In December the County Council Meals Officer visited the School and improvements were made.

The New Year brought familiar weather problems – on 21st January 1963 "no school meal arrived. Biscuits, Ryvita, butter, cheese, drinking chocolate and Ideal Milk purchased from stores and a cold meal with hot drink was supplied to the children. School closed 2.30pm. Drifting snow on all roads."

In March 1963 the County Architect called, promising to install hot water over the sink some time soon! Encouraged by this, the managers resolved to send further letters on "the desirability of having a telephone… and a fire extinguisher".

Money had been raised at a Christmas Entertainment. The managers planned another jumble sale. Both teachers were often ill throughout Spring and Summer Terms. Supply teachers included E. Clayton, E. Allen, and Mrs. Ball. Mrs. Proctor resigned from her post as infant teacher in July 1963. One child had gained Grammar School Entrance. The L.E.A. undertook to repair and paint the School, fit a water heater and install a telephone during the Summer holidays. Maybe the School was at last moving into the 20th century!

In September 1963 Miss Shelton, Supply teacher, took charge of the infants. Roll must have been in the thirties, since 32 took daily milk, and 28 had school dinners. Rev. Darwin moved away; the new rector was Rev. Westbrook.

The Managers' Minutes of a meeting in October 1963 contain a startling comment. A psychologist had been sent by the Education Committee to test the I.Q. of pupils. The Minutes say "the report from the school psychiatrist had proved that 20% of Suffolk children are sub-normal".

Whoever wrote this had first written "psychologist", then thought better of it and scrubbed the word out, writing "psychiatrist" on top. Nobody at the Meeting, not even the Headmistress, appears to have challenged this so-called "proof". I have an uneasy feeling that this view was tacitly held by many people in positions of authority, who expected test results to substantiate this belief.

I remember that when I was a student at Training College, there was general belief that a person's I.Q. or intelligence quotient was an unchangeable part of their make up (rather like eye colour), and that it could be accurately established through certain types of test. Half a century later, researchers, educators and psychologists no longer hold such a simplistic view. By any standards this statement about "Suffolk children" is unjustifiable and derogatory. If widely held at the time, it goes some way towards explaining why the education of country children of labourers was given such low priority. The resourcing of village schools was not regarded as particularly important because the village children would never amount to much! What a sad state of affairs. What a different picture is presented by the descendants of these families, educated in today's schools. They have a huge range of skills and qualifications and go out into the world as well equipped as the children of top professionals.

I felt affronted by this bald declaration of "sub-normality", on behalf of those industrious and able children whose work from 1910-12 and 1929 I had so enjoyed reading. Also, in dozens of conversations with adults born in Drinkstone during the first half of the twentieth century, I have constantly found myself full of admiration at their intelligent and generous attitudes. They have huge wisdom and a fund of knowledge and experience. Clearly they continued learning all their long lives. As children, they must have had enormous potential. I feel ashamed that any such comment should ever have been made.

The same Minutes record that £1-1s was collected from pupils for a leaving present (rose bushes) for Mrs. Proctor. The Managers' Fund paid for children's prizes. The Jumble Sale raised £20-9s-4d. "The helpers had worked very willingly and the schoolchildren had helped by the distribution of notices". The Chairman thanked everyone for their co-operation.

THE VILLAGE

In the year 1963 The Old Rectory was sold. This grand house had been the scene of so much fun and laughter in the old days, when the rector and his wife would throw open their home and garden for choirboys, or Sunday School, or Women's Club, or Young Men's Bible Class, entertaining them to games and races, parties, suppers, and every kind of jollity. The house was described as "a fine Georgian house on the edge of the small picturesque village of Drinkstone", with entrance hall, 3 reception, 5 bedrooms, 2 dressing rooms, 4 bathrooms, domestic offices, a garage and a staff flat. The grounds include a lodge cottage, outbuildings, orchard and walled garden, a well-timbered park and meadowland, a total of 21 acres. Occupies a pleasant high position. Approached by gravel drive and forecourt."

During the 1960s a steady stream of new houses and bungalows began to appear in the village. Green Farm, home of John Jewers, and then of Captain Horne, was sold in 1959 to Mr. and Mrs. Land. Some of the land and tied cottages were also sold. On a meadow, formerly Green Farm land, twelve new bungalows were built. This new road was aptly named "Green Close". A few more houses and bungalows appeared in Cross Street, at least eight more in Rattlesden Road, two in Park Road, and a scattering in Beyton Road and Woolpit Road. These would bring a few more pupils to the little School.

THE SCHOOL

At last, in March 1964, came news of the permanent appointment of a teacher of infants ready to really become part of the school and stay for years rather than weeks. The L.E.A. asked the managers to approve the transfer of Mrs. Kozlowski from Thurston to Drinkstone School. She had already been interviewed by Mrs. Collins. Everyone was in favour, and Miss Shelton, Supply, was thanked for her "much appreciated" work.

The L.E.A. asked for an extra payment from all Church Schools towards Insurance costs. The managers agreed to pay "a few shillings each year". The first payment, 7s, was sent in June. Mrs. Frost of Hessett resigned from the Board. Roll was 31 pupils.

In September 1964, a letter from Hessett parents caused concern. They had written to the L.E.A. requesting that their children should attend Beyton School rather than Drinkstone. Mrs. Valentine, a manager from Hessett parish, said she had talked with these parents "and gathered that they were worried about sanitation arrangements at the School". Mrs. Collins said there had been no cleansing fluid for the lavatories and they were in "an unpleasant condition on the day of the parents' visit to School – a hot summer's day". There had been a delay of some weeks in delivery of Elsinol.

The matter was reported to the Chief Education Officer. Probably this incident prompted the managers to ask the L.E.A. about the possibility of having a septic tank. They requested a survey. They were informed the cost would be between £300-£400, and the matter never went any further.

1965 began with 32 children on roll. Mr. Calthrop had joined the managers. The children enjoyed special visits, first to see a puppet show, and later to explore Grimes Graves in Norfolk. They took part in a Singing Festival, and in the Autumn Term attended special events commemorating St Edmund's Day and the signing of the Magna Carta. The infants visited the Abbey Gardens and ruins in Bury St. Edmunds, while the juniors visited the Cathedral, St. Mary's Church, the Guildhall and the Abbey ruins. "The School closed on 22nd October for a holiday in honour of the Magna Carta and all it stands for."

This was another year of poor health for Mrs. Collins, and Supply teachers Mrs. Catchpole and Mrs. Kay were often called in to take her class. The L.E.A. funded improvements to the school playground. The managers kept up their support and fund-raising efforts. In February 1966 Mrs. Land held a coffee morning and raised £8-3s-10d for prizes and parties at the School. At this date there were only 25 pupils.

In June two students from London came to work with the children. Pupil numbers had increased to 34. For some reason the managers didn't meet for a whole twelve months, their next meeting being May 1967, when they discussed repairs to the water heater, finally carried out "after considerable delay and inconvenience".

In February 1967 there was a bit of excitement when "John Irving tripped over hummock of grass in meadow – ricked ankle rather badly. 3pm very swollen so I took him to Hospital". Mrs. Collins took John to the hospital for two follow-up visits, on 3rd and 8th of March. After their third visit she was able to write "ankle OK."

I imagine Mrs. Collins herself was in more robust health in 1967 since she organised a trip to Belgium and Holland for 15 pupils! This was possibly the whole of her class (or at least, all those whose parents were able to pay, and happy for them to go). The children were away from May 28th until June 1st – presumably the whole of a school week. This was an extremely enterprising venture for the 1960s in a small village school, and this time the managers offered no criticisms, but approved the visit and her suggestion that a prize should be given "to the pupil giving the best account of the holiday". Mrs. Valentine offered to donate this prize.

In the Autumn Term 1967 Miss McGregor joined the Board as representative for Hessett. There were 8 children on roll from Hessett, 20 from Drinkstone. The School roof was a cause for concern, roof tiles were slipping down and there were fears that they might fall on the children. The Log Book states, 29th September: "Mr. Nunn completed the safety wire fixed around the school to catch falling slates. The nails holding the slates are rotten and the slates dangerous and always needing repair."

In November the managers organised a jumble sale with produce, teas and cakes, to boost their Fund. By February 1968 they decided to try other methods – a box was placed in School whenever a Prize Giving was held, in the hope that parents might contribute. They wrote to the L.E.A. asking for a grant towards the cost of prizes (this was turned down). Each manager gave 10s to the Fund. Pupil numbers were steady at 31/32, although one day in September the village was flooded, only 13 children were present, and no school meals arrived. Familiar weather problems occurred in the New Year – "February 11th 1969, heavy snow. School closed at 12.30pm after school meal had been served."

THE VILLAGE

In October 1968 the *Evening Star* put Drinkstone on the map with an article about the post mill, entitled "Big Sails Keep Turning". A photograph showed Mr. Wilfred Clover climbing the ladder up to his mill. The article says:

> "With the help of a gust of wind and a little corn, one of the oldest post windmills in the country was grinding away merrily at Drinkstone in West Suffolk this week, as it has done since the 17th century. And working in the mill – which he has done all his life – is 61 year old Mr. Wilfred Clover, whose great-great grandfather Mr. Samuel Clover bought Drinkstone mill in 1760.
>
> "Mr. Wilfred Clover said he was sure his mill was the only post mill working in East Anglia. The only other one he knew of was Pakenham mill which is a tower mill. Now, says Mr. Clover, the mill is only a hobby, and more a liability than an asset. But he recalls the old days when he and his father, Daniel, were working from seven in the morning until eleven at night. They would be out in the morning collecting grain from local farmers and returning it the same day. 'At one time we had about five men working at the mill,' said Mr. Clover. 'During the 1930s I can remember spending many a winter's evening grinding by candlelight. The mill – on an average – would grind about 60 cwt of grain in a day.'
>
> Although Mr. Clover has made many repairs to the mill, the timber is all original. The woodwork, which is all well-seasoned oak, has not been repaired. Mr. Clover explained that of the four sails on the mill, two were cloth sails and two shutter sails. The cloth sails were rolled tighter if the wind became stronger. The corn is ground by two pairs of stones, the head stones and the tail stones. The heaviest weighs about a ton. When the corn begins to run out, a bell rings to warn the mill keeper to stop the stones making contact."

THE SCHOOL

It is easy to get side-tracked when looking through the School Log Book. Some names recur more than others, and I noticed a certain Mrs. Haill who helped with school dinners was mentioned over and over again. Reading these entries it seemed that she and her children were rather unlucky healthwise, all the "Haill" entries relating to absence through illness. I first noticed her name in 1955, when on February 14th she was absent because her son was taken to hospital. She was absent in order to visit him on February 23rd. Then on March 23rd she was once again "absent – took son to hospital", and exactly the same reason for her absence was given on April 4th. Then in 1962 Mrs. Haill was absent to visit the hospital again, but this time the patient was her daughter! Among entries for 1963 I found "10th June – Keith Haill tripped while running in the meadow and hurt his shoulder. Mrs. Proctor took him home in her car with a suspected broken collar bone. 11th June – Mrs. Haill confirmed Keith was suffering from a broken collar bone. Report sent to office".

Poor Mrs. Haill! In 1967 it all started again. She herself was absent no less then seven times in the summer term to visit the dentist, and once for "illness – hospital". Was there ever such an unlucky family?

During the late 1960s the managers visited the School regularly. There were new County Council-appointed managers, Mrs. E. Gunnett and Brigadier Wight.

In 1969 there was depressing news. A letter dated 14th April from West Suffolk Education Committee said that their Education Sub-Committee "recommends that Drinkstone School be permanently closed" and they "have written to the Under-Secretary of State at the Department of Education for procedures to be put in place (Public Notices of Intention etc – two months for objections)." At the same time Rev. Westbrook, who had been acting as correspondent, announced he was leaving the village. A huge party from the Education Department met with the managers to view the School – 22 visitors, 31 pupils!

DRINKSTONE BECOMES A 5 - 9 FIRST SCHOOL

In 1970 numbers increased despite the ominous rumblings! There were 37 pupils. February brought details of the proposed Comprehensive three-tier system:

In September 1971 Beyton School would become a "Middle School".

In September 1972 "Thurston Upper School" for pupils over fourteen would open.

In September 1973 Drinkstone children aged ten and over would transfer to Beyton Middle.

The daily business of school life carried on regardless. There were always plenty of distractions and small excitements, such as Fire Drill in January 1970 – "Fire Drill carried out – Exit No. 1, both classes out to corner of playground away from school. Also Exit 2 – infants passed through window into playground, bigger children through window from small room". Sounds like fun!

THE VILLAGE

Drinkstone village was seen by millions of television viewers in 1970. Once again, the reason for fame was the post mill. In July, the *Star* contained two photos, the caption under the first reading – "Captain Mainwaring, played by Arthur Lowe, pictured during filming for 'Dads' Army' at Drinkstone Mill."

The second photo shows a startling scene – a man clings desperately to the turning sails of a windmill. Underneath are the words:

"Lance-Corporal Jones (Clive Dunn) being filmed clinging to the sails of Drinkstone Mill. There was quite a shock in store for anyone glancing towards Drinkstone windmill... from the nearby A45 Bury to Stowmarket road it looked as if a man was clinging to one of the sails spinning round. But no-one need have run to the nearest telephone to dial the fire-brigade since it was all part of a stunt set up by a T.V. crew filming an instalment of the BBC series 'Dads' Army'. The figure on the sail was, in fact, a dummy representing one of the stars of the series, Clive Dunn, who was supposed to be trapped on the sail."

So why was Drinkstone mill chosen? I think, because the two cloth sails needed adjustment by hand, Drinkstone post mill had unusually low sails, which can be reached from the ground for furling, and can be made to turn slowly. I'm sure this event was the talk of the School and featured in many a "News" diary.

Around this date, the *Bury Free Press* published a feature on the village. The writer described Drinkstone as "a green and pleasant place. Its houses, Church, School and shop nestle among trees, gardens and fields... resulting in an effortless harmony of what man has built with what nature has provided". The village was described as three distinct areas, Street, Green, and Park. The Street had no new houses at that date. Church Cottage is described as "thatched and pretty as a picture, one of the oldest in the village. It is three cottages in one, and is full of beams, and interesting nooks and crannies." At the time, owners Mr. and Mrs. Harold Scroxton ran the Post Office and general stores there.

The Old Almshouses, then known as "Church Close", is described as "six Tudor cottages in one". It was the home of Brigadier and Mrs. M. Jenkins, and was in the process of being re-thatched with reed.

The School, having 42 children from Drinkstone and Hessett, "is faced with eventual closure... it is impossible to install modern sanitation there" (not true, it was to prove difficult and expensive but possible!) "Mrs. Collins, Headmistress, says 'numbers are on the increase... there are plenty of opportunities for the children to get individual attention ...which is the great strength of the small village School'.

Of course, there is a picture of the post mill – "one of the few fully-operational mills left in this country", still being worked occasionally "as a hobby". Miss Wynifred Clover was living in Mill House and was organist at All Saints. Her brother Wilfred and his wife were living at Windmill Bungalow.

The article describes The Park and its lake as "idyllic", and says "Mr. and Mrs. Blewitt Robinson of Garden Cottage, Drinkstone Park, fell in love with their home at first sight. The Mansion was demolished after the Second World War, and now only a few reminders of past glories remain, among them stately trees and the impressive walled garden of the cottage".

The section on Drinkstone Green mentions "the new estate of chalet bungalows in Green Close" and "several new houses in Rattlesden Road, where there is also a shop run by Mr. and Mrs. W. Cooper". The Cherry Tree was going strong, but the Chapel had closed. Moving on to Garden House Farm, a photo shows "Mr. Fred Barcock in the office of his sixteen-acre nursery, planning gardens for his customers". Mr. Barcock, a former tea-planter in Malaysia, bought the Farm in 1932, and the family lived there until 1991. There is a very informative paragraph on Drinkstone House, then the home of Mr. and Mrs. Vansittart – "it is on the site of a lath and plaster house existing in the reign of Queen Elizabeth I. It was faced with Woolpit white bricks in the Georgian period." After a fire, it was "rebuilt in a much smaller form using cleaned bricks from the burnt-out original. Mr. Vansittart breeds British Landrace pigs… and has a herd of pure Norwegian Landrace". A photograph shows Michael Cocksedge "keeping a careful eye on one-day old Landrace piglets. A Grade II Listed, 300-yard long avenue of lime trees, is thought to mark the drive to the ancient house."

At Rookery Farm, Mr. Ben Dunning was also keeping pigs, but with less public approval since his was apparently a particularly smelly farmyard!

At this date, the W.I. was very strong, having recently "won the West Suffolk Women's Institute Rounders League, and a Darts League shield". The president was Mrs. Edna Gunnett of Chesil Cottage, Cross Street, who said "I never want to live in a town again". Her two children attended Drinkstone School, and her husband was Clerk of the Parish Council. "Raymond Bland of Whitefield House, whose family has long connections with the parish, going back at least until the 1800s" was Chairman.

Altogether, the village was given a very positive public image in this article.

THE SCHOOL

By 1971 pupil numbers had increased to 42. Mrs. Collins remained optimistic that closure would not take place. At Managers Meetings she said new classroom cupboards and a Staff Room were needed. Locally, there were rumours that a site for Travellers might be set up at Rookery Farm so that far from closing, the School might be enlarged! In November 1971 came "an Inspection of the fabric of the House".

On April 19th 1972 Mrs. Wendy Collins (wife of Constance Collins' son Geoffrey) was appointed Ancillary Helper to the infants, a post she held for the next 14 years. No one was acting as if closure would really take place. In October 1972 a letter to managers said School Closure was "Scheduled on completion of alternative accommodation". The managers replied: "It would be very unfair for pupils to be transferred to any other school before provision of a new Primary at Beyton. It was regretted that it should be necessary to close any village school of a reasonable size."

The managers were surprised to learn that Mrs. Collins had sent a letter of resignation to the Education Office. She must by now have been of retirement age. She was to leave on October 20th. Miss Raynham was to take over as temporary Headmistress. Mrs. Kozlowski remained as Infant teacher. The Minutes record: "The Chairman voiced the thanks of the managers to the Headmistress for her almost 25 years service to the School and invited her to a small presentation on Thursday October 19th at 7.30pm."

Constance Collins was the longest serving Headteacher in the history of Drinkstone School, with Ruth Gobbitt a close second. Both left their indelible mark in the memories of many a pupil and parent.

One of the council bungalows built in the 1950s. The village now has between 40-50 bungalows (mostly privately built after 1950).

Council houses, Gedding Road, built in 1947; many are now privately owned.

Southernwood, Rattlesden Road, built in 1974, one of dozens of new houses constructed in the village since the 1950s.

Ivy Cottage, Rattlesden Road, was the White Horse Beer House.

Fyfers, Rattlesden Road – 15th century.

The Gables, Rattlesden Road – built circa 1600.

Green Farm, Rattlesden Road – built circa 1500. Home of "John Jewers Junior" 1892-1951, then of Captain Michael Horne 1951-1959.

Potash Cottage, Rattlesden Road

Brookside, Chapel Lane.

Bellrod, Chapel Lane – built circa 1800.

Rear view of "Haverigg", converted to a residence circa 1950 from part of the coach house and stable block of Drinkstone Park – a mansion built in 1760 and demolished in 1949.

Park House, built as stables and coach house to Park Mansion in 1760.

Above and below:
Elm Tree Cottage, Gedding Road, built in the 14th or 15th century. Was a shop selling arts and crafts in the 1980s. In the early 20th century it was divided into two cottages, and was then the home of 'The Twins', Teddy and Jimmy.

Above and below:
The Old Almshouses, built in the 17th century as an L-shaped block of six dwellings. Bought by the Rev. Horne in 1870 for use as almshouses and refurbished in 1949. When the cottage nearest The Street was demolished a huge brick chimney stack was revealed at one end.

Home Farm viewed from across the pond where Drinkstone School pupils went pond-dipping in the 1980s. A meadow belonging to Home Farm opposite the school was used at playtimes until the 1970s, when it was sold and three houses were built on it.

Bridge Farmhouse/old tithe barn in The Street. Sold to the owners of The Old Rectory after the death of Douglas Bland in 2003 and now called Tithe Barn Farmhouse.

The Blacksmith's Cottage, The Street, built in the 16th century. Grade II Listed.

Church Cottage, formerly a shop and general store, built 15th-16th century.

Stone Cottage, Park Road, home of Gerald Mayes since the 1930s.

Marsh Green Cottage, originally used by labourers at Burts Farm as a tied cottage.
Built in the 15th or 16th century.

Above and below:
Drinkstone Lodge, The Street, built circa 1650. For many years members
of the Horne family lived there.

Chapter Eighteen

PERSONAL STORIES
Michael Smith, Betty Blumfield, Alan Bradley, Margaret Plummer, Dennis Bradley, Richard and Virginia Bradley, Violet Cocksedge, Judy Frost, Wendy Collins

---

MICHAEL AND BETTY

Michael and Betty are the children of Tom Smith of Chapel Lane, whose story is in Chapter 11. Both attended Drinkstone School, it was the only School they ever knew. Neither really enjoyed their school-days. They endured the experience philosophically, and looking back, both remember some good and useful experiences. Michael is the older of the two. Now retired, he lives in Elmswell, and like his sister he regularly visits Drinkstone to help his father, now in his nineties.

MICHAEL SMITH

"I was born 1937, in Drinkstone. We moved to 14, Council Houses, Gedding Road, within a few weeks of me being born. I'm the oldest, Betty's a year younger.

"I hated school, more or less from the word go. I got on all right with the other children, and with the teachers. They were Miss Jackson and Mrs. Collins. I kept in touch with Mrs. Collins and her son Geoffrey. I knew Geoffrey right to the time he died. But I didn't like being restricted indoors all day. Playtime was great fun, we had the run of both the meadows opposite the School (where the houses are now). We'd play football, and chase the girls, annoy them probably!

"There were some big families went to the School in those days – Cocksedges, Nunns, Mertons... I was always keen on sports. I played for the village football and cricket teams, later I played for Rattlesden. I enjoyed tennis. Now I'm reduced to the old man's game – bowls! I've had two operations for arthritis in my ankle. I couldn't walk, it was so painful. But luckily I could drive. I'm divorced now, I'm quite happy on my own. My oldest son Martin lives at Finningham, Andrew's at home with his mother, and Richard's recently married, he's living at Thetford.

"I didn't have problems at School, it's just that I was much happier messing about in the fields with my Dad. He worked at Hill Farm as a horseman. As I got older I used to lead the horses, using a horse-drawn hoe between the sugar-beet rows. Then I'd lead the horses home. I left School when I was fifteen. I was one of the few of my age who worked with horses after they left. I worked for Rev. Blencowe at Meade Farm. He was a director of Greene King in Bury. I don't think he ever worked as a parson. He was a gentleman farmer, an eccentric. He wouldn't cut any hedges or trees. His house was surrounded with them, that lane to Tostock

Working with horses

was all arched over and shady with trees. He'd walk about with an old pulp sack or corn sack over his shoulders.

"I was one of the last National Servicemen. I went in at eighteen, I was posted to basic training at Catterick, then to B.O.A.R. in Osnabruck, Germany. That's still a garrison town, I think. I was in the Armoured Corps, I was allotted to C Squadron, HQ Squad. When I got there I marched up in front of the Squadron Leader. He didn't look up from his papers. This is how the conversation went-

"He just said: 'Trooper Smith?'

"I said: 'Yes sir!'

"'I see you come from Drinkstone!'

"'Yes sir!"

"'Well, I come from Drinkstone originally!'

"He was Major Oliver Horne from The Rectory! His father was rector of Drinkstone and my Mum had been in service there. From that day on I couldn't do no wrong! When he came out, he opened an antique shop in Long Melford.

"I signed on as a three-year Regular. I got a little more money that way, and I came out with two stripes. I often regretted not staying in the army. You had to have two trades. I got Driver Grade One, Signaller Grade Two and Gunner Grade Two. Every trade you passed was worth a few shillings extra. We'd go on training schemes, five or six weeks long, in different parts of Germany.

"I was in the army during the Suez crisis. I'd just got home on leave on the Friday, and I was called to report to Liverpool Street on the Sunday night! But I didn't bother going to London, I went straight to Harwich. The lorries and tanks were all loaded up ready to go to Suez but we never did go. We were on stand-by for three weeks! After that I came home and finished my leave.

"I came home two or three times a year escorting prisoners to Colchester. I got a few extra days of leave that way. National Service makes a man of you, gets you away from mother's apron strings. If I'd stopped at home I'd probably have worked on the land all my life like my Dad – though it never did him no harm. There wouldn't be half so much trouble in this coun-

try if they'd kept up the National Service – even if it was only for one year. That was the worst thing they ever did, stopping it.

"I came home and went into civil engineering with T. C. Stewart, Bury St. Edmunds. We were building at I.C.I. eight years. I was a plant driver, being a tank driver was a good introduction for that! Then I set up my own plant business.

"I still go over to Drinkstone once or twice a week to see my Dad. He had a hard time with Mother's illness, it wore him out worrying about her and caring for her. But he still comes out with stories about his life that I've never heard before."

BETTY BLUMFIELD

Betty (née Smith) is now a widow and lives in Great Barton. She was born in July 1938 at number 14, Council Houses, Gedding Road – the first council house ever built in Drinkstone, Here is Betty's story:

"I can remember a long way back, right back when I was three years old. I can put a date to my first memories, because I remember sitting on my Nanna's bed, talking to her, and she died when I was three. She was Nanna Bullett, my Mother's mother, and she lived at Green Farm, Hessett. I remember the day she died, my uncle Fred took me out of the house to go for a walk with him so I wouldn't see what was happening.

"I started at the School in 1943. Michael's 16 months older than me, so he was already there. Mum walked with us at first, you walked everywhere then, until you could afford a bicycle. We only ever had second-hand bikes but we didn't mind that, we were just so glad to have any kind of bike. It was a long walk for us, our house was just to the right of Cherry Tree Lane, and our neighbours each side were Mr. and Mrs. Rose, and Mr. and Mrs. Brinkley.

"Miss Stiff from Norton was infant teacher when I started at the School, and I can just remember Mrs. Winsall being in the top class, but she never taught me. I went up to the top class when I was about nine, and Mrs. Collins was my teacher from then until I left at fifteen. Miss Pearson came later on, to teach the infants, by then I was with Mrs. Collins. Although I didn't really like School, and I was glad when I left, I did all right. I just didn't get on with Mrs. Collins really. But I liked doing essays and reading and English. I didn't like arithmetic, and yet when I left School I went to work at Plumpton's Draper's shop in Bury St. Edmunds (it's Palmer's now). I did a five-year apprenticeship there, with hardly any pay, and I coped all right with the money.

"At School, I loved needlework and knitting. We made clothes, we had one or two machines and once I put the needle through my finger, I'll never forget that! We did a lot of country dancing and I liked that as well. We made our own dance costumes in School. I had a white blouse (probably made by Mum) with coloured ribbons which we stitched on ourselves. We made black dirndl skirts and stitched coloured ribbons all around. We used to go to different fetes in the villages round about to dance, with Mrs. Collins in charge – that was her way! Thinking back now, she did a lot for us, but at the time I didn't enjoy it. She'd come along with the ruler and she'd soon hit you on the hand if she didn't like what you were doing. We never had to answer back if we didn't agree with what she was saying. But although she was quite strict she did a lot with us, like taking us to London. I never went to London with my parents, we hadn't got money for that. But Mrs. Collins would take us all, it was the highlight of the year for us. I think Mrs. Collins came from Teddington, and when we went on our trips to London we used to meet up with her elderly mother. I remember we went to Hampton Court, and once we went in a boat on the Thames. She took us to Kew Gardens and the Tower of London as well.

"When we were older, we girls would cycle to Rattlesden Village Hall on a Friday, to do domestic science with Miss Taylor. I can see that woman now, she was a spinster, and was she strict! She was so old-fashioned. We'd be about a dozen girls, six from Woolpit and six from Drinkstone. That Village Hall was set up, one half like a kitchen, the other half like a sitting-room. We'd cook a dinner in the morning, then we'd eat it. In the afternoon we made cakes, to take home – but there'd not be much left by the time we got there, we'd be nibbling them all the way! Mum used to say, 'Bring it home this week', but we'd be walking up Rattlesden Hill

pushing our bikes, and we'd say, 'Go on, just have a little taste...' and there was never much left!

"We'd learn how to keep a house clean, polishing everything. Miss Taylor would come along and test for dust with her finger. If it wasn't good enough we had to do it all over again. It didn't matter if it was rain or snow, we still cycled to Rattlesden every Friday. You didn't say 'no' in those days, you had to do as you were told.

"After I left School I worked at the shop in Bury St. Edmunds, then in 1960 I married Tony Blumfield. He was from Rougham, his father was a policeman. Tony was a builder, he was a person who'd help anyone, ever so kind. My Mother thought the world of him. At first we lived with his mother, at the Old Police Station in Rougham. We bought this piece of land by the woods in Great Barton, and built this bungalow ourselves. It took about a year. Every evening and every week-end, we'd load up the motor-bike. We'd have all sorts of things tied on the back! After we moved into the bungalow, we went on extending it year by year – I was the labourer!

"We had two children, Sarah and Adrian. They played in the woods all the time, they grew up there and that's where I'd walk the dog. People are afraid to let children play alone there now, it's a different world. Sarah and Adrian went to Great Barton Primary, then Ixworth Middle, then Thurston Upper School. They got on really well. Sarah worked at Greene and Greene's, starting as a junior. She had to walk all around Bury St. Edmunds delivering letters. She was always saying, 'Mum, I need new shoes!' She became a Conveyancing Secretary; she stayed there until she had her son Kieran. He's three and a half now. Their little daughter Asha Jade was born in 2004.

"Adrian's had a lot of jobs and some bad luck, he's been made redundant several times. He trained as an electrician, he's a Jack-of-all-Trades a bit like his Dad. He can turn his hand to anything. We're all the same, we never say we can't do a thing. We have a go. Adrian worked for a Security Firm, which closed down. Then he was taxiing at Newmarket, he was always having to move prisoners so I used to worry about him. He worked in printing but was made redundant. He had his own business, in security, at one time. Now he's working in computers. He's a bell-ringer, he's done that since he was seven years old, he's very keen. He's got two sons, Aaron and Alex.

"My Tony had cancer and he went through four years of treatment. Then just when he was getting over that he died of a heart-attack, twelve years ago. He was a lovely man. I still go to work, I couldn't just stay at home alone all day, and I visit my Dad several times a week to clean up and cook for him and do his shopping. I've got friends, and my children and grand-children, and I see quite a lot of my brother now."

ALAN BRADLEY

Alan and his family were the last people to live in the Schoolhouse. Since the death of his wife seven years ago, he has lived alone at Elmswell. Many members of "the Bradley clan" live within easy visiting distance, and his two sons, three grandchildren, and many friends, keep well in touch. Photos of his family hang in his home. Recently retired, and with some heart and circulation problems, he takes life easily, but copes well on his own.

This is his story:

"I was born in Stoke Bridge Street, Ipswich, on November 18th 1939. Our home was a tied cottage right near the docks. The docks were a target in the war, so when my father joined the R.A.F. in the early Forties, my mother and I went to live with her mother (my Gran) in Drinkstone. My mother was born Phyllis Robinson, she went to Drinkstone School as a child. She told me that Miss Minns, the infant teacher, would sometimes give children the cane. But before the end of the school day, Miss Minns would go across to the shop that was beyond the Church, to buy an orange and a handkerchief for any children she had punished, hoping that

would stop them from complaining to their parents!

"My father lived at Hessett, in one of the thatched cottages known as 'The Wash'. The Wash was a river that ran alongside Hessett Street, in front of the row of cottages. It was more like a rough track than a road, and those cottages are gone now. My mother and her sister Betty (who was caretaker of the School before me) married two Bradley brothers, Herbert (my Dad) and his brother Alfred (Dennis's father).

"When my Dad came out of the services, he got a job on a farm in Drinkstone. He never talked about his war-time experiences. We were lucky, we were given a council house in Drinkstone. I was the eldest in our family. After me came Margaret, Dot, Richard and Elsie. My sisters Dot and Elsie did the same as my Mum and Dad – they married two brothers! So they both became Mrs. Peck. Dot lives at Thurston, and Elsie lives at Woolpit, and works at the school with the youngest children. Margaret, who's now Mrs. Plummer, lives in Stott's Cottage, Cross Street, Drinkstone. My brother Richard married Virginia Woods, who went to Drinkstone School and was one of the very few children who passed the 11-plus. They live at Gedding now.

"Well, I'll tell you about my schooldays. I didn't really enjoy School, I didn't get on with the Headteacher, Mrs. Collins. To be honest, boys were less important to her than girls, and she had her favourites. If you didn't happen to fit in with her way of thinking, it was tough! If you did well in your education, she had all the time in the world for you. But if you found the work hard, you were ignored or pushed to one side. She was a strange lady, there was more than one side to her. I think she did her best for us, in her way. I remember the trips she took us on. We went to London, to Kew Gardens and Hampton Court, and up the Thames on a boat.

"At the School, we had assembly first thing in the morning, outside because there wasn't room for everyone to be together inside the School. The partition between the classrooms was hardly ever opened in those days. So if it rained, we missed assembly. There was a little hole in the wall, 'the loop', between the kitchen of the Schoolhouse and the big classroom. Mrs. Collins would send her favourites round to the house to make her coffee. They'd pass the coffee and biscuits to her, through 'the loop'.

"Really I think Mrs. Collins should have been a menagerie keeper, not a teacher, because that place was full of animals. She had ducks, hens and geese, and in the classroom there'd be her two dogs, asleep under her desk. There were cats, they had their kittens in the school cupboards among the school books! And she had a pet jackdaw that used to fly around the place. Once it was flying around and it messed on my work, and I tried to rub my book clean and that just made it look worse. So then I got the ruler from Mrs. Collins for having an untidy book. In the end someone shot the jackdaw and Mrs. Collins wasn't too pleased!

"The animals were very important to her. In the mornings when we got to School, if some of her ducks had gone missing, we boys would get sent to look for them in all the local ponds to bring them back. But if we found them, we didn't bring them back! We fed them instead, because if they were still missing the next day we'd get another morning off School! I skived off a lot. One or two afternoons a week, the older boys would walk to Woolpit School, across the fields, to play football or cricket. We didn't have sports at Drinkstone although we were allowed to play on Thurlow's meadow across the road at playtimes. Anyway, about a dozen of us would set off walking and there was no teacher with us. At the end of the afternoon, we were meant to walk back to Drinkstone and report at School before we could go home. Well, I remember one time, Anthony Lingwood and me decided to give the football a miss. We went off moorhen-nesting, to get eggs for our tea. All the boys used to go birds' nesting in those days, it was a hobby, we had collections and we swapped eggs with each other.

"There was an Attendance Officer who'd come to find out about any boys who didn't arrive at Woolpit. I remember him chasing me and Anthony in his little car! We called him 'the kid-catcher'. Mrs. Collins couldn't cope with me and Anthony, and when I was eleven or twelve, we got expelled and sent to Rattlesden School. My parents didn't mind, they knew the Bradleys weren't at the top of Mrs. Collins' list of friends! I liked it better at Rattlesden. A teacher called Mr. Foat taught us agriculture and gardening. That was something we hadn't done before and *it interested us. We did metalwork and woodwork with Mr. Cass and I enjoyed that too. Beyton Secondary Modern School opened just before I got to school-leaving age, I had just one term there. Some of the teachers from the small schools transferred to Beyton, so Mr. Cass taught us metalwork and woodwork there as well. I remember Beyton School amazed us, we just couldn't comprehend the size of the place and the number of people, we'd never seen anything like it before.*

"When I left School, my father said to me, 'You need to have a trade.' So I went to J.A. Deacon electricians in Rattlesden, as an apprentice. I got one day off a week to train at college at Bury St. Edmunds. That's when I first realised my education had been pretty basic. When they talked about fractions, and decimals, and algebra, and Ohm's Law, I found myself completely at a loss. I thought, 'Whatever are they talking about?' Really, I had only been taught to read and spell, add up and take away. At School I always looked forward to leaving and going to work. That was something new to look forward to, a big adventure.

"One of the first jobs I did as an electrician was wiring up a new bungalow for Mr. Cass, my teacher from Rattlesden and Beyton! In those days, you kept meeting the same people everywhere. Villages were a very close community. Every lunch-time, and straight after school, Mr. Cass would come to the bungalow to check my work. He'd get the spirit-level out and check everything I'd done to see that it was right.

"When I was twenty-two I married Gwendoline (Turner) from Haughley. We were looking for somewhere to live, and I heard that the Schoolhouse was empty. Mrs. Collins had moved to a cottage in 'The Wash' at Hessett. (Later she moved to Rattlesden, and after that to a farmhouse at Norton with her son Geoff. One of his sons, Keith, lives here in Elmswell now). So I negotiated with the rector, Rev. Darwin, who worked in Drinkstone and Tostock. He gave us the Schoolhouse to live in, at about five shillings a month. At that time my Aunt Betty and her husband were still doing the cleaning and caretaking, but after a while they decided enough was enough. As someone to work for, Mrs. Collins was hard to please. But my wife and I took it on. The job was in two separate parts, one hour a day for cleaning, and another hour for looking after the fires and the toilet buckets. The pay was in shillings, rather than pounds. Of course I had to do a full time job as well, at one time I worked six till six at Ivor-Jones' farm up the By Road. I was pig-man, I worked with Tom Smith there. So my wife had to do some of the work with the stoves, and that was hard for her, carrying the scuttles, she wasn't very big or strong. The coal dust and smoke and fumes made her breathing troubles worse. She was on a nebuliser in the end.

"We took on the caretaking of the Church as well. I'd go into All Saints' in the early hours of Sunday morning, about 1am. usually, to light the fires so it was warm enough for the services. And sometimes I'd know Rev. Darwin was sitting in the Church, because I could smell his pipe! He'd say, 'Hallo,' then he'd say, 'I thought I'd just come in here and see my boss!' And we'd sit and have a good chat about this and that – mostly about the difficulties of keeping the Church and churchyard maintained.

"It wasn't easy, cleaning the School. All we had was a broom, a bucket and mop, and dusters. Smoke and coal dust blew everywhere, and you'd keep moving the dirt from place to place. There was a cold tap in the School porch, but if you wanted hot water you had to carry it round from the Schoolhouse in a bucket. You could work really hard at the cleaning and get nowhere.

"In the holidays, we'd have a list of jobs to do – washing all the walls, right up to the high ceiling, top to bottom. Cleaning the windows. Scrubbing the wood floors with a brush, then putting on oil to stop the wood rotting, a horrible job. If there were builders or decorators in the School, we had to clean up after them. The big old tortoise stoves were terrible things to look after, and they gave off dreadful fumes. The coke was outside, not under cover, so it was usually wet. We were given firelighters, but when you used them and added the coal or coke, the fire would go out. We had open wood fires in the Schoolhouse, so I'd get some wood kindling from our fires on a shovel, and carry it round into the School to get the stoves going. For

three months in the winter we'd try to keep the fires going day and night to keep the place warm enough. When it got warmer we'd light them every morning. It was a no-win situation really. You'd get into trouble because it was too hot or too cold, or because you'd used up your quota of fuel. There weren't any Health and Safety regulations then, and we weren't in a Union. But in those days you weren't brought up to complain, and everyone in the country had it hard. We had paraffin lamps, the electricity only came to the village about 1953, and even the council houses had earth closets until the early Sixties. It was just a part of life. At the School you had at least50 people using the toilets each week, and I had to dig holes round at the back, on the left-hand side. The right-hand side used to be Mrs. Collins' vegetable patch. We were allowed to grow vegetables there.

"Our two sons Mark and Richard both started School at Drinkstone. The house was in poor condition. The floor in the room nearest the Church was bad, with dry-rot. The Church got that repaired. The wood was taken up and a solid floor put in. The room nearest the road was rotten too, and getting beyond repair. I had the Authorities out, and they put a closure order on the Schoolhouse, in 1972 I think. That worked out well for us because the Council gave us this house in Elmswell, and I was already cycling over here every day to work in the bacon factory. Our boys were aged about six and eight then.

"I had some happy times in Drinkstone. It was a good community. You'd see little clusters of people chatting together outside the houses. People tend to shut themselves away more now and live their separate lives."

MARGARET PLUMMER

I visited Margaret (née Bradley) and her husband William in their home, No. 1 Cross Street (one of the pair of cottages that are the subject of Chapter Ten). William was born in Great Barton. Margaret was born in Drinkstone, at No. 1, Council Houses (next door to the Village Hall) on 7th August 1941. Her parents were Phyllis and Herbert Bradley. Margaret is the second of five children (sister to Alan). Here are Margaret's memories:

"I started School in 1946, we'd tramp down there every morning in all weathers. There used to be a whole gang of us, and on the way we used to take a sugar beet off the heap, one each, and we'd skid all the way down, using our beet as a skate under one foot, and then we'd see who'd made their beet thinnest by the time we got there!

"At School, I didn't like Mrs. Collins, and she didn't like me, or any of our family. She said we were all 'a load of wasters'. Some other families she thought were wonderful. But she was quite wrong about our family. We've done really well. We've got trained nurses and even a doctor among us now.

"Mrs. Collins was always on at us. When we wriggled about in class she'd say, 'For goodness sake sit still! Your father must have been an earwig and your mother an eel!' She had some horrible punishments. She used to have a great big tongue she'd made out of cardboard. It was bright red. If you did anything wrong you had to wear this tongue, which hung round your neck on a bit of elastic. It went from under your mouth down to your waist, and you weren't allowed to take it off in School, only at home time. You'd have to sit in the corner, facing the wall, wearing this tongue. You had to wear it for a certain length of time, depending how bad you'd been, maybe a whole week. I think she kept a list of whose turn it was to wear it next.

"Of course I liked playtime on the meadow, we played hopscotch, and Tag, all the usual games. I always enjoyed the maypole dancing, which is something they don't do now. I remember after Mrs. Collins moved out of the Schoolhouse, she bought the old School at Hessett. After that she lived in a house in the Park at Great Barton.

"I was about thirteen when Beyton Middle School opened and I went there. It was a lovely

School, and all my children and grandchildren went there.

"*Sundays we'd go backwards and forwards to Church all day. We used to love being in the choir. We'd walk down to All Saints' in the morning, home for dinner, then to Sunday School at the Chapel, then back to All Saints' for the evening service. I think we went to All Saints' Sunday School as well. We all had to go! These days we don't go to Church much – maybe at Christmas or on Armistice Day, and for funerals. But I feel quite proud of myself when I do go, because I still know all the words of the hymns by heart.*

"*When I left School, I worked at the egg-packing factory in Elmswell. I went down on me bike – we were a fit old generation then! I married William, a panel-beater by trade. We had two daughters, Belinda and Julie Ann. They both went to Drinkstone, there was a lovely teacher then, Mrs. Kozlowski, in the infants' class. I can't remember who taught me in the infants, we had a lot of different teachers.*

"*Our family moved from No. 1 Council House up to No. 21, next door to Nell, when I was about twenty-two. My mother wanted to have a few more neighbours. William and I moved into this cottage in 1965, it's still rented from the Council. It's very comfortable, we've got two good living rooms, the kitchen, a downstairs bathroom, and there's a little den where William has his old clocks and his radio equipment. The bedrooms are upstairs. There's views over the countryside, we've still got meadows opposite. When we came, these cottages stood all on their own. Now this side of the lane's all built up between here and the playing field. There's only one house on the opposite side of the lane, and we've got a lovely conservation wood with a pond, and horses in the meadow opposite our cottage.*

"*Our neighbour Cora was living here with her mother and father when we moved in. Now Cora's in her seventies, and her parents are gone. They were always lovely neighbours to us, Cora's a brilliant lady. My children used to go round to Cora's mother if they couldn't do their homework and she always knew the answers!*

"*When we came, the old cottage at the end of the lane* [formerly Widow's Cottage, then Slug's Hole] *was derelict, just a shell. Terry Kirby from London bought it and did it up, it took him years. He had a tent down there and he'd come and go until the cottage was fit to live in. His wife Peggy did a lot of the work, she's a clever person, she did most of the electrics and the plumbing. They lived there a while with their two little girls, who used to come and play with our daughters. Then they sold the cottage on, to Lynne and Duncan Hannett. Lynne and Duncan bought up some of the fields when Billy Land gave up his farm. The meadow and horses are theirs. They bought more land and made the conservation wood up the lane. It's private, but they had a proper Opening Day when we could all go and walk around. Their cottage is really nice now, it has been made larger and much more comfortable.*"

William joins in to tell me about the former state of what is now Lane End Cottage.

"*There was a reservoir with tin sides, all falling in. There were wet slippery wooden steps down to the water where you had to take your bucket. I think there's a natural spring, but it was dangerous really. Now it's all been filled in. Up the top of the lane towards Rattlesden Road, there's a cottage we call the Fish Scales because of the pargetting, and that's where old Ozzie used to live.*"

Margaret takes over to tell me:

"*Ozzie had an old cart, and a horse, and if his horse got tired he'd pull the cart himself! And he used to have his old horse with him in the house. We were a bit afraid of Ozzie when we were children. We've seen all the new houses go up. Some of them – like the one with a wood front – went up almost overnight. They built the chimney first, then put up pre-fabricated panels for the walls. But it looks all right, and some of the new people have done a lot for the village. Mrs. Beswick and her friends made the Village Hall look wonderful for Christmas this year. They organise things, like the over-sixties meal paid for by Wrenn's Charity, but we missed that this year. We've got four grandchildren, all boys, and we had to go to one of their school Christmas concerts. You can't miss those, you have to go.*"

There is a delightful pencil drawing of daughters Belinda and Julie Ann, done during a holiday in

Teneriffe, displayed in the living room. Many photos of grandsons Matthew, Adam, Bradley and Jordan adorn the walls. William has to take great care of his health after a brain haemorrhage finished his working career; he spent 14 weeks in Addenbrook's and now has an assortment of daily medication. But Margaret has spent a happy life in Drinkstone and the couple enjoy life in their Tudor home.

DENNIS "SOOTY" BRADLEY

I talked with Dennis in the home he built for himself and his family in Cross Street (he is a brick-layer by trade). Wife Sue (whom I interviewed separately, with her sister Joyce) was listening and helping Dennis remember. Daughter Rebecca, whom I had taught at the School during the 1980s and who lives in Germany with her R.A.F. husband and two daughters, phoned her parents during the evening. Rebecca told me some of her Drinkstone memories too.

Here is Dennis's story:

"I was born in 1946, in the council house right next to the Village Hall. My Auntie lived there with her husband and five children. The doctor suggested that my mother should go there for her first child to be born, so she would have family all around her to help. After a few weeks we went home to Church Cottages (now Old Almshouses) where we lived. Those cottages belonged to Mrs. Summers. When I was about a year old, we moved up to 15, Council Houses, in Gedding Road.

"My mother was at Drinkstone School until she was 14. She started off cleaning, as scullery maid in big houses. Then during the war, she was a waitress in the NAAFI up the yankee airbase at Ashfield. Her name was Ethel Elizabeth Robinson, she was always called Betty. My father Alfred was a Hessett man. He started off as a brick maker at Woolpit brick factory, but later on he worked at Blencowe's farm [Meade Farm on Park Corner]. Rev. Blencowe was a character, he bought the rights to the oak trees up there so they wouldn't be cut down. They grew along the roadside, and he had the tree trunks and telegraph poles painted white to reflect light at night. There's a few of these trees still standing today.

"There were two Suffolk Punches on the farm then, and my Dad worked with the horses at first. Later they changed over to tractors, they were little grey 'Fergies'.

"That done my father out of the job he liked best, with the horses.

"I can remember when I was about seven I was in the harvest field with Dad, taking a load of sheaves back to the stackyard on a cart, pulled by the tractor. My father was the stacker so he was on top of the load, and I was with him lying on top of the sheaves. We were on a narrow bit of road up by Hessett House when we met the local bus going towards Bury St. Edmunds. The tractor and the bus were trying to edge past each other and my Dad jumped up, took his pitchfork, and banged on the top of the bus. The people inside screamed, they thought we'd fallen on top of them! My Dad was a joker, he liked a bit of fun, he'd surprise people letting off bird-scarers along the road sometimes.

"My grandmother cleaned the School in the late Forties and early Fifties, then my mother took the job over. I was lugged up there when I was about three or four. She took me in a basket-work seat on the back of the bike. So I had the whole School and playground to play in, it wasn't a new place to me when I started there. My father did all the emptying of the school toilets on his way home from work. There was a big plum tree in the corner at the back of the bike shed, he used to dig holes in that back corner for the bucket contents. There was a coal shed round the back of the School, and about six or seven toilet cubicles. Father used to help with the stoves as well, going into the School about seven in the morning on his way to work, and put a scoopful of coke on the old tortoise stoves. My Mum went in about eight o'clock and made up the stoves again.

"When I was old enough to start School, I used to walk down with all the other children who lived round us. We didn't play about, because we were always in a hurry! At first I took sandwiches for lunch time, but when I was older I was allowed to go home for dinner. So that meant we walked the mile to School four times every day! When I was about ten my Mum got me a second-hand bike.

"Mrs. Collins the Headteacher had two dogs, Scamp and Ben, and they used to howl in the mornings when we sang our hymn! She had two cats that used to lie on her big old desk, she'd push the desk right up to the stove to keep warm. Then there was her pet jackdaw, it used to fly right up into the rafters above our desks, and do its droppings on us children below. It followed Mrs. Collins everywhere, and it learned to say a few words in a funny squeaky voice. It went missing one day and she was really distraught. I think it got shot.

"I remember the milk we had, sometimes it was so cold the ice would rise up and burst the cardboard tops off the bottles. We used to put them near the stove to get warm. There was a little hole in the wall between the Schoolhouse kitchen and the classroom, only about nine inches square. We called it 'the loop' for some reason. I remember once Mrs. Collins locked herself out of her house, and she asked little Rosemary Bird to crawl through the hole! Rosemary was tiny, very skinny, and she went in head-first and wriggled her way through. We all watched her and somehow she got down onto the kitchen floor and opened the house door from the inside.

"About once a year, the doctor and nurse would come to the School to weigh us and measure us and examine our eyes and ears and hair. All the infants would go in the big room, and the doctor and nurse went in the infants classroom for the day. To try and get out of having to go in there and get undressed, I told a lie. I said my Mum was coming, when I knew she wasn't. So I was waiting, sitting on a bench. But my cousin Alan who was seven years older than me, was going to be seen by the doctor and his mother, my Auntie, came to the School to go with him, and she knew my Mum wasn't really coming! So I had to go in with my Aunt and Alan. Alan was standing by the stove in just his underpants, when two of the older girls came in. Their job for the day was carrying in papers, and calling the next child to come in. Alan went mad when the girls came in and saw him in his underpants! He shouted at them to keep out, then he wedged the door shut by shoving a chair under the door handle. His Mum was trying to calm Alan down, and the doctor and nurse were grinning a bit.

"Because my Mum was the caretaker, once or twice when the fires had gone out Mrs. Collins would get me to empty out the ashes and the clinker. I didn't appreciate that. And a couple of times she told me to come to the Church (on a school day) to pump the organ, when she was playing for a funeral. I was a bit of a jerky pumper, she blamed me for her bad playing! I wasn't getting enough air in. At the end of the sermon she'd put her head round the corner and hiss at me 'PUMP!' She was pressing the keys and no sound was coming out. She didn't ask me to do that job many more times! School and Church were very close in those days. Rev. Lilley came into the School a lot, and I was in the choir. We got two pennies a time for singing. My Dad used to give me three pence to put in the collection, and my mate said to me, 'Just put two pennies into the collection, then you're a penny in profit!' None of the money got home, it all went on sweets at the shop next to the Church.

"On a Friday afternoon, Mrs. Collins would send us bigger boys to do her garden. We'd have to weed her vegetable garden at the back, and cut the grass. We got fed up with that, so one day we pushed the mower into the lily pond and told her it was an accident! She told us off, and made us drag it out again. We had to clean it up and dry it down, but we didn't have to do any more mowing that afternoon! I got into trouble once, because I aimed my spade at a frog, and missed and chopped one of her best trees down instead. That didn't go down too well!

"We used to get sent up to the shop to get anything she needed, like a big green tin of Lyon's coffee, and some sugar, just anytime she needed it. I didn't like her much, and one day three of us boys tied her to her chair! She was sitting down and first we wrapped the rope round her ankles and round the chair legs, and then we wrapped it round and round the whole chair. Of course we were in trouble, she wasn't too pleased about it! Sometimes we boys just hooked off School, we'd play in the fields at Drinkstone Park, or go down to the farms and spend the day with the men.

"We had some good times too. We used to play on Thurlow's meadows opposite the School. They had apple trees, a pear tree, and a small pit where we used to slide down if it was icy. From the corner of that meadow we could look down into the farmyard and see the men working. I can remember watching them burning off the lambs' tails with a hot poker. The teacher could stay on the high lawn in front of the School, she could see us well from there. She'd blow the whistle when playtime was over.

"The older girls used to have a Maypole and I was fascinated by this when I was little. They seemed to get the ribbons in a terrible twist and tangle, and if it went right, they would all untangle again. There was a flag pole in front of the School. The flag was hoisted on St. George's Day, and for Queen Elizabeth's Coronation. I think it was at half-mast for the death of King George. Mrs. Collins arranged a trip for all of us, to go to the old Odeon in Bury St. Edmunds to see the Coronation film, all in colour. I remember seeing the Pathe News come up, and there was Hillary and Tensing, they'd conquered Everest. So she tried hard for us in some ways. I liked the infants classroom, there was a big wooden sand box, you could get about four children kneeling along each side.

"Mrs. Collins did some really good things for us. Like she had a television in her house, it was a rarity then, and she had all her class – about thirty of us – in there to watch the Trooping of the Colour (in black and white!). She'd take us on nature walks to find as many different flowers as we could. Her dogs would come along for the walk. We used to go down to the marshland. We went on trips, she took us to Lowestoft, up the light house. I remember Douglas Carter – when he went up the light house he was eating a stick of rock, and the keeper went mad! He was smearing all the lovely polished brass with his sticky hands. The keeper told us how much candle-power was in those lights. Then we went to some kind of sea defences, a big bank, and we had to pick salt-marsh flowers. I was more interested in throwing stones in the sea really. Then we went up the Oulton Broad with her son Geoff, he took six of us at a time in a little motor boat. One year we joined up with Ashfield School and went in a coach to Felixstowe. We went on the ferry, across to the Harwich side, and back.

"The big classroom was full of furniture. There were big tables near the partition, where we did art work, and had school dinners. Over by the front wall of the room, opposite the door to the porch, there were shelves for the dinner equipment and an old gas or oil cooker where the plates were warmed. The big partition doors were always kept shut.

"In the holidays, my mother was given certain jobs to do in the School, and I'd be there trying to entertain my sister Brenda in the playground. She was six years younger than me. Sometimes Mum would leave us with our Gran or our Auntie. She had to oil the wooden floors to stop the splinters coming up.

"When Beyton Secondary Modern School opened, everything at our little School changed. It was strange – all those big girls and boys, the 14 and 15 year-olds, were gone, and suddenly I was almost the oldest one there. It seemed like a different place. I went to Beyton for four years and left at 15. I went to train as a brick layer, with W. J. Baker's at Thurston. I took a professional with me to help me buy the right equipment, from Andrews and Plumpton's tool shop near the Corn Exchange in Bury St. Edmunds. Camborne's Charity gave me £9 towards buying stuff, I got a trowel, a level, hammer and chisels and some sets of brick layers' lines. Carpenter trainees got more, about £16- £17. £9 was a lot then, about three weeks' wages. Our daughters got help from Camborne's too, Rebecca for art materials, and Helen for knives, catering equipment and overalls, she was given about £100.

"I was at Drinkstone School with Peter Smith, and I went into partnership with him when we both finished our apprenticeships. We were apprentices together, and we worked together from 1962 – 1990, first for W. J. Baker at Thurston. Then we worked together freelance, as work partners. I've worked on some interesting jobs. I worked for Lord Ivor, he was a multi-millionaire and he owned acres and acres of land worth millions. But he didn't live in the mansion. He preferred to live in a little cottage. I remember one day he bought an old fridge from his game keeper for just five pounds! And he said he'd rather have a little ordinary cheap car

– when he used to have Bentleys they always got scratched and spoiled.

"After I left Drinkstone, I started to get a better relationship with Mrs. Collins. It happened because one morning, when my mother went into the School, she found Mrs. Collins really ill, just lying there looking bad. I biked down to Woolpit, to the little cottage surgery opposite The Swan, where the fish shop is now. I got the tablets she needed. After that, we started to get on with Mrs. Collins in a more friendly way. It sort of broke the ice between us.

"There's been such a lot of changes in Drinkstone, it's like a different place. In the old days no one had any money, but there were charities to help people. I remember about a stone of flour being given to my mother when I was a boy."

(Here his wife Susan adds that her mother was always given money for coal by the British Legion, and there were some very poor families in "tin town", Rattlesden, where some families had moved into the old nissen huts left over from the war.)

Dennis continues:

"Land around the back of the Church was given to Drinkstone village to be farmed for the poor. Lane End Cottage down the end of Cross Street (formerly Slug's Hole, and before that Widow's Cottage) used to be a whole row of cottages. Some were knocked down. There used to be a footpath running in front of those cottages. It joined up with the winding track to Hill Farm. That footpath's all ploughed up now. All the fields and lanes had names. Where my Dad worked at Blencowe's, I remember there was Ten Acres, Blomfield, Moss, and lots more names of fields there. On our walk down to School from the council houses, we'd go down the Queach, then nearer the School there was Coupson's Corner, Coupson's Hill, and Coupson's Pond – just where you turn up to the By Road. It was a little pond by an oak tree that was always over-flowing in winter-time.

"There is not such a community feel about the village now. When the Cherry Tree was open, there was a cross-over between the old and the young. You'd get the old boys sitting there, play-ing draughts, cards, shove ha'penny and darts. And then you've got the young lads, and there's a bit of bantering between them and the old chaps. Old and young knew each other then. There's not many who were bred and born here, still in the village. We used to do all things together. When the sewers were laid at the Village Hall, some of us – Derek Cross, me and Michael Smith and some others – we dug the drains, just for a crate of beer. Arthur Munford, Cora's father, was chairman of the Parish Council and he'd go up the Cherry Tree and bring us a crate every lunch time. And John Donaghy did the plumbing. Now there's talk of having a community centre at the Old Cherry Tree, and getting rid of the old Village Hall, but difficul-ties keep coming up. The land for the Village Hall was sold to the village for around £26 by Mr. Thompson of Rookery Farm. But now that farm's been sold and divided three ways. If the old Hall's not used any more, there's a problem with who to sell the land back to. So the vil-lage is thinking of keeping it, and building behind it."

Here his wife Sue joins in to say:

"Rattlesden and Drinkstone always used to communicate, through the clubs. That's how we met, remember? You used to cycle over from Drinkstone to Rattlesden to the Village Hall dances, and that's how we got together. We married and had our daughters Rebecca and Helen. They shut the School soon after Rebecca had gone up to Beyton School. Helen was still a pupil at Drinkstone when the closure was announced. We got together and formed a protest group, there was several meetings with the Council but it was useless. After the closure, the parents didn't often meet, the School had joined everybody together more. Sad day!

"The whole family still remember some of the things that happened at the School, like study-ing the wild white mallow plant, that's a beautiful flower. We still gather the seeds and scatter them in new places to make sure it won't die out! Rebecca remembers a day when you praised her for drawing a wonderful picture of a tree – all your class were drawing the trees in the back meadow. Rebecca loved drawing and she went on to study art. There's a photo of Helen in the 'Sports Day marathon' when children used to run four times around the School. They were good days."

RICHARD AND VIRGINIA BRADLEY

I talked with Richard and Virginia at their home in tranquil Orchard Close, set among the fields and green open spaces of Felsham. The couple were both born in Drinkstone and were pupils at Drinkstone School. I was pleased to be able to meet them because Virginia is the first ex-pupil I have met who passed the dreaded 11-plus exam for Grammar School entrance and stayed there until age 16. There were others (for example Peter Newdick, see page 169); but previously I had only met those who either passed and didn't take up their place, or who passed and detested the Grammar School, leaving as soon as possible!

Richard told me that his Grandfather Charles Frederick Robinson (known as "Chesty") was "a bit of a lad. He'd buy up old cottages, clear the rubbish out of them, and sell them on later, sometimes for twice as much, without really doing much work on them". But as a young man in the years following the First World War, Charles Robinson could find no regular work in the Suffolk villages. Like many others he set out for Yorkshire, where he found not only work, but a girlfriend named Muriel. Muriel had been fostered out as a child to a lady with a large number of children in her care. The first-born child of Charles and Muriel was born in Yorkshire, and was named Phyllis. She was about three or four years old when her parents set up home in Drinkstone. Phyllis was to become Richard's mother.

Richard's father Herbert Bradley was born in a farm cottage in Quaker Lane, right on the parish borderline between Hessett and Beyton. When Herbert left school, he did a variety of jobs, first looking after the vicar's pigs, later doing road work, building, "a bit of everything". He joined up in the Second World War, spending some years in the R.A.F. Richard says his father told the family very little about his war time experiences. When he was discharged he found work at I.C.I. in Stowmarket, where he stayed until retirement. The family lived in No. 1, Council Houses, Drinkstone (next door to the Village Hall). Richard was born in December 1948, the fourth of five children.

Unlike his older brother and sister, Alan and Margaret, Richard enjoyed his time at Drinkstone School. He says:

"I remember Mrs. Clayton in the infants' class, and Mrs. Collins in the big class, she treated me all right. Mrs. Clayton was the wife of the Headteacher at Beyton. I sat the 11-plus exam with Sandra Cocksedge and Derek Warby. We had to take it at Beyton School and it was a bit daunting. I don't think we'd been taught what we needed to know to pass. Anyway, I was quite happy to go to the Secondary Modern at Beyton with my friends. Beyton seemed big at first but I soon got used to it. I left when I was15, in March '64. I went to work with T. H. Nice doing motor repairs, in Eastgate Street, Bury St. Edmunds. One of the director's sons set up on his own, as 'Anglia Bodyworks' in Mildenhall Road, and I went to work for him, and that's where I've been ever since."

Virginia told me about her family:

"My Mum and Dad moved to Drinkstone from Cambridgeshire, a couple of years before I was born. My father had been working for Rushbrooke Estate farms, then later at the Experimental Farm at Lolworth. Mum missed Suffolk and wanted to return there, so Dad got a job with Mr. Ivor-Jones of Burt's Farm in Drinkstone, and they moved to Chapel Cottages in Gedding Road in 1950. There were eight or nine other men all working at Burt's in those days. When we were children, we'd know what time of day it was by seeing all the farm workers cycling home for their dinners. When I was old enough to start School, I'd walk down with my older brother Richard. My brother had a bike, so he'd cycle home for dinner, but mostly I stayed at School. If we got a bit weary maybe in the afternoons, we'd just rest our heads on our folded arms on the desks, for a bit. In the infants' class, I remember Mrs. Lomax, and Mrs. Proctor – she had red hair, and she'd give you a bit of a shake if you mis-behaved! But I liked most things, we used to do knitting and sewing, clay work and painting. My favourite lesson was always English. And I used to really love that big wooden sand-tray.

"In the big class, I remember Mrs. Collins used to stand behind her desk pulling her stockings up, and she had her hair in a roll around the back, and she'd pat it into shape. Everything had to be just so! She was strict, she used to get very short with the ones who couldn't do things right. If you were given the honour of making her cup of coffee it had to be just right! I used to

get sent across the Churchyard to the Post Office to buy the Savings Stamps, and Mr. Allen would give me a jelly snake to eat while I waited."

Here Richard joins in to say:

"Mr. Jim Allen, he had no teeth, and he was friendly with my parents, and I remember one day he came to tea with us and he was trying to eat some cake, and his jaw just kept wobbling up and down, and me and my sisters just couldn't stop looking and laughing! And the more you're told to stop laughing, the worse it gets."

Virginia resumes her story:

"When I got a bit older, my Mum did cleaning for Mrs. Le Roux down Cross Street. I think she'd been a teacher at some time. She had some old 11-plus exam papers. I used to go down with my Mum, and while Mum was cleaning, Mrs. Le Roux used to sit me down with some of these exam papers to see what I could make of them. Adrian Bland took the 11-plus the same time as me, and his father Ronnie Bland took us to Beyton for the exam, in his car.

"I passed, and my parents were pleased, they really wanted me to do well. My mother signed a paper to say she undertook to keep me at the County Grammar School for Girls until I was 16. She said, 'Now I've signed, and you're going!' The uniform all had to come from certain shops in Bury St. Edmunds, the expensive shops of course, which was quite a headache for my parents on farm worker's wages. I had a navy skirt, navy jumper or cardigan, blue blouse, and striped tie which all had to come from Plumpton's (Palmer's, now), and a dress for summer that had to be made of the right material. I had a blazer for summer, a gaberdine mac that I never wore out, and a horrible little beret. Then there was all the sports gear, that had to come from Day's.

"The first day, I waited for the bus in my horrible beret and all this gear, not knowing anyone. The bus didn't turn up, they didn't know they had to pick me up! There were children from all the schools, the Catholic ones as well, and there were boys on the buses too. At first I felt quite lost. When I got to the School I had no idea where to go, but Penny O'Brien from Rattlesden (she's Penny Otton now) was in the Sixth Form and she took me under her wing and helped me. Nobody had told me you had to provide your own pens and pencils. Somebody had to lend me those on the first day. My sister Adele who worked in Bury St. Edmunds had a mad rush around to see what she could get for me.

"That first year (1963-4) the School was in Northgate Street, but then a brand new School was built in Beetons Way. You were supposed to keep your beret on at all times outside the building, never be seen without it. But the boys would always be whipping them off and pulling off the little tuft on the top. One day a boy got hold of mine and filled it with sugar. When I put it back on I had all this sticky sugar in my hair!

"My Dad helped me with homework, especially the Maths. I got some O–Levels, so when I left at 16 I had an interview at Southgate Street in Bury, at the office of the Ministry of Agriculture, Fisheries and Food (it's DEFRA now). The job was mine! I was temporary clerical assistant at first, and I earned £6–2s–6d a week. After my exam results were confirmed I was promoted to Clerical."

Both Virginia and Richard have fond memories of their days at Drinkstone School, particularly the outings to London organised by Mrs. Collins. They saw the Royal Tournament, the Tower, the Zoo, and Kew Gardens. They remember the "comfort stop" in Baldock on the way down. In London, they would all visit Mrs. Collins' daughter Sandra's home and amuse themselves in the playroom, while mother and daughter shared a chat and a cup of tea together.

Richard told me about his father-in-law John's close friendship with Nicholas Cribb:

"Old Cribby, John called him. He had a pet goose which was suffering, and John had to go round and put it down for him, because he couldn't bear to do it himself. Cribby was a lovely man, he used to help out when we were between rectors – first we were with Rattlesden, then Tostock, then Woolpit. Cribby always had time for everybody. John knew him well through the British Legion. John was very active in the village, in the darts club, and everything that went on in the Village Hall."

Virginia remembers fun at the Rectory, when a Mrs. Shaw lived there (unconnected with the Church):

"Mrs. Shaw used to invite the whole village there for free tea and sports. The Mums had a trifle competition; my Mum often won the prize. Then the trifles were part of the tea! And my Mum won a beautiful tea-set of bone china. Nell Cocksedge and the others, they used to be all dressed up, walking around the big lawns for the Fancy Dress Competition."

Richard adds:

"You could have as many free ice-creams as you liked, you could keep going back for more – at least until your mother stopped you! Later Mrs. Shaw was killed in a car accident, that was very sad.

"We had a lot of fun on the farms. We used to go at harvest time, up to Burt's Farm maybe, and pretend to help a little bit – try and lift some of those huge sacks of grain, or pile up some sheaves. Suffolk always seemed a bit behind the times – we'd still be using a binder here when everywhere else had combines. We'd wander about all day and no-one worried about us, so long as we turned up for meals. The Recreation Ground (we called it 'The Cricket') was rough then, we had a lot of fun digging holes, and making tracks for our bikes. There was a patch where you could play football or cricket, but it was rough, and there was no play equipment. There's an old car buried there, I know whose it was and where it is but I'm not telling!

"The Blands owned Bridge farmhouse. They used to do thrashing in 'The Damlan', that field opposite the farmhouse, by the bridge. There were a lot of old wrecked cars and vans to play in, some of them stripped down but with the steering wheel still in, and we'd play on those. They were mostly old Morrises and Austin 7s.

"Ruby's family, the Rogers, had Yew Tree Farm in Cross Street, and they owned the fields around there. Ruby and her sister Daisy were friendly with all our parents. It was a proper old-fashioned farm with a dairy, and chickens running about. They'd come round with a milk churn on the back of the car, and you'd have a tin measuring jug to pour the milk into your own container. They had a big old carthorse by the name of Dolly, the children could go up and ride her. She used to get out sometimes!

"You could walk across to the farm from where Field Close is now, and there were old sheds and barns and cart-lodges full of old wagons and tumbrils and two-wheeled carts – at least 15 altogether. The whole place was cleared in the late Sixties and sold off, but the farmhouse is still there, and the old dairy was made into a studio.

"Well, Virginia and I got married in 1975 and couldn't really afford to buy anywhere. Then the Council built these houses to sell, and we were lucky and bought one. We had three children, Nicola, Robert and Lucy. Nicola's got one child (our first grandchild), and she's a full-time mother. Lucy works in Administration. Robert's a doctor, he's working at St. Mary's Hospital, Paddington."

Virginia tells me:

"Mum and Dad are both buried in All Saints' Churchyard, so we go down to Drinkstone to do the graves. And we visit Ruby, and Richard's sister Margaret in Cross Street. Sometimes we'll walk the old footpaths, around Burt's Farm. I still work part-time for Kevin Mayhew in the warehouse at Buxhall."

Richard says:

"As children we knew everyone in the village, and we both have very happy memories of our childhood."

VIOLET COCKSEDGE

Violet Cocksedge, affectionately known as "Vi", was caretaker at Drinkstone School during its final years, wonderfully supported by husband Jim who did the necessary with the Elsan toilets week by week! Now widowed, Vi lives several miles from Drinkstone, in Haughley village, and despite troublesome knee problems she still cycles over to chat to friends and relatives in Drinkstone. This is her story;

"My husband Jim was born in Hessett, two miles from Drinkstone. When we were first married we lived in Sicklesmere, my home village, six or seven miles from Drinkstone. Jim was working as a lorry driver. We lived in rented accommodation and never had much money. We had three children, Susan was the first, born in 1949 when I was aged twenty. Then our son Roy arrived in 1951, and Mary in 1953.

"The children were still very young when we heard that a couple was required to run the Cherry Tree Public House at Drinkstone Green. This looked like a good opportunity for the family, so we applied. We scraped together £70 and offered ourselves for the job. We were told, the valuation for the pub contents, furniture and everything there, meant we would have to find at least ten pounds more to have a chance of being accepted. Somehow, we found the money, and in 1954 we had the excitement of a new home and a new way of life.

"The first year in Drinkstone was traumatic for us all. Roy, our middle child, had only just started at Drinkstone School when he became dangerously ill. He was rushed to Addenbrooks Hospital suffering from polio. I was terrified. I felt terrible guilt in case I myself might be the "carrier", and dreadful fear that our other children would contract the disease. The polio vaccine was just being introduced locally, Drinkstone children had not yet received it. Miraculously, no-one else in the district became ill so the whole thing is a mystery. We were so relieved to eventually bring Roy home again, suffering only slight back problems and some stiffness in the legs. When he was fit enough to return to School, the County Council provided a taxi for him. Strangely, my other children were not allowed to ride with him, so continued to walk the mile to School and back each day! Nearly all the children from The Green walked to School in those days, very few had bicycles. They would walk with their friends. There was hardly any traffic on the roads in those days, everyone expected to walk.

"When Roy left School he became a Site Agent for building firms, and he's very active. He does all the things the doctors said he must never do, heavy work and lifting, whenever he has to get jobs properly finished himself.

"My children were happy at the School. In those days, they had to learn all their times tables. Susan always found that hard. So we'd be sitting down to dinner, and her Dad, Jim, would say, 'Now Susan, say your seven times!' and she'd try, then he'd call out, 'What's seven times seven, then?' and she'd be in a muddle. He'd tell her, you won't get much of a job if you can't count properly". Susan says that made her determined to prove him wrong one day!

"When she left School, Susan found a job as Nanny to some children. She soon wanted a change, and was offered work in a small shop. Later she worked in Marks and Spencers, and her maths just got better and better. Her husband says to me, 'Susan only has to look at a list of figures and she knows whether they're right or wrong!'

"One winter time in the snow, the school dinners didn't arrive, so the headmistress gave the children cream crackers with margarine. I was disgusted my children were not given butter and I wrote to the teacher to complain! But I can't have been so bad because later on I was asked to be on the Board of School Managers. Susan and Roy went on to Beyton School when they were eleven, but Mary passed the 11-plus and went to Bury St. Edmunds Grammar School. She hated it. She said, 'Mum, it's all doctors' and dentists' children, and I'm just from the pub! You must let me leave!' We wanted her to stay, but she said, 'If you don't let me leave I'll get myself expelled!' so we had to give in.

"It was hard work at the pub, but I enjoyed it. Jim was still working as a lorry driver, first for the Civil Defence, and then for the County Council, going to all the Schools.

"So I had to run the pub. I had to fit it in with all my other work. It would take me all day to do the washing on Mondays. I'd go into the shed at the back and put all the white clothes and sheets in the copper, and light the fire underneath using faggots, then wood or coal, whatever we had, to burn. Then I'd go back into the pub, and when the men came in the middle of the day they'd say, 'Come and have a game of dominoes with us, Vi!' - or sometimes, it was darts. There was one old chap in his seventies, he always wanted me to play him at darts and he always won. If you won the game, you'd have to buy everyone a half-pint of beer, so if I won *that was the lunch hour profit gone from the pub! I didn't mind stopping to play the games, that was my duty really, part of the job. Afterwards when I went back to look at the wash copper in the shed, it would have all boiled over and maybe put out the fire!*

"We knew everyone in those days. Villages are so full of newcomers nowadays. Then we knew everyone who came in and we had some laughs. I remember once a couple came in with a dog and it started fighting. I was so scared I jumped up on the table! But they were good times. You had to work all evening of course. When the farmers held a shoot, about twice a year, the men used to come in afterwards for a meal, just cold meat and pies and cakes. They weren't easy times, but they were good times.

"I remember we had this tin bath. In summer we'd use the bath in the outhouse. But in the winter, we'd bring it into the sitting room in front of the fire. We'd all use the same water, going in one at a time, the cleanest had to go in first!

"Jim used to work on our patch of land as well as driving. We had a good patch front and back, he'd grow sprouts and potatoes, swedes and sugar beet, some for us to use and some to sell. I had to help him, so did the children. We had the pub re-furbished, that cost money, and we had to pay our rent, and something off the valuation money, bit by bit. It was hard work. We were there fourteen years as landlords. But what we really wanted was a place of our own, so we kept looking out to find somewhere.

"At last there was a piece of building land came up for sale in the village, down the Rattlesden Road. Jim was talking to the farmer that owned it, and he said, 'If you want that land, Jim, don't bid for it yourself, because people know you haven't got much money.' That land was going 'under the hammer'. We managed to borrow £1000 from the Bank. Jim went to the Solicitors Banks Aston, and asked them to bid for him. At the auction, the plot went for £800. Someone said to Jim, 'That chap from Banks Aston was bidding like he had plenty of money, I wonder who it was for?' and Jim told him!

"We got friends to help us build our bungalow. We knew everybody with having the pub. We'd have bricklayers go and do a bit late evening, after their day's work, and we'd pay them cash there and then. That's the way we got it built. Then we could move in and give up the pub.

"Then – I think it was in 1974 – I saw the advertisement for the job of caretaker at the school, in the Bury Free Press. *It said:*

CLEANER-IN-CHARGE (10 hours per week) and MALE PART-TIME
TOILET CLEANER (Two hours per week, Term-time only)
Required at Drinkstone C. E. Controlled Primary School.
Wage 77.10p per hour and 75p per hour respectively.
Applications to Miss A. G. Raynham, Headmistress at the School,
SUFFOLK COUNTY COUNCIL

"We applied, and got the job. The caretaker couple before us lived in the School house, but they'd moved out and gone to live in Elmswell.

"I'd get to the school for 7am every morning. I'd go down on my bike in all weathers except icy days when the hill was too slippy – then I'd walk. We had those tortoise stoves then and they were dreadful to look after. We'd try to keep them in all night, but sometimes I'd go down in the morning and they'd be out cold, with all the clinker stuck at the bottom. And then I'd have to get them cleaned out and light them all over again before anyone came. Then I'd go and clean up after School ended.

"When I first went to that School it was filthy. Jim and I went and scrubbed the floorboards in those two big classrooms, we had to keep changing the water and we did a lot of unpaid over-time. Then Jim varnished them all over. I was flabbergasted when someone in the village said to me, 'Well, it's all right for you, they've put in a new floor for you!' There was a Sunday School at the week-ends and we cleared up for them as well. We did a lot of unpaid over-time but we didn't mind.

"I remember when Miss Raynham left, Jim and me gave her an azalea, and there were tears in her eyes, she really appreciated it. Mrs. Barbara Wright took over as Head. Her husband worked in the Council, so between them they got a lot of repairs done to the School and the Schoolhouse. Mr. Nunn was the builder who did most of the jobs. Mrs. Wright started to use the empty Schoolhouse rooms for storing things, and she used one room as her office. The toilets were just ordinary buckets when we started, but she got us the proper Elsan ones. Emptying those buckets was hard work in the winter, finding some sheltered corner of the garden soft enough to dig, but Jim never made a fuss. Then he would have to go in the School cloakroom to get fresh water to rinse the buckets out.

"When I was cleaning the School, I was working on the land as well, doing fruit picking, potato picking, chopping out sugar beet. A van used to pick the women up around the village at 8.30am and I would be on it, but by then I would have done an hour down at the School. I was always used to outdoor work, when I was a child my Mum and me once picked a whole tin bath full of blackberries. My Dad took them to a little greengrocer's shop in Hatters Street, Bury St. Edmunds, and they'd sell them for us. Nothing was wasted in those days. When my Dad was working shifts at the sugar beet factory, he would go into North Hill Woods at Rushbrook and pick up a few stone of sweet chestnuts to sell. In the war, I remember school-children all got time off to single the beet. There was always some way to earn a bit extra. I remember going plum-picking when I needed money to buy my children new wellington boots.

"Do you remember, Sheila, when you were teaching at the School, one day you left me a note saying, look out for the little Russian hamster, he's got out of the tank! That was a tank full of leaf-mould for the hamsters to dig their burrows. I looked everywhere. I found a lot of chewed-up paper scraps under that big book-case in the corner, but I couldn't find the hamster. Somehow he got back in on his own! And you had stick insects, and once you had new-hatched chicks in the classroom.

"I worked for so many teachers and they all had their different ways. I remember when you and the children were planting the wild white mallow flowers and so many other little memories. Then there was Mrs. Shirley Hall, and after her Mr. Connolly – he still sends me a Christmas card every year. It was a good little School really, I was happy to work there all those years."

JUDY FROST

Judy Frost (née Cocksedge) is the eldest daughter of Nell Cocksedge, whose memories are in Chapter Eleven. Judy now lives in Haughley village, with her husband Dennis. This is her story:

"I was born on 25th March 1939, third in the family. My brothers Brian and Michael were older than me, after me came four others. I was born in Hessett, at the 'Black Cottage' which has been knocked down since those days. I started at Hessett School when I was five. We moved to Drinkstone in 1947, to live at No. 23, Council Houses, in Gedding Road, so I started at Drinkstone School. I was eight then, so I went straight into the big class. Mrs. Jackson was my teacher. I always liked School, though I never liked maths much. At playtime in summer we played on Thurlow's meadow. We played stool ball, it's a bit like cricket, but instead of stumps you had a stand with a square of wood on top. You had a little bat and you had to hit the ball and run! There was Doreen, Anne, Betty – about six of us girls, all around the same age, all great mates. I don't think we had any enemies really!

"I remember after Mrs. Jackson left, we had a few Supply teachers, then Mrs. Collins came. Mrs. Collins had her moments, she'd have a bad day when she'd pick on you, but I got on all right with her. I liked the afternoons, when we'd do singing, country dancing, and art. Some afternoons, the boys would go outside to do gardening, and the girls would stay in the classroom with Mrs. Collins, doing needlework. We'd make costumes for the country dancing displays she took us on – we danced at fetes, in a lot of villages round about. The boys never came *with us. Some of the girls would take the part of boys for those displays. Girls wore a white muslin blouse with puff sleeves, and a black dirndl skirt. We sewed bias binding in different colours all around the bottom of the skirts, above the hem. We used Mrs. Collins' sewing machine for that. The boys' costume was a white shirt, black shorts, and a sash in bright colours. Those were my favourites – dancing, and needlework. We even used to go back to the School in the evening, about once a week, and do sewing or dancing. If Mrs. Collins' daughter Sandra was at home (she went to the East Anglian School, a private School in Bury) she'd join in with us.*

"Out of school time, we had a lot of fun, just playing, usually in the road because there was hardly any traffic then. We'd play skipping, and hopscotch, and ball. The lady opposite would never give us back our ball if it went in her garden. She'd give it to my cousin Joyce Levett (now she's Joyce Rouse) who lived next door to her. Joyce's Mum, our Aunt Mary, would let us have it back! We went down to 'The Cricket' sometimes on summer evenings. We'd play cricket, boys and girls together. In winter we were never allowed out after dark. We'd play ludo, snakes and ladders, draughts and cards at home. Mum and Dad taught us to play Cribb, and we still enjoy that now. We'd read comics, we used to argue who'd read the comics first. Usually the boys got their way, and we had to wait until they'd finished!

"I took the 11-plus exam, with a boy my age called Peter Newdick, who used to sit by me in class. I failed, he passed – he was a very clever boy. He had an older brother Stephen, and a sister Helen. They lived in a cottage further up the Gedding Road, on the left, one of the last cottages before you're into Gedding parish. Peter went off to the Grammar School, but I stayed on at Drinkstone. When I was 14, the Secondary Modern School at Beyton opened, and I went there, but only for two terms. I started in September, and left the following March, after my 15th birthday. Beyton was a good School too.

"When I left School, I went with my friend Doreen Boreham from Drinkstone, to work as a waitress in a restaurant in Bury. I don't think that was for me, really! It was a long bus ride. I left, and went to work at Mills and Son, the grocery shop in Hessett. I cycled down and that was a bonus – not having to pay out on bus fare. I still worked there at first, after I married Dennis in 1959. Dennis came from Beyton, and he worked on Mr. Mitcham's farm in Hessett, as a tractor driver on the arable side. We lived in a caravan up Hubbard's Lane off Hessett Green, on land belonging to Mr. Mitcham. There was an old fella lived in an old cottage there, and when he died, Mr. Mitcham had the cottage demolished. He let us put the caravan on the brick base where the cottage used to be. We had electricity put on, and there was a stand pipe. We had lovely neighbours in the other cottages. Mr. Bullett lived there, he worked as stockman on the same farm as Dennis. His wife was really kind. If I was out, and it rained, Mrs. Bullett would take my washing off the line and put it near her Rayburn. She'd give it to me all nice and dry when I came home!

"Our daughter Roslyn was born in October 1960. The next Spring we moved into No. 5, Council Houses at Drinkstone. Josephine was born in 1963. Our daughters went to Drinkstone School and went on to Beyton when they were eleven. Then they went on to Thurston School, because the three-tier system had started. They're both married now, Roslyn has two boys, and they live in Elmstead Market near Colchester. Josephine has a daughter, and twin boys. They live at Aberporth in Wales.

"Dennis left farming after a while, and worked in Woolpit, at Derby's sand and gravel yard. They excavated on the site, and made breeze blocks. Dennis used to deliver all around the area. That yard's built over with new houses now. He went on to work for Biggswall, Civil Engineers. The depot was at Semer. In 1979, in April, we moved into The Cherry Tree Pub at Drinkstone, renting it as landlords from Greene King. Dennis still worked for Biggswall for the first two years, while we built up the trade, then he left and helped me at the pub. We thoroughly enjoyed it but it was very hard work. It's like 24 hours a day work really. If you weren't working in the pub, you'd be at the Cash and Carry, buying odds and ends. Then you'd be working all evening until midnight.

"People were all beginning to have cars then. Before so many had cars, the village did more things together. They'd go on coach outings in summer, usually to Felixstowe. Sometimes two coaches would go, all full of Drinkstone families. In the evenings, it would be Drinkstone people at the Cherry Tree too. But now, with so many having cars, we'd get customers from other villages, and the Cherry Tree wasn't the only place for Drinkstone people to go in the evenings either.

"Most evenings there'd be something going on at the Cherry Tree. We had a men's Quoits team, mixed teams for dominoes and Cribb, and two darts teams – one for men, one for women. As time went on, the drink-driving laws made it harder. People wouldn't spend the whole evening in the pub, they'd come in around nine or half past so there was less trade. After twelve years, in 1991, we thought 'enough's enough' and we moved here, to Haughley. Dennis still does some part-time work here and there, he can put his hand to anything. I work two days a week at Palmer's Bakery in Haughley. We're both bell-ringers at the Church here.

"I do go back to Drinkstone, to visit Mum, but it's not the same. There used to be three shops, the pub and the School. It is nice the way they keep the Village Hall going. It's great there's things going on there. That's thanks to Sheila Beswick and her friends, they take a lot of trouble to keep a feeling of community."

WENDY COLLINS

Wendy was classroom assistant when I was teaching at Drinkstone, and we have remained friends ever since. This is her story:

"I was born Wendy Secker in Bury St. Edmunds, where I spent my childhood.

"My first contact with Drinkstone School was in 1960. My future mother-in-law Mrs. Constance Collins was head teacher and was organising a concert. She said to me, 'If you really want to be a teacher you'd better come in and see what we do!' She wasn't the sort of person you could say 'no' to, you did what she said. So I was roped in to dress and make up the 'Tar Baby' played by Elsie Bradley. I remember I used cocoa mixed into a paste to cover her skin – what a mess!

"Mother-in-law had lived in Teddington with her husband, who worked for Mobil in the City. When war started he joined the Home Guard in Teddington. One day in 1940, on his journey home from work, he collapsed and died as a result of a brain haemorrhage. He was only forty-two, and his wife was thirty-four, with two young children. My future husband Geoff was five at the time, and his sister Sandra was a couple of years younger. Fortunately mother-in-law had already trained as a teacher at Goldsmiths College. I think being widowed at such a young age and having to fend for herself led to her developing such a strong, independent character.

"Mother-in-law moved to Drinkstone in 1948 when Geoff, my future husband, was thirteen years old. The family lived in the School house at first. Around 1961 Mrs. Collins moved to a bungalow in The Park at Great Barton. Sandra and Geoff were not pupils at Drinkstone. Geoff attended a boarding school in Middlesex, near his grandfather's home. Sandra was a day-pupil at the East Anglian Girls' School in Northgate Avenue, Bury St. Edmunds. That School has now been moved to Culford, sharing the site with the boys' School.

"There was a small pond in the front garden of Drinkstone School where frogs were encouraged, this was used for Nature Studies. At one time Mrs. Collins had a pet rook, and it used to follow her. Even when she went shopping in her car, it would follow her, wait for her up a tree, and follow her home again! The back garden had a vegetable plot which the older children worked, the boys doing most of the digging. They learned how to grow vegetables. They went on nature walks so the children could learn the names of flowers and birds, and see the farm workers in the fields and learn what sort of work they did. Cows were pastured on the meadows over the playground wall, and ducks and geese swam on the pond at Home Farm. The farmer, Mr. Thurlow, allowed the meadow opposite to be used for playing games like rounders,

as the playground wasn't very big. Mrs. Collins taught maypole dancing in the playground, and once a week the tall partition between the classrooms was pushed back and all the children learned to do country dances. The children enjoyed this.

"Until 1954, the children's parents could keep them at Drinkstone until school leaving age – in 1953 some children stayed until age 15. At that time everything in the village revolved around the School, their parents would have been taught there as well. After 1954 they had to move on to the Secondary School at Beyton at age eleven. After 1973 they had to go to Middle School at the age of nine so the School became much smaller. I started working at Drinkstone as classroom assistant at Easter 1972. At the time I started, most of the villagers, young and old, had been taught by Mrs. Collins, even some of the grandparents had been her pupils. Most of them had stayed in the village and whole families would turn up for concerts and carol services. I worked two mornings a week. When I started, Mrs. Collins was still head teacher and Mrs. Kozlowski (Mrs. K.) was infant teacher. Mrs. Kozlowski was known as 'Mrs. K.'. because it was easier to remember, for children and parents alike. Her husband was a Polish refugee. They lived on Beyton Green, alongside what was then the A45 trunk road. There was a bus stop outside her house, where older children waited for the Eastern Counties bus. She used to complain they kicked her garden wall, she could never stop them! Part of her house was a shop, run by her husband.

"There were tortoise stoves to warm the classrooms, great big pot-bellied things with fireguards. On wet days we'd put the children's clothes on the fireguards to dry. The heating was always appalling; it just depended which way the wind was blowing. We had outside lavatories with Elsan toilets – very cold and damp, and it didn't encourage anyone to hang about longer than they should! By this time Mrs. Collins had moved out of the School house, and the caretakers Mr. and Mrs. Bradley lived there with their sons. So we didn't go in the School house at all. Mrs. Collins would put a saucepan on the stove to warm the children's milk, and that's where she made her coffee. We just had the cold tap in the cloakroom, an electric kettle, and a telephone in the big classroom. There wasn't any staff room. The postman in those days was Eddie Coe, he was quite a character, rather round and rosy. He used to bring the mail right into the classroom and hover about for a while, maybe to get warm. He lives in Woolpit, he's got arthritis now. I see him going around on a little motorised scooter.

"When Mrs. Collins retired after twenty-five years, the School changed. I don't think much fuss was made when she retired. People tended to regard her as feeling superior to the country people, and they didn't necessarily agree! She went to Australia, where she died several years ago. Someone said to me, 'What does it feel like, now she's gone?' Well, it's like having a lid lifted off a boiling saucepan – I can get out and be me! Really, she always did what she thought was best for the children. She'd take them on trips, to Hampton Court and Tower Bridge, and once even to Belgium. It couldn't have been easy for her. Her husband died young and she was left high and dry with two little children. At Teddington she'd taught in a girls' Secondary school, a lot different from teaching in a little village school.

"After Mrs. Collins retired, Mr. and Mrs. Bradley moved to Elmswell, leaving the School house empty. Mrs. Cocksedge (Vi) and her husband Jim, took over as caretakers. Miss Raynham came as temporary head teacher. My duties were to help the little ones with their reading and writing and handicraft and painting – making sure they had aprons or old shirts on, and cleaning up the mess. I helped them change for P.E., put their shoes and coats on, go to the toilet, wash their hands and so on.

"During the 1970s the School house was brought into use. The front room became the office, back room and bedrooms were for storage. The kitchen was used for school meals, which were delivered there and served, and that's where the washing up was done. Postal deliveries were made to the secretary, Mrs. Cady, who dealt with them instead of disturbing the head teacher.

"Later, when Kevin Connolly was head teacher, I used to take several little ones into the kitchen and we cooked buns and biscuits which they enjoyed, especially licking out bowls! Most Mums were working then and they missed this treat at home. We had a piano in the big

room and the teachers used to play for singing lessons. Later Meg Jack came to do this once a week. During the 1980s I used to take the children to Bury St. Edmunds Swimming Pool on Wednesdays, with the infant teacher, and one of the mothers. The children soon overcame any fear of the water and were soon trying to swim – some with success. We'd often take the children on walks and visits in the village – I remember visiting Mrs. Jones with her goats. She lived near Mrs. Pocock, up the lane beyond the Church. Her older children, Tom and Emma, came to the School. Before her in that cottage, the Boulton family lived. The older children, Michael, Zoellii and Bianca came to the School. Bianca was very artistic (like her mother). She was a dear little thing, she'd just wriggle up to you and tell you things.

"When I first started at Drinkstone I was trained as a first-aider so I could deal with any problems. This was renewed every three years to keep me up to date. I also went on lots of courses in dealing with infants, helping with speech therapy and so on, organised by the Education Department.

"Drinkstone was a Church School, situated right next to the Church. The children would go to the Church for religious festivals. The rector was involved with the running of the School, he would be one of the managers or governors as it was later called. The Rev. Nicholas Cribb was a dear – such a kind man, he'd really listen to the children. I remember many names over the years – Rev. Darwin, Rev. Rodgers and Rev. Wall, also Mary Pocock, Miss MacGregor and Geoffrey Wilding.

"Head teachers I worked with were Mrs. Collins, Miss Raynham, Barbara Wright, Shirley Hall, Kevin Connolly and Sheila Wright. Rosemary Cady and Lynda Steward were school secretaries, both were mothers of children at the school, Lynda taking over when Rosemary transferred to Elmswell School. Dr. Wilson was visiting doctor, and Ann Peacock the School Nurse. Dinner ladies included Joyce Cocksedge, Wendy Baker and Mrs. Raison, who all lived in the village and had children at the School. I remember Mr. Ken Gilbert used to take a lot of photos for the School.

"When the School closed, I had to find another way of earning some money! I asked around, and found work in several large Drinkstone homes. I worked at Rookery farm as general housekeeper and cook for a French family for a while. They only came at week-ends, with their three gorgeous children. The parents were Monsieur and Madame Paul-Renaud. Monsieur's father had been in the war-time government of France. Madame was a very glamorous model from the south of France. She was so nice! She would phone me on a Friday and say how many would be coming because they often had house-guests. She'd bring some food from Harrods, and I'd get what else I needed from Sainsburys – which was much better quality than those little dried-up lettuces from Harrods! Their Nanny was from Morocco, she would do breakfast. Then I'd go in about 9.30am and start doing lunch. I'd do all the cooking including dinner parties. When they left, I'd clean right through the house, which was lovely – a big hall with Suffolk pantiles, and fitted carpets in most of the other rooms.

"I worked at Drinkstone Lodge sometimes, I cooked for dinner parties, and the lady would say, 'Do plenty so you get a meal as well!' About once a month I stayed to look after the house and their two Jack Russells while they were away. In the end they moved to the east coast. I even looked after The Rectory once or twice, that was a beautiful place, but some of the furniture was a bit used-looking. The first time, the owners had gone to the Champs-Elysées Races. They had huge Airedale-cross dogs. I could eat what I liked from the enormous old-fashioned pantry, I poked around and found some extraordinary things, not all too fresh! They were very kind, the lady said, 'You can sleep in any room you like, but this bed here is all made up ready.' So that's where I slept, in a four-poster! I looked out down the long drive before I got into bed, then I pulled the curtains close and snuggled down. I was a bit scared of the dogs but I was glad they were there!

"After a while I decided it was easier just to work in Sainsburys! All those families I worked for had moved away by the Nineties, I don't know any of the new owners. Over the years I've stayed in the district and seen a lot of the children grow up. I worked in Sainsburys and a lot *of the parents and pupils did their shopping there. They all seemed to do well in life. Several now have their own businesses, like Jonathan Bland with his office equipment. Some trained for professions; Vanessa Bland became a nursing sister at Ipswich Hospital. Lucy van den Bruel became a T.V. News Reporter. I got such a surprise one day when I recognised her on G.M.T.V.! I often see the Sobkowiak children, who lived at Hessett. Their father was also a Drinkstone pupil (his father was a Polish refugee).*

"I've come across several of the governors since the School closed. I went to work as a carer in old people's homes in Stowmarket. It's quite sad to see what happens to people. There was a man I knew in Norton when he was the village cobbler, a big, strong man. He suddenly had a stroke and became quite helpless. Some of the patients can be strange, you sometimes got knocked about a bit. I remember one day I just bent down to a lady called Alice, to do up one of her blouse buttons. Without warning, she knocked me on the chin and gave me whiplash! But I didn't mind, I thought, one day I may be like Alice, and I'll be so frustrated when I can't do what I want to do. I loved looking after them. These days I just go in once a week to do their mending. I used to see one of the Drinkstone governors, Geoffrey Wilding, who suffered from Parkinson's. He was a very gentle, generous man, and he could still talk right up to the end despite being so ill. I've got so many memories of Drinkstone School and many people connected with it."

CHRISTINE CATLING (NÉE BLAND)

Christine is one of Raymond and Vera Bland's three daughters, and spent her childhood in Whitefield House farm in Park Road. She was a pupil at Drinkstone School in the 1960s, and sent me these memories of those years:

"My earliest memory of Drinkstone School is of days in what was known as the 'Little Room'. This was a strange name, as this was actually the larger of the two classrooms! My teacher was Mrs. Kay (her real name was Mrs. Kozlowski, but Mrs. Kay was a lot easier for little people to say).

"Our days in the 'Little Room' were very enjoyable as we had many things to do. There was a sand-pit in a large wooden box with a fold-down lid, a shop in the corner which had shelves full of cardboard packets which looked just like the real thing, and a large selection of books to read, all lined up in a hanging library.

"The day usually started with assembly. Everyone came into the 'Little room' and Mrs. Collins played the piano. We usually sang 'All things bright and beautiful' or 'There is a green hill far away' as these were fairly wellknown hymns and quite easy to sing. Mrs. Collins however on many occasions would stop playing and tell us we were singing too slowly and not loud enough. Her favourite saying was that we were just like a 'load of lemmings' all singing the same!

"One of my favourite things in Mrs. Kay's class, was listening to stories. The one I remember most was 'The Three Billy Goats Gruff'. I liked this because I remember having large pictures which went with the story, pinned on the board at the front of the class. Another nice thing we did was making things with clay, then painting them when they were dry.

"My first lesson in Maths (as it is now known, but called Arithmetic in my early school days) was learning to do 'sums' with a rather nice abacus with lots of coloured beads on it. We learned to write using an exercise book with lines in, and I remember finding it difficult keeping my letters small enough to fit between the lines.

"Mrs. Kay was a lovely lady who was very kind to us all. I don't remember her ever being cross with us, although I'm sure we must have tried her patience on lots of occasions, especially when she had to deal with someone who wasn't feeling very well and was sick in class. For this we kept a box of sawdust in the cupboard, which was sprinkled over to make it easier to clean up. And she had to deal with 'small accidents' when someone didn't like to ask to go

to the toilet in time! For this we kept a rather fetching pair of long black shorts in the cupboard. The unfortunate thing was that you had to wear these for the rest of the day, until you were picked up by Mum. Thankfully, I didn't have to suffer this!

"Our toilets were not very nice as they were outside and were quite dark. We had a chemical toilet in a cubicle with whitewashed walls (this came off on your clothes if you touched the walls). I remember the scratchy loo paper which I think was Izal or something. To get to the toilets, you went through a little courtyard. This had a large pile of coal in the corner which was used to fuel the fires in the classrooms during the winter.

"We had little bottles of milk every day at break time in the morning. During the winter these were brought into the classroom and placed in front of the fire to warm up, because the milk was very often frozen in the bottle and the lids had lifted up. I think having warmed-up milk which I was made to drink, put me off for life!

"When we went up to the 'Big Room' we were taught by Mrs. Collins. She was a very different lady to Mrs. Kay. She was a lot stricter with us but I don't think this did us any harm. We had to behave, and if we didn't, we had to go out to the front of the class and hold out our hand, palm upwards, for a whack on the hand with a wooden ruler! I must confess to having had this punishment on one occasion as I was messing around at the back of the class behind my desk lid, with Brian Lark.

"Another thing I remember about Mrs. Collins was that she liked to listen to classical music. We always had one lesson a week where we sat quietly and listened to either Grieg's 'Hall of the Mountain King' from 'Peer Gynt', or Tchaikovsky's 'Nutcracker Suite'.

"Mrs. Collins always used to bring her two dogs to School. These were a rather large corgi called Amber, and a small hairy terrier, called Podgy I think. She used to take them for a walk during lunch time. The rest of the time they would sleep behind her desk. The corgi was a bit yappy and I remember it would sometimes run after you when you opened the door to go out of the classroom. One thing she used to do which was not too nice, was wash the small dog's bottom in the sink in the cloakroom – where Mrs. Haill used to wash the plates after lunch! Another thing I recall about the dogs was having to take them and put them in her car, which she always parked in the small lay-by near the Church. We had to do this when the School Inspector was coming to look at the attendance register. After he had gone, the pupils who took the dogs to the car went and fetched them again. We were often given some money to buy ourselves something at the shop near the Church, before going back to School with the dogs.

"Another memory of Mrs. Collins, was seeing her adjust her stockings and suspenders behind the desk! Also, how her neck went red when she gave someone a talking-to on the telephone. We always had to go and sit in the 'little room' when she did this as she didn't want us listening to her conversation. We could however hear most of it as there was only a wooden screen between the classrooms, which didn't stop the sound of her raised voice!

"Mrs. Collins was a very go-ahead lady who took some of us on a trip to Holland and Belgium. For this we had to make dresses with some material especially chosen for the trip. I remember it being brightly coloured with green, purple and white shapes all over it. We had to make matching hats which looked like scarves, with ties which did up under the chin. We went by coach down to Dover where we boarded a ferry which took us over to Calais, and then we went on to Holland. We went to see lace being made, also chocolate. I have still got a pair of wooden clogs that I bought on the trip.

Another thing Mrs. Collins did was encourage us to learn to swim. We did this at Beyton School which had a new outdoor pool at the time. I remember her walking along the side of the pool shouting encouragement when I managed to swim my first length, for which I received a prize at the end of term. If you behaved yourself you would get on well with Mrs. Collins, and she would encourage you with your work and praise your efforts. If you misbehaved, you would see the other side of Mrs. Collins, which was not something you wanted to do! I think she had to assert her authority in the early stages of our time at School, because she had to have respect from us when she took us on trips out of School. I think she was a brave lady when she took a whole class of children on her own, to somewhere like London Zoo. We went there by coach, and then went to her daughter Sandra's for tea afterwards.

"Another thing we did with her, was go on nature walks around the fields near the School. This was very enjoyable as she was very informative, and we were encouraged to collect things, including wild flowers which we pressed and put into a book on our return to School. We were also encouraged to go to Church, and we used to take our various vegetables there for the Harvest Festival. My other connection with Mrs. Collins and the Church was that she used to come and pick me up to take me to Church at Hessett, where she was organist for quite some time. I was in the choir there, and am very thankful to Mrs. Collins for taking me to choir practice and to the service on a Sunday morning.

"My other memories of Drinkstone School are of the playground where we spent our break times. We had one swing which was fixed into the ground, which was concrete covered in black asphalt. We also had a large climbing frame which was made of iron, I think. This was on the asphalt, which was not that safe really and would not be allowed in a playground these days! I don't remember anyone injuring themselves seriously, but a few people fell off the climbing frame and ended up with bumps on their head!

"We used to play games during breaks, mainly 'I sent a letter to my love', and 'The farmer's in his den'. It seems very unfair now when I think back to some of our games and remember that the same person always seemed to end up being 'the bone' in "The farmer's in his den"! This was usually the most unpopular person in the School at the time – I won't name names but if they read this they'll know!

"We used to make a pretend hospital in the bottom corner of the playground, using fallen leaves from the holly trees that surrounded the playground. We used the leaves to make the outlines of 'wards', and we girls were the nurses. The boys were pilots in their planes, which would crash every now and then. The pilots would then be rescued by some of the other boys who played the part of ambulance drivers. The 'drivers' would then carry the injured to the hospital where we would lay them out in the ward and care for them! I think this would seem very dull to children at school today, as it doesn't involve a computer or a mobile phone – but it called for a very vivid imagination!

"Finally I would like to say that I don't have any nasty memories of my time at Drinkstone School. I think it's a shame it had to close (as has everything else in Drinkstone)."

Chapter Nineteen

SCHOOL AND VILLAGE, 1972 - 1983

THE SCHOOL

In October 1972 there was a managers' meeting at which agenda items had a familiar ring: cupboards and trays for children's work had not arrived, since the L.E.A. was "awaiting available finance". There was never enough money, the L.E.A. was always juggling insufficient funds. It was difficult for them to properly support small schools in old buildings. This was depressing for staff at the School, who were kept constantly aware of the possibility of closure. This was a vicious circle, because the likelihood of closure made the L.E.A. reluctant to commit more than a minimum amount of funding to schools such as Drinkstone.

The managers again feared closure. For many months they had been complaining of "lack of information, and uncertainty regarding the future of the School". Into this atmosphere Mrs. Collins then dropped her bombshell: she was resigning from her post as from 22nd October. Mrs. Collins assured managers that "Miss Raynham would act until the closure of the School which is still indefinite". Miss Raynham was a member of Supply staff, already well known to the children. Mrs. Kozlowski would remain as infant teacher.

So, Mrs. Collins made her farewells, and life went on. On 20th November Miss Raynham was writing in the Log Book: "The School was closed, the children had a holiday for the Royal Silver Wedding Anniversary."

When the managers met in May 1973, the Rev. Daniel Gooderham was in the Chair, apologies were received from Brigadier Wight. Present were Miss MacGregor, Mrs. Gunnett, Mr. Sharratt, Mrs. J. Smith, and Miss Raynham (Acting Head). One welcome item was the appointment of Mrs. Meg Jack for two hours per week, from January 1st (Mrs. Jack continued teaching music until the closure in 1986). Not so welcome was a letter from the Department of Education and Science, in reply to the managers' letter of objection to the closure of the School. A new School was to be built at Beyton during 1974-5 with 130 places, four to five classes at most, having approximately the same catchment area as the present Beyton and Drinkstone primary Schools. So the future of Drinkstone School looked brief, and motivation among managers must have been undermined. Miss Raynham would continue to hold the fort cheerfully whatever happened.

The School numbers were good, 49 on Roll (24 infants, 25 juniors). At the start of the Summer Term three more entrants were expected. Thirty-six of the pupils lived in Drinkstone, and 17 in Hessett. Forty children took school dinners, supervised by Mrs. Smith. The dinners cost 12 pence a day, and were brought from the kitchens of King Edward's School at this time – good meals and ample helpings. Miss Stiff was in charge of serving and washing up. Mr. and Mrs. Bradley "keep the School and grounds clean, tidy and warm". Miss Raynham commented "We are most fortunate in having Mrs. Jack as music specialist, and Mrs. Wendy Collins as ancillary helper two mornings a week". Four juniors had completed a 12-mile sponsored walk, raising £81.48 for Help the Aged. Children's entries in the South Suffolk Show had won prizes. They had entered modelling, flower arranging and collage items. The juniors entertained at the Church Fair, playing recorders and singing. This does not sound like a school in the doldrums, more like a school going courageously onwards.

At the next meeting, a letter from West Suffolk Education Committee outlined re-organisation of schools: Drinkstone would become a First School in September 1974, but would definitely be closed "as soon as alternative accommodation for the children is available at Beyton. As yet, building has not commenced."

There were 54 children on roll, (14 children from Hessett transported by taxi). The use of the meadow for play was proving a great advantage. Staff worked happily together. Mrs. Jack was teaching singing, percussion, recorders and musical appreciation (through records). The children regularly saved with the National Savings stamp scheme. Eight children had gained cycle proficiency certificates.

Visits were made to Norton "Petsenta" for infants, and Bury St. Edmunds for juniors in connection with Magna Carta studies, to see the Norman Tower, Abbey ruins and the Cathedral. The rector took weekly assemblies. The winter Term closed with "a simple Carol Service in the Church", and entertainment by a conjuror. Under difficult circumstances, the School was doing a grand job.

Mrs. Bradley had cleaned the School well in the holidays, but the change of heating fuel had not proved satisfactory. (Those stoves were a perennial problem!)

By March '74 another letter from the Education Office had arrived, "concerning the proposed closure of the School as soon as alternative accommodation is available at Beyton". It's just as well the School carried on as normal, because this new primary school never materialised! Managers requested the installation of an outdoor light to help Mrs. Bradley with her work during the winter, when re-fuelling the stoves. No new cupboards and work trays had arrived, but at least the blackboards had been replaced. The Thedwastre Rodent Officer had been called in to deal with shrews which were "troublesome in the infant cupboards". Managers discussed a report in the *Bury Free Press* on the state of the school toilets, "but there have been no complaints from parents about them." The Education Office "cannot sanction improvements in view of the pending closure of the School" – a familiar refrain!

The next meeting was in June 1974, by which time, including 16 Hessett children, there were 51 on Roll. Numbers would fall when Beyton Middle School became fully operational in September. Meanwhile, the School continued to flourish. Two girls had played recorders in the Breckland Music Festival at Brandon. "Credit is due to Mrs. Jack for training them … both gained good adjudications and one gained first place. Certificates will be sent to both". Also "Sergeant Cadge and P. C. Upson tested 10 children who have been having Cycle Proficiency training, and nine passed."

Another major change occurred in the mid-Seventies. The dreaded, socially-divisive and demeaning 11-plus was phased out as Comprehensive Schools were established.

DRINKSTONE BECOMES A 5-9 FIRST SCHOOL

In September 1974 children aged nine or ten years were enrolled at the new Middle School at Beyton. Drinkstone's roll was only 38, 19 in each class.

From my personal experience as a teacher of young children, I know that small classes spanning only a small age-range enable appropriate, first class education to be offered in a friendly secure environment. Teachers need to be well-trained, flexible and enthusiastic for a small school to work well. Multi-talented also, you might think! But in a village school friendly and welcoming to parents, the parents' talents can also be called on. The school becomes even more "owned" by the families using it. Parents and friends can become a huge strength, offering special skills, and individual support for children who need it. At this stage in Drinkstone School's history, there were improved resources all round – a specialist music teacher, cover for the Head during her hours of office work, and professional ancillary help. By the 1970s, teachers were no longer left to flounder or vegetate for years on their own, but had up-to-date professional training available from the L.E.A. even including supply-teacher cover for all-day courses. Drinkstone could have remained a viable First School adding considerably to the village sense of community. During the last two decades of the School, all these aims were achieved, most of the time.

What was lacking was commitment from education authorities, from Parliament down to grass roots, towards the ethos of small village schools. I think this lack of commitment was basically fuelled by insufficient funding. Changes were made on short-term economic grounds, not because they would benefit children and their communities.

However all this is now history! So back to the story of the Seventies and Eighties, as told in Log Book and Managers' Minutes:

Autumn 1974 - "Towards the end of Term, parents were invited to visit School, where they saw some of the normal activities of their children". The children were to organise their own Carol Service in the Church.

During these years, the managers' Rota was faithfully observed, with regular visits to the School. In January 1975 Brigadier Wight reported "all seemed to be in order and reasonable repair, considering the imminent closure of the School".

Sometime during Spring – Summer 1975, the proposal for a new First School to be built at Beyton was finally dropped. Drinkstone would remain open, and at last a permanent Head could be appointed. Miss Raynham had run the School pleasantly and very successfully, but was employed on a temporary basis.

The Log Book for Summer 1975 says: "The County String Quartet visited on 5th June, and gave a short concert. Our recorder players joined the strings for three items. The children also sang with the Quartet."

At a meeting in October 1975, Miss Coleman of the Education Office was present. New managers were appointed – Mr. John Bell and Mrs. C. Button. The big news was that the post of Headteacher would be advertised by Suffolk County Council, to commence at Easter 1976 (by which time Miss Raynham would have run the School for three and a half years.) There was discussion regarding a Parent-Teacher Association and "possibility of self-help in improving the School generally now that the closure of the School has been postponed indefinitely."

In January 1976, the appointment of Mrs. Barbara Wright, from April 27th, was confirmed. Mr. Carnall, the Chief Education Officer, asked to be notified of dates of all future Managers' Meetings. Miss Raynham reported 45 on roll (11 from Hessett). Up to 38 children took school dinners each day, the rest bringing packed lunch. She said: "Staff and children were very pleased that several parents joined them for the Carol Service in Church at the end of term. Such an occasion, and weekly visits by the rector for assembly, strengthens the link between School and Church."

Mrs. Button, visiting manager, reported the School to be "in good shape, although the motor tyres have perished and are dirty". These tyres were used in play by the children (providing much fun, as Andrew Smith recalls in the Personal Memories of the next chapter.) Another problem was early arrival by taxi of Hessett pupils, before any member of staff was present. It was agreed that a letter be sent to the Office pointing this out, and repeating the request for "a suitable light for the coal shed, for use in winter months".

At the Meeting in March 1976 (Miss Raynham's last) a letter was read from Mr. Carnall "regarding provision of lights for the benefit of the caretaker. Mr. Nunn explained that an estimate for two lights, including one on the outside corner of the School building, had been obtained from the Architect's Department, of £65".

Miss Raynham reported that parents were dealing with the tyres used at playtime, and that "the matter of the children travelling from Hessett by taxi and arriving at School before a teacher was present, had been resolved, since Mrs. Kozlowski now travels in the first car".

At the meeting in May managers were shown "a letter of thanks to the managers from Miss Raynham, for the book token and flowers given to her at the end of term". Certainly her efforts had a positive effect on the School and she was probably sorry to be leaving. During her time as Acting Head, she had introduced a termly Newsletter for the benefit of parents. Children and parents appreciated her, as my interviews with ex-pupils showed. Her successor, Mrs. Barbara Wright, was an enthusiastic and energetic lady, who continued the work of bringing the little School closer to modern expectations.

One of Mrs. Wright's first entries in the Log Book (April 28th 1976, her second day as Head) was the startling announcement: "Mrs. Kozlowski absent today due to a lorry crashing into her house"! At the first Managers' Meeting Mrs. Wright attended, in May 1976, a letter was read from the Diocesan Solicitor about use of the School house. At last this looked possible, and there could not have been a more likely person than this new Headteacher to make it a reality, since her husband worked for the County Council as Area Building Surveyor. He knew where surplus or cheap materials could be found. The couple also had the practical knowledge and expertise to organise the work themselves. During the Easter holidays Mrs. Wright had already sent a list of requests to the Office. The School had received very little attention or help during the previous few years due to threat of closure. Now that threat was removed, and hopes were high.

The Head's Reports presented to the managers at the first few Meetings after Mrs. Wright took up her post show her all-round enthusiasm, so I give them in detail.

Head's Report to Managers 27/05/1976:

I have appointed Mrs. Bithray as clerical assistant, and Mrs. R. Troll as Head's Relief (teacher when the Head is involved in office work)... I have ordered drinking glasses for use at dinners as I feel the children need a drink with their meal.

In the holidays my family and friends turned out the cupboards and re-painted all wall-boards, and moved all furniture in an attempt to update the School. I have re-organised the classrooms so that as soon as the equipment is available we may use the hall for movement – especially in the winter. The best tables are now used for dinner as I felt the old ones were unhygienic. I am aiming to share resources and equipment between both classes which will conserve space and provide continuity of work. We are very badly off for equipment and junior books but I hope to obtain quite a lot from Beyton (First) School when it closes, and am due to visit Mrs. Betterton with this in mind after half term. I have ordered some basic maths and reading books to work with for this term, also I have on loan some reading books and an SRA Lab for use with slower and younger children... Mr. Foreman has been to School and tested the children who will leave to go to Beyton Middle in September.

No adequate reading records or maths records by my standards have been left for me so I am working through the children and making a complete set of my own. I hope next term to introduce an internal record book for use throughout the School.

The attendance of juniors for swimming at Bury pool has been 100% and the children are making good progress and having a most enjoyable time. We have been having an "Eye Spy" quiz on the bus en route and doing some follow-up work on our return.

Mrs. Jack and I are taking a party of seven juniors to the Breckland Festival. I have invited Mr. Shaw, Music Adviser, to visit the School with an eye to providing us with more musical apparatus. Mrs. Jack is most enthusiastic and deserves encouragement.

The children and I enjoy folk dancing outside and I feel this compensates somewhat for the lack of a games area. We have started a gardening programme, each junior has a small plot of garden, seeds are coming up at last! I should like to make the area at the back of the junior room more attractive so that it might be used as an outdoor work/play area.

I wish to extend the dinner hour by ten minutes, until 1.20pm, as such a short time as at present gives insufficient time to prepare an afternoon lesson; to open School at 9 o'clock and close at 3.30pm. I have ordered three new Elsan toilets, I hope to press for a Portaloo unit after. I have got the firm approval for the acquisition of the house. This is of primary importance and needs to be pushed at once.

I hope to move the climbing frame from the playground onto the grass in front of the house. This will be safer and give more play area.

New equipment obtained so far is as follows – paper trimmer, second-hand duplicator, typewriter (in need of attention), telephone installed.

I have requested the following from Mr. Carnall (some may be available from Beyton) – 22 replacement infant tables and chairs, 2 wire book racks, floor-standing cupboard or shelves for infant reading books, new storage cupboard, new teacher's chair. I have not received any extra money from the County for the School as promised by Mrs. Dunning at my interview.

I had a visit from the press, who under the pretence of doing a feature on small old village schools, took photos of the children at work, and then published the article attached. I feel it is best to ignore the whole episode, but it may be relevant when I apply for a Portaloo later.

"I have erected an old tennis net as an experiment along by the fence onto the road. This has so far been quite effective as a 'ball-catcher'. Perhaps later we may raise some money for a better net to take its place. I hope to have an open afternoon at the end of term, possibly a combination of stalls, games and entertainment."

Head's Report to Managers 08/07/1976:

Swimming programme excellent, seven children gained awards. Mrs. Jack and I took seven juniors to the Breckland Festival. I was delighted that from our group two children went into the final. Sally Anne King was the overall winner in her age group, obtaining distinction.

Mr. Shaw (Music Adviser) has promised a new set of chime bars, a glockenspiel, and some more music books for next term. A new tape cassette has been received from Mr. Sheppard (Senior Adviser). The large P. E. mats promised, have been received, and are being used for some basic gymnastics outside. The new Elsans have been installed. We have started using the new maths books and the children are working enthusiastically. I obtained four unwanted book racks from Thurston First School, also a Baby Belling cooker. I hope to introduce cooking as part of the curriculum next term if we obtain the use of the Schoolhouse.

The acquisition of the Schoolhouse is proceeding very slowly. I have telephoned Mr. Carnall twice this week and have still received no firm reply to my enquiries. I feel a letter from the managers may help. If we are to use the house next term, work needs to be in hand during the holidays. I should like to appeal to parents for help in decorating the rooms and covering the floors. Curtains and furniture may be available from Beyton, but without the firm approval for the use of the house I am unable to make any further moves.

Items to be requested from Mr. Hill are as follows: the garden at rear of School to be grassed for use by the children as we have no playing field. A Portaloo to be installed to replace the Elsans, the old toilets cleared, and the area to be included in the grass at the back of the School. Also, something must be done about the dreadful furniture in the infant room. I had hoped to acquire some from Beyton but it is not of a suitable size. Also we need improved heating to both rooms.

We have been invited to Sports at Beyton School on 21st July and they are paying us a visit for an informal afternoon of music and drama. A successful parents' evening was held – all families except two were represented.

A visit was made on Monday 5th July by Mrs. S. Mowat, School Meals Supervisor, to observe dinner arrangements. We need further equipment and more time for Mrs. Andrews to clear away. I have requested improvements in the kitchen to the sink and drainer and the floor as they are all in a poor state and unhygienic.

At this Meeting, the managers were informed of a letter from Mr. Hill (Education Office) inviting them to express their views concerning urgent work needed on School property. They agreed to send a letter to the County Land Agent, to Mr. Carnall, and to Mr. Hill "in an effort to get some urgent action on the acquisition of the house, which has been offered rent-free to the Education Authority for use by the School".

Possession of the Schoolhouse was finally confirmed in a letter from Mr. Carnall, dated July 16th.

At the next Meeting, which took place on November 4th 1976, Miss J. Coleman (from the Office) was present. One "urgent matter" under discussion, was "action on the heating apparatus". Mrs. Wright reported that "the new caretaker, Mrs. Vi Cocksedge, takes great pride in the new appearance of the School", and at her suggestion, the managers agreed to send a letter of appreciation to Mrs. Cocksedge "for all her hard work during the School summer recess and at all times."

The Mini-Sports afternoon at the end of Summer Term was well attended, the white elephant and cake stalls raising £44 "to start our School Fund". Also the school groundsmen had cleared and seeded the garden at the rear of the School to make a grass area for play. They were asked to mark out additional games on the playground "to encourage incidental learning of reading and number facts".

The doorway through from classroom to the house had been completed by Mr. Nunn, also further repairs to the roof. Mrs. Wright's Report continues: "My family and I cleared the rotten floor from the T.V. room, and replaced this with a solid floor. Old students and Mrs. J. Smith came to help me cart sand for use in the room, their help was much appreciated. Some of the old students have returned to see me this term to see how we are progressing. The house has been re-wired, with lights and plug points for the downstairs rooms. I acquired two heaters on loan from Sudbury Evening Centre. I have roughly re-decorated the office so that it is fresh and bright. The old cupboard in the infant room has been replaced by a tall book rack."

The outcome of a visit by Mrs. Brain, School Meals Organiser, to discuss improvements to the servery arrangements in the back porch, was that the kitchen in the house might be adapted for this instead. (It was even suggested by another member of Office staff, that Drinkstone might become a "cooking kitchen", subject to County Architect's approval. Mrs. Wright considered this unlikely unless drainage arrangements were improved. It never happened.) Mr. Crane had also paid a visit "to examine the stoves and discuss the possibility of a new form of heaters".

The Report goes on: "A Harvest Gathering was held in School on 24th September. A good number of parents and friends attended. The produce was later distributed to the Over-60 Club in the village. The Open Evening on 12th October was very well attended, and very complimentary comments were received regarding the appearance of the School and work seen".

No outside lighting had been provided, but "a torch has been ordered for Mrs. Cocksedge to use during the winter!"

There were 40 pupils on roll at this time, 18 infants and 22 juniors. 32 dinners were provided each day. At the end of this meeting, the managers adjourned to the Schoolhouse "to appreciate the improved facilities".

At the next Meeting of managers, in March 1977, Mr. Harris from the Office was present, and confirmed that taxi transport for Hessett children would continue. Mr. Bell announced his resignation as manager, the new manager to be Mr. Cady. Mrs. Button, visiting manager for the term, reported all well with the School, excepting uneven floors in the infant room and the back porch. Improvements and repairs were going well. Oil heating was to be installed during summer 1977, the coal shed removed, and an oil tank sited behind the Schoolhouse. Rotten trees in the playground area were "felled by Mr. Lockley's team". The new servery in the house kitchen was "a great help to us all". Mrs. Bullett was now mid-day supervisor.

That summer, May-Day Festivities raised £15 "despite rain". The County String Quartet performed to the children. Janice Pickering "won the Community Council Prize for the best poster depicting village tidiness. Prize to be presented in the marquee when the Queen visits Ipswich on 11th July. We are all delighted for her and for the School."

By the Meeting held on 10th November 1977 "the new heating is fitted at last after a lengthy interval between commencement and completion of work. The flues have still not been cemented in. We are keeping the temporary heaters, on loan from County Architect's Department, in case of further problems." This turned out to be a wise move! Outside painting and repairs were reported to be almost complete, and a fence had been erected in the back garden to enclose the Elsan emptying area. Mrs. Wright said: "I am concerned about the boys' urinal area. In wet weather there is no protection. Could this be covered in?" The poor condition of the path up to and around the house was noted. Approval was given for improving the scullery/ entrance porch, and for a second electrical point in the juniors' room.

"Mrs. Francis, Schools Adviser, called. She was pleased with improvements made, and gave £20 to be spent on equipment. She borrowed some work to show at one of her Courses." At Harvest time, children organised an afternoon for friends and parents. Produce was given to the Church for their Service, and passed on to the Meals on Wheels scheme.

The Log Book graphically describes problems with the new oil heaters that winter. Despite new chimney cowls, and "stabilisers" to the flue pipes, the new heaters "emitted clouds of blue smoke and black soot, but little heat." Six weeks after installation, Mrs. Wright reported "temperature of large room 39 degrees Fahrenheit at 9.15am. Calor heaters and electric fires were brought in and the temperature "peaked" at 58 degrees by 3.30pm. These heaters had electric time clocks. Power cuts were frequent, some days they didn't come on. By May, Mrs. Wright had learned to switch them on herself.

There were more changes among the managers by the next Meeting, February 1978. Mrs. Joyce Cocksedge and Mrs. Mary Pocock took office. In December, "a letter had been written to Mr. Carnall, expressing disappointment with the new heaters". Due to unexpected electricity cuts, the children had to be sent home on January 30th. The Rodent Officer had dealt with "troublesome mice". On the plus side, the Christmas Concert had been greatly enjoyed and appreciated, the scullery/ cloakroom area had been re-equipped to include a practical maths and home play area. New fire extinguishers had been provided and fire drills practised. Children would have a "Spell-in" for the Blind, and perform a play at Thurston School.

Rev. Gooderham was leaving the parish. Mrs. Wright thanked him for his help and encouragement during his time at Drinkstone.

By June, a new manually operated heater was installed in the large classroom. The heater in the smaller room remained "rather erratic at times!" Floors in rear porch and infants room would be re-laid using industrial vinyl.

A great many visitors had been received at the School, including Miss Wickham, Church Schools Adviser, Mrs. Browning to talk on Japan, Mrs. Cooper from the Children's Society, and Mr. Brand, H.M.I., who "expressed what a pleasant school this is!" "Sponsored Tables" had raised £60.

The children enjoyed several outings. They visited Moyses Hall, and Colchester Castle and Zoo. The Log tells us "all children and some parents spent a happy time at Norton Bird Gardens". Mrs. Kozlowski was retiring, having taught at the School for 14 years (second only to assistant teacher Caroline Minns, who had stayed 22 years). Mrs. Scott, already well known to the children, would teach the infants class from September 1978.

Mrs. Wright reported that September roll would be only 24 children, but "as yet we are not included on the closure list". This fluctuation in numbers was a constant factor at Drinkstone School. Now, taking only pupils aged 5–9 years, and with families smaller than in the past, the arrival or departure of just one or two families, or an extra-large year group going up to Beyton, could make a drastic difference in numbers. There had been 45 on roll when Mrs. Wright started at the School two years earlier. Now she felt bound to seek a post elsewhere. At an Emergency Meeting of managers called on 15th June, she announced her resignation as from December 1978, this being accepted "with much regret".

Autumn Term 1978 came and went, with the usual round of events – Harvest Gathering, a visit from the County Wind Quartet and a visit to Ipswich Theatre to see a puppet show, "Animal Magic". Mrs. Scott settled in well, even the stoves were functioning! Sadly, in December the time came to bid Barbara Wright farewell. The managers thanked her "for all she had accomplished at the School" and wished her all the best for her new employment.

I think it likely that without this lady's wonderful efforts to improve buildings, grounds, and resources, the School might not have managed to stay open until 1986.

THE VILLAGE

During the 1970s the village grew in size and population. Much new building was of "executive homes", expensive dwellings with numerous "en-suite" bathrooms, not the kind of home young parents with small children can afford! There were also smaller homes, and bungalows. A high proportion of new homes were bought by older couples. The appearance and character of the village continued to evolve towards modern attitudes and lifestyles. Some new residents had a suburban-commuter life-style, so that in-comers often remained somewhat apart from village community life, having work, leisure, and family links elsewhere.

In contrast, some newcomers were keen to be active in the community. Mr. and Mrs. Beswick moved into No. 2, Cross Street, in 1974 (their home was built on land purchased from Greene King, at the rear of The Cherry Tree pub). This couple involved themselves with Church, Sunday School, clubs and pastimes in Drinkstone. Sheila Beswick, with some friends, set up a Local History Group which attracted both old and new residents. Mr. and Mrs. Gilbert moved into "Kimberley", a bungalow built in Beyton Road in 1977, and Ken became a School manager. Mr. and Mrs. Medcalf moved into Green End,

High Barn

The Old Rectory

Cambourne Cottage

The Chestnuts

Rattlesden Road, in 1972, David becoming a churchwarden. These and others were ready to give to the community and helped keep Drinkstone a good place to live.

Most new building was concentrated in Rattlesden Road and Cross Street, but a few new homes appeared in Gedding Road, Beyton Road, and The Street (opposite the School). "Mr. Thurlow's meadow" where school children had spent so many happy playtimes, was sold for the building of three imposing new homes. Home Farm, the Thurlows' farmhouse, was also sold off separately from the farmlands (which are still farmed today by members of the Thurlow family, but from Moat Farmhouse and Moat Cottage, which stand in the former parklands of Drinkstone Park). Down-sizing of farms and their properties was happening everywhere. For example, in Beyton Road, the bungalow built as a tied cottage for Meade Farm in the 1930s, was sold off privately to Roger and Lynda Steward in 1974, and re-named as "Whispering Winds". Yew Tree Farm in Cross Street had been sold, and new properties built on the land. Ruby Bland (née Rogers) whose family owned that farm, wisely kept the field on which her home stood, alongside Gedding Road. The Rogers' bungalow home was in fact an adapted building from a World War Two air base, which I am told Ruby kept in immaculate condition and comfort.

Other changes were unstoppable, such as the closing of the Wesleyan Chapel, which had celebrated its Centenary in 1966, and which in the 1860s was said to have been "crowded to excess, many being unable to gain admittance, at every service". Like others in villages all over East Anglia, the Chapel was converted into a four-bedroom home, in 1974.

The Anglican Church of All Saints' no longer had rectors who were allowed to stay for decades. During a long interregnum, the Rev. Nicholas Cribb, a widower who lodged in High Barn in Chapel Lane with Mrs. Margaret Hazell, unofficially stepped in to keep things going, and was to do this again in a later interregnum. He had worked as lecturer and chaplain at Trent Polytechnic in Nottingham, and had a great love of children, becoming a School manager and regularly visiting just to chat with the children (doing more listening than talking). He was a real friend to the children. Mrs. Hazell, now in her eighties, says "every Saturday the children used to come round, I'd sometimes find them sitting on the doorstep! The Raison family, the Williams family, Matthew Bullett and many others would come, they'd bring frogs for Mr. Cribb to put in the pond. We fenced it round to keep it safe. They came here for confirmation lessons, and they used to sit on my rocking chairs, and I think they used to rock across the room! Afterwards I would have to put the carpet straight. Rev Cribb had endless time for children, he thought they were important. I remember the last service he took, he was 'fading', and two of the boys were his 'bearers', each holding one arm!"

Margaret Hazell had been a good friend of Constance Collins, the widowed head teacher who served so long at the School. Her home at High Barn is an example of a surprisingly early barn conversion. The barn was built around four hundred years ago, as a typical four-bay timber-framed barn, then was converted into two farm cottages around 1850. In the years following the Second World War it was sold off for private use and made into a single house. Mrs. Hazell bought it in 1955, adding a small extension in 1978 (tiled, whereas the main barn area is still beautifully thatched). Great care has been taken to retain, and even add, period features. The living room has an amazing carved wooden fireplace, bought from Culford Hall and elaborately adorned with foliage, men and lions (similar to a fire surround in Strangers' Hall, Norwich, Margaret Hazell says). The heavy studded wood front door with grille is said to be a relic from Rattlesden Gaol!

Landmarks of Drinkstone, such as The Old Rectory north of the School, also underwent changes. This Grade II Listed building was advertised for sale by auction, at The Angel Hotel in Bury St. Edmunds, described by the *East Anglian Daily Times* (November 1973) as a country house "built of red brick in 1760, with a later northern wing". In 1976 the house was again for sale, now described as having three reception rooms, seven bedrooms, four bathrooms, and an outside stable block providing two receptions, three bedrooms, and garaging for six cars. The Lodge Cottage was to be sold off as a separate lot, standing in a plot of one third acre. Not many years later, the coach house and stable block were also sold off separately.

In company with many Suffolk villages, Drinkstone acquired a stylish "village sign" in 1978. The *East Anglian Daily Times* showed a photo of the unveiling, which took place on 29th October, at the junction of Green Close and Gedding Road. The article reads "Residents at Drinkstone yesterday saw the unveiling of their new village sign by the oldest inhabitant, 83-year-old Mrs. Anna 'Pansy' Mayes. The sign was designed and made by local craftsman Mr. John Gibbs who lives in the house in Chapel Lane where Pansy was born. The sign was dedicated by the priest-in-charge of the parish, the Rev. Nicholas Cribb. The sign was paid for by the Drinkstone Jubilee Committee from funds raised last year and handed over to the Parish Council by the Committee's Chairman Mr. Malcolm Robertson."

1975 saw the much-regretted closure of the village shop in Rattlesden Road, run for many years by the Cooper family. The cottage housing the shop was built by Mr. Cooper senior in 1913, and is now known as Bramble Cottage. The Post Office Stores run in Church Cottage, The Street, was also closed by this time. At least the village still had its pub, The Cherry Tree, where meals were available. But everyone was now forced to shop for daily needs outside the village, or rely on the few goods available from the milk-man. and a handful of shops delivering by van. The village was no longer a self-sufficient community. There was still one shop in the village, at Elm Tree Cottage in Gedding Road where Anne and Geoffrey Wilding ran a craft shop and gallery of art, also selling greetings cards and small items suitable as presents. Geoffrey Wilding was a valued member of the Board of Managers of the School.

Those who bought older properties in Drinkstone often had a great interest in the history of their homes (and the village), and spent time and money lovingly restoring and maintaining them. A good example of this is Blacksmith's Cottage, north of the School, in The Street, thought to date from the early 16th century. Purchased by Randall and Eileen Bell in 1974, these new owners made extensive repairs which included replacing the roof (decayed thatch covered over with corrugated iron!) with splendid new reed thatching. None of the character was lost during repairs and restorations: the right hand side of the roof is lower than the "parlour block" (with half-hipped roof) to the left. The two roof levels, gabled thatch dormer and small-paned casements are charming. The cottage (now owned by Louise Todd and Robin Sharp) is a chocolate-box example of pink-washed thatched cottage. Without this timely help, it might have been demolished (the fate of many others). Without the expedient action of previous owners, who used corrugated iron to avoid the expense of re-roofing, it might have disintegrated through damp. Now it is Grade II listed.

Other venerable cherished homes in The Street include the row just south of Blacksmith's Cottage. These started life as three terraced cottages built circa 1640. The cottage now known as The Old Post Office was built on at the north end in the early 19th century. The 1839 tithe map reveals that the cottage (then owned by David Bull) was inhabited by James Hawkins, William Bennet and Joseph Manfield, and was a wheelwright's shop. The last postmistress to live here was Maria Craske. A wheelwright also lived in the older, southern section of the row at one time, and a stone fireplace here bears the inscription "Joshu Hawkins 1785". Unusual horizontal-sliding Suffolk sash windows in some of these cottages is part of the reason for their Grade II listing. The present owners keep them in wonderful repair.

In the same 1970s decade, Cambourne Cottage in Rattlesden Road also changed hands. Originally a row of three rather humble thatched cottages dating from the late 16th or early 17th centuries, the building was bequeathed to the parish in 1693 under the Will of Rev. Thomas Cambourne, one-time rector of Drinkstone. This Will is now in the Records Office. Mr. and Mrs. Wilson, who bought the cottage in 1970, obtained permission for extensions to both ends of the cottage – looking from the road, the left-side or east extension cannot be seen as it is to the rear, but on the right (west) end, a new two-storey wing extends from front to back, and beyond into the rear garden. This "west wing" has an impressive tall window, continous through upper and lower storeys, and makes the cottage appear quite a grand building.

In 1976, Peter and Anne Norman bought the cottage. They were fascinated by its history, and even had a weather-vane designed and made, bearing the exact signature of Rev. Cambourne, taken from his Will written in 1692, plus an effigy of a clergyman of the period. A second effigy stands in their entrance hall, in recognition of this generous priest whose gift still enhances the lives of young people embarking on work or training. Grants are given for tools and equipment.

Several pairs of semi-detached cottages in Rattlesden Road were converted into single dwellings. Some had their old thatch replaced by tiles. "Needle's Eye" is one example. Originally a pair of farm labourers' cottages belonging to Green Farm, they had become semi-derelict, their thatch green and rotten. In the Seventies, the cottages were stripped down, totally renovated as a single dwelling, and given a tiled roof. "Chimbleys" was also renovated and tiled. This was a better fate than that which befell the pair of cottages which once stood in the garden of Lyndhurst cottage in Gedding Road, last owned by William Canham and occupied by William Steff and John Palfrey. Mary Horrex (née Palfrey) speaks of a row of thatched cottages opposite Chapel Lane, where she was born. There is no trace of these today.

Brick cottages were also knocked two-into-one during the 1970s, one example being "Woodend" in Rattlesden Road, built of Woolpit brick circa 1830. The building was extended, making a family home now occupied by the Lane family.

Also in Rattlesden Road, changes during the 1970s literally turned up the past! There had been two cottages, each not much more than a single room, used by long ago itinerant Quaker preachers. Quaker Cottage was the preaching room, while Hazel Cottage provided sleeping accommodation. Both are now incorporated into one dwelling, known as "Quaker Cottage". In the garden of these Quaker buildings, in 1973, "Green End" was built, becoming home to David Medcalf and his wife Susan. One November in the late Seventies, builders who were extending some drains in the garden of "Green End" dug up some body remains (parts comprising about one and a half bodies). An inquest declared the remains to be over 100 years old, so they were buried elsewhere. It is probable that this land was used as a Quaker burial ground.

Another change of use during the 1970s had unexpected results for the parish. "The Chestnuts", far along the Rattlesden Road, beyond Barcock's Nursery, was a 16th century farmhouse, constructed like most Tudor buildings of heavy oak timber framework infilled with wattle and daub. A lean-to at the rear was thought to be built simply of straw, muck and mud, and a long pond along the road side of the garden showed where clay had been dug out for the building. By the 1970s, the outer walls were rendered and colour-washed, and the original thatched roof had been replaced with tiles. It is a fine historic farmhouse; in one ceiling a leather shoe sole had been discovered, reputed to be a charm to repel witches. This house, in several acres with fine oak barns, actually stood in the parish of Rattlesden, although many fields separate it from the houses of Rattlesden village.

In 1971 the owner farmed pigs, but profits were poor. So during the Seventies Mr. and Mrs. Barber, helped by Mr. and Mrs. McSweeny of Woolpit, set to work converting the barns into workshops, display areas, a craft shop and a cafe. An article in the *East Anglian Daily Times*, March 1974, tells how skills such as corn-dolly making, wood-carving, pottery, candle-making, copper and silver-smith craft, could be observed and learned at the centre, which also had a children's play area. It was an ambitious project, intended as a tourist attraction and venue for school parties. It was hoped that one day other crafts such as 'lapidary' (work with polished and semi-precious stones) would be included. Peter Gunnett, an artist from Drinkstone, was one of the artisans. It was an imaginative venture, but sadly it did not attract enough customers to pay for itself long-term, and had to be discontinued.

However, there was an interesting spin-off for Drinkstone parish! Feeling themselves to be much more a part of Drinkstone than of Rattlesden, the place was advertised as "Drinkstone Craft Centre". It was confusing for visitors approaching through Drinkstone village, to find themselves staring at a "Rattlesden" boundary sign before they reached the "Drinkstone Craft Centre", and Rattlesden Parish Council objected to the name. The result was that County authorities actually moved the parish boundary further along the Rattlesden Road so "The Chestnuts" and its land (together with several properties on the opposite side of the road) became part of an enlarged Drinkstone parish.

The great outside world impinged on the parish to the south, on the Gedding Road, in various ways. One of the Kray Brothers' henchmen lived for a short while at "Stone Cottages"! Further south along the road to Gedding, the wealthy Tolman family moved into Abilene Lodge, and every now and again Mr. Tolman would give Drinkstone children a ride in his helicopter! And a little further on, at historic Gedding Hall, the new Lord of the Manor was Bill Wyman of The Rolling Stones!

THE LAST YEARS OF DRINKSTONE SCHOOL

Returning to events at the School: Mrs. Shirley Hall, new Headmistress, took up her post in January 1978, with 24 children on roll. The managers at this time were Mrs. Button, Mr. Parrin (from Hessett Six

1979: back row – Mrs Barbara Wright, Mrs Rosemary Cady, Robert Sibley, Peter Chater, ? ?, Andrew Jack, Justine Gridley, Mrs Andrews, Mrs Cathy Scott. Third row – Susan Lingwood, Tracey Cornish, Lynn Tipple, Tressa Sobkowiak, Samantha Cocksedge, Nigel Button, Ian Crick. Sitting on chairs – Ian Wilmshurst, Gary Wilmshurst, Zoe Wilmshurst, Matthew Cady, Stephen Wells, James Charter. Sitting on floor – Karen Cooper, ? ? ?, Claire Cocksedge.

1980: Back row – Mrs Joyce Cocksedge, ?, Tressa Sobkowiak, Gary Wilmshurst, Matthew Cady, Justine Gridley, Sarah Lingwood, Tracey Cornish; Third row – Kerry Parrin, Mandy Smith, James Charter, Samantha Cocksedge, Zoelli Boulton, Stephen Wells, Zoe Wilmshurst; sitting on chairs – Karen Cooper, Debbie Cooper, Mrs Rosemary Cady, Mrs Shirley Hall, Mrs Cathy Scott, Rebecca Bradley, Darren Haill; sitting on floor – Daniel Steward, Arabella Thomas, Tracey Foster, John Foster, Amanda Sobkowiak.

Bells), Mrs. Pocock, Rev. Nicholas Cribb, Mrs. King, Mr. Cady, Mrs. Cocksedge, and Geoffrey Wilding, acting chairman. David Medcalf, in his role as churchwarden, also attended meetings. At the meeting in March 1979 Mrs. Hall reported that Mrs. Scott, the young infant teacher, was "excellent", that Mrs. Cady was new School Secretary, and Mrs. Andrews and Mrs. D. Smith were lunch-time supervisors. The new Reading Scheme was good, and Standard Reading Tests for the older children resulted in above-average scores, one child only needing special help. Educational visits included trips to West Stow Nature Trail to observe the seasons, and a performance by a Theatre Dance Company. There would be a Candlemas service in All Saints' to which parents were invited. Mrs. Hall invited voluntary help from parents, with or without any special talents.

On the negative side, the roof was still leaking, Hessett parents now had to pay for their children's transport to School, and pupil numbers were low. Rev. Cribb was asked to keep in touch with the doings of the National Association for Support of Small Schools (NASSS). Mr. Cady had written to the County Council representative asking him to vote against the closure of two other small Suffolk schools.

At the meeting in June 1979 thanks were proposed to various voluntary helpers – Mr. Crick with football, Mrs. J. Cocksedge with swimming at Bury pool, Mrs. Donaghy with the infants, and Mr. Bell and Mr. Medcalf with cycling proficiency training sessions. In Maths tests for older children, all but one had gained average-or-above results. Mrs. Francis, adviser, had borrowed the School's Science Project for display. All but two four-year-olds had attended swimming classes. Pupils had been congratulated on their behaviour at the pool. Children had taken part in Breckland Music Festival, and Area Sports at Pakenham. They had visited West Stow, and Clare Country Park. The children would attend an Ascension Day service at the Church. A group of pre-school children attended on Tuesday afternoons.

This does not sound like a disadvantaged education! Even the building had received attention. Mr. Nunn had repaired walls and roof to prevent rain entering. There was talk of injecting damp-proofing. Mrs. Cocksedge was keeping the School "looking clean and bright" and several compliments on its appearance had been received.

By Autumn Term 1979, a new incumbent, the Rev. David Wall, had arrived, and his small son was enrolled at the School, which even so had only 21 on roll (nine had gone up to Middle School, two had moved to Norfolk). Rev. Wall and Rev. Cribb both visited the School regularly. Community links were strong, and the village over-sixties group had attended the children's Harvest service.

Mrs. J. Cocksedge was now lunch-time supervisor. Repairs to the Schoolhouse had resulted in the removal of a demolition order imposed in the early Seventies. Many minor repairs to buildings and playground had been completed.

The Theatre Royal in Bury was celebrating its 160th "Birthday"; pupils enjoyed a puppet show there. At Breckland Music Festival, Andrew Jack came first out of 82 entrants. Children's work had been exhibited at the village Craft Exhibition. For the end of term, a Concert, a Children's Party, an Open Day, and a Christmas service in All Saints' were planned.

By the time the managers met in the Spring Term 1980, there were 30 pupils on roll. Parents had given books, dolls, a painting easel, and a carpet for the infants' reading corner. Volunteer parent-helpers now included Mrs. Boulton, Mrs. Clark, Mrs. Donaghy and Mrs. Budden. Nine pupils took the County Reading Test for eight-plus children, and six of these were found to have reading ages over ten years.

The Minutes conclude with this statement:

"The managers noted the happy working spirit in the School, and also the high estimation
in which it is held locally, and... are determined to keep the School open".

During the Summer Term 1980, all children made flower arrangements to decorate All Saints' pews for a Flower Festival. Due to a fire at Bury pool, swimming now took place at Rougham Primary School. Mrs. J. Cocksedge had resigned as manager, but had presented the School with a trophy for achievement to mark her time in office.

In the County Maths Test for older children, all were graded average or above.

It was announced that "for reasons of uniformity" the L.E.A. had re-named managers "Governors", a change involving much new training, rules and paperwork. Also, the valued provision of daily milk to younger children was withdrawn by the L.E.A. in March 1980. ("Maggie Thatcher, milk-snatcher!" I recall!)

By the end of the Summer Term, 33 children were on roll. This reduced to 26 in September. However during Autumn four children living in Rattlesden transferred to Drinkstone School, bringing the roll once again to 30. In the Autumn Term, children studied the Church with Rev. Cribb. They were to entertain the over-sixties club at a party in the Village Hall (given by the Women's Institute ladies). They would take part in All Saints' Carol service. Claire Cocksedge did "exceptionally well" at the Breckland Music Festival. Children collected tree seeds, and sent a donation of £28 to the Woodland Trust.

On the down side, slates were falling from the roof, the protective wire-netting around guttering needed renewing, and Groundsmen's hours had been cut. Parents agreed to help with maintenance of the grounds, and painting and decorating the building. School meal price was to rise from 45p to 50p in 1981.

By the first Governors' meeting of 1981, there were 30 on roll. Miss A. Moll from Western Area Education Office was present. Most items were positive news – a dangerous plum tree had been felled; a parent, Mrs. J. Crean, had given a screen to go with the projector already owned by the School; money set aside for a screen could be used for musical equipment. Parent helpers included Mrs. Charter, Mrs. Frogley (from Rattlesden), Mrs. Gill (from Hessett) and Mrs. L. Steward. Miss Rosemary Hazell (daughter of Margaret Hazell) brought a brass and woodwind group to play for the children. Hessett playgroup, comprising ten children with their mothers, visited the School. A policeman visited to talk on road safety. Children watched "Gulliver's Travels" at the Theatre. There would be an Open Evening for parents, and an Easter service in the Church.

The only bad news concerned a leaking window in the juniors' classroom!

The Summer Term 1981 was exceptionally eventful. Matthew Cady and Edward Crichton excelled in the Schools' Chess Tournament. Children's art was exhibited in the Bury Schools' Exhibition. The County String Quartet visited, children took part in Music Festivals at both Breckland and Rougham, and held a musical afternoon for parents. A new television was purchased, to be paid for in part by parental donations. A School outing to Kilverstone Wildlife Park was greatly enjoyed. Children attended Area Swimming Day at Rougham, and Area Sports at Bradfield St. George.

A letter from Her Majesty's Inspectors complimented Mrs. Hall on "the high standard of the work exhibited for them".

By Autumn Term 1981 Mrs. King and Mr. Cady had retired from their governing role. Mr. Wilding was again elected chairman. School roll stood at 27. There was news of the usual events – Harvest Festival Service, visit by County Wind Quintet, an afternoon watching "Da Silva" puppets. Mrs. Button's Coffee Morning raised £45 towards the cost of the television.

"Matters Arising" included "the appointment of Mrs. Sheila Wright of Wickham Skeith as maternity supply teacher in the absence of Mrs. C. Scott". Also, the news that Shirley Hall would be leaving to become Headmistress of Bacton First School. Rev. Cribb proposed a vote of thanks to Mrs. Hall for "raising the standard of teaching in the School, especially on the mathematical side, for raising the prestige of the School in the area, and for making it a happy place for all children who attended". Mrs. Pocock seconded this, and it was passed "by acclamation!"

A presentation to Mrs. Hall, planned to take place at a School Concert, was made impossible by closure of the School due to ice and heavy snow. The presentation was made at the children's party instead. "Leaks in the roof" were reported!

At the first meeting of 1982, Kevin Connolly, the new Headteacher, was warmly welcomed. This was about the only good news at the meeting – apart from "improved drainage outside the School gate". Governors learned that Mrs. Scott would not be returning to School, that the heating was "not very efficient" (grand understatement!), school meals were going up to 55p. Finally, dire news – the L.E.A. were withdrawing taxi transport for Hessett children, claiming that "Hessett comes into Thurston catchment area". Governor Mr. Neil Parrin, a Hessett parent, said he felt most parents would prefer bringing their children to Drinkstone rather than putting them on an 8.15am bus to Thurston. But with only 27 pupils on roll, this was serious news.

Things looked brighter by the Summer Term. Six hours weekly of Ancillary help (Mrs. Wendy Collins) and three hours Head's Relief cover (Mrs. Meg Jack) were confirmed, and my own appointment was made permanent. Seven Hessett children would continue to attend in September '82 (five others would

1982: Back row – Mrs Sheila Wright, Philip Harris, Emma Crichton, Zoe Wilmshurst, Mandy Smith, Stuart Frogley, ?, Kerry Parrin, Mr Kevin Connolly.
Third row – Amanda Sobkowiak, Heidi Robinson, Debbie Cooper, Nigel Baker, Darren Haill, Rebecca Bradley, Daniel Steward, Oliver Crichton.
Sitting on chairs – Geoffrey Green, Bianca Boulton, Kim Blackburn, Cassie Smith, Matthew Bullet, Naomi Baker, Helen Bradley, Mark Steward, Jonathan Brown.
Sitting on floor, Nina Holden, Damien Sobkowiak, Corinne Parrin, Sara Monk, Rachel Crean, Daniel Smith, Gregory Raison.

transfer to Thurston), making thirty on roll "so rumours of Drinkstone School Closure were unfounded". Mr. Parrin was thanked for his work encouraging Hessett parents to continue bringing their children to Drinkstone. But governors felt dis-satisfied with the Education Office since no representative had attended the meeting to answer questions regarding closure of schools: "According to the brochures and training sessions run by the Office, governors were important. In fact, the Office disregard them."

The School continued to flourish. A "Sinclair ZX81" computer had been purchased (now a museum piece, then state of the art!). There was a concert, an Open Evening, swimming once again at Bury pool, weekly gymnastics for the juniors at Beyton Middle School, Area sports, visits and outings. Mr. Connolly wrote his notes on the term with flair, saying:

"22nd June, Fighting in the Falklands ended. Princess of Wales gave birth yesterday to a boy. The children were excited by this.

"9th July, The whole School and many parents visited Orford Castle and Thorpeness. The outing was a great success even though some of us were stranded in the middle of the lake when we should have been on the bus.

"14th July, Visit from a guitar duo – very enjoyable, although the children seemed obsessed with how much everything cost."

The Autumn Term brought news that Rev. Wall would be leaving the parish. Eight Hessett children were attending, five parents' cars bringing them by rota. The twenty-nine pupils enjoyed a Ballet performance, Nativity play, Christmas party, and a Bazaar to raise funds. Mr. Connolly recorded: "Mr. Carnall (County Education Officer) visited to examine state of the School. Like all visitors he commented on the chemical toilets. No-one here seems to notice."

The threat of closure seemed ever worse after Christmas. In the New Year 1983 an Area Review of Schools was announced. Ironically, the continued building of new properties in the village seemed to have no impact on County planning for education. There was neither will nor money to maintain or extend small Schools in neglected buildings.

Chapter Twenty

PERSONAL STORIES
Muriel, Rex and Sylvia Plummer, Janet and Andrew Smith, Barbara Wright, Joyce Cocksedge and Sue Bradley, the Steward family, the Blackburn family

MURIEL, REX AND SYLVIA PLUMMER, JANET AND ANDREW SMITH

Muriel and Janet have been friends over many years, and shared their memories as parents of Drinkstone pupils with me. Rex, Muriel's husband, and Andrew, Janet's son, were also part of this convivial group, so stories flew back and forth, each reminding the others of times past. We met at "Cyrena", home of Muriel and Rex, in Rattlesden Road. Their children Sylvia and Bruce, and Janet's sons Martin, Andrew and Richard, were all pupils at Drinkstone. Janet also served as a manager.

MURIEL, REX AND FAMILY

Muriel gave me an outline of her own life from childhood; here is her story:

"I was born in May 1938, in Langham. My mother Shirley (née Stannard) was only sixteen when I was born, and my father David Wilding wasn't much older. After they married, they lived in Long Thurlow. Dad was only nineteen when he went off to war in 1939, with the 'Suffolks'. At one time he was pronounced 'missing, presumed dead'. I didn't know him at all, until he came home in 1945. By then we had moved to Walsham-le-Willows, and my first glimpse of my Dad was when he was biking up the hill in Walsham with my Nan. I didn't know who this strange man was.

"When he got home after the war, Dad was ill, he was in hospital at first. Then he went to live with his mother at Wyverstone, because he didn't even know where my mother was, and she didn't even know he was still alive.

"My Dad had been captured at Singapore, and he was a prisoner of war in Burma. He came back very thin. He didn't have a very happy childhood, and with that and what happened to him in the war, he wasn't easy to live with, he was difficult to please. You didn't know where you were with him, he kept changing his mind. He was a bit strict. I remember, after he came home from the war, he went down to the shop and bought some bananas. They were as green as anything, but he made us eat them! But you wouldn't dare say anything, we had to do what he said. To this day bananas still don't appeal to me!

We had a council house at Walsham-le-Willows. At first we had oil lamps. Then Dad paid to have electricity put in. We couldn't believe as kids, that you could just press a switch and light would come on! We still weren't on the sewers for ages, it was a bucket in the privy down the garden. At Walsham, when they were putting the mains water in, my Mum would always offer the workmen a cup of tea. When she was out, they'd brew up themselves. One day when Mum

193

was out, a workman came and asked me for a bag of sugar. I was used to bagging up sugar in those blue bags, helping my Dad; I took a bag and went into the garden and filled it up with earth, then folded the top down very neatly and took it to the workmen. I couldn't resist staying to watch them open the bag, to see their faces – but I made sure I was ready to run!

"My Dad was working at Badwell Ash at Pryke's (later Minter's) as a delivery man. We children would help deliver the papers all around Badwell Ash, Long Thurlow, Hunston, Ashfield, Daisy Green and Walsham, and we'd take customers' orders for groceries at the same time. In the late Forties the rationing from wartime still went on. On Saturdays we had to wash down the delivery van, and sometimes we had to bag up dried fruit, weighing it out on the scales first, and bag up sugar in the blue bags. In the school holidays we'd go with Dad every day to deliver boxes of groceries to the houses. Even after rationing finished, we never had much – we might have an ice cream one week, then a bag of Smith's crisps the next week.

"It wasn't easy for my mother. Dad used to work on an allotment to help out, and he'd give her a little money to go shopping for seeds, but he'd always want to know how much she spent, and make sure he got the right change back. I'm the eldest of four, my sister Margaret was next, two years younger than me, then Ron, then Douglas, who was born after the war.

"My Dad's mother (my Nanna Sophie Wilding) lived at Wyverstone, and Dad spent a lot of time with her. I loved it in the school holidays, all summer I was over at my Nanna's at Wyverstone. My Grandad and my two uncles worked on Russell's Farm over there, with the horses. I used to be with them all day, we used to ride the horses when they were carting the wheat. After they were unharnessed, the horses used to go in the pond to cool off after their long working day. At home, I was a bit defiant to my father, so I was glad to be away, I had a fabulous time at Wyverstone. There was Nanna Sophie, Grandad, four of the family still living at home, and me. I remember my Nanna doing a huge colander of beans for us all. They used to keep chickens, so I used to go gleaning for grain with my Nanna, after harvest.

"When the sheaves were taken to the farmyard to be threshed, I remember Grandad wore wire glasses over his eyes to keep out the dust and chaff. Once, me and another girl climbed the stack, and I fell off and hurt my back. I was a proper tomboy. The girls (my aunties) worked at Black's farms, and I sometimes went with them, picking apples and plums. I loved going up the ladders. We'd go on the bus from Wyverstone to Stow once a week, and I liked that.

"My other Gran and Grandad Stannard, at Langham, had a huge garden, and they grew all the different kinds of currant bushes – red, black and white. Grandad used to walk from Langham to Walsham-le-Willows to take us to Congregational Chapel. His neighbour always gave him a nice flower, a 'buttonhole', to wear on Sundays.

"I had some good times at home in Walsham too. At the back of our house there we had a field of cowslips, and oh! the smell! I don't think they smell the same somehow, today. Mum's Mum, my Nan Minnie, was an invalid. She came to live with us after Grandad died, and she loved the flowers. We'd go down the lanes and allotments for them, violets were the first, then bird's-foot trefoil, then ox-eye daisies – we knew all the names. We had a big Show every year in Walsham and we'd have to put seven different wild flower species in a jam-jar, all labelled, and we'd try to find rare ones. Someone (I think he was a cobbler) used to pay us to catch cabbage-white butterflies, and there was a prize for the one who caught the most! We'd work for the Show at school as well, with writing, painting and sewing, and there'd be races and sideshows.

"I used to like 'Uncle Mac', on the radio. We had a travelling cinema come to Walsham once a week, it was sixpence to get in. We never missed. I loved 'Flash Gordon', and 'Old Mother Riley'. I had a job, so I used to treat my brothers. While I was still at School, I worked for a London family who owned a garage in Walsham. They were well off, but the wife couldn't even cook! I'd cook for her, after School, and if I didn't know how to do something, I'd run up the road and ask my Mum how to do it. I took after my Mum in so many ways. She died in 1986 when she was 64, so I've already lived longer than she did.

"The woman I worked for sometimes went away to give lectures, and then I'd have to give

*her children their tea. They always had to have Marmite on their first piece of bread and but-
ter. After I left School, I worked for this family for a while. Then I went into domestic service
at Stowlangtoft Hall. That was an L.C.C. Children's Home. My job was to look after the Sister
and the Matron. The Inspectors came regularly. We had our own well, excellent water, and
they'd check that, and also the nurseries, the kitchens, the cleaning, everything. My work was
good. I never needed a written reference, all my life I've got jobs on a 'word of mouth' reference.*

*"We'd go to dances at Pakenham, Ixworth and Bury. We'd all pile into a taxi together, so it
didn't cost much. Rex came from Essex. He was still in the Navy when we met. He was courting another girl up at Stowlangtoft Hall, I was best of friends with her and that didn't change
when I started going out with him! When we married, we started as lodgers with an old lady
in Bury, in a terraced house, out Risbygate. The old lady became ill with a heart condition and
went to live near her son at Sible Headingham."*

Rex takes over the tale at this point:

*"As we were basically sitting tenants we had first offer on buying the house. This was £1000
and the most I could get was a £900 mortgage with a repayment of £5-2s-6d per month.
Council rates were £26 per year. My wages at George Burlingham Seed Merchants were £8-5s
per 48-hour week, with one week per year paid holiday. Five months of the year we could do
an extra 12 hours overtime, so from midsummer we worked a regular 60-hour week. During
this five months we did roughly two months of 8-hour Sundays. For these 68-hour weeks the
wages were about £15."*

Muriel resumes her story:

*"Money was tight, it was quite hard. I used to have to stagger my shopping, I couldn't buy
everything we needed every week. By then, my parents had moved to a Brewery cottage in out
Westgate Street. For a while, my Dad had worked at Ixworth Cider works as a driver, then that
firm closed down and he worked as a drayman at the Brewery in Bury St. Edmunds. My Mum
and Dad moved to a Brewery cottage in 1959. Their first one was in Whiting Street.*

*"Once some blokes came to the Brewery to clean the vats, a young lad and an older chap
called Ted. And Ted had been a prisoner of war with my father! So Father invited them home
for a meal. The young lad was a picky eater, he hardly touched his food. But Ted ate all his own
plateful, then he went on and finished up all the lad's food as well! They'd been half starved in
the camps so he couldn't bear seeing food go to waste.*

*"Our daughter Sylvia was born in 1959, in Bury. She was a breech baby, hence she was hard
of learning. She was a very good baby. My brothers and sister used to help me buy her clothes,
or I don't know how I would have managed. Sylvia didn't pick up language easily. I worried
about her, but no-one suggested looking into the reasons. She was brilliant at some things. I
did a bit of seasonal fruit picking, on those days I'd leave her with my mother. A bus would go
all around Bury taking women to William's Farm at Sicklesmere. Sylvia had auburn hair so felt
the heat very much on really hot days. When she was old enough she started at Victoria School
in Albert Street".*

Rex takes over the narrative at this point:

*"Our house needed decorating, that was all. I did a lot of work on it, and six years later we
were able to sell it for £2,200! We moved to Ixworth for a bit, to live with my parents, then to
a caravan in Bakers Yard, Thurston, while our bungalow was being built. We bought this bungalow in 1966, the year our son Bruce was born. It cost us £2,900. There weren't nearly so
many houses along here then, just Green Farm opposite, and on this side The Homestead and
The Gables. There was a ditch all along this road, and apple trees all along the side of the garden. Now it's all filled in with houses, there have been 40 houses built in this road since we
moved here."*

Muriel continues the story:

*"I hated living in a town, we always wanted to be in a village. When we moved, first to
Ixworth, then to Thurston, Sylvia had to change schools. She could say a few words by now,*

but those two schools didn't do much for her. But when Sylvia started at Drinkstone School, Mrs. K. (Kozlowski) was brilliant with her! Really, the only way you could make Sylvia under- stand was to smack her on the hand. I don't agree with teachers not being able to smack chil- dren, today. Sometimes they need it. Mrs. K. helped Sylvia no end, and once she learned some thing, she never forgot it. At first she'd listen more to Mrs. K. than she would to me.

"Our bungalow is about a mile from the School, so Rex would take the children to School when he could, but he was working shifts at ABM the Maltsters (now Paul's) at Bury St. Edmunds, so he couldn't always take them. Vera Bland from Whitefield Farm would help out, or sometimes Janet Smith or Victor Jack would take them by car. But if no-one could help, I'd walk down with them myself. I remember Sylvia and Martin both wore 'Doc Martens' shoes, and they couldn't walk far in them!

"I hardly knew anyone in Drinkstone at first, so I joined the W.I. to get to know people. We had a good life with our children mostly, with a lot of fun. Every other Sunday we'd go to Lowestoft with my brother and all his family – that was our favourite place. And we used to go up to Ipswich for the Country and Western shows. Our favourite was Slim Whitman when he came on tour.

"Well, to go back to the subject of education. Sylvia never complained about School, but it was hard for her sometimes. Because she's hard of learning, people would put on her, and she couldn't express herself well enough to tell tales. When she went up into the big class, Mrs. Collins hadn't got time for her so she didn't do so well there. Sylvia went on to Beyton for a while, but she was unhappy there. No-one helped her. When I met her after School she'd be crying her eyes out, but she couldn't say why. I think she used to get lost in that School. She was assessed at Beyton, and they decided she needed a Special School place. But the Priory Special School in Mount Road was still being built, she couldn't go there straight away. So she was given a temporary place as a boarder at Pield Heath School in Hillingdon, Middlesex, a Special School run by nuns. She calmed down a lot there, I think it did her the world of good. She was ten when she went, and she stayed a year. She's very clever in some ways, she's very good at crochet, and jigsaw puzzles."

Muriel showed me a charming letter, written by Sylvia to her family during her time at Hillingdon. Among the rather jumbled, disjointed sentences are phrases such as "Thank you more sweets and bis- cuits…. please write to me…. goodbye and God bless you…. lots of love to Daddy and Bruce and Mummy….and a big hug for you Bruce." The letter is decorated with neat drawings of a house, trees and a vase of flowers. I'm not surprised it has been kept and treasured by Muriel for thirty-five years!

"Once the Priory Special School opened, Sylvia came home again, and went each day in a mini-bus. That was in 1970, when she was eleven, and she stayed there until 1978, when she was given a place at Bury Adult Training Centre in Hollow Road. She did a lot of gardening there. She transferred to Stowmarket Education Centre in Crown Street, in 1980. The staff try to 'meet the social, educational, training and occupational needs of adults with learning dis- abilities'. That Centre was brilliant for her. The teachers would let her go and do the shopping and she was allowed to take money out to buy the things. At first she'd have no idea whether the change would be 5p, or 20p, or whatever – but she did learn to get it right in the end, she's quite good at numbers now. She was there two years.

"The next place she went was Unit 9 at Moreton Hall, Bury, where she was trained in pack- ing and printing. That was in 1989, it's an Advanced Work Unit for people with learning dis- abilities, and they do light industrial work. Then Mencap got her a paid job, packing, at Clare Craft Design in Woolpit. One or two people kept an eye on her there; she does remember what she has to do once she's finally learned it. She's like the proverbial elephant, she just does not forget! She was only made redundant well after people who'd been there longer had gone. She was given a good Reference: 'During your employment you have proved to be a considerable asset to the Company'. Then she went to work for 'Fragrant Memories' in Borley Green, start- ing when there were only three people – the man in charge, Sylvia, and another girl. By the time the firm moved to the Isle of Wight five years later, they employed about 150 people! Sylvia

went back to Clare Craft for a few months, then she stayed at home for about a year, until Paul Bridges at Mencap's Pathway found her work as a packer at Taylor Barnard in Mendlesham (under the mast). This company is now known as TNT. They look after Sylvia extremely well although the work is hard, there's a lot of lifting.

"When Sylvia had done six week's training at Taylor Barnard's, with no pay, I phoned up and said: 'Are you going to take her on or are you just after cheap labour?' and they took her on. Once the Manager said to me: 'She works well, but she's always bossing people about!' I told her: 'You won't stop her, she's always been like that! You've got to tell her what to do, and tell the others to ignore her.' In fact she's often right, she does remember what to do once she's learned it. Sylvia's done well really, it's important to her to have a job and be paid like everyone else. She likes social clubs, gardening, jigsaw puzzles, and listening to music.

"Our son Bruce liked being at Drinkstone School. His first teacher was Mrs. K., then he had Mrs. Raynham and he really liked her. After leaving school he tried office work, and didn't like it. He went on the market in the end. He married, and he has one son, Shaun, we see a lot of our grandson. Bruce has a Heavy Goods Vehicle Licence now, and he works at Ridley's, in Rougham.

"Rex, my husband, is a Jack-of-all-trades really, he's worked at so many jobs and been made redundant time and time again. He did a proper training at Sainsbury's in London, to become a butcher, then he worked at Sainsbury's shop in Bury for eight years. He does all the electrical work around the house, and for other people. He put in our central heating in 1967, and upgraded it with more radiators and an oil-fired boiler in 1997. His interest in woodwork started at the age of about ten, and now he teaches carpentry part-time at West Suffolk College. He started teaching in 1979 with the Community Council for Suffolk, doing everything from basic brick-laying, painting and decorating to ground working, at various G.N.V.Q. Levels. He taught computers when very few people had ever seen one, most computers at the time cost about £6,000, apart from the Sinclair which was very basic. The BBC Micro B came out about the same time. The washing machine still gets repaired, but he doesn't repair the car any more unless it's something easy! Gone are the days of lying under the car.

"I've always done domestic work but I find plenty of time for gardening. We're members of Rattlesden Garden Club and one year I won the over-all prize, a lovely glass vase. I started with 3rd prizes, but I've got better results each year."

ANDREW AND JANET SMITH

Andrew Smith (grandson of Tom Smith), Janet's middle son, was next to tell his memories. Andrew was born in Drinkstone in 1967, his older brother Martin in 1963, and Richard, the youngest, in 1969. These three were known as the "MARS" boys because of their initials. Martin is now married and lives in Finningham. Richard is a driver for Glasswells, and lives in Thetford. Only Andrew has stayed in Drinkstone, where he lives with his mother Janet. These are some of his memories:

"Mrs. K. was my first teacher. I liked the sand-pit best. I hated winter-time, having to go outside to the toilet! Learning to read and write was hard for me, I was dyslexic I think, and because I was left-handed, I had to turn my book sideways and curve my hand round so I didn't smudge the ink. In the big class, I remember Mrs. Raynham and then Mrs. B. Wright were my teachers. We had the vicar come in at least once a week to do a service. I remember a little cubby hole in the School roof, where bats lived.

"At dinners, I hated the semolina with orange peel in it, and the tapioca pudding, and the lumpy gravy, but I loved the custard. I hated the school milk, it always tasted funny to me. I loved playtimes, I had some good friends at the School. I remember we used to play dodgems with old tyres. I slit my eyebrow open playing that game. In the winter time, when the leaves fell, we'd play houses. We'd gather up the leaves and put them down in lines to show the walls of our house and the rooms inside.

"When we were a bit older, we'd jump down over the playground wall into the field and go to the oak tree in the middle of that field (that was out of bounds). We'd have races to see who

got there and back the quickest, but we had to keep away from the cows, and the bull! At lunchtimes, sometimes we'd jump the other wall, into the graveyard, and we'd sneak to the shop just past the Church and buy sweets.

"Once us boys had been playing ball, and the ball got stuck in the troughing around the school roof. Richard Bradley got a bit of metal off the climbing frame to poke the ball off, and it slipped backwards and hit one of the Crick boys, and he had to go to hospital! After school, sometimes Bruce and me would go conkering at Old Hall Farm. We'd get over the barbed wire fence, and once I went up to my knees in mud there, it was where the old moat lies! We used to play cricket on the field at Old Hall Farm. In them days we had so much freedom. We could go on push-bikes, all over the place, me and my little brother. You can't do that now."

Here Rex recalls the state of the Schoolhouse at the time when the Bradley family lived there as caretakers – just before the welcome advent of Headteacher Barbara Wright. He tells me:

"When the Bradleys were in the Schoolhouse, they heard a strange noise in one of the rooms, and when they looked in, they saw a hole about five foot square had opened up in a corner of the room, and the leg of the table had gone through the floor! That was when the Church still owned the house but they wouldn't do anything about it. That's why the Bradleys moved to Elmswell. When Mrs. Barbara Wright and her husband came, they didn't have any choice – they had to do the repairs themselves".

Janet adds: *"I remember carrying sand through the house for Mrs. Wright!"*

Andrew takes up the story of his education:

"When I went up to Beyton Middle, I was with Mark Armstrong, he was a year older than me and he took me under his wing. I was behind with the work when I went there, so I got special help. There were three of us who went by taxi once a week from Beyton, to St. John's Church up Hospital Road. We did reading and writing, and made models. It really got me on. Because I was at these special classes, I missed out on the first French lessons at Beyton. When I stopped going to St. John's, I was a year behind in French.

"When I left School I wanted to be a chef. I got a place on a Youth Training Scheme, I was paid £25 a week and I worked at The Angel Hotel. Then they took me on permanently, and I had to train one day a week at Ipswich College. After that I worked in the revolving restaurant at Centre Parks, until it burned down! I got another job, at P.P.G. Stowmarket (that's a paint factory near I.C.I.) filling tins of paint. There's a lot to remember, there's a lot of numbers involved. I get paid twice as much at this job, and the hours are better, three shifts over the twenty-four hours".

The reminiscences ended with nostalgic remarks from these gathered friends, about "the old days", and the many changes that have taken place in Drinkstone:

"There's so many new houses now. It used to be all meadows, just a few farms and cottages. I think there's now about 470 electors, and quite a lot of new children in the village.

"The Chapel closed, then the shops, then the pub. The Post Office, it moved so many times – first it was down near the Church, then it was at Mrs.Thurlow's in Gedding Road."

Muriel remembers:

"I used to go to Mrs. Cooper's shop to buy sweets, and birthday cards, and ice cream, and little surprises for the children's birthdays. It was olde worlde, she'd talk to you, the atmosphere was so friendly in her shop."

BARBARA WRIGHT

Barbara Wright, whom I have never met, was kind enough to reply to a letter I sent her, with this vivid account of her short time at Drinkstone School:

"I was only at Drinkstone for a little over two years – but very active ones and the most enjoyable time of my teaching days. I have no doubt that you have gleaned loads of tit bits from Vi Cocksedge who was an invaluable help to me.

"When I arrived at Drinkstone it had been expected to close from time to time and had been let to go very badly. The house was derelict and closed. There was a tarred urinal outside for the boys, and Elsan toilets which reeked of Jeyes Fluid, kept very clean by Mr. Cocksedge. There were old sheds and dumped rubbish from various sources in the area behind the School. This area was very overgrown. There was also an old coal house. Inside the Schoolhouse, one of the rooms had severe dry rot, one of the upstairs floors was very shaky, and the kitchen-scullery was impossible. As for the School, the hall and small room were habitable, the porch had one cold water basin, pegs all round, a concrete floor, and flaking walls with damp patches. Each room had a large Rowesse coke stove which was temperamental. The telephone was in the small room, lighting was from one bulb in a white shade.

"I had fancied being head of a small village School, but when I arrived I was appalled at the state of it. In the small room where the biggest children were crowded, the furniture units were stacked two high to make enough space. The few infants were in the hall which was dominated at the far end by a vast dolls' house – a period piece on loan by Mrs. Collins who had been a previous head. A tall library cupboard and a piano were also there. A large desk was by the stove. Some old tables were set out near the desk. A screen which was there when I came was closed, separating the two rooms. Vi Cocksedge did her best with it all with polish etc. She loved the children.

"I was appointed to start after Easter, so I spent the holiday changing the School round. My husband and two sons and a group of friends from the School where I had been deputy, came over to help me. We moved the infants to the small room and the older children to the hall. They were better able to cope with the upheaval of preparation for dinner, which was served from two trestle tables. We removed the doors from the large cupboard and painted it inside and out so that the children could get things out for themselves, painted all the display boards to freshen them up, made a reading corner in the far end of the hall, and used a clothes horse with covers, with pockets to hold work cards. I also found a bright carpet from home, and we were almost ready. The cupboard had held many old fusty out-of-date books, and some bean bags eaten by mice. I sorted through the rubbish bit by bit. I acquired some books and equipment from Beyton Primary which was due to close in July. Mrs. Bettinson, the head, was very helpful with various items, including a maypole.

"I contacted most of the advisers at Bury requesting equipment and money, and had fair success in all areas. The children were thrilled with some P.E. items and balls and hoops for playtimes, also painting for hopscotch and number lines, on the playground. I discovered a better type of toilet fluid which I bought in from a caravan centre near home. Fairly soon the ground at the back was cleared by county groundsmen and laid to grass. Then we tackled the house. I obtained permission to have a doorway knocked through to join it to the School, and to use one room as an office, the other for T.V. etc. Before this was done, my husband, who was area building surveyor, supervised a local builder, Mr. Nunn, to 'do' the door, which was obtained from another school. Then the rotten floor was taken up one weekend by my husband and sons, and buried out the back. We then got two tons of sand and enough paving slabs from one of the parents, Mr. Charter, who was in charge of Suffolk County Council Highways Department, and I asked for volunteer parents and children to come over one week-end, to bucket and barrow the sand in. At that time it had to come up a slope to the front door of the house. This was then used to make a base for the slabs, which made a good surface for the floor. Some school carpet was found to finish it off, and two electric fires were given by parents. The wiring was then made good and safe. School meals service was contacted for some surplus stainless steel items to make a working servery. A hatch was cut through into the hall, and things were looking better.

"As far as I can remember, this was completed in the first year, but the details are in the Log Book. Mr. Carnall, the Chief Education Officer, was very helpful to me. I think the people at the Council rubbed their hands together and thought, 'this is a cheap job!' My husband knew where there were surplus materials and left-overs that we could use.

"*The children were lovely! Interested and excited with all the change. They were well-behaved and generally used to working together in family groups. They loved having P.E. and games which had not been very common. They enjoyed music and drama. They were knowledgeable in country ways – farms and animals – and had done a regular amount of oral arithmetic and tables. The piano was fair; singing was popular. Mrs. Jack, also a parent, came in one afternoon a week, which gave me a little time out. She was a lovely lady who loved music, and also did recorders. We acquired a few items for percussion, which I took, and we had a great time. Art was something they enjoyed, having mainly previously worked with crayons.*

"*We had Harvest Festivals, May Day with dancing, Open Days, Mini Sports afternoons, Christmas Concert and parties. Parents joined in to help. Parents had not been allowed into School property before and had to wait in the playground, and if pouring wet would come into the tiny porch. Many of them walked, only about two came by car to collect the children. Five children came by taxi from Hessett. The infant teacher, Mrs. Kozlowski, caught the taxi at Beyton, arrived at 8.55am and left at 3.15pm with the children.*

"*After a short time I invited parents to call in after School to see the changes. They all came and I had many letters and comments of approval. They knew they were welcome to call in after School if they had a problem. We had an Open Afternoon each term.*

"*The vicar was Chairman of Governors and lived in Rattlesden. He was Rev. Gooderham, and he was a great support, coming every week. Later he was moved away and a gentleman who lived in the village unofficially took his place. He was Nicholas Cribb, and he was very good with the children and encouraged them to be interested in the Church, holding services there for the School. Some of the children brought mushrooms from the churchyard which he pronounced safe to eat!*

"*After a while I was able to arrange for swimming at Bury, sharing a coach with Woolpit. We also joined in the Sports Days with Thurston and Cockfield Schools.*

"*School meals were brought in containers, I think from Woolpit. We had one lady serving and washing up, and one dinner lady, she came from Felsham, and the other, Mrs. Andrews, from Culford. Both were loved by the children.*

"*Wet days were trying until the porch was improved. There was very little to occupy the children, but an appeal to parents brought forth scrap paper, old toys, jigsaws, etc. Before long the dolls' house was claimed and we had more room. Also, as it probably was quite an antique, I was glad to see it go.*

"*The Christmas Concert was the high spot. We had a large Christmas tree with decorations, a party afterwards, and all children took part. Mrs. Jack had done magnificently with the music, which had been taken from the BBC schools programmes. Every parent and grandparent who could, squeezed in. We had a very happy Christmas. We had a school picnic at the end of the Summer Term.*

"*Our final claim to fame was when Janice Pickering from Hessett won a place in the Best Kept Village poster competition, with her painting of litter collection, and went to meet the Queen and Duke of Edinburgh at Ipswich, and of course had her picture in the local papers.*

"*I was at Drinkstone for just over two years, then left for a new School with an old one to close down, at Acton nearer to my home. Drinkstone was never a dull moment, I loved it. Hard work, loads to do, excellent parents and children. I was sad to leave. In my last year, Mrs. Kozlowski retired and I appointed Mrs. C. Scott, an excellent young teacher, to join us. The Managers had given generous support at all times.*

"*It is a long time ago now, I really had to think to remember all this. I did consider writing a book about it but took up painting instead!*"

JOYCE COCKSEDGE AND SUE BRADLEY

Joyce and Sue are sisters, born in Rattlesden, who have lived in Drinkstone throughout their married lives. They married David Cocksedge and Dennis Bradley, two Drinkstone boys who attended the School together and were always good mates. Joyce gave me a photograph of all the pupils taken 1956 /57. Twenty-eight smartly dressed, happy and mischievous looking children stand smartly in line, their two teachers (Mrs. Collins and Mrs. Henley) in their midst. David and Dennis stand side by side, in the back row at the extreme left. Living only a few hundred yards from each other, the families have remained very close.

Joyce and Sue's mother and father came from very large families, around a dozen children in each. Joshua Plummer, their father, was born in Rattlesden. Their mother, Ada Gowers, came from Middleton, near Manchester. Ada would come down to Suffolk for family "wakes" held in "The Brewers' Arms" at Rattlesden, where one branch of her family were landlords, and that's how she came to meet and marry a Suffolk lad.

Joyce says their mother was really a rather sad, lonely little woman, due partly to extreme deafness, and partly to the fact that in Suffolk, she was far from her own family, and lacked that life-time knowledge of her neighbours which most Suffolk families had. She was embarrassed about her deafness, and "wouldn't say 'Pardon?'". Being reluctant to ask people to repeat what they said, she often responded strangely, saying "yes" instead of "no" and finding it hard to become part of the group and develop close friendships. Joyce, "a war baby", was born in 1945, at Bury St. Edmunds hospital, the maternity unit at that time being located in a group of Nissen huts. Joyce was a favourite with the Plummer grandmother because in looks she resembled that branch of the family. The sisters remember this grandmother from Rattlesden coming over with little gifts for Joyce, but nothing for Sue (born in 1948) because Sue was "more like the Gowers!"

Tragedy struck the family in 1947. Joshua was working on Jewer's Farm in Rattlesden, and while herding the cows one day, a nearby shot startled the animals, causing one heavy cow to turn suddenly, knocking him down and trampling his unprotected body. His heart and lungs were so badly damaged that he never worked again, and spent the last few years of his short life an invalid at home. He passed the time reading, and taught Joyce to read before she started school. Ada taught him to knit, since he could do little else, and his mittens won prizes at Felsham Village Show – a great event for which all the schoolchildren would paint pictures. Now the sisters laugh and say, the best entertainment they knew as children, was knitting mittens round the fireside!

Sue was very young when her father died in 1954, and has only hazy memories of him. After his death, the young widow Ada bought one-way tickets for herself and her daughters to return to her family in Middleton. Unused to travel, the trio boarded the Liverpool Boat Train (steam) running from Harwich to Liverpool, but failed to notice when the train steamed into Manchester station, ending up at the Liverpool terminal! For once, their shy little mother did what was necessary, pleading with station staff until the three were allowed to board a train going south to Manchester, where anxious relatives waited to receive them.

For a short while the family stayed with the Gower grandparents, aunts and uncles. At one time they stayed in Oldham Road near the Warwick Cotton Mill where the Gower family worked. They enjoyed the big May Day Parade and the maypole dancing. There were pubs, shops and bustle, and Aunt Lily would walk to work in her wooden clogs. The girls would lie in bed at night listening to the clip-clop of workers' clogs as they went to and from the factory. But Ada soon decided country life in Suffolk was more peaceful, and brought the sisters back to live in Rattlesden. It was a hard childhood with little money, but then no-one in the village had much. There were only two cars in the whole village. Hopgood's van would come once a week bringing everything needed, paraffin, mops, brooms, groceries. The girls would walk up to Rattlesden Mill to buy flour for the baking. Ada didn't have much to say to her daughters, but they never lacked love. Sue says Ada was a kindly woman, generous to others, and when a poor family who had been living in "tin town" (temporary war-time accommodation at Brettenham) moved into a council house near them, Ada carried over some basic furniture and provisions from her own meagre possessions.

The Plummers' household belongings were battered and second-hand, but the girls remember a huge extending gate-leg table with carved legs, which could seat sixteen. With the drop-leaf sides folded down, this made a wonderful hiding-place for them when they were in mother's bad books! "Tally men" who called at the house would offer to buy it, but Ada refused. After her death, the table sold for over £800.

The girls remember getting away with plenty of mischief, playing in the road (forbidden) and climbing the huge trees in the meadows to swing and slide down leaning boughs. There were accidents, too, as when Susan was riding Joyce's tricycle, and Joyce hid behind the tank until she passed, then jumped out and leapt onto the back, causing the whole to tip over and breaking Sue's arm. Another nasty accident occurred in Rattlesden playground when Sue was six. Some children blocked her path, knocking her down and causing another break. Seeing Susan's arm at a strange angle, one of the children pulled it straight, causing a sharp end of bone to gash the flesh and protrude. The scar, several inches long, can still be seen, so this must have been a traumatic event for teachers as well as children! The sisters laugh as they tell me these stories, because lately it has been Joyce's turn. She fell over the handlebars of her bike outside her Drinkstone home, breaking both wrists, and Sue was "an angel" after the accident, coming round to help her sister get up, wash, dress, and eat, good humoured and endlessly supportive.

After their father's death, some aunts from the Plummer side of the family "took over" the two little girls, doing what they thought was best for them. This meant regular attendance at Rattlesden Strict Baptist Church (founded 1813), Sunday School and Bible classes. The girls had been christened at St. Nicholas, Church of England. Now began intense Strict Baptist indoctrination with no let up. Sue remembers the cottage where the aunts, Lydia and Anne, lived and ran the village Post Office (across the road from the present Post Office in Rattlesden) as being always dark and gloomy. On the huge table with its heavy fringed cloth stood a tilley lamp, but it gave little light. She says "when I remember how people lived then, it's a wonder there weren't more fires, everything was sombre and cluttered".

Visiting the home of these aunts, the girls would have to stand on chairs and recite Bible verses which they had learned – if correct, they were offered an elderly biscuit from a musty tin. Susan asks her sister "do you remember those horrible mouldy biscuits?" It was a scary place, and the privy was "out the back in the wash house, with the mangle". Joyce remembers a little rhyme stuck on the door, which read:

When to this little place you come,
To do two jobs that must be done,
Before you leave, please do two more –
Cover the seat and shut the door!

In due course the girls were baptised. The sisters have fond memories of the pastors and teachers, despite the hours spent in Church listening to long sermons. There were Bible-searching sessions. A text (Book, chapter and verse) would be called out with the rally cry "Draw your swords!" The children raced to be first to find the page. Miss Bragg and Yvonne Ball at the Sunday School were very kind. Every year there was an outing to the sea-side. Joyce remembers Mr. Hitchcock the pastor swimming out to sea with her on his back! This was their only, annual, day out. Each sister experienced one week's holiday away with the "Fellowship of Youth" (just once each) in Paignton and Somerset. They would have one new dress annually, worn first at the Sunday School Anniversary. When the time came for them to go to Beyton Secondary School, it was Mr. Hitchcock, pastor and miller, who paid for their uniform. Joyce says "everything we did was organised through the Church, and there were a lot of people looking after us in the background". She remembers in Drinkstone too there was much training by non-conformist believers, and the sisters attended Bible classes at "The Homestead"in Rattlesden Road, run by Mrs. Saunders. (Victor and Meg Jack, also staunch Free Church Christians, now live there).

The Church people of that time had very demanding standards for their members. Eventually both sisters were "excommunicated" because they failed to attend Holy Communion during three consecutive months. In a rather guilt-inducing letter the pastor remarks: "I did ask you to meet me some time back, but at the last minute you cancelled the visit… to be quite honest I feel you have treated the Church and your fellow members rather badly, but would say very definitely, if some recognition of fault was admitted, coupled with a return to the services and ordinances of the Church, you would be welcomed back with Christian love." Both sisters ceased to attend in their early twenties, and in any case, both lived in Drinkstone after marriage.

The sisters say "everyone knew your business, your life was never your own, but at least everybody knew everybody else, and they really cared".

In 1959 Ada remarried. Albert Pettit, known as Jack, was much older than Ada, and had two grown-up daughters, who seemed to Joyce and Susan like two more aunts added to the tribe. A teenage son, also named Albert, came to live with them. The sisters never regarded their step-dad as a caring father. He had owned cottages in a very run-down state, and sold these before moving in with Ada and the girls. The money he had was not spent on his new family, but on his son Albert, for whom he bought expensive presents such as a motor-bike. Young Albert soon left to join the Royal Marines. The step-father died in 1977, and his presence had only added to a sense of confusion and bewilderment about exactly whose family they belonged to. The religious aunts Annie and Lydia eventually died, having omitted to write a will, so that their small savings were divided between a horde of relatives and Joyce and Susan each received the princely sum of £3!

Education was never a priority for their mother Ada. Her own schooling had been sparse, interrupted by long spells in hospital due to ear infections. Thus she floundered in the classroom, and became adept at copying neatly the work of those sitting near her! She probably heard very little of the teaching. She went to work in the noisy Cotton Mill. So it is not surprising that she showed little interest in the school work of her daughters. If they were given homework, she would be unwilling to help, saying "You should have done that at School". However she did her very best for her girls. Despite her ear trouble, she had been a good swimmer as a girl. She taught Joyce and Susan to swim, not entering the water herself, but demonstrating from the side of the pool. She had been a little thing, only eight stone, when she married Joshua, but in Suffolk she expanded to twelve stone and was embarrassed about her size.

Ada saved up to buy one good present for her children each year – they remember hunting the house to discover what they were getting, before Christmas, despite being sternly warned "Do not search!" Once they found a "Tessa" doll with stiffly-bending legs; another year, a red toy piano with about twelve keys. Both loved music although there was no chance of lessons. Susan says,"How I loved that doll with its funny legs, I could make her sit or stand, I thought she was marvellous".

Joyce remembers doing well at Rattlesden School, and was one of the few chosen to sit the 11-plus exam. No-one told her she had passed! She remembers "Mr. O'Hagan, the teacher, came round to see my mother and ask why I wasn't going to take up my place at Bury Grammar School. But I didn't even know I'd passed until one of my father's family told me. I didn't know anything about the Grammar School or what it could have meant for me. I didn't know anyone who went there. It's only in retrospect now, I think about lost opportunities.There were others like me, in those days, who passed the 11-plus but who were not able to take up a Grammar School place due to home circumstances. I didn't have strong feelings about it, at the time. All the family have made a success of their lives, we've taken training opportunities. I went on to College after School and obtained certificates in shorthand, typing and book keeping. We both received training in connection with our work (like computer skills), and our children have all done really well."

Susan recalls mainly "playing about" at school, but remembers "at Rattlesden I was good at times tables, and because of my loud voice (having a deaf mother) they put me in the middle of the class when we used to recite the tables so I could lead everyone, and I was proud of that. At playtimes in the winter, we made horrendously dangerous icy slides right across the playground, and we used to swap little treasures, red reflectors off bikes were a favourite".

Beyton Secondary School, says Susan, "seemed immense – I feared getting lost, with all those rooms and stairs as well. I had mischievous friends when I went there. We'd get wet on purpose, rolling in the snow, so we'd have to go in the drying room and miss the lesson. We were so naughty at School, we missed a lot of work. Some-times we'd hide behind the hedge and deliberately miss the bus. That bus would go on from Gedding Road Drinkstone, to pick up at Gedding and Felsham, and we'd jump off and run down the hill, trying to beat the bus to the bottom."

Joyce remembers being taught Religious Instruction at Beyton, by Audrey, one of Fred Barcock's daughters from the Nursery in Rattlesden Road, but says "I wasn't very good in her lessons because I already had a crush on David, my future husband, and he'd be playing football on the playing field outside the classroom when we were having R.I., and I was more interested in watching him!"

As adults, both sisters have seized every opportunity for education. Susan currently studies French at Drinkstone Village Hall. She says "I love living here in the country, but what else is there to keep your brain alive stuck in a village?" She and her husband Dennis built their own home in Cross Street between 1970-2. Joyce and David bought their home (ex-council house) in Gedding Road, Drinkstone, and extended it themselves.

All their children, Paul, Claire, Rebecca and Helen, attended Drinkstone. The mothers usually walked the mile down to School with the children in the mornings – "one child walking, one in the pram, dressed or not!" – and the same at home-time. Occasionally kind neighbours might offer a lift. When the children were older, they would ride down with their mothers, on bikes. Because both became dinner-ladies (Joyce regular, Susan relief) there were six journeys daily – there and back, morning, lunch-time, and home-time. Poorly paid work, but they loved it, being immensely sociable and fond of children.

Joyce says: "My children loved it at Drinkstone School. Mrs. Hall the Head teacher taught Claire the flute and the piano, she taught Matthew Cady as well, in school time. They both won awards for music in their first year at Beyton, and they were allowed to go straight into the orchestra. It was all down to the teaching at Drinkstone. Mrs. Jack used to give Claire piano lessons after School as well. Then I learned the piano, after I was forty, with a neighbour." Both sisters now enjoy keyboard playing.

Susan says: "When we had parents' evenings and they asked if we had any problems it was only things like 'my Rebecca gave Matthew Bullett a bite of her cream Easter egg, and he took too much, and she was ever so upset!' We never had any real problems, the children were happy. The saddest thing when the Village School closed is, you don't have the same rapport between the families. When I meet those mothers I used to talk to at the School gate, we've got nothing in common any more. We used to be more together." Joyce remembers how everyone practised together for sports, and in Jubilee year she was tipped to win the hundred metres. "Lots of people bet on me to win – then a girl we didn't know who'd gone to a private School somewhere, came along and beat the lot of us!"

Joyce's daughter Claire was the first ever girl of the Cocksedge family to go to university. She studied at Bristol, and her Grandpa Sindal John Cocksedge couldn't see any sense in a girl studying for a degree: "What's the sense in it, she'll probably get married and have a baby!" The sisters are wonderfully proud of the achievements of their children, who spent their early years happily learning at Drinkstone School.

LYNDA, ROGER, DANIEL AND MARK STEWARD

Lynda and Roger Steward bought their bungalow in Beyton Road, Drinkstone, in 1974. The bungalow was built in 1937 as a tied cottage belonging to Meade Farm. Their sons Daniel and Mark grew up in the village and were pupils at the School. Lynda was always a willing volunteer when extra help was needed. During the final terms before closure she was School Secretary, so was very involved with all the special events. She shared with me the difficult task of sorting papers and records, and totally emptying the office and store rooms in July 1986.

She and her sons have kept in touch with many parents and ex-pupils and were able to update me on the lives of many of them during the last twenty years. It was lovely to learn that Peter Rodzian, a jolly little rascal at age seven, is now a competent nurse at West Suffolk Hospital; Scott and Lee McInnes whose father worked at Meade Farm, have followed in their father's footsteps, both working with cattle at West Winch, Norfolk; and David Button became a fire-fighter.

I took some School photos to the family, hoping they could help me remember names. Daniel showed one to his girlfriend Julie, asking if she could recognise him among the thirty or so small children. Julie said: "I thought that was one class!" and Daniel explained: "No, that's the whole School!"

Lynda's response was "That's how it should be!"

Daniel shared some memories:

> "On my first day, they told me my Mum was just around the corner! Nigel Baker, David
> Button, Debbie Cooper and Hannah Gill all started the same time as me. But Hannah and her
> brother Simon moved to Newmarket a couple of years later. I met up with Hannah again, at

Debbie's twenty-first birthday party a few years ago.

"I can remember some of the things we learned, I've always been interested in history. It was brilliant, the best time, the only time I ever learned anything really! I liked learning all about the Romans and Pompeii. We learned about the Greeks and the Olympics in 1984 – was the Olympic Games at Los Angeles that year? I remember making medals in clay, showing athletes doing all the different sports. I liked going to the castles at Orford and Framlingham. And when they were lifting the Mary Rose out of the sea the whole School watched on the television.

"All the trips were good – at Kilverstone Wildlife Park the otters and miniature ponies were my favourites. And we went to so many windmills! I remember camping out behind the School. It was a big tent and there were lots of us in it – I think Mr. Connolly was with us so we had to be good! We all went for a long walk round the back of the Church and along the footpath. Then we went in the big classroom and played 'Dead Indians', all lying on the floor as still as we could. It went so quiet I was afraid they'd all gone away and left me, so I opened one eye to make sure I wasn't alone, so then of course I was out! I was quite disappointed, I was doing well till then! At the end of term, every term, we used to pester the teachers to let us watch the 'Star Wars' video. The teachers were so tired of it, in the end I think they told us the tape was broken!

"I did a project on Donald Smith's vintage cars – two Humbers, one was his and the other belonged to Mr. Lightfoot, the dentist. One was a 1929 model, the other 1931, and there's only four that old in existence. I remember Janet Smith coming in (her children were Cassie, Daniel and Lydia) and doing pewter and copper work with us. We traced a picture on first, then hammered out the shape".

The results of this craftwork are still displayed around the house – Mark's lovely avocet, hedgehog and fungus plaques, as well as Daniel's fine metal work. Several tiny clay cottages, also made at Drinkstone, stand on shelves. Given pride of place is a photo of Mark, aged seven or eight, totally absorbed by the lighted candle he is holding during our Candlemas service at All Saints'.

Mark now has his own business, specialising in traditional upholstery. His memories of the School include seeing Mr. Nunn repairing the roof, fixing loose and fallen slates and throwing down lost balls stuck in the guttering, together with toy cars and other bits and pieces thrown up by the children. Talking of School visits to castles, Lynda says:

"Poor old Mark, you know how he is with heights – at Framlingham we walked around the curtain wall, and there were some very narrow places along the walkway. It took a lot of courage."

Roger, father of the boys, is a plumber, and recalls coming into the School to talk to the children about his trade:

"I took a tripod bender in, and tried to show them how to bend a copper pipe; we had some children hanging on the handle trying to bend it. We let them try using the pipe-cutters and I remember worrying someone would cut their fingers off!"

Lynda talks of the antiquated office equipment she had to make do with:

"It was hard work trying to get copies out of that old machine with the drum, the cyclostyling machine. You had to write with a sharp point, press down so the carbon got on the back of the sheet, then make copies on the roller of all the letters for the children to take home. The typewriter was a museum piece, it was ancient, with very high stiff keys. You had to press the keys right down from above. I couldn't press most of them down hard enough to make a mark. I used to bring a lot of the work home to finish."

Both boys trained as Pool Life-Guards and were employed at Bury Pool. Later Daniel did a gardening course at Otley College and now works at historic Ickworth House, where the hotel garden is his special responsibility. He says: "I'd like to put things back how they should be, one day, if I ever get the chance. I'd like to restore the summer house down by the lake." Lynda tells me the Educational Charity set up with the proceeds of the sale of the School paid part of the cost of a computer for Daniel to use during his college training.

Lynda talks about her own school experiences. She grew up in Shimpling village and went to the little School there. She has bad memories of the "11-plus" era:

> *"When I failed my 11-plus I'll never forget how awful I felt. My Aunt was a teacher and I was meant to pass! A letter came to my parents, and they said to me, 'Lynda, that's it, you'll just have to walk down to your Aunt and tell her why you've failed.' And I felt I was pretty useless and couldn't do anything."*

We reminisced about the pupils we had known at Drinkstone – Nina Holden, who sang so beautifully; Stephanie, who was so disappointed after her very first week in the infants' class because "You STILL haven't taught me to read!" And five-year-old James with his cherubic round face, looking up under long dark eyelashes to tell me he couldn't do his writing since he had lost his pencil (he was always sitting on it and was nonplussed when given another one!). The children were a lot of fun, and we will never forget them!

PADDY, DAVID, KIM AND MARK BLACKBURN

Paddy and David Blackburn, who live at Mill House, Rattlesden, sent their two sons to Drinkstone School, both boys attending until the closure in July 1986. Both parents had very close involvement with the School and gave unstinting support in many aspects over the years so I was glad to be able to visit them and share memories.

Paddy was an invaluable volunteer-helper in School activities. David was a staunch member of the group of parents, governors and friends who fought against closure.

Kim was born in June 1977, and Mark in October 1979, so both were still very young at the time of closure, yet it is surprising how much they could recall! Living in a homely mill house dating from the 1830s, with the ruined base of a windmill in their own back garden, they were an obvious venue for School visits. In those days bureaucracy was less heavy. We could take the children out at short notice and with minimal expense.

I had a three-way conversation with Mark and Paddy, recorded on tape, so in presenting it below the name of the speaker (mine included!) precedes each remark.

Paddy: *We all remember the School fondly. Neither David nor I will ever forget all you did for us, not least when our baby died. David has many memories of the Save our School campaign and the friends he made through it. I will never forget the fun of listening to readers! Mark went to the School very young; we started coming in about a month after the baby died, so that would make it about November 1982, just after Mark's third birthday. I got a letter – in fact I've still got it somewhere – from all the children in the School, they all signed it, saying they were so sorry about the baby, and would I like to come in and hear them read when I felt well enough.*

I remember Jonathan Brown, when I was listening to readers I used to welcome him because he had a reading card with a Giles cartoon of "Grandma" on it, and I just loved that picture, the expressions on the faces. Jonathan would say, "I know, you don't want to listen to me, you just want to look at my card!" When his reading card was full, he said to me, "Mrs. Blackburn, I've got a present for you!" And he solemnly handed me his reading card to keep. I've kept it all these years and it still makes me laugh! I used to meet Jonathan sometimes after the School closed because he'd work on his father's market stall as a Saturday boy. Later, I met him in Sainsbury's, just before his first baby was born, he was so excited! I remember when we were still at the School, we all teased Jonathan because he'd gone to play at Geoffrey Green's house in Hessett, and in the garden there was a climbing frame with a safety rail around it, and Jonathan tripped over the safety rail and broke his arm without even getting on to the climbing frame!

Mark: *I remember we used to keep words to learn in old tobacco tins.*

Sheila: *But at first you just played, you were a tiny little chap then, Mark.*

Paddy: *A belligerent little chap! The little girls tried to take care of him and he wasn't having any!*

Mark: *And on my first day, someone was giving Kim a hard time, and I stomped right up to them and said, "Don't you bully my brother!"*

Paddy: *That's right! In the classroom, you used to absolutely love that sand and water tray. I remember you went through a spell of getting an awful lot of ear infections, and if the worst came to the worst we just used to shove you on the floor under the desk and you'd go to sleep and I'd just carry on listening to readers!*

Mark: *I remember, I absolutely didn't want to go to playgroup. I hated it – I was used to playing with an older child. If Kim had friends to play here, I always ended up playing with them, and Kim would play with the younger ones.*

Paddy: *I still think that for children from country homes, a School that size is perfect [Mark agrees], because if you've only lived with just one brother, or on your own before going to School, thirty other children is daunting enough, you don't want three hundred!*

Sheila: *I think the work you did with the children out of doors was really valuable, Paddy, because you could work with a small group.*

Paddy: *Yes, we did a lot of nature work and practical work with them, in the churchyard. Never will I forget getting Ollie to estimate the height of the Church tower! He had to lie on the ground and hold up a ruler, and it had been snowing! And being Ollie, it was a full-scale theatrical performance, it really was!*

Mark: *I remember very well when we went into the churchyard with you, Mrs. Wright, in lesson-time, to try and build a stick-house and a straw-house in there like the "Three Little Pigs". We built them up against the wall near the holly trees, in the overgrown patch. We spent either an afternoon, or maybe a whole day – I know I built the stick house, because I was very proud of myself, and we could all get inside our little house and hide from the wolf. That was the first time I saw the grave of the headteacher who drowned in a pond.*

Sheila: *I was very grateful to the churchwardens Gerald Mayes and David Medcalf for letting us use their churchyard. One year they even let us plant sunflower seeds in there – it was for a charity fund-raising effort.*

Mark: *I remember the wild white mallow that grew in there. When we'd finished that project I think the district was over-run with it! I was sorry to see they've mown the churchyard now.*

Paddy: *But the white mallow still grows around the graves. It's rare, you don't see it much anywhere else. But it still grows locally, I've got a photo of it flowering in James Bland's garden. We even exported it into South Africa, a thoroughly illegal import! It did very well there in my sister Anne's garden. Shall we say, it's a fairly strong weed there now!*

Sheila: *I remember once, we were going for a nature walk, and you were walking with me, Mark, and I said to you "That flower there is called Jack-by-the-hedge – and this boy here is Mark-by-the-hedge!" And you nearly fell over giggling – it was lovely to hear you! And I remember how Daniel Steward could always tell us the names of any birds we saw or heard on our walks.*

Paddy: *It was Kim who came up with a wonderful idea: "You know what we should do in the afternoons, Mrs. Wright – we should take the Lego outside!" But then we'd have to find it all afterwards. I remember going up to the School one afternoon to pick up Kim and being told that he hadn't been in the classroom that afternoon and I was absolutely convinced he'd done something perfectly appalling, and I said "Er...why not?" But then you explained that the children had started watching them baling the hay in the meadow at the back, during the lunch hour, and Kim was trying to understand how the baler worked. And it was perfectly obvious he wasn't going to listen to a word anybody said to him, so you left him there!*

Sheila: *Yes, it was quite easy for us to take out some toys and the children's reading books and drawing things and spend the afternoon on the back grass.*

Paddy: *I think Kim finally worked it all out, and it stood us in good stead because we had a baler on site here which he has to sort out every year to get the hay. Now, as well as his day job he's "moonlighting" for Channel 5's "Fifth Gear" programme. He and his friend James Brighton devise the radio control and drive the cars used for the crashes that appear to be done by Tiff Needell. Great fun and fairly profitable but dreadfully time-consuming.*

Mark: *Do you remember that time when Kim was doing clay work, and the* Times Educational Supplement *was protecting the table, and he found a special free offer of Teachers' Packs of*

Lego and tore it out and brought it home? He sent off the application form and got a lovely col-lection of gears, sprockets and other wonderful technical bits, all free, gratis and for nothing! Mrs. Taylor wasn't very pleased, because he'd found the advert and she hadn't, and he more or less said "Tough!"

Paddy: *I don't think it showed quite the right attitude to clay work!*

Mark: *I don't know, maybe it did, considering Kim's lack of talent in that direction!*

Sheila: *Do you remember walking to the Mills? And to see Mr. Baker's collection of old tractors, and Mrs. Jones' goats? And how we walked to the water meadows to see the early purple and spotted orchids, and found hundreds of yellow flag iris and buttercups, and ragged robin grow-ing there as well?*

Mark: *Yes. And I remember the windmill drawings were still on the blackboard long after the School closed. We went to the Tide Mill at Woodbridge. Once we all went over to your place to see your puppies, and we found a hedgehog.*

Sheila: *Yes, and Laurence fell in the mud at the edge of our village pond, "the Grimmer", and I had to kit him out in my daughter's trousers, socks and jumper. He was pink with embarrass-ment because although they could well have been boys' things, he knew they really belonged to a girl!*

Paddy: *Sometimes we'd pop the children in cars and go a bit further, to see James Parker's pigs, and of course to Bradfield Woods. I remember once we had Alexander Boudry with us, in a push chair, because his mother was one of our drivers. He was only four but he was a big lad. Right down the far end of the woods, in the mud, the flipping wheel came off and we had to carry him all the way back to the cars! We looked at dogwoods, and hazels, some coppiced trees, some pollarded, and we found dog's mercury, and fragrant orchids, and tway-blades with creamy-white flowers.*

Mark: *Yes, some of those are quite inconspicuous, you wouldn't think they were orchids at all.*

Paddy: *What's that indicator species? I know, one of the umbelliferae, pig-nut, we found some right under a pollard. People used to eat those.*

Mark: *Yes, and you can eat cow-parsley roots as well.*

Sheila: *I remember those big old fish lakes left by the monks. I used to think they looked as though a dinosaur might come out of the swamps any minute – they were so overgrown with greenery, it was such a lost place – as if people weren't really invading the planet just yet.*

Paddy: *I used to know the children so well. I remember little Corinne, she was the one who had a thing about Kim, she kept chasing him! His only refuge was the boys' loos. I think it was Corinne he wouldn't invite to his birthday party; he invited everyone except her, but he would-n't tell me why! Kim fancied the boys' urinal, especially in the snow, because you could make patterns! And he did treasure the memory of the caretaker one Friday evening, chucking the contents of the bucket loos over into the meadow! He must have been in a hurry that evening, because he didn't dig a hole. Kim happened to be there quite late for some reason. Kim said there was this great "Whoosh!" and over it all went!*

Mark: *I'm not sure if you ever knew this, Mrs. Wright, but at playtime – you know if you're stand-ing with your back to the School, on the right-hand corner of the playground there used to be a wall, and a lot of the kids, including me, would pop over the wall. And you could get between the hedge and the fence of the next-door house, and there was a kind of den area in there. We used to be moaned at by the dinner-ladies: "You shouldn't be going in there!" Of course we all did, but I don't think we ever did any harm.*

Paddy: *I knew a lot of the parents because I was doing the post at the time. There was a couple at Lodge Cottage, Rose and Murray Clark, he was a gamekeeper. They went to Stowlangtoft, and a while later I heard the father died tragically.*

Sheila: *Yes, they had a dear little son with curly red hair, Christopher, and a baby girl. I was sorry they moved away, and what happened later was very sad.*

Paddy: *There was a much-married lady in Lodge Cottage later. Every time she found another man, she added his surname to the existing ones so the name just got longer and longer, and I said to her "If this goes on, you'll only be able to get letters in foolscap envelopes!" She kept goats – I remember Kim going round there once to play with her children – she had four – and he was given goat-burgers for supper. He was absolutely stunned!*

Sheila: *Do you remember we had eggs hatching in School, in an incubator?*

Paddy: *Yes, Scott and Lee McInnes brought them in. Their father worked at The Meade, he lost his job when the farm was sold, and they moved to Wiltshire. They were a lovely family.*

Mark: *I remember mushroom-picking with Scott and Lee, there were a couple of fields that were absolutely full of mushrooms at Meade Farm. They reared beef cattle, and Richard McInnes was Head Herdsman.*

Sheila: *We took all the children down to see the pedigree Charolais herd, and I still have a letter from Tom Isaacs who owned the farm. We sent thank you letters and drawings and some white mallow plants after our visit."* (Later I unearthed the letter from Mr. Isaacs which says: "We were delighted to read the quite varied comments of the letters, and the pictures which were fun. Cattle are very difficult to draw. We much enjoyed your visit with your delightful, well-behaved and interested party. Do come again.")

Mark: *Wasn't it Kim who took in the mole for showing time? We found it dead.*

Paddy: *That's right, and I think it was you, Sheila, who persuaded him to take it home again, because it was really offering to walk out! But then it got left behind on the wall – I think it had been put out so that Kim didn't forget it. Janet Smith got to School first that day – she of course being a staunch vegetarian – and took off the lid to see what was inside the box and found it was this heaving mole! Utterly repellent!*

Mark: *I remember taking in a grass snake that I found. It was fascinating, because how many people have actually seen a grass snake? We'd find feathers as well. I remember you showing us once, how on a magpie you think the colours are just black and white, but when you actually look at the feathers you see they're multi-coloured.*

Sheila: *Do you remember when we were practising for Sports Day on the back field, how baby moles would run across the track, and we'd carry them back to the sandy holes under the hedge?*

Mark: *Yes, and I remember the sack race, which was done with proper hessian sacks.*

Paddy: *That round-the-School race was lethal – especially if you happened to be official time-keeper and they decided to take a short cut. And some of them were very competitive. I always managed to avoid the Mothers' Race – I never joined in – I was tempted to have my leg put in plaster just for that day!*

Mark: *I remember one Christmas, Kim thwacked an angel on the head!*

Paddy: *Yes, Kim was in the pulpit at the Church, doing the narration for the nativity story one year. Around the pulpit were the Heavenly Host – little girls in angel outfits that were a bit grubby by that stage. They were chattering, they'd forgotten Kim was there. And he leaned over and walloped Natasha on the head with the script! She must have thought it was the hand of God!*

Kim was no actor but he loved being on the stage doing the narration. Another year he did it for "The Tailor of Gloucester". I remember one Christmas you said all the boys had to have plain grey trousers for the Play, and in the end I had to make some out of an old piece of material – we were pretty skint at that time. I remember going to Haughley Park at bluebell time, dressed as Red Indians. We had to contrive Red Indian gear for both boys, and Kim already had a head-dress. We were on our uppers at that time, but we had a fortuitous road accident so Mark had a head-dress made with pheasant feathers! I cut the feathers off the pheasant, instead of plucking them out, and stuck them in corrugated cardboard. I remember cooking sausages over the camp fires at Haughley, it was great fun!

I remember you had Watch Club on Saturday mornings sometimes. We went pond-dipping in Mr. Penrose's old moat [at Home Farm]. Janet Smith used to help, she'd bring Cassie, Daniel and Lydia. There wasn't any sloping shallow part so we had long-handled nets and jam-jars. I remember bringing microscopes, and we went back into School to identify what we found. We put drops of water under the microscope so the children could draw water fleas.

Mark: *We did life-saving lessons in School. You had to rescue children the width of the big room, crossways, on the end of a rope. I've never rescued anyone since, but I have done a bit of rock-climbing. It's one of the lessons you never forget, how to coil and throw a rope. What you learn when you're really young, that's the knowledge that really stays with you. That's when children should learn foreign languages.*

Paddy: *The Candlemas Service in Church – letting all those children loose with candles! We had cardboard candle-holders – when I think of all the things that you did with the children that just wouldn't be allowed now! Candlemas was lovely, very moving.*

Mark: *That sand-pit we used to have in an old tractor tyre, round at the back of the School – there was a time when we had a gale and a tree fell down behind the sand-pit and damaged the wall.*

Sheila: *Yes, we had some bad winds that actually broke the frame of one of the high dormer windows.*

Mark: *I think we were sent home early that day. We couldn't go to that end of the classroom because the whole window was wobbling, some glass fell into the room.*

Sheila: *The L.E.A. had that window boarded up – they didn't attempt to repair it, we were too near the closure date.*

Paddy: *I remember that wonderful last day out when we did – was it Framlingham castle? – Orford, and Thorpeness, I think.*

Sheila: *Yes, we got Mr. Crichton to auction an old pine dresser that had been given to the School, and we used the money to hire a coach to take everyone, children, parents, and friends of the School, on a free day out. We felt they deserved it; all that fighting against the closure and getting nowhere.*

Mark: *It was a really good day, fantastic, I'll never forget it. At Thorpeness we all went in the boats.*

Paddy: *Yes, because Kim and I were rowing, and he said "Let's go to the Pirate Island" and I said "Fine!" but we nearly came to blows! It turned out there were two Pirate Islands and we were each trying to get to a different one.*

Sheila: *Do you remember getting to Orford Castle* [it might have been on an earlier trip], *and as we arrived a whole lot of people in medieval costume streamed down the steps and disappeared over the grassy hillocks? It turned out that they were spending a week there, living in tents like in medieval times. I couldn't help wondering if any of the children might think, since this was a medieval castle, people might live there dressed like that, all the time.*

Paddy: *I remember the work the children did for the closing Exhibition. The top class all had alter egos from the past. They made figures of themselves – they lay on the floor on a huge piece of paper and drew around each other, twice for each child. Then they dressed one figure in their current costume, and the other in whatever outfit went with the occupation of a person from the 1861 Census* [just after the School opened]. *They each twinned up with an actual historical person mentioned in that Census – such as a laundress or a backhouse boy – and found out about their work and their way of life.*

Mark: *Our class made puppets to tell stories from the Log Book. I can't remember much detail.*

Paddy: *I've still got your puppet somewhere, Mark. And I've got a lovely photo somewhere, of me with Lydia Smith and Clare Monk, out in the playground, sitting on a rug, sorting out some old books and papers.*

Do you remember rigging the flag for the last day of the School, Mark? We did it as a surprise.

Mark: *I was only about seven, but I can just remember. The week-end before, I think it was on a Sunday, we lowered the flag pole just to make sure that we could lower it, and that it didn't need repair, or was so rotten that we couldn't use it. We found out what fixings we needed but we didn't put the fixings on because we thought that would give the game away.*

Paddy: *Then we went up the evening before the last day, and put all the ironmongery on and put the ropes on. The next morning we went in early and put the Union Jack on, and flew it from the top of the pole. That Union Jack dated from the Coronation, it came from David's parents. They ran a grocery shop and we had their bunting out as well, on the hawthorn hedge between the School and the road.*

You wanted to know about the protest group, and our fight to prevent closure. David can tell you more about that. I suppose it was the Mums who started it, but as Mums of small children, how much time do you have? It involved a lot of committee work and the men seemed better at that.

[Mark says he thinks the men were more patient with the bureaucracy!]

Paddy: *I remember meetings in our sitting room. Don Smith was there, and Geoffrey Green's Dad, whom I always liked immensely because his firm did all the art work and printed the posters. We put those posters all over the place. But of course we couldn't win, however hard we worked, unfortunately."*

David Blackburn kindly sent me his thoughts and memories:

"Like most parents, we always wanted to do the best we could for our children, so it was natural to us to make the most of our rights to "express a preference" about the boys' first school. First, it meant listening to what other parents had to say about their children's experience. We'd only lived here a couple of years when Kim was born, so we didn't know many folk when it was time to start thinking about schools. Gathering experiences made us quite a few new contacts and helped us to decide. We counted a lot on reputation, and Drinkstone's fitted with our ideas about how to go on. The kind of welcome we got mattered a lot. I'll never forget another head teacher telling us that the parents' involvement should stop at the school gate. We didn't choose that school!

"The relatively small number of children on the roll mattered too. It meant that the classes worked well together as groups, and even the whole school could do things together very readily. Then again, when one of the children needed a bit of time on its own, it could have it while still being within range of a teacher or "mum helper". Impromptu outings could be put together quickly and were of enormous value to the children. When, as they usually did, these expeditions involved a good handful of parents, it gave the adults a real sense of contributing to the school and what it was trying to do.

"Finally, I learned a lot about small-scale politics from the campaign to save the school from closure. I'd never before been such an "activist", but I was surely prepared to do all I could to defend what seemed to me such a successful organisation, so important to our community. I'm still convinced that we managed to refute every point put forward to justify the closure. I still believe it wasn't a logical exercise – the numbers as published didn't add up; but at least we were listened to all the way up to a Minister of State – in person and face to face. I do know that as well as educating our children, Drinkstone School did a great deal to educate me."

Chapter Twenty-One

THE CLOSURE OF DRINKSTONE SCHOOL

A SOMBRE GROUP of governors met in March 1983, to discuss the imminent visit of a "fact-finding party" connected with the Area Review of Stowupland catchment schools. In April a group with power to decree closure would visit. The Parish Council had sent a written promise of support in the fight to keep the School "open and safe". However the picture was bleak, the comments from authorities worrying. Basic facts were these – all First Schools in the Review were housed in Victorian buildings. Elmswell was to have a new building. Maintainance of Drinkstone, Rattlesden and Woolpit had been neglected. Decisions would be made on economic, rather than educational grounds. Drinkstone had little space for re-building, stood on a bank, and had no parking facilities. Of the 34 pupils at Drinkstone, only 21 lived in the parish. There was a surplus of 15,000 school places in Suffolk primary schools, and 7,000 must be abolished.

The governors passed "a vote of thanks to Mr. Connolly and Mrs. Wright for maintaining a high standard of teaching in the School, with happy children and modern equipment", and the meeting was closed.

The Area Review party duly arrived on 25th April and asked a great many questions. Mr. Connolly reported that "the outside toilets were once again prominent in discussion, but no child, parent or teacher has ever complained about them". The following day Mr. Duncan Graham, Chief Education Officer, visited unexpectedly and "expressed great satisfaction at the work going on".

It was really no surprise when on 19th May, the Consultation Document produced by the Area Review body arrived, proposing closure of Drinkstone School and transfer of children to Rattlesden or Woolpit. Mr. Connolly commented: "After so many years of threat of closure this definite proposal is still a shock".

An Extraordinary Meeting was held on 27th May. Chairman Geoffrey Wilding's suggestion that a public meeting should be called was unanimously approved. The date was fixed – 15th June at 8pm in the School.

Forty people attended the Public Meeting. Parents from Drinkstone, Hessett and Rattlesden came, also governors, and members of Drinkstone Parish Council and Thedwastre District Council. It was decided to form an Action Group, completely independent of the governors. Those nominated were Mr. Blackburn and Mr. Boudry, from Rattlesden; Mr. Green, from Hessett; and from Drinkstone, Mrs. Isaacs, Mrs. Parker, Mr. D. Smith, and Mrs. Vansittart. The Secretary was instructed to issue press releases. The new Action Group held their first meeting at the close of the Public Meeting, under the chairmanship of Mr. Don Smith.

At the next governors' meeting, on 21st July, a letter to the L.E.A. was composed, asking for clarification of certain points in the Consultation Document. Normal life continued at School, the children enjoying the usual summer trips and visits – to Chadacre Agricultural Institute, a Festival of Song, a Music Day at Beyton, and so on. All children were now doing clay work, all attended weekly swimming sessions in Bury. Mrs. Wendy Collins' hours were increased to nine per week, and Mrs. Bradbrook took over as mid-day supervisor.

In October there was an emergency meeting of governors, to meet representatives from the Education Committee. Mr. Carnall and Mr. Hedley from the County Education Department were present. There was "free and animated" discussion! The governors unanimously agreed to oppose closure. A few days later, the Diocesan Education Committee visited, but said they were unable to support the School in its fight against closure. On 1st November Michael Lord, the local M.P. (Conservative) visited, staying three hours. Mr. Connolly commented "he seemed to enjoy himself".

At this time, the School was preparing a curriculum document, a "statement of intent to turn out children with confidence in themselves". The governors were preparing a Document with their views on the proposed closure, to be circulated before the next Education Council meeting in January 1984.

As usual, the heaters were causing problems! The infants' room heater had an erratic time-switch. Various repairs were carried out – the path to the front door was re-paved. Rev. Cribb resigned from the governing body due to ill-health. We would miss him; he was invited to continue visiting the School, anytime.

In May 1984 the governors agreed to have their Document "Objections by the Governors of Drinkstone VCP School to the Suffolk County Council Proposal to Close the School under Section 12 (1) of the Education Act, 1980" printed, and sent to the Chief Education Officer. The paper contained a thoughtful, well-researched response under the headings Buildings, Social Context, Use of School Buses, Resources, Staffing, Educational Quality, Financial Considerations, Access, School and Church, and Catchment Area.

The governors set to work producing an attractive leaflet, comprising four large pages of photographs taken by Ken Gilbert, with descriptions of life in the village and activities at the School. Entitled "The face of Drinkstone – a place where people care", it presented Drinkstone and its School in a very positive light and brought in new supporters for our cause. The designer of this leaflet was Sarah Gunnett, a past pupil of the School. The first paragraph reads "Drinkstone – A pleasant rural village near Bury St. Edmunds, having a wide spread of occupations, and many young people. There is a church, village hall, public house and school. All are essential for community life." An excellent case is made for the School – "Children work in a happy and relaxed atmosphere where the process of growing up and learning to take a place in the world is fostered, with teachers and parents working together for the same end. The curriculum is broadly based, music, drama, science and computer usage, are all part of the normal studies; such variety makes learning so enjoyable, and fits children for adult life through the high quality of primary education which they receive. Why subsidise buses to take children away from the village when they can go along with their mothers? What makes a village? People and the things which they do together; whether it be at home, in the church, public house, village hall, or the school, it is essential for the community. A village without these things is no village at all. Drinkstone does not intend to become yet another dormitory."

The content was convincing, the presentation professional. The trouble was, the School was about to close not because of unsatisfactory performance, but because the expense of bringing the building up to modern standards was just too great for the L.E.A. to contemplate. The L.E.A. had no intention of entering any debate about what makes a good local community. The fate of the School was already sealed. Nothing we could have done (short of somehow building a smart new school ourselves!) could have made a difference. And we could do nothing to counteract the number facts: we had only kept going because pupils came to us from Hessett and Rattlesden, and the Authority's contention was that Hessett children should go to Thurston School, and Rattlesden children should attend the School in their own village.

Chapter Three of this History tells of the need for village schools to evolve and adapt to changing circumstances and requirements through the decades. Drinkstone had done just this. From being a typical village school of the mid-century decades, in which teachers reigned supreme in their own little kingdom, it had become a place of open doors inviting community input and involvement, where the individuality of pupils was not squashed, and children were not made to conform to some official blueprint. This was why several families from other villages sent us their children and gave us such whole-hearted support. While such a small school would not be the choice of every teacher, nor every parent, it worked well for many and was highly valued. None of this cut any ice with authorities, when set against the cost of bringing buildings up to standard.

Meanwhile everyone tried to stay positive. A wine-tasting evening was held in May, to boost funds, and Mr. Connolly commented "Peatling and Cawdron did us proud – a splendid evening, I think. We made £25 profit, but this was nothing compared to the boost to morale as we await our fate". In July, Mrs. Francis, adviser, called to say goodbye before her retirement, and "thoroughly enjoyed herself. Now we may be closing there is nostalgia for small schools", reported Mr. Connolly.

The Action Committee made stupendous efforts. They produced counter arguments against every reason for Closure cited in the Consultation Document. They canvassed and campaigned, gaining supporters on all sides. They created and displayed "Save our School" posters. They produced and circulated leaflets. They attended a public consultation meeting at Stowupland School. They organised an evening of one-to-one consultations between parents and a few Councillors who were members of the Education Committee. They organised a postal lobby of every County Councillor, with a tailored approach to those on the Education Committee.

Finally came the County Council meeting at which the Education Committee recommended closure of Drinkstone School. David Blackburn attended to observe proceedings from the public gallery and was pleased that "at least one Councillor spoke in our favour… but the vote went pretty much on Party lines".

In July 1984, David Medcalf, David Blackburn and Don Smith went to the Houses of Parliament with Michael Lord, our local M.P. They met Sir Keith Joseph, then Secretary of State for Education, and presented him with their carefully prepared reasons for keeping the School open. This document, entitled "Are you Sure?" contained many irrefutable arguments. For example, under the heading "BUSSING" they wrote:

"We are told that hundreds of children are bussed to and from school every day, and we are expected to be satisfied that no harm will come from extending the practice. We are not. Surely no-one thinks it a good thing in itself, especially for five to nine year olds. The children are exposed to considerable danger on narrow country roads; the buses are unsupervised and young children are at the mercy of older ones; it extends the school day appallingly… Too often buses have to do more than one round and children are dumped outside a locked school. Do we really want this? NO, we endorse the findings of Professor Lee from his extensive study of the subject:

"BUSSING IS UNDESIRABLE – Bussing destroys the possibility of parents becoming involved in the school unless they too have transport. We consider this involvement beyond price… Bussing is not going to get any cheaper. Transport costs are rising all the time and it is unfair to add this burden on the Education budget… At best, bussing is a necessary evil."

"As far as Drinkstone is concerned, this evil is not necessary."

Next, they discussed the building:

"THE BUILDING – is it 'poor and neglected'? Neglected, yes, we agree. Why has this been allowed to happen? It almost looks as though the L.E.A. have been trying to close the school for years… and have deliberately allowed the buildings to become run down to further their cause. Why else have they left us the distinction of "the last chemical toilets in Suffolk schools?" For the rest, the school is a substantially sound Victorian brick building with two classrooms, kitchen, office, library, storeroom and a cloakroom. There is a tarmac play area and a grassed area large enough for school sports. The garden is used by the children. In short, no worse than many another primary school, and better than some".

Under the heading "THE TEACHING" was written:

"Drinkstone is a school in and of its community… Parents and others help… by listening to the children read or sharing any special skills that they might have… there is a regular rota of mothers and other adults from the village who attend the school to help… Fathers are involved too… one has recently helped the whole school study his collection of vintage tractors. It is such community involvement that Head teachers value most, it gives the community a better understanding of the aims of the school… and encourages the teachers to be more responsive to community needs… the school is small enough to achieve "the intimate family atmosphere so helpful to young children". (This last was a quote from the Plowden Report of 1967, which recognised the damage done to small communities by closing their schools).

The Report concludes with the words:

"The L.E.A. should be grateful that it has a Community School in its midst. Repair its roof,

All Saints' Church, Candlemas Service

The Infants perform "Sleeping Beauty".

Left: Drinkstone Post Mill

Botom left: wild White Mallow flower

Bottom right: The Infants tell "The Story of Flour"

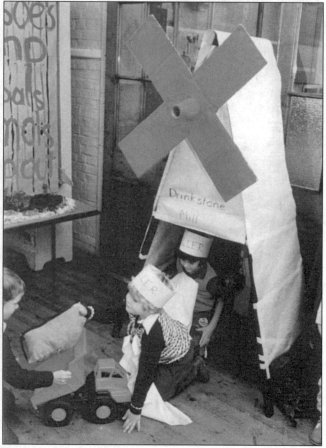

install proper WCs, encourage it in every way, but UNLESS YOU'RE SURE, DON'T CLOSE IT."

Those who visited London to deliver this message felt they "had a fair hearing" from Mr. Dunn, the Under-Secretary of State for Education. As Mr. Connolly said "no-one could have worked harder than these people, to win their case. Now all we can do is wait." So day-to-day School life carried on regardless.

Summer Term saw the usual exciting programme of events for pupils – visits to Bradfield Woods, on-going nature study in the churchyard, establishing a herb-bed in the School garden, close encounters with a flock of Jacob's sheep, and plays performed for parents and friends ("Robin Hood" by the juniors, "Sleeping Beauty" by the infants). At a visit to West Stow Saxon village we tried our hand at ancient crafts – using a spindle and trying to card wool with teasels was interesting! Back at School, we experimented with dyeing, boiling up some of the wool acquired from the Jacob's sheep (collected from hedges) with various plants such as sumac bark, bracken, lichen, and nettles. The odour of wool left to boil and soak in these strange mixtures is still with me! We made some delightful subtle shades and the children wove patterns, on card wound about with string.

More visits took place as soon as we were back from the summer holidays – to Pakenham water-mill and windmill, in connection with Harvest and a project on wind-and-water power. We tried milking goats belonging to Mrs. Jones, a parent living near enough to School for even the youngest children to walk there across the fields. At our Harvest event, "Little Red Hen" was performed by the juniors, and the infants enacted "The Story of Flour". Coins were collected in Smartie tubes to help the drought-stricken people of Ethiopia, £42 was sent. The children attended a guitar recital; they performed a Nativity play, and the story of Baboushka. Mr. Connolly reported "it is my proudest boast that every child has a significant part in our concerts. This is the great strength of a small school. After the concert I was presented by the governors with a personal stereo. I was very moved and felt it was I who should give a present". By this date, he had found a new post, as Head of Woolpit School. Mrs. Maggie Barber was to take over as Head from January 1985.

On the 20th December 1984, Geoffrey Wilding was first to learn that the School was definitely closing. Mr. Connolly reported: "I immediately phoned every member of staff, and some parents. I felt most strongly that it was discourteous not to inform the staff and governors before the press". A sad note on which to start the Christmas holidays! The actual closure date would be the last day of the Summer Term 1986.

The roll in January 1985 was 31. The children, who had greatly enjoyed the Da Silva Puppeteers' performance of "Alice in Wonderland" the previous year, this year were delighted by "James and the Giant Peach". Farm visits continued, this term to see James Parker's pigs at The Green. Pupils were learning to use the ZX81 Computer, and this was almost paid for, thanks to £145 from the P.T.A., £100 from the L.E.A. and £90 from a Jumble Sale held in School. As always, heaters caused problems! "The new stove in the infants' room does not always ignite and sometimes the children have to vacate the room due to unpleasant-smelling emissions".

Maggie Barber and the children were just beginning to know one another, when she obtained a permanent Headship, at Bacton (Shirley Hall having moved on from there to a post at Hoxne). At this point, I felt most honoured to be asked to hold the fort as Acting Head until the closure. Of course I said: "Yes please!" Mrs. Sylvia Taylor was appointed to teach the juniors. Faithful Meg Jack and Wendy Collins still came, Meg to teach music, Wendy as Classroom Ancillary. We had extra Ancillary help, used to support children with special needs, for the last three terms: Beverley Parker (a parent) agreed that despite her teacher's qualification, she would give the hours allowed us for Special Needs, for the lower rate of pay Ancillary Staff receive. This was typical of the generosity towards the little School shown by so many well-wishers. There were other changes – Mrs. Raison (a parent) worked as kitchen assistant. Mrs. Steward (also a parent) was employed as School Secretary, Mrs. Cady having moved on to Elmswell School. Mrs. Baker (a parent) was lunch hour supervisor. There were 35 children on roll, with three or four pre-school children coming in one afternoon a week.

We started planning a stimulating programme for these last four terms. The School was to take part in the "Domesday Study", a nationwide project involving detailed observation of the locality. Mr. Wilding and Mr. Ken Gilbert visited to show footpath maps, to be used in our study. In April the whole School walked to see the post mill and smock mill, by kind invitation of Miss Clover, and "several excellent sketches of the structure and machinery were produced". I will never forget the quiet charm of that kitchen at Mill House, with blue and white china on a dark wood dresser, everything so neat yet far from modern, like a picture from Beatrix Potter's stories.

The churchyard was like an extension to the classrooms for us, we were allowed great freedom there. This spring, the children planted sunflower seeds in pots, then transplanted them to the churchyard by kind permission of the churchwardens. We had noticed beautiful mallow plants growing wild there – large white blossoms with a hint of mauve and pink around the stamens. We decided to study these lovely plants as a whole-school project for the "Cyril Grange" Competition run by the Bury St. Edmunds and District Naturalists' Society, for natural history and conservation studies. We set to work to observe, draw and measure systematically. We collected seeds and tried to spread this lovely plant around the neighbourhood – I still have some in my garden today! In July 1985 we learned we were judged joint second in this Competition. Six children were chosen to attend the celebration in Bury St. Edmunds, when the Mayor presented us with a certificate and a book token. The children's work was put on display at Belstead House in September. We felt very proud!

Also in July the whole School took part in a Red Indian Day at Haughley Park, with schools from all over West Suffolk. Each school brought tepees and a totem pole. Our tepee was made of sacking over bamboo poles, and was decorated with drawings of bison, bears and other wild life. Our totem pole, brightly painted with warriors in war-paint and mythical creatures, was constructed of cardboard boxes stuck one above the other. We made camp fires and cooked sausages on sticks – all rendered perfectly safe by the presence of our usual strong quota of voluntary parent-helpers. The children had visited this beautiful park to walk in the bluebell woods as part of the Domesday Study. Now they had a chance to enjoy climbing and rope swings, tracking, target shooting, weaving, printing, and clay work, in the open air. We had a Pow-wow, every school singing one song to the rest. Our children so much enjoyed this that tepees, cardboard canoe and totem pole came out again for a summer concert to parents on the grass at the back of the School. Everyone wore home-made Indian head-dresses and war-paint. Our pupils designed the programme leaflet.

Ironically, with just three terms to go, July 1985 was the month when two documents were produced to comply with Education Department and L.E.A. rulings. One was a detailed account of the School Curriculum. The other was a fine new up-dated School Brochure for parents, in splendid yellow covers, for the Year 1985-6. (There was no mention of imminent closure in this Brochure!) Both were dutifully read, and approved, by the governors.

Mr. Connolly had not forgotten the children of Drinkstone! During each of our last two Summer Terms he invited Year Five children to join those of Woolpit on a week away in Norfolk, sleeping in a Youth Hostel, and visiting the Broads, Norwich Castle and Cathedral, and the coast. They had a lot to tell us on return! The juniors all went to Woolpit one afternoon a week for outside games, so would be familiar with many peers when they eventually moved on, either to Woolpit, or to Beyton Middle School.

We had School trips to Saxtead and Woodbridge Mills during this term, filling up the coach (55 seats) with parent helpers. Sports Day was a real family day, with Mums, Dads and toddlers all keen to enter their special events. Altogether fourteen parents came in to help during this term.

The Autumn Term was equally busy, highlights being extra swimming at Rougham, visits to Bury Art Gallery and the Abbey Gardens, to my home at Wickham Skeith to see geese and puppies, and to Mrs. Raison's home to see aviaries of exotic birds. The School "Watch Club" met some Saturdays, and we were able to enjoy pond dipping in Mr. Penrose's large pond (he was an Advisory Teacher, living at Home Farm, who took a great interest in the School). Records reveal that at these Saturday meetings we sometimes had 19 children – half the School!

We raised £69 for "SOS Children's Villages" with our sponsored sunflowers, gave to "Aid for Africa" at our Harvest Service, and to the Church of England Children's Society at the Carol Service. The School Fund paid for art and craft materials, music, and gifts and crackers for the Christmas Party to which Santa always came!

In January 1986 we set to work seriously planning Closure events. We decided to have an Exhibition about the village and the School, and a Thanksgiving Service in All Saints'. There would be two Open Days, one extending into the evening with drinks and a buffet. Governors and all staff were eager to help.

Right: "Watch Club" Pond-dipping

Left: In the orchid meadows

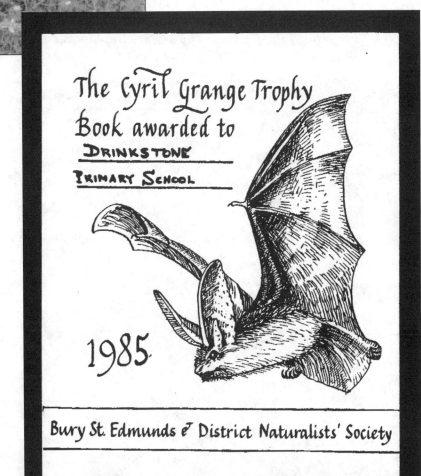

Right: the Cyril Grange Trophy

Above: This way to the closing exhibition.
Below: Each pupil was "twinned" with an actual child or young person who had lived in Drinkstone at the time of the 1861 Census. They made two life size collage cut-outs of themselves – one "dressed" in today's clothes, the other in the likely costume of their "twin's" trade.

Ideas came thick and fast. We would contact as many people as possible who had past connections with the School, and study with the children past life styles, and major changes during the 127 years the School had been open. Mrs. Pocock and Mrs. Taylor volunteered to visit the archives to investigate history of School and village.

The usual termly events took place, with a Theatre visit to see "The Snowman", Water Safety Training from County Staff, String Quartet Recital, Police visits to tell the children about road safety, and a Maths Open Evening. Our Candlemas service, so entrancing in the ancient Church with wonderful carved oak rood-screen background, before which our children stood spellbound by the lighted candles they were given, was an example of an activity from the past, repeated in modern times. This was to be the pattern of the next six months. We read Log Book entries and discussed the stories – Mary who got a counting bean stuck up her nose was a favourite (but we did not imitate Mary's behaviour)! We searched the Log Book for activities and outings that we could copy with the children.

After half-term, a letter arrived from Meg Jack. It said (in shaky hand):

Dear Sheila, so sorry to welcome you back with bad news. I won't beat about the bush but tell you that I shall be away for the rest of the term! I am in Ipswich Hospital at the moment with a nasty fracture to the back of the head. The Doctors have taken it very seriously, demanded "Bed Rest" and ordered "no work" for several weeks. A head cannot be put into plaster and rest is the only cure (I'm not very good at resting!! I think I shall have to be sat on!!).

I am so sorry to let you down. Do get someone to use my hours. I don't get sick pay anyway so there will not be a double pay out.

I fell during a Barn Dance to celebrate my son's 21st birthday. Someone fell on top of me and my head was smashed on the concrete, laying me out cold! It was all very dramatic. I had a BAD 24 hours but am now picking up quickly. I'm sure they will send me home in the next day or two. A new head is the only thing I need!!

My love, Sheila – will pop in when I can drive again – Meg.

Poor Meg! Children and Staff sent cards and good wishes – we would miss her. Meanwhile, Angela Connolly, wife of our ex-Headmaster, kindly came into School to teach class music and recorders every Friday morning.

The children joined Woolpit School for an excellent performance on Suffolk Legends, which included the "Green Children of Woolpit" and the "Green Merman of Orford". Educational visits during these last two terms focussed on past times, in preparation for our Closure Exhibition. We visited Easton Farm Park, with its wonderful octagonal Dairy built in 1870, Victorian Laundry, and Smithy. We saw Suffolk sheep and Suffolk Punch carthorses and various rare breeds from the past. We visited Colne Valley Steam Railway, rode in fine restored carriages, and climbed on the huge locomotives – this was relevant because the first Headteacher of the School, back in 1860, travelled from Exeter to Elmswell by Steam Railway, with his wife and baby son. They stayed overnight in London, and made the final leg of the journey from Elmswell to Drinkstone by horse and carriage. At the East Anglian Museum of Rural life we saw horse drawn vehicles, admired the rooms set up with furniture and equipment from past times, and wandered through the stark "Victorian Schoolroom" with its comfortless benches and desks.

Mrs. Bland (a parent), came in to help older children stitch samplers like those sewn by Victorian schoolchildren.

Mrs. Easdown, our Speech Therapist, visited to tell the children her experiences as an evacuee in the Second World War. The children tried on my gas-mask, which accompanied me to school as a five-year-old, also my father's "Air Raid Patrol" helmets.

Meanwhile our building reminded us that it too was Victorian! One wild day, gales loosened slates, some falling into the playground. Electricity failed, and several rotten bits of wood fell into the classroom from a high dormer window, leaving a pane of glass swaying precariously above us. The infants spent the afternoon in the library and we were glad to see everyone safely home that afternoon. The very next day, electricity was restored, workmen boarded up the window, replaced around 40 roof slates, and sawed up two large trees that had fallen on to the grass behind the School.

Summer Term, our last, saw visits to Bradfield Woods and Norton Bird Gardens (like pupils of the past). We walked the meadow footpath behind the School, down to the marshy meadows near the Mills.

We found orchids, yellow flag iris, ragged robin, red and pink campion and masses of buttercups. Our children were allowed to pick buttercups and campion, not the orchids! We had many visitors – Mr. Gilbert showed the children slides of recent events at School, and helped them prepare a commentary for the end of School slide show. Mrs. Bell, a local authoress, came to show us her children's story books, and told us about her country childhood (in Oxfordshire) and her home in Drinkstone, "Blacksmith's Cottage", with a wheelwright's cottage next door. Mrs. Austine (née James), an ex-pupil now aged seventy, cycled over from her home in Woolpit, and showed us where the pump and the school bell used to stand.

Meanwhile, Mrs. Taylor and Mrs. Pocock took the older children to the Record Office to study Census Returns for Drinkstone in 1861. In the village, they mapped those houses surviving from the 1860s, and each pupil was "twinned" with an actual child or young person who had lived in these homes at the time of the 1861 Census. They studied occupations, clothing and lifestyles of the 1860s. Then each child made two life size collage cut-outs of themselves – one "dressed" in today's clothes, the other in the likely costume of a trade – laundress, milk-maid, scullery maid, gardener, boot-boy, blacksmith's boy or bird-scarer. They compared a day in their own lives with the long hard days of the past. It was tremendously productive work and made a fantastic display. These collage portraits, picture maps, paintings and accounts of our visits covered the walls of the classrooms as high as a person on a step-ladder could reach! The infants meanwhile made puppets illustrating characters and events from the Log Book. We had fun!

These are some fascinating details of Drinkstone households from The Street (around the School) from 1861:

> PLACE FARM (now HOME FARM)
> Thomas Sorrell, Bailiff, Lydia Sorrell, Housewife, Ann Blines, Servant, Son, 11, Scholar
> SCHOOL HOUSE
> John Knott, Headmaster, Charlotte Knott, Wife, Son, 6 months
> TUDOR COTTAGE (now ABBOTT'S LODGE)
> John Smith, Carrier, Mary Smith, Laundress, Niece, Laundress
> THE OLD POST OFFICE
> William Presland, Painter and Glazier, Mary Presland, Grocer
> BATH HOUSE (now DRINKSTONE LODGE)
> Henry Hoggitt, Gentleman, Marianna Hoggitt, Wife, Son, 1 year, Hannah Felgate, Cook, Sarah Makin, Housemaid, Maria Hinnell, Nursemaid
> RECTORY HOUSE
> Maria Carey, Housekeeper, Frederick Cresswell, Gardener, (Rev. Maul not at home)
> COTTAGE
> Edward Ottewell, Farm Labourer, Rosanna Ottewell, Housewife, Children 15, 12, Farmworkers, Children 10, 7, 4, Scholars, Baby, 2 years
> GLEN COTTAGE (now BLACKSMITH'S COTTAGE)
> William Nunn, Blacksmith, Mary Nunn, Housewife, 3 children, Dressmakers, 3 children, Scholars
> CHURCH COTTAGE
> Morris Korde, Farm Labourer, Jemima Korde, Housewife, Children 10, 6, 3, Scholars, 1 Baby
> THE ALMSHOUSES
> Robert Squirrell, Labourer and Pauper, Elizabeth Squirrell, Pauper, Elizabeth Wright, Pauper, George Rowe, Labourer and Pauper, Sarah Rowe, Housewife, Harriet Gill, Laundress, Susanna Gill, Scholar, Esther Osborne, Pauper, Ann Bunker, Pauper

It was a very busy time! Throughout the term, governors and parents helped with visits for each child to the school they would attend in September. Those going to Woolpit got a chance to play outdoor games, and future pupils of Rougham even swam in the pool! Teachers from all these schools visited Drinkstone to see the children and their work. There were invitations to send out, for our closing events, programmes to organise, buffet lists and rotas of helpers. I enjoyed designing a commemorative mug

An exhibit in the closing exhibition

with a drawing of our elegant front façade and the dates 1859-1986. We ordered 120 of these, to be presented to children, parent-helpers, governors, staff and special friends of the School. We sought out elderly ex-pupils, and visited some of them – Mr. O. Squirrell, born 1906; Mr. Cyril Smith, born 1904 (unfortunately, when four children called, he had been taken to hospital); Mrs. Mary Halls, born 1901; Mrs. Ada Lee, born 1894! Two of our youngest children, and two of our oldest, visited Ada in her Elmswell home (see page 227).

There were other tasks for me – an inventory of all contents of the School was made and circulated to other Schools, and I spent many evenings delivering furniture, toys, books, games and equipment. Those benefiting were Woolpit, Rougham, Beyton, Great Barton, Chilton Road, Cavendish, Elmswell, Bacton, Walsham-le-Willows and Rattlesden. We were happy that a few items ended up at Drinkstone Village Hall and All Saints' Church. Of course much had to be kept until the end of term. People called to select items, and the L.E.A. dealt with major equipment. We were very busy.

We had an early sports day, concert and prize-giving so as to concentrate all efforts on end-of-School events. No less than 15 children received certificates and badges from the Royal Life-Saving Society! Happily Mrs. Jack was with us again to lead the musical performances.

By July it was all systems go for the special events. The School was open for the Exhibition on 9th and 10th July. 157 visitors signed their names in the Log Book but we had many more visitors than this, and it was wonderful to see ex-pupils meeting old friends and sharing memories. On 14th July we had a splendid outing, to Framlingham Castle and Thorpeness Mere, where the children revelled in landing on one island after another! We invited all parents and governors who wished to come, a full coach load. This trip was entirely funded by our School Fund (coach, boat hire, ice-creams). The Fund also paid for prizes, gifts and certificates, commemorative mugs, and refreshments for end of School events. The small remainder of the fund went to Woolpit School.

The children spent many hours creating floral arrangements and practising our songs for the final Thanksgiving Service. On a sunny afternoon, we all trooped into a crowded Church. It was a happy afternoon – we were giving thanks for 127 years of school life, and for all the fun and learning of hun-

Signatures of parents, governors, friends and pupils at the school

Children's signatures

dreds of children – most of it, hopefully, good to remember. Rev. Rodgers conducted the Service. We sang "The journey of life", "One more step along the world I go" and "The wise may bring their learning". The children sang "Light up the Fire" and "The earth is the Lord's". Bishop Eric so enjoyed the percussion accompaniments that he asked for an encore! He gave a most heartening address and presented the mugs, and the whole event was videoed. Back in School, there were refreshments, a final exchange of heartfelt thanks and gifts, and a chance to watch the video of the service! This was not entirely a sad occasion; we had received so much support and appreciation through these last days.

The children dispersed to six schools – Beyton Middle (9); and primary Schools at Woolpit (10), Rougham (8), Thurston (3), Tollgate (1) and St. Edmunds (1). Two gentlemen, one from the L.E.A. and one from the Ministry of Education, called to discuss the effect of closure on staff, children and community. I was able to tell them that our children had coped well and had mainly happy memories, and would most likely settle quickly into the new schools, BUT that the loss to the community, ALL age groups, was great, and was deeply regretted.

Many kind words were spoken and written during these last days. Mrs. Cocksedge was thanked for her "splendid and unstinting care" as cleaner for eleven years. Gifts and thanks were exchanged all round. Mrs. Taylor said she "felt honoured to be a participant in such a wonderfully warm and happy reunion of past pupils and friends of the School." Mr. Wilding congratulated staff on their positive attitude and said "no pupils have been prematurely lost to other schools and all the children had gained an especial and rewarding experience". Drinkstone Parish Council said our Exhibition had "given tremendous pleasure to so many older residents, and... the children have been given something of their heritage which they are not likely to forget." Mrs. Easdown, our friendly Speech Therapist, said she would miss our children, and the Exhibition had been "very interesting and very beautifully done – just like walking into a history book!"

From Mr. Peter Northeast, Head of Rattlesden School, and Chairman of the Executive Committee of

Press cutting of pupils with their work for the closing exhibition

Another press cutting: Kim Blackburn, left, and Helen Bradley, both nine, with their pictures of former village characters. Kim's is of the Rev. Spencer Woodfield Moul, who gave the land for the school to be built, and Helen's is of former village grocer Mary Presland.

Suffolk Local History Council, we received a letter to all staff saying:

"Wearing both my major hats I feel I must let you have a note about your outstanding exhibition we so much enjoyed... without the slightest element of exaggeration, it really was the best display of historical work I've ever seen in a small school. What a pity you didn't enter the 'Jack Carter' competition – you'd have walked it!... It's that quality of work that makes this government-inspired headlong closure of small schools so obviously crass."

There were so many moving and kind words from various friends of the School that we could not be too sad. Geoffrey Wilding wrote a lovely letter, thanking staff for their loyalty, determination and hard work, and saying:

"Your positive approach to closure has seen the School reach a zenith of achievement... the display of the Open Days had to be seen to be believed, and it opened many people's eyes to the School's standard of achievement."

Two of the letters, both written on the actual last day of the School, 18th July, were utterly heart-warming. Nicholas Cribb wrote:

"...the name of the School stands higher than ever as a happy place for children, and a place where the foundation of a sound education has been laid. The children loved to go there... I also owe you a debt of thanks for I have spent so many happy Thursday mornings in school... it was a personal joy to sit with the children, to hear them sing, and see their obvious joy in what they were doing. I owe the school so much, and I owe you a debt of thanks... above all, for your great kindness to me."

A letter from dear Meg Jack summed things up beautifully;

"Thank you for the many happy hours shared at school with you – today has been perfect! Let's not be too sad. Drinkstone School has fulfilled its purpose – and we must be thankful for the privilege of serving God there. We must look forward – trusting that the children will build on what they have learnt.... With my love and my thanks for your friendship."

I treasure all these letters, also the photograph of the School given to me, cleverly made into a book, with the signatures of those friendly, lively little pupils, their parents, the staff, the governors and many friends from those years at Drinkstone, written inside. The video of the Thanksgiving Service now belongs to the History Group and the little School will never be forgotten.

On the first day of the summer holidays, Lynda Steward and I packed up Log Book, Managers' Minute Books, Attendance Registers and so on, leaving them (as requested) to be collected by officials from Shire Hall, and thence to safe keeping in the Record Office. It is a puzzle to me that somehow, the second Register of pupils (1947-1986) subsequently vanished. We certainly used it up to the last months of

Schooldays recalled

Things have changed a lot since 91-year-old Ada Lee was a pupil at Drinkstone's tiny village school.

She had to write with chalk on a little slate, books were few and far between and a large brass bell summoned the youngsters to school.

These were just a few of the memories she shared with modern-day pupils to mark the school's closure on July 18 at the end of an era spanning 127 years.

The school's youngest pupils, Mark Hale, aged 5, and four-year-old Kelly Sturgeon, pictured, visited Mrs Lee as part of activities to mark the closure.

An exhibition of its history opened yesterday and is open today from 10 am to 11.30 am and 2 pm to 3 pm.

the School, whenever pupils arrived or left. A mystery now of the past!

Chapter Twenty-Two

A STRANGE STORY

IF YOU WANDER UP The Street southwards, beyond School, Church, Church Cottage and Drinkstone Lodge, you will come to a narrow lane known as the "By Road". This lane winds uphill, with first Lodge Cottage, and then a bungalow, on the left, arriving at a T-junction. Turn right here, and you eventually come to some Tudor dwellings, Burt's Farm and Marsh Green Cottage. If you go on past these two you find ancient Hill Farm (where the lane comes to a dead end). Amazingly, there was a farmhouse on this site dating from Saxon times, recorded in the Domesday Survey of 1066, when a Freeman was tenant here, under one of William of Normandy's supporters, Robert Earl of Moretaigne. The land was named for St. Etheldreda, held by the Abbot of Ely. The Gossard family who now live at Hill Farm, recently unearthed an extremely ancient horseshoe, assessed by experts as dating from "pre-Roman times."

Returning to the T-junction – if you go north here, towards the Mills, you come to Burt's Farm Cottages, and finally to Woolpit Road. Near Burt's Cottages a track known as Deadman's Lane also leads to Woolpit Road.

Very little traffic (apart from tractors) is seen in this lonesome part of the village, but it has a fascinating history. Lodge Cottage originally belonged to Drinkstone Lodge (home in the19th century to members of the Horne family), as housing for workers. I was surprised to be told that there is a restrictive covenant preventing any building on the Lodge Cottage site without the permission of the owners of Drinkstone Lodge; this covenant was imposed as a result of dubious goings-on at the Cottage, giving rise to rumours that the place might one day be used as a Night Club!

The second dwelling up this lane, the bungalow, is the real subject of my story. This was built early in the 20th century, originally to house the curate. At an earlier date, curates of All Saints' lived in Chesil Cottage in Cross Street (formerly known as Spring Cottage). Chesil is a timbered dwelling, originally thatched, later extended to accommodate a housekeeper. Part of Chesil Cottage is flint-faced, and a pond in the garden shows where flints for this were excavated.

Returning to the isolated bungalow in the By Road: I don't know at what dates it was home to a curate. It was known simply as "The Bungalow", and was constructed entirely of corrugated iron with a lining of wood. In 1981, when I began to teach at the School, I was introduced to Mrs. Mary Pocock (a widow), much-respected governor of the School, who lived in this bungalow. Mary was born on January 10th 1915 and at the time of writing has recently celebrated her ninetieth birthday! She is as charming and as lucid as ever, a wonderful lady.

Back in the 1960s, Mary was employed as resident Housemistress at Headington Boarding School near Oxford, and was beginning to wonder where she might live during her forthcoming retirement. Her daughter, who was teaching in Cambridge, said "come East, it's cheaper!" So Mary wrote to Lacy Scott, Estate Agents, explaining that she had very limited opportunity for house-hunting but wanted a country home not too far from Cambridge. Weekends were spent rapidly viewing properties from lists supplied by Lacy Scott's. Mary says: "I was furious when they sent me details of a tin bungalow! But since I was in the area, there was no harm in looking. Arriving in Drinkstone, I came to a windmill, and there in the garden an elderly lady was weeding her flowerbeds. So I stopped and asked directions. She turned out to be Wyn Clover, and she became a very great friend. It's really thanks to her kindness that day that I ever saw the cottage, and ended up buying it. Later on I said to her, 'I can't thank you enough, it's just wonderful!' Really I fell in love with the site, the fantastic view from my living room and bedroom windows. Where would you find another place like this?"

From the front windows of the bungalow a landscape of rolling fields, hedges and trees stretches uninterrupted to "Lane End Cottage" (once Widows' Cottage, then Slugs' Hole) which in today's splendour of white-painted walls appears idyllic. For Mary, the beautiful setting of her new home far made up for details such as lack of central heating and the fact that both walls and roof were of corrugated iron (now painted a warm dark green). Set in a verdant country garden of shrubs and flowers, with three ancient wells on the site, the total effect is charming. Mary moved in with delight, in 1971, and was soon immersed in village life.

Mary gave her home a new name, "Monk's Hoot". I asked her what lay behind this evocative name, and she told me "I had a fantastic Italian midwife when my daughters were born. We were living in Surrey at the time. My midwife's name was Albertella Paravicini. When my eldest child was born, Albertella said she looked like a monk. When the second arrived some years later, Albertella said, 'This one's a hoot!' – because she looked so comical (my younger daughter was a bit of a drama queen as a child, but now she's a responsible headteacher in Warwick). Well, I said to Albertella, 'One day we'll live in the country, and I'll have a house called 'Monk's Hoot'. Sadly, she died just before I found this place so she never knew about it."

Back in the 1980s at the School, Mary quickly became a friend. One day she told me about a peculiar experience from her early days at the bungalow. She had soon discovered that one room in Monk's Hoot somehow wasn't quite right. Although it was heated and furnished just like the other rooms, she was never comfortable in there. The room felt cold and hostile. She could only remain in it for about ten minutes before feeling chilled to the bone and surrounded by unhappiness. Her little dog, Frodo, was equally uneasy in the room. So Mary concluded that an unquiet spirit inhabited the room and didn't want company.

Well, Mary thought, since the cottage was not very large she would like to be able to use all the rooms. Besides, she could not get the thought of the grieving spirit trapped in the house out of her mind. So one day, she decided to say prayers for the unhappy one and ask that it might leave the cottage and be at peace. She used no special form of words, just simple prayers that came into her head... but after a few moments of prayer, Mary's power to think was suddenly snatched away. She seemed to lose all self-control and even all knowledge of her actions....

Some time later Mary came to herself again, and was astonished to find herself running headlong across rough pastureland, her agitated little dog criss-crossing frantically in front of her as if heading her off from danger. Mary could not remember how or why she came to be in that particular meadow, but she was aware of an overwhelming urge to reach a pond in which to drown herself.

With a huge effort, she forced herself back to normality and managed to stop at the brink of a muddy pond to which she had been running in a state of inexplicable desperation. She stood, breathless, scratched and bewildered, taking in the reality of her situation – as she said to me, if she had not managed to stop her headlong rush, if she had indeed stumbled into the water and drowned, no-one would have guessed the true cause. Probably her death would have been judged a simple accident to a smallish woman trying to reach and pick sedges and reeds for flower-arranging.

Somehow she pulled herself together. Still shaky with fright, she trudged back to the cottage to have a hot bath, a cup of tea, and calm herself down. She was so thoroughly mystified and un-nerved by the experience that for some time she told no-one. Besides, it sounded so fanciful; not in keeping with her character at all.

But somehow a change had occurred in the cottage. In the next few days every trace of the unhappiness that had filled that small room completely vanished. It became like the other rooms, a peaceful, welcoming friendly place to be.

Eventually, Mary found the courage to tell the rector of Drinkstone and Woolpit, Canon Rodgers, the full story – the chilling atmosphere, the simple prayers, and then the terrifying and dreadful emotions that engulfed her and dragged her towards danger. She was told she had done a dangerous thing, for in effect, she had attempted a lone exorcism. But on the other hand, her prayers had brought peace and blessed release to a tormented spirit, who hopefully was now in the arms of God. And the bungalow was from that day on, a warm and happy home.

Well, Mary began to ask questions about the history of Monk's Hoot. What mystery did the "tin bungalow" conceal? She discovered that around fifty years earlier, the bungalow had been home to Miss Caroline Minns, assistant teacher at Drinkstone School, whose sister Ruth was Headteacher at the School for 22 years. Delving further, Mary learned that during the summer of 1927, Ruth had been staying with Caroline, sleeping in the bungalow. Ruth had been in a distressed state and had poured out her troubles to her dear sister. Then one sad night, Ruth had crept silently out of the bungalow to drown herself in a nearby pond.

When Mary told me this story I knew nothing of the existence of these two sisters. Ruth's grave is easy to find, standing apart near the School wall, not far from the gate into the road. However, it was not so easy to discover details of Ruth's years at the School. The first School Log Book disappeared around the date of Ruth's death in 1927. The only Log Book known to exist today dates from the Autumn Term 1927.

However we did have three "Managers' Minute Books", the earliest of which recorded the appointment of "Mrs. Gobbitt of Norton" as Headteacher, in January 1905. As recorded in this history, she was a most energetic and talented Headteacher, unsparing of her time given to School, Church and village, and unbelievably generous of heart. After all, how many Headteachers in charge of an overflowing village school and living in a modest Schoolhouse with her sons and daughters, would unhesitatingly take in orphaned pupils to live with her own family? I was intrigued, and saddened by what I was learning. In both 1920 and 1926, the Minutes record that Ruth Gobbitt tendered her resignation, only to change her mind soon after and be re-appointed. Obviously the managers held her in highest esteem, but equally obviously, Ruth was far from happy at this time.

In keeping with attitudes of that era – which decreed that sorrows, deaths, depression, and above all suicides, should be decorously passed over, not dwelt upon, and survived with a stiff upper lip – no mention whatever is made in the Minute Book of this tragedy. The meeting following her death was mainly concerned with repairs to the building. In October 1927 the managers met "to consider Mrs. Hockley's application for the post of Headteacher at Drinkstone School". Obviously since that sad day in June, steps had been taken to find a temporary teacher and to move the bereaved family out of the Schoolhouse. But there is no record of any of this, nor any statement of regret or sorrow over Ruth's death, nor any expression of appreciation for her 22 years of dedicated service to the School. This reinforced my impression of the disgrace and shame attached to mental unrest and suicide in those days. It all seemed inexpressibly sad, and the whole episode seemed lost in the past.

Then in 1984, when the proposed closure of Drinkstone School had become

The display in the closing exhibition

Mrs. Ruth Gobbitt was Headmistress here from about 1905 until 1927 public knowledge, we were delighted to receive the first of several letters from Dorothy Lee, one of Ruth's six children (see Chapter Six). We exchanged letters, and had some telephone conversations with this vibrant lady in her eighties, so that by the time of the closing exhibition in July 1986 we could present a very positive picture of Ruth Gobbitt and her time at the School. We could tell our little pupils about this teacher's lovely singing voice, how she taught the children beautiful music, how villagers could hear the singing from way across the meadow. We could tell them six children lived in the Schoolhouse, some were born in the upstairs rooms, the little ones used to escape from the house and join the children in the classrooms! We could tell them that Ruth loved flowers and made a wonderful garden around the Schoolhouse.

We did not of course tell the pupils all of Dorothy Lee's memories – how her mother drowned in a pond, how Dorothy and her brothers and sisters received little explanation or comfort at the time of the tragedy. How no-one talked about their mother any more. How everything was hushed up, swept under the carpet. How they had to move on in life hurt, bewildered and upset. Privately I pondered on the feelings of Carrie Minns, that "kindly and painstaking" teacher, and how she also must have suffered.

A newspaper report now in West Suffolk archive reads as follows:

Bury Free Press July 2nd 1927

DRINKSTONE SCHOOLMISTRESS'S SAD END
Drowned in a pond

THE TRAGIC story of the death of a schoolmistress, Mrs. Ruth Elizabeth Jane Gobbitt, who was found drowned in a pond at Drinkstone on Friday morning, was told at the inquest held by the Coroner for the Liberty of Bury St. Edmunds, (Mr.) Thomas Wilson, on Friday.

Caroline Emma Amelia Minns, sister of deceased, stated that Mrs. Gobbitt was living apart from her husband – Henry Moyse Gobbitt – a commercial traveller.

"She had been very ill for about a year and could not sleep without a draught."

On Thursday night she went to bed about 10pm, but was missing on the following morning when witness took her a cup of tea, about 7.45. After searching the house, witness at last discovered her sister's body in a pond. Witness had often heard deceased say she was tired of living.

Police Sergeant W. Dunnett, Woolpit, said that he recovered the body from the pond, with assistance.

Dr. E. C. Hardwicke stated that he had attended Mrs. Gobbitt, who had had a nervous breakdown last term, when she had to give up work. She had been mentally unstable for some months past. Signs of death were consistent with drowning."

Poor Ruth, poor family, and poor Carrie! Carrie was last to speak to her sister, last to see her alive, endured the horror of searching for her and finding her in the water, and then attended the inquest as witness. It was unbearably sad; and Carrie continued at the School another 13 years, no doubt often recalling the happy days of working in the little School alongside Ruth.

When preparing the closing exhibition in 1986, we devoted the wall dividing large classroom from Schoolhouse to these two sisters. A rubbing of Ruth's tombstone was displayed, wreathed in children's paintings of flowers. Ancient photographs of Ruth were loaned and displayed. I received a postcard from

Dorothy Lee at the beginning of July, saying she intended to be with us for the valedictory service in All Saints'. Bishop Eric (Eric Davenport, Bishop of Dunwich) mentioned Dorothy in his address and said kind words about Ruth Gobbitt. Everyone clapped as Dorothy went up to receive a commemorative mug. She came back into the School for tea and biscuits, explored her old home, and was most touched to see the children's pictures and stories about her dear mother. She actually told us it was the happiest day of her life, because after so much silence her mother was being publicly appreciated and remembered with affection.

This was one small incident at a very busy time, but I will never forget it. I felt we had helped to replace sadness with joy, maybe even helped to heal some of the pain of long ago times. We were so lucky the story turned out this way enabling Drinkstone children to play a part at the end.

In 2004 I received a letter from Margaret Minns, Great-niece of Carrie and Ruth (whom I later met). A second letter came from Josephine Newman. Josephine is Ruth's granddaughter, Dorothy Lee was her mother. Dorothy died in 1997 (aged ninety-one) and her daughter says "my mother was indeed a very great character… we still miss her, although I always feel she is not far away from us." Dorothy had made her wishes for her interment and memorial clear before her death: instead of being buried near her home at Southsea, she wished to share her dear mother's grave at Drinkstone. She is recorded on the tombstone under her married name, as "Dorothy Violet Lee". She is described, not as a wife, but as "daughter of Ruth Minns" (Minns being her mother's maiden name). I believe Dorothy wanted to demonstrate great love and sympathy for her mother – perhaps her way of trying to cancel out some of the sorrows of the past. That lonely tombstone so close to the School playground wall, has now been inscribed with Dorothy's name and dates and she has returned to Drinkstone, the place of her birth. Now Josephine regularly sends money for flowers for the grave, and occasionally visits the village.

It is nearly 20 years since Dorothy's return to the School to share the Closure events, when she described her memories so poignantly – how she and others in the family were born in "the churchyard bedroom", that little room whose lancet windows look onto the churchyard; how she loved the place, the School and her mother; how it all came to a tragic and bewildering end, all their memories darkened by grief. Her choice to return to this place in death was a marvellous gesture of love and solidarity with her mother Ruth. Dorothy's daughter Josephine has admired the present day "Church Pyghtle" (the former School and Schoolhouse).

This is the full tombstone inscription :

IN LOVING MEMORY
RUTH E. J. GOBBITT
The beloved daughter of
Richard J. and Ruth Minns
Born December 25th 1876
Died June 24th 1927
"Blessed are the merciful for they shall obtain mercy"
DOROTHY VIOLET LEE
Daughter of Ruth E. J. Minns
Died 4th July 1997
Aged 91
R.I.P.

What of Carrie Minns, who lived in Drinkstone until her death and taught the infants for 22 years? I learned more from Margaret Minns in 2005. Margaret is grand-daughter of John George, a younger brother of Ruth and Carrie. John George is the brother who is remembered by several contributors to this history as a kindly man who continued to pay visits to Carrie throughout her 22 years at the School. Margaret tells me George would always visit sister Carrie at Christmastime. There were other sadnesses in this family, the youngest two sisters, Victoria and Bessie, having both died, one aged five and one seven years, in July 1894. Their graves are in Ashbocking churchyard. Probably they died from one of the childhood scourges of the era such as diphtheria. Margaret also has photos showing some of her aunts (daughters of John George Gobbitt, and nieces to Carrie), named Doris (Dollie), Gladys, Elsie and Olive, visiting the "tin bungalow". Carrie stands with them in what was then, and is now, a "lovely garden". So Carrie did have some happy times before her death in 1958.

Ruth, Carrie and John George were the second, third and fourth children in a family of eight. John George went on to have ten children (only Olive now surviving). So there may be other relatives of Ruth and Carrie who may read this book. If so, I hope it brings pleasure!

Mary Pocock says other curious events have taken place in the lane, one of these seeming to illustrate the uncanny instincts of animals. Mary was in the habit of walking her little dog Frodo up the By Road towards Burt's Farm. Often her cats would come, just as far as a holly bush at the junction, and settle down to wait until dog and mistress returned. But one morning, all three animals simultaneously began to walk one behind the other along the centre of the lane, in a slow and stately way as if in procession. Even faithful little Frodo took no notice when Mary called him. Then all of a sudden, over the brow of the hill appeared a hearse (the lady who had died had been a friend of Mary). The men driving the hearse watched the three little animals in amazement, as they continued to lead the hearse for about 100 yards.

The story of Monk's Hoot continues, eventful to this day! In 2003 Mary was lighting an oil stove to take the chill off her dining room, when the stove suddenly flared up, setting furniture and curtains alight. Mary seized the phone to dial 999, but was interrupted by the terrifyingly rapid spread of flames, and had to pass the burning area to reach the door and the safety of the garden. She ran as fast as she could along the lane to Lodge Cottage, where the fire-engines were summoned. By this time the bungalow was well alight and was an alarming, dismal sight when I drove past a few weeks later. However I was soon reassured that Mary and her cat had escaped miraculously unscathed. Mary spent the first night at the home of her friend Maggie Ivor-Jones of Burt's Farm, and says everyone was marvellously kind to her after the fire. She later found temporary accommodation in Woolpit.

The insurance firm, says Mary, "were fantastic – they haven't quibbled about a single thing". The corrugated iron roof was replaced with neat grey tiles. Now, in 2005, whereas before the only reliably warm place was the kitchen, the whole house is kept comfortable by safe and efficient central heating. Walls and ceilings are re-lined and all rooms are sparkling bright with new paint. Even the scorched pictures have been cleaned, re-framed and re-hung, although Mary has regrets over several aerial photos of her home which were lost and cannot be replaced. An old chest of historical treasures mostly survived, a few articles only being "singed beyond repair". Mary has done considerable research into the history of the village, particularly into links with monasteries in early times. She now anticipates more happy years at Monk's Hoot; a very special lady in a special place.

Chapter Twenty-Three

AFTER THE CLOSURE
Drinkstone Village; Church Schools in the modern world; Drinkstone Charities

THE FOLLOWING REPORT appeared in the *Bury Free Press*, on July 25th 1986:

"Drinkstone School Closes – Another chapter in the life of Drinkstone has come to a close, first the village shops, next the post office, and end of term saw the life of the village school come to an end after 125 years. The 32 pupils, together with their teachers, staff and school governors walked in procession from the school to the church for a special service of thanksgiving. They were met at the church by rector Canon Rodgers who conducted the service. The church had been decorated by the schoolchildren. The address was given by the Bishop of Dunwich, the Rev. Eric Davenport, who said it was a very sad day to see the school closing, but it was also a day of thanksgiving for all the care given to past and present pupils by the teachers and staff. The Bishop presented commemorative mugs to pupils, staff and governors, and one to a special visitor, Mrs. Dorothy Lee, aged 80 years, who had travelled from Lincoln for the service. Mrs. Lee's mother, Mrs. Ruth Gobbitt, was headmistress at the school from 1905 – 1927. There was a large congregation of parents and friends together with former pupils, some now senior citizens. After the service refreshments were served at the school, and presentations made to the teachers by chairman of the governors, Mr. Geoffrey Wilding. Mrs. Wright received two stone garden urns and a stone garden seat, Mrs. Taylor a collection of classical records, both had a picture of the school signed by all the pupils, and a bouquet, and all the staff were presented with a Victorian posy."

The next part of the Report describes the W.I. visit to a herb garden – so at least they were still doing well in Drinkstone!

The closure may have only merited a short newspaper article, but in the hearts and memories of those involved in its last months and years, the closure still evokes strong feelings. I spoke to Anne Wilding, wife of Geoffrey our Chairman of governors (sadly no longer with us). She wrote down for me (20 years after the event!) her understanding of Geoffrey's views:

"As you know, he fought hard to keep the School open, as he felt that it performed an important role in the community. There can be a more nurturing approach within a village school because the children are well known to everyone – and not just a name in a register. It was a happy environment for the young children and it received a lot of support from parents and villagers alike. Taking the children to School enabled parents to meet up with each other on a regular basis, and once the School was closed it seemed as though the heart of the village died too."

It's ironic that in several Suffolk villages I know well, an increase in new house-building has followed hard on the heels of closure of the school! In Drinkstone, throughout the Eighties and Nineties, and into the 21st century, the village continued to grow and change. More houses in Rattlesden Road, including a development of 12 new houses in "The Meadows". More open spaces filled in along Cross Street with houses and bungalows (some of these on former Yew Tree Farm land). Field Close, a development of four pleasant bungalows in Gedding Road, replacing the airfield building on the meadow owned by Ruby Bland. Tithe Barn Farmhouse sold, modernised and extended. The face of Drinkstone was changing, and is still changing.

At Rookery Farm, the farmhouse was sold off, separate from most of the land, and the wonderful farm buildings were converted into dwellings. The 16th century three-bay Oak Barn has become a very special home, with inglenook fireplace built of thin Tudor bricks. Great Barn, dating from the 17th century, an exceptional five-bay oak barn, was also very sympathetically converted. The original thrashing-floor in the central bay remains in all its glory, the beautiful roof still exposed to view. The pairs of bays on either side have been converted into four comfortable living units. The stables, built from red brick, flint and stone in the 1840s to house the Suffolk Punch farm horses, have become a pair of charming homes. The brick and timber cart lodge and stable block built in the 1870s and altered for use as a dairy in the 1920s, was further transformed, into a unique home. The brick and stone buildings stand around a lovely courtyard. Mr. Thompson who farmed the Rookery for over fifty years would not believe his eyes!

16th century Whitefield House in Park Road, home of Raymond Bland and his father before him, was sold off in 1986, once again separately from most of the farmland. Raymond and Vera Bland kept a meadow, located at the end of Chapel Lane, and on it built a fine modern house. They have stables and keep horses. In fact there are probably almost as many horses in the village as there were 100 years ago, since horses are also kept down Cross Street, at The Chestnuts in Rattlesden Road, and in several other places – but no longer are they of the Suffolk Punch breed!

Home Farm stockyard sprouted a large new brick residence in the 1980s, and now (2005) five more fine houses are going up there. Home Farm (the house) is undergoing extensive renovations. It's good to see sheep in the fields at this northerly end of the village still – both commercial breeds, and a small flock of Jacobs. But the rural atmosphere has certainly undergone change.

In 1984 Street Farmhouse, dating from the 18th century, was sold by owner Mr. Sydna Parris, separately from its land. Mr. Parris built a new house further along Beyton Road. In 1990, the pair of thatched cottages on the opposite side of Beyton Road (set well back in the former parklands of Drinkstone Park) was rescued from self-destruction in the nick of time! This was the ruined building where for many years Reggie Wells made his home, with neither water nor electricity on site. He had to leave in 1980 when the property was condemned. Now the pair of cottages was restored and converted into one very desirable home in its own extensive meadow, with a lengthy new drive now linking it to Beyton Road.

Burt's Farm and Hill Farm lands have been sold off, separate from the farmhouses. Gone are the days when most men of the village were employed at local farms, eight to a dozen local men cycling to each farm to work together for farmers living in venerable farmhouses surrounded by their own fields. Seasonal piece-work for women and children has also disappeared.

Hall Farm was run decades ago as part of "Tostock Farms", by an owner living elsewhere. Now many other farms are run in the same way. Robert Baker at Whitefield Barn farms a few of his own acres, but also farms much of the former Park lands, now owned by "Tostock Farms". David and Paul Thurlow still live on their own land and farm it themselves, but not from Home Farm. That is sold off, and the Thurlows live in Moat Farm and Moat Cottages (formerly tied cottages belonging to Drinkstone Park). There is still a thriving plant nursery at Garden House Farm (once Barcock's Poultry Farm, and later Barcock's plant nursery, where Gerald Mayes worked). Mr. Frederick Barcock's daughter Mrs. Maureen Ridge still lives in Drinkstone, at "Treaclebenders" in Cross Street (formerly tied cottages belonging to Green Farm). The ancient garden at "Treaclebenders" is a picture in Springtime, thousands of snowdrops nestle there and the garden is open for charity at the height of the snowdrop season. Green Farm lands are all sold off, and in 2002 the farmyard at Green Farm sprouted three smart new dwellings.

Here and there the charm of old-world thatch remains – Dene Cottage in Beyton Road, Blacksmith's Cottage and Church Cottage in The Street, Elm Tree Cottage in Gedding Road, a couple of thatched dwellings in Chapel Lane and in Cross Street, and a handful in Rattlesden Road. The Tudor farmhouses are still a feast for the eye. A variety of tiled older properties, built of clunch, or wattle and daub, or flint-faced, or brick-built cottages from the early years of last century, mix shoulder to shoulder with the many

"Treaclebenders", Cross Street (formerly Medway Cottage)

Rosy Hayward's drawing of the Mills for a fund-raising notelet.

modern homes. The grand country houses such as the Old Rectory, Drinkstone Lodge, and The Meade remain, but are no longer the venue for community junketings. No longer are their spacious gardens lovingly tended by teams of full-time gardeners, producing bounty such as exotics, flowers for the house, all the fruits, nuts and vegetables a large household could eat, and even eggs, poultry for the table, and a private spply of pork and ham, as in the days of the Reverends Horne. The glory of those gardens is not forgotten, however. Members of the Charity "Suffolk Gardnens Trust" completed in 2005 an intensive survey of the walled kitchen garden at the Old Rectory, which stood on two levels and contained a nuttery.

The story of change, restoration and innovation is much the same in every corner of the village. No longer are the Clover family in the mill house. In 1997 an enterprising young couple, Rosy and Alex Hayward, bought Drinkstone Mills and set about lovingly restoring the place. They applied, and received, a grant from English Heritage, and set about fund-raising, determined to do everything properly. Rosy even designed a "notelet" to sell around the district as a fund-raiser. On the back of this notelet are the words "Drinkstone Mills, Suffolk, 'without doubt the country's most important windmill site', (Mark Barnard, Suffolk Mills Group)".

In 2002 the Haywards had to remove the sails of the post mill, which were rotting, for restoration. Their aim was to keep all original timbers that could possibly be saved, and restore every part as carefully as Daniel or Wilfred Clover would have done. A newspaper article showed photos of Rosy and her children standing in front of the post mill with previous owner Jack Clover. Another showed Wilfred and Daniel Clover pictured at the mill in 1935, and a third showed the mill house and smock mill in 1926. The text explained that:

> "The smock mill began with horse-power turning the grinding stones, and the smock was added on top later, converting it to wind-power. It saw conversion to steam and oil-engine power by the turn of the last century and still has a working 1929 Ruston oil engine. Animal feed labels still hang from pegs in the rustic, atmospheric mill and an 1860s railway carriage is another authentic feature of the site."

Sadly, at the time of writing, Rosy and Alex are having to move to Edinburgh! However they are bound to continue with the restoration for at least ten years, as this is a condition of the grant. So although the mill house will be sold, they will remain in charge of the mills' restoration which they began with such enthusiasm. One day the sails will once again turn gently in the blue skies of Drinkstone.

The closure of the School ended an era and left a yawning hole in the social structure of the village. But it was by no means the only sad ending in Drinkstone at the end of the 20th century! Next to go was the Cherry Tree public house. That patch of land so lovingly tended by Jim Cocksedge and others through the years, is now (2005) up for sale – "2.25 acres with outline planning permission for nine dwellings". The once-cheery pub has "blind" windows, boarded up and depressing. But in Suffolk, we've learned to look forward. Villages everywhere are constantly adjusting to their changing populations. Likewise, facilities, institutions and voluntary groups evolve with the times.

I have a copy of Drinkstone Parish Magazine of May 1998 (nearly 12 years after the closure of the school). At this time the rector, the Rev. Alan Taylor, was retiring after ten years in the parish. His letter, on the first page of the magazine, explains how Church services, including baptisms, weddings and funerals, also pastoral visiting, will all continue thanks to a strong team of (mainly voluntary) workers, during the inter-regnum. The article goes on to say :

> "But this alone will not meet the challenge facing all of us who live in Drinkstone, which is, to foster an active, caring, sociable, neighbourly community. The context is that Drinkstone's remaining institutions, All Saints' Church and the Village Hall, both need substantial commitment and investment. It could be very depressing, but it is not. There is a mood in the Village to meet these challenges, able people are becoming involved and new, positive ideas are emerging. The Church in the Village must take a leading role. The Parochial Church Council intends to implement a plan of action to increase its caring role in the community. Church activity, attendance and giving have all risen. There is reason for optimism."

The PCC report mentions fund-raising to provide better heating in the Church, and eventually, running water and toilets to allow "more versatile" use of the Church building. There have been lively Festivals and a Harvest Supper. The Village Hall (run by the Drinkstone War Memorial Institute) reports improvements to the kitchen and hopes that an entertainments licence will soon be acquired. There are (1998) regular meetings of Drinkstone W.I., the Royal British Legion and the Windmill Club. There is an Age Concern representative in the village.

What of the children? Well, the Sunday School's contribution at special Church services is described as "delightful", and the P.C.C. hopes "to introduce a range of activities to attract older children". Sport and leisure are not neglected. The charity Drinkstone Educational Trust, the Parish Council, Drinkstone Funday committee and various national bodies combined to fund a full-size basketball court for the village. This Educational Trust can be approached for help for any young person or child, giving financial support for musical training or any special interests and needs, including individual sports. For the very young, a Toddler Group meets (at Felsham).

A report by "Ofsted" on Rattlesden School, now attended by a few Drinkstone children, speaks of "a very successful school where standards of attainment are frequently high… behaviour is very good… and children have rich cultural experiences and produce high standards of work…" Most young children living in Drinkstone today attend Woolpit First School. But without doubt, Drinkstone remains a stimulating, friendly and caring corner of Suffolk despite the loss of all shops, public houses, and the School. It's very much up to the residents now and they seem "up for it"!

Five years on, a 2003 Parish Newsletter reveals that although, sadly, the W.I. is "suspended indefinitely", other groups have started up. These include the Local History Group, Computer Class, French Class, Art Class, Pilates (physical exercise) Groups, Music Club, Junior Club for children aged 5-12 years and Youth Club for older ones, and Table Tennis Club for all ages. All these meet in the Village Hall. There has been community fund raising and a welcome grant from "Drinkstone Educational Charity", enabling creation of an Adventure Playground on "The Cricket" (alongside Cross Street and Rattlesden Road). This has a safe slide, two sets of swings, and climbing apparatus for younger and older children.

I read about the Grand Opening of the Wood and Conservation Meadow in Cross Street, where trees, shrubs and bulbs have been planted to encourage wild life. There was an Open Week-End at Drinkstone Mills, with old-time farming demonstrations, reaping, binding, threshing, heavy horses and goats, proceeds to be shared between Woolpit Health Centre and Drinkstone Mills Restoration Fund.

At All Saints', the Priest-in-charge is Rev. Hocking, based in Woolpit. The Organ Restoration Fund will benefit from an evening's entertainment and lecture, in All Saints' Church. The giving is generous, there's to be a hog roast and Wild West Evening in aid of "Wheels for Africa", a Macmillan Cancer Relief Coffee Morning, and a British Legion Plant Sale, while the Sunday School children have been making up parcels for children in the Third World.

It's impressive reading. The village is going from strength to strength, determined to remember and cherish the heritage of the past while keeping well up with the times. There are today around 470 adults on the Register of Electors. So probably the total population is quite near to the 1851 population figure of 543. Of course, there are now far more homes, but with a much-reduced average number of persons per household. The average age of inhabitants now is far greater than in those 19th century days of large families. It is a very different type of community now; but there really seems to be something for everyone in Drinkstone today. I feel proud that I have some small connection with this village that adapts and survives through all the chances and changes time brings.

CHURCH SCHOOLS IN MODERN TIMES

Drinkstone School, like the majority of small village schools, was a Church of England School. It started when and where it did because of the Anglican Church. During the last half of the 20th century, thousands of small rural Church of England schools shared the fate of Drinkstone. So is the era of Anglican Schools in England at an end?

The answer is a resounding NO! The glowing "Ofsted" Report on Rattlesden School, historically Drinkstone's "partner" School, is proof that some still survive and flourish today. Look in any telephone directory under "Education" and most primary schools have letters following their names, denoting some link with the churches.

Here are some recent facts and figures, taken from the weekly *Church Times*:

1995 – Of 22,598 maintained schools in England, 4,858 are Church of England schools, 21.5% of the total. At primary level, the C. of E. provides one quarter of all schools. Many of these are small schools: 59% of schools in England with 60 or fewer pupils are Anglican schools. At secondary level, C. of E. schools are of average size, but are thinly spread: 200, representing 4.2% of the total. In total, around 850,830 children are educated in C. of E. schools, 12.2% of all pupils.

In Voluntary Aided schools, governors still have to find 20% of capital costs.

In Voluntary Controlled schools, all costs are met by the state via L.E.A.s. In Grant-Maintained schools, funding is from the state, but trustees continue to own buildings, and must comply with the terms of their foundation with regard to worship and R.E.

There are 11 Anglican colleges of higher education, educating 53,145 students out of the total 1,500,000 young people in higher education. There are 212 Anglican chaplains working in higher education colleges.

This is encouraging, but the best news is that Church schools in this country are thriving, and increasing, especially at secondary level, because they do such a good job. The following facts come from the Church Times of 2004:

Since 1998, 18 new C. of E. comprehensive schools have been opened. Twelve of these were "conversions", i.e. former community schools that have chosen C. of E. Voluntary Aided status. Reasons for this include:

* the wish by staff, governors, parents and pupils to formalise the Christian values that are already a strong influence in the school, or -

* an L.E.A. with several C. of E. primaries but no C. of E. secondaries co-operates with the diocese to remedy this, usually in the name of parental choice.

Governors of C. of E. schools currently appoint inspectors, with the guidance of the diocese, for the inspection of worship, ethos, R.E. (in Aided schools) and the spiritual, moral, social and cultural development of pupils. These inspectors are separate from Ofsted inspectors, but the two groups try to work together, sharing information. The "National Society" (which supported Drinkstone during the 19th century) has produced a framework for inspection and trains these inspectors.

Today's Church of England schools are not narrow or insular in outlook. Not all give admission priority to C. of E. families. There is no exclusion of children from families of other faiths, and staff may include those of other faiths (most often Muslims). Some former "Roman Catholic" or "Church of England" schools are now combining to form joint "Church Schools".

Many local clergy work with their local schools, for example visiting or taking assemblies at the invitation of the Head, even where the school does not have official Church School status.

A few other excerpts endorse the impression of popularity, sound aims and successful learning at Church schools:

The Minster School in Southwell diocese, which provides choristers for Southwell Minster, and which was formed from an old Grammar School combined with a Secondary Modern, is receiving £60,000,000 from diocese, L.E.A., Government and governors, to expand and update. This includes "appropriate worship space". This school is over-subscribed [i.e. has a waiting list of would-be pupils], as is Emmanuel School, which was a "failing school" when the diocese took it over in 2002.

Many Church schools continue to have close connections with their founder churches. For example, in 2004 at Yattenden Primary in Oxford, all pupils were involved in creating new perspex windows celebrating St. Peter and St. Paul.

The schools also take great pains to foster a sense of community, with pupils learning to value each other and provide mutual support; also, to instil appreciation and care of our world, as at the Bishop King School in Lincoln which "has a strong ecological bias."

Drinkstone School came about partly through the Church of England, and partly through certain local charities and bequests. So what about these charities, in the year 2005?

DRINKSTONE CHARITIES

The various charities in the parish continue to exist. Cambourne provides grants for tools and equipment for young people starting out on training or a new career. Wrenn's is drawn on for social events for elderly parishioners – coach trips, special meals and so on. "Drinkstone Allotments" has a balance between four and five hundred pounds. "Widows Cottage" and "Perambulator and Causeway" have balances of about £28.

The largest charity of all is Drinkstone Educational Trust – to learn how this came about, read the next chapter!

Charities are not easy to run, all need trustees and all present problems from time to time. With this in mind, the "Parish Council News" in the November 2005 Newsletter contains the following statement:

"Amalgamation of Village Charities. The meeting had been held during which it was proposed that the Cambourne Charity would be amalgamated with the Education Charity; Perambulator and Causeway would close and the held funds be used for maintaining footpaths; and Wrenn's Charity to absorb the Widow's Charity.

"It was also proposed that the aims of the charities be broadened to be of benefit to a wider range of parishioners. It was agreed that no further action would be taken until legislative changes had gone through."

So where did the Educational Charity come from? I talked to the Rev. Alan Taylor, who was rector of the parish from 1988 until his retirement in 1998. He and his wife Dorothy have been friends of mine since they cared for Wickham Skeith parish church during an interregnum. This is what Alan told me:

"I was the last actual rector of the parish. Rev. Hocking who lives at Woolpit, is now Priest-in-charge, not rector. When I arrived in the parish in 1988, after a lengthy interregnum, nothing much seemed to be happening in the village, I thought it seemed rather dead.

"The empty School next door to All Saints' was in a poor state. I assumed the School was going to be sold, I didn't even know it was a Church School. I then had a letter from the Property Department of Diocesan Office, saying that they wanted confirmation that, as the previous rector had indicated, the parish had no interest in the property.

"When I enquired – asking the churchwardens – quite a storm blew up. They went up like rockets! They had tried to find out what would happen to it and could discover nothing. We discovered what the status was (I'd had similar experiences in Lincolnshire). It didn't belong to the Church, but to a local trust, the trustees being the rector and churchwardens. It did not belong to the Diocese. I visited Diocesan House and managed to walk out with the whole file on Drinkstone School under my arm!

"We had a lot of local expertise. David Medcalf, one of the churchwardens, was a solicitor with the firm Greene and Greene in Bury St. Edmunds. Louise and David Stewart (whom I had married in All Saints' Church) both had legal training and were very helpful. I first got to know Louise when she came to me asking to be confirmed, and when Gerald Mayes retired I proposed her as new churchwarden. They've now gone to live in Ixworth, but they, and David Medcalf, were a great asset.

"We had to make a variation in the original Trust Deed, because the gift of the property had been for the village to have a school. So we were able to change the purpose of the Trust so it would still be of benefit to the whole village. The 'privileged area' was the parish. So the proceeds of the sale would go into an Educational Trust for the whole village, people of all ages. The interest only may be used, each year. It took some time to sort out, but we got there!

"At first they applied the fund very strictly. For instance, there was a proposal that money

should be used to fund a school bus, and we couldn't do that because it would have involved children from outside the parish as well as Drinkstone children.

"Now it's used for as wide as possible a brief within the parish. It can be used for Youth Clubs, sports, anything that can be called 'educational' for any age group.

"Villages today have undergone such great changes, they're not the places they were 50 years ago. I remember talking to Wyn Clover from the Mills. She told me how she worked at Clare during the war, and because transport then was slow, she stayed there all week, coming home every Friday night by train and arriving at Elmswell station between 6.30 – 7pm. From there she would walk home. She used to love 'the walk across the valley' from Elmswell to Drinkstone, because 'everything was so peaceful and quiet'. Can you imagine anyone walking that route now? There's the roundabout and flyover, crossing the A14. There's no footpaths or crossings, and cars and lorries zoom everywhere! You just couldn't do it today and it certainly wouldn't be peaceful!"

So, thanks to a lot of hard work, the School was put up for sale. What happened next? The next chapter brings us to the end of the long story.

Chapter Twenty-Four

A LABOUR OF LOVE

DRINKSTONE SCHOOL stood empty through the autumn and winter of 1986. Lengthy discussions had begun about the possible sale of the building. Nothing could proceed until the Charity Commissioners agreed where the money from any sale should go. Wind, snow and rain left their mark. The position of the building, high above the road, on a bend, and screened by trees, made it easy to ignore. A stranger passing through the village would be unlikely to notice its existence, although occasionally some curious passer-by or nostalgic ex-pupil would wander up the neglected path to peer through the cobwebby windows at the dismal scene within.

At some stage, mild vandalism added to the damage done by the passage of time and weather. In an attempt to preserve the battered building, the windows were boarded up and the place looked even more desolate. The little School that had seen so much fun and laughter, mischief, endeavour, and the whole range of human emotions over the years, seemed doomed to a lingering demise through the ravages of neglect, damp and decay.

But this was not to be the end of the story! Like the phoenix, the School was destined to spring back to life, an exciting new life with new inhabitants who would cherish and enrich the old building.

The churchwardens had established a Charitable Trust under the title "Drinkstone Educational Charity Trust" to receive the proceeds of the sale. But who would be prepared to buy the old School in its neglected state? Years passed, prospective buyers came and went, the building deteriorated further. Youngsters took pleasure in throwing stones at windows and roof; then some enterprising soul decided to remove and carry away a large number of slates from the less visible rear of the building. Rain poured in, the floors became sodden. Nick Lane, a local builder and developer, considered it beyond repair. Eventually it was decided that since no-one in their right mind would buy the School as a restoration project, the best hope was to seek planning permission for the site. Mid-Suffolk County Council had placed a Closing Order on the Schoolhouse in 1976, and its condition had worsened over the years. The plan was to demolish both School and Schoolhouse, then build two houses on the site. Drinkstone School seemed destined to become only a memory.

Enter the heroes of the hour, Sue and Chris Wright. As a boy, Chris had been a pupil at a Suffolk boarding school. His parents had lived in Theberton, near Leiston. Chris and his wife Sue were now living in Essex, but Chris was based in Bury St. Edmunds for his work as a civil engineer. They had begun to dream of restoring some old building, preferably within easy reach of Bury, to create a home of character.

In the Spring of 1992 they were staying with their friends Michael and Sylvia Williams at their home in Rattlesden Road, Drinkstone. The two families had been friends for many years, first meeting in Essex. They felt a close bond since both families had a daughter with Down's Syndrome. Hearing of their search for somewhere requiring creative restoration, Michael remarked: "If you really want to restore something that's derelict, why don't you look at the old School in the village?"

At this time, Chris says, the building was totally overgrown and almost hidden from view. But the seed of an idea had been sown!

The next opportunity came during a camping week-end at Pakenham, on August Bank Holiday 1992. Chris re-visited the old School with a friend, Vic Beadle, a building surveyor. Chris says that despite hav-

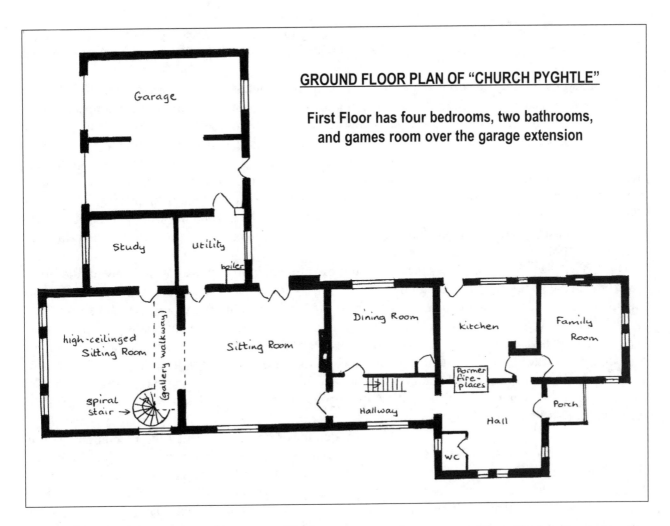

GROUND FLOOR PLAN OF "CHURCH PYGHTLE"

First Floor has four bedrooms, two bathrooms, and games room over the garage extension

ing to climb a wall and fight their way through the undergrowth, they were immediately attracted by the pretty windows and soft red brick-work. The charm of the Victorian building was still evident, to them if not to others! The lancet windows of the Schoolhouse, their shape exactly echoed in the brick archway of the porch, were a particular delight. At the North gable end of the School, they admired the symmetry of the huge arched window, in Victorian pine frame; perpendicular in style, with elegant interlaced curves.

Later, during the restoration work, the family were able to trace some of the history of the building, and discovered that this infants' classroom and its rear porch, were a 1912 addition to the original School. This new room, with a ceiling height of 15 feet 6 inches, had been built to join seamlessly with the original structure, and was entirely in keeping with the original design. A sash window (matching the two in the large classroom) was built into the west wall, facing the road. The gap between old and new classrooms was closed off with tall sliding doors with glazed panels.

At the same date, the cloakroom annexe at the back of the School, through which children entered the building, was extended to create separate cloakroom access for each class. These 1912 extensions account for the fact that one section of the cloakroom had a lean-to roof, and the other, a pitched roof.

On this exploratory visit, such discoveries were way in the future for the Wrights. Most of the windows were boarded up entirely to minimise dangerous vandalism and the entry of rain, but light still streamed through the upper panes of the elegant north window, since the protective boarding did not extend to those beautiful high curves.

The amount of brickwork on the site was astounding. The Victorians did not stint on bricks, and the main buildings were solidly constructed, being one and a half bricks thick on a two-brick plinth. Brick walls enclosed the hard playground, and at the back of the building a labyrinth of high brick walls enclosed small yards containing brick-built stores, oil tank, garden sheds, sheds for kitchen use, and of course the notorious chemical toilet cubicles and urinal. The various walls, around seven or eight feet in height, created a kind of maze, some of the original sheds having lost their roofs many years ago. These gloomy remains, overgrown with brambles, did nothing to enhance the rear appearance of the place! Between these walls and the surrounding fields a jungle of growth rampaged over the grass play area and garden.

Undaunted by the obvious disadvantages, Vic Beadle pronounced the brick structure of both School and House to be basically sound. The setting among the fields was delightful despite the rampant growth everywhere. The friends returned home thoughtful, their heads full of ideas and possibilities.

Chris describes the next moves as follows: "We made enquiries as to ownership and the possibility of a sale… during the period of negotiations we were able to survey the third of an acre site and all the derelict buildings therein… draw up detailed plans, and submit them to the local authorities, so that by the time we obtained possession we knew exactly what we wanted to do… our main priority was to clear the site and find out exactly what it was that we had bought whilst negotiating with contractors to provide access, basic services, structural alterations and the re-establishment of a watertight shell. In addition, a new 10m x 7m wing was to be added."

This makes the project sound reasonably straightforward, but in reality there were many hurdles to be overcome, as anyone else with the courage and vision to attempt such a project will know. After this August visit, various urgent enquiries began. David Medcalf, Churchwarden, was approached, and said he did not know the asking price, and anyway the School was not yet officially on the market. Nevertheless, Chris, Sue and family continued to dream and plan. On their next visit to Drinkstone School, they managed to open a door, and have a good look around inside the building. On the walls of the schoolhouse still hung (or rather drooped) a display of children's writing and careful drawing depicting "The life cycle of the white musk mallow". Soggy and mildewed though it was, the display conveyed a flavour of past times in the darkened rooms.

The family explored, exclaimed variously with delight or horror, navigated the precipitous narrow stairway to the bedrooms, now dangerous underfoot but with light flooding in, since the first-floor windows had not been boarded up. They discovered an ancient well in the grounds, south-east of the Schoolhouse, near the kitchen door. The family took photographs and measured dimensions, then returned home to draw up exciting plans. They continued to correspond with David Medcalf, so that when the School was put on the market by agents Lacy Scott early in 1993, Chris was first on the scene.

Sue remembers one mind-boggling moment, during Maundy Thursday morning, 7th April 1993, when she received a phone call from a person with a most unusual voice, who asked:

"Is that Mrs. Susan Wright, please?"

"Sue Wright speaking," she replied, a little mystified.

"Then I have to tell you that you are now the proud owner of a derelict ruin!"

It was Chris, her husband, speaking, of course. With a mixture of exhilaration and trepidation the family, complete with enthusiastic Labrador, plunged into their new project. To the astonishment of friends and onlookers, things began to happen!

There was no way the family could take up residence in their new acquisition. The Closing Order had to be lifted. The restoration had to meet environmental requirements as well as building regulations. Vehicle access was the first priority – not easy – Chris says "a curved and steeply rising access road was established linking the playground to the street some five feet below". By this time, he says, having "spent every available moment in Suffolk", the family had "completely cleared the site and demolished a number of the dilapidated outbuildings no longer required. As we progressed around the building it appeared to get bigger and the extent of the task became readily apparent!"

Undaunted, they forged ahead. The interior would have to be gutted, floors replaced, roof completely re-worked, windows altered or added, new first-floor rooms created over what had been the large classroom – but the first job was to get the brick shell repaired and weatherproof. For this, Chris hired a contractor. But after the first optimistic planning meeting, the contractor abruptly withdrew. So there was nothing for it but to organise the work scheme piecemeal, unaided. Chris sub-contracted a roofer, a bricklayer, and a carpenter.

The slates had to be lifted off the roof for repairs and alterations. On the day the roof came off, in November 1993, there was a heavy snowfall. But nothing stopped the work; two new dormers were constructed on the east side, and the three existing dormers on the west side (facing the road) were replaced

The school house, showing the boarded-up lancet windows and the remannts of children's work on "The white musk mallow".

Left: The maze of old brick walls was removed to make room for the new wing.

Below: New dormers and one sash window lowered, at the front of the school, and a new driveway laid.

The Wright family toast their new venture.
L-R: Rebecca, Sue, Nick and Chris

Rebecca tackles demolition – in a corner of what is now her bedroom!

Original chimney stacks preserved.

Work on the roof begins.

School toilet block in 1993.

to match the new ones. New battens were fixed, new felt laid, and the slates replaced, Chris scouring reclamation yards to find additional matching slates. The huge chimney stacks were repaired, the chimney pots removed, and the flues cleared of rubble and debris, most of this consisting of jackdaws' nests!

Floorboards, floor tiles and wooden parquet blocks had to be lifted so that new concrete sub-floors, damp-courses and under-floor heating could be laid down. Where possible tiles and wood-blocks were lovingly dried, cleaned, polished or waxed, and eventually replaced in the refurbished rooms. Nothing was wasted, and wherever some lovely old feature could be retained, no effort was spared. For example, the tall sliding doors of wood and glass between the classrooms were removed during restoration work, then reduced in height so they could be re-fitted once the first floor was constructed above the large classroom. When opened, they slide neatly into slots in the side walls. (When I was teaching at the School, we made use of this feature for dramatic productions, using these doors like stage curtains.)

Some tasks inevitably required the calling in of professionals. A heating engineer checked the central-heating plans, and contractors installed steel girders to underpin the new first floor areas. But the family – Chris, Sue, sons Tim and Nick and daughter Rebecca – valiantly tackled the bulk of the work themselves.

The steep and tortuous staircase was removed. Chris says: "We worked endlessly, stripping the old building of rotten ceilings and plaster, re-glazing windows and generally clearing up after the sub-contractors. By the Spring of '94 their work was substantially finished and we were on our own, the sub-contractors only returning to build an inglenook fireplace out of reclaimed bricks to house our wood-burning stove, and install the main staircase." These new stairs were constructed in pine, in an airy open stairwell, in the south-west corner of the high main classroom. East of the stairs a dining room was created. A gracious lounge spanned the full width of the main classroom. The extra space resulting from the removal of the original staircase allowed the Schoolhouse kitchen to be enlarged and modernised. The other two Schoolhouse ground-floor rooms became, to the south a "snug" or family room with its own wood-burning stove, and to the west or front of the building, nearest to the road, a welcoming entrance hall with adjoining cloakroom. Although some of these areas have new Chinese terracotta floor tiles, these look entirely in keeping, as if they have lain there for years. All the enchanting lancet windows have been lovingly repaired and painted (retaining the original cast-iron frames).

The original bedrooms were beautified, and a new bedroom built in the new first-floor area above the large classroom. The graciously curved trusses spanning the roof area east to west, a few feet below the peak of the roof, are just sufficiently high above the new first floor to allow a tall person to pass beneath them at their centre. These pine trusses were stripped to expose the wood.

Much highly specialised planning and work took place. For example, Chris says: "A load-bearing division wall incorporating a new flue was built to divide the original hall and provide bearing for new steel purlins needed to support the roof once the tie-bars were removed from the pine timber roof trusses." Definitely not a venture for the ignorant or faint-hearted! Planning was meticulous and detailed. The most modern methods of insulation were employed. Space was found for two en-suite bathrooms – the old tin bath concealed in a corner of the kitchen, under that alarmingly steep and narrow staircase, was consigned to the past! The transformation was amazing!

Needless to say, basic work such as installing a septic tank and drainage system, re-connecting electricity, water and telephone, treatment of all timbers and injection of a damp course, was achieved as soon as possible. When demolishing the depressing jumble of brick sheds and walls at the back of the School, the best bricks were saved, and used in the building of the new wing. One three-sided section of the toilet block was retained and re-roofed with reclaimed pantiles. At the rear of this block is a new storage area, while the mellow front section (facing the house) has become a delightful feature of the garden. Chris says: "The south facing courtyard with views over the old Church, created by the new wing joining the remains of the old toilets to the main building, proved to be such a sun trap that a large vine-covered pergola was added to provide a shady outside dining area." The long east wall of the School, which faces this light and spacious garden area, was enhanced by new, wide windows, a new French window, and a new half-glazed stable door to the kitchen. These replace one tiny original window and two plain doors.

The major tour-de-force was yet to be seen as dreams turned to reality in the infants' end of the build-

Drinkstone School has now been transformed from dereliction into a beautiful home.

Facing page and this page: photos show some of the artistic features of the now light and spacious Church Pyghtle

ing. The high infants' classroom was left intact. The wonderful high arched window was repaired in situ. No glazier could be found who would risk replacing the new, extra strong, heavy panes of glass, meticulously cut to fit the curves of the frame. Chris had to construct a safety-frame for the glass in order to refit each piece, heart in mouth, with the assistance of his family. A grand piano now graces this beautifully light and spacious room.

When the Wrights purchased the building, the dank and draughty cloakroom with its ancient sink, water fountain, and coat pegs, still adjoined the rear classroom wall. Unbelievably, washing-up after school meals took place here from the mid 1940s until 1977, in the only sink the School possessed, with its one cold tap. These awkward cloakroom buildings were demolished. In their place arose an entirely new wing on two floors. From the house at ground-floor level original doors lead to a study and a utility room with central heating boiler. Beyond lies a double garage with workshop. The long room above has three dormer windows set into the south-facing roof, and is fitted out as a games room with full-size table-tennis table for daughter Rebecca, who has twice represented England against France. An interesting feature here is the recessed fluorescent lighting which provides even illumination for table tennis, or for Sue's needlework.

When the new first floor was constructed over the main classroom, the floor joists were laid to extend several feet into the former infants' classroom, (this room being left at full height). This was part of Chris's imaginative plan. He ordered the component parts for a spiral staircase in cast iron, with matching balustrade. He erected the open staircase in the south-west corner of the infants' room, leading to an iron walk-way supported by the extended floor joists. This galleried walk-way leads directly to the games room on the first floor of the extension. Chris designed and assembled the whole iron structure himself, and painted it a tasteful mid-green. Who would have thought this old Victorian building, left untended and empty for many sad years, would ever be adorned with such modern and artistic features?

I am writing this account in the winter of the year 2004-5. The Wright family moved into their unfinished, but habitable, home in November 1996, having sold their Essex home. They named it "Church Pyghtle", the name coming from the original Deed. Today "Church Pyghtle" is a unique house with every comfort. The garden is entrancing, especially on the east side, hidden from the road, where plants entwine mellow brickwork. To the south, the orange-red brick tower of All Saints' rises above the churchyard trees, while to the north, visible from some of the windows of the house, is Drinkstone windmill. This is an idyllic corner of old England, and it is heartening to know that the story of Drinkstone School was not at an end on the sad day of its closure. The grand enterprise achieved by the Wright family was, as they say themselves, truly a labour of love. Long may they enjoy it!

WHITE'S DIRECTORY for 1844

Drinkstone is described as "a neat and pleasant village, built round a large green", with a population of 505 persons. At this date John Mosely, Esq. was lord of the manor of Drinkstone Lovaine, and Rev. Dr. Kilderbee was lord of the manor of Drinkstone Timperley; while a "great part of the land" belonged to the Grigby, Franklyn, Powell, Hart, Boldero, Steggall and other families.

In 1840 a rent charge of £546 was awarded in lieu of tithes (stated in White's 1855).

In 1844 the Rectory was the seat of Henry Franklyn, Esq, while the Rev. Edgar Rust, MA, was patron and incumbent of All Saints' Church. The Church land of 5 acres was let, the income used for repairs to the Church. There is a list of landowners, professional and trades people:

Barrell Robert, butcher
Clover John, corn miller
Cocksedge William, land steward, Drinkstone Place
Cottingham Lionel, surgeon
Franklyn Henry Esq, Rectory
Grigby Mrs. Anna, Drinkstone Park
Hawkins James, wheelwright
Jewers John, maltster
Manfield Joseph, shopkeeper and carrier
Manfield Martha, schoolmistress
Mortlock William, shopkeeper
Nunn John S. maltster, Tyshurst
Nunn William, blacksmith
Rust Rev Edgar MA, rector
Steggall Rev John, incumbent of Great Ashfield
Whiten Hannah, beerhouse
Farmers (owners) –
Cottingham, Lionel
Craske John, senior, Timperleys (also Craske John, junior, and Craske Mrs. M)
Jewers John
Nunn James
Tenant farmers –
Boldero William
Cooper William, Whitefield House
Death George
Nunn J. S.
Raynham John, Drinkstone Hall
Whiten Samuel Winter Mrs.

KELLY'S DIRECTORY for 1846

The only notable difference in information from White's 1844 Directory above, is that Miss Emma Sidney is listed as "school", which presumably means she was teaching – possibly as Headmistress, or possibly as the only teacher.

WHITE'S DIRECTORY for 1855

John Mosely esq. is lord of the manor (manor not identified).

All Saints is in the patronage of Rev. Spencer Maul, while the incumbent is Rev. G. Peloquin Cosserat, who holds 90 acres of glebe.

The list of landowners, professional and trades people is as follows:
Clover John, corn miller
Cocksedge Henry Le Heup Esq., Drinkstone House
Cosserat Rev. George Peloquin M.A., Rectory
French Robert B., schoolmaster
Frost John, parish clerk
Hawkins James, joiner and wheelwright
Manning Robert, beerhouse
Morris William, land steward
Mortlock William, shopkeeper
Nunn William, blacksmith
Powell John Harcourt Esq., Drinkstone Park
Presland Mrs., shopkeeper
Sidney Emma Maria, schoolmistress
Owner-farmers –
Boldero John
Jewers John (and maltster)
Tenant-farmers –
Cooper William, Whitefield House
Fitch Thomas, Drinkstone Hall
Grosling John Edward (and maltster)
Payne Samuel, Rookery Farm
Whiting William (and beerhouse)
Craske John

MORRIS'S DIRECTORY for 1868

1861 Census gives 496 inhabitants. Clergy and Gentry:
Cocksedge Henry Esq., Drinkstone House
Horne Rev. Frederick E. M.A., Rectory
Horne Captain W. H., Drinkstone Lodge
Parker John Oxley Esq., Park corner
Powell Captain Thomas Harcourt, J.P., The Park
Trades and Professions –

Ardley Edward, farmer and maltster, Ticehurst
Bird William, farmer
Bull Benjamin, wheelwright
Burt Thomas P., farmer
Clover John, miller
Cooper Mrs., farmer, Whitefield House
Coulson J., farmer
Craske Mrs. Martha, farmer
Frost John, parish clerk
Jellins John, farmer, Rookery
Jewers John, farmer
Manfield Joseph, farmer
Manning John, shoemaker
Nunn William, blacksmith
Presland William, shopkeeper
Sorrell Thomas, farmer
Whiting William, farmer and beer retailer
Postal delivery from Bury St. Edmunds 8am.
Collection 6.30pm. Money Orders from Woolpit.

KELLY'S DIRECTORY for 1869

National School has in 1868 been placed under
Government Inspection.

Thomas Mingay Golding is lord of the manor. Main
landowners are Captain T. Powell J.P. at Drinkstone
Park, Nunn Boldero, J. O. Parker, Henry Cocksedge at
Drinkstone House, Captain William H. Horne at
Drinkstone Lodge, Rev. Frederick Horne at The
Rectory, J.O. Parker at Park Corner.

Ardley Edward, farmer and maltster, Ticehurst
Bird William, farmer
Burt Thomas, farmer
Clover John, miller
Colson John, farmer
Cooper Mrs, farmer, Whitefield House
Craske Edmund, farmer and landowner
Frost John, carpenter
Jewers John, farmer and landowner
Jillings Harry, farmer
Manfield Joseph, farmer
Manning John, shoemaker
Nunn William, blacksmith
Presland William, shopkeeper
Rowe Mary, shopkeeper
Ruddock Jonathan, wheelwright
Sorrell Thomas, farmer
Whiting William, farmer

WHITE'S DIRECTORY for 1874

492 inhabitants, 2,172 acres.

1564 – John Wrenn gave 15 acres of land, to be
ploughed, tilled and sown by poor householders of
Drinkstone for their own profit; but it is let for £30 p.a.
which is distributed in bread-corn by the rector and
Churchwardens.

In 1692 Thomas Camborne's Charity – the property

belonging to this charity is partly copyhold, and consists of a house and about 29 acres of land, let for £58
a year which are mostly dispensed by the trustees in
apprenticing poor children.

A cottage, garden and a piece of waste ground are
appropriated by ancient usage to the relief of poor widows, and let for about £4 a year.

The National School which was built by voluntary
contributions in 1861 is attended by 50 children and is
under Government inspection.

Ardley Mrs. Louisa, farmer and maltster, Ticehurst.
Bell John, victualler, Cherry Tree
Blake John Bennington, shopkeeper
Bolders John, farmer
Burt Thomas P. farmer
Clover Daniel, corn miller
Cocksedge Mrs. Mary Ann, Drinkstone House
Cocksedge William Henry, farmer
Coldham William, farmer, The Bucks
Colson John, farmer
Dixon Miss Maria, National Schoolmistress
Cooper Mrs. Emma, farmer, Whitefield House
Cooper William, farm bailiff
Craske Edmund Robert, farmer
Craske William, farmer
Grimwood Thomas, farmer, Lower Bucks
Horne Rev. Frederick Edward, B.D., rector, The
     Rectory
Horne Captain William Henry, Drinkstone Lodge
Jewers John, farmer, maltster and landowner
Jillings Harry, farmer
Manfield Joseph, farmer
Manning John, shoemaker
Nunn William, blacksmith
Parker Mr. John Oxley, Park Corner
Powell Captain Thomas Harcourt J.P., The Park
Prigg Mr. John Edward
Revens George, parish clerk
Roe Mrs. Mary
Roe Richard, shopkeeper
Ruddock Jonathan, joiner and wheelwright
Sorrell Arthur, farm bailiff, marine store dealer, and
     carrier
Sorrell Mrs. Lydia
Wallace Robert, beerhouse
Whiting William, farmer
Carrier – A. Sorrell to Bury Wednesdays and
     Saturdays.

KELLY'S DIRECTORY for 1875

Mrs. Maria Willis is mistress at the National School.
Landowners/ Gentry – Captain George Blake at
Drinkstone House, Captain William Horne J.P. at
Drinkstone Lodge, Rev. Frederick Horne at The
Rectory, Mrs. Parker at Park Corner, Captain Thomas
Harcourt Powell J.P. at Drinkstone Park, Edward Prigg.

Ardley Caroline Mrs, farmer, Ticehurst

Bell Judith Mrs. Cherry Tree
Blake John Bennington, shopkeeper
Clover Daniel, miller
Coldham William Annis, farmer
Colson John, farmer
Craske Edmund, farmer and landowner
Jewers John, farmer
Jillings Harry, farmer
Manfield Joseph, farmer
Nunn William, blacksmith
Rowe Richard, shopkeeper and carrier
Ruddock Jonathan, wheelwright
Wallace Robert, beer retailer
Whiting William, farmer

KELLY'S DIRECTORY for 1888

The living – held since 1865 by the Rev. Edward Horne M.A. of Trinity College Cambridge.

The village is two and a half miles from Elmswell Station in the Eastern Union Railway. There is a Wesleyan Chapel.

Charities distributed by Churchwardens –

1692 Thomas Camborne's; also, another charity benefiting "poor widows".

Landowners – Captain Thomas Harcourt Powell, D.L., J.P., Drinkstone Park,

The Trustees of Frederick Nunn Esq,, Mrs. Parker, and Mrs. Cocksedge.

Chief crops – wheat, barley, oats, peas, beans, roots.

Area 2,172 acres. Rateable value £2,917. Population in 1881 was 463.

National School (mixed) erected in 1859, for 70 children; attendance 60. Mrs. E. S. Pullin, mistress.

Baker Lady, Drinkstone House (which was owned by Mrs. Cocksedge)
Horne Mrs. Drinkstone Lodge
Horne Rev. Frederick Edward M.A, Rectory
Parker Mrs. Park corner
Powell Captain Thomas Harcourt, Drinkstone Park
Alderton Charles, farm bailiff to Captain Powell
Bland Charles, shoemaker
Blake John Bennington, shopkeeper and Post Office
Boldero Edward, farmer
Clover Daniel, miller (wind and steam)
Coldham William Annis, farmer
Constable Arthur H. farmer, Rookery Farm
Craske Edmund, farmer and landowner
Death Thomas, farmer, Ticehurst
Halls Marquis, shopkeeper
Jewers John, farmer and landowner
Jewers John junior, farmer, Whitefield House
Long James, Cherry Tree Public House
Nunn William, blacksmith and assistant overseer
Plummer Henry Roberts, wheelwright
Reader George, shoemaker
Taylor Thomas, farmer, Hall Farm
Theobald John, beer retailer

WHITE'S DIRECTORY for 1892

(463 inhabitants in 1881)
Ager, victualler, Cherry Tree
Alderton Charles, farm bailiff
Baker Lady, Drinkstone House
Barrell Charles, farm bailiff
Blake John Bennington, shopkeeper
Bland Charles, shoemaker
Bolders Mr. Edmund, Raynham
Burt Thomas P., farmer
Clarke John Thomas, day and boarding school
Clover Daniel, miller and farmer
Coldham William, farmer, Green
Constable Arthur Henry, farmer, Rookery
Craske Edmund Robert, farmer and landowner
Craske William, farmer
Grimwood Fred, beerhouse
Halls Walter Charles, shopkeeper, The Green
Horne Rev. Frederick Edward M.A., rector, The Rectory
Horne Robert, wheelwright and carpenter
Jewers Mrs. Emily, farmer
Jewers John, farmer, Whitefield House
Nobbs Walter, farm bailiff
Nunn William, blacksmith
Palmer George, gardener, The Park
Parker Mrs. Caroline, Park Corner
Phillips Edward, waiter
Plummer Henry, joiner, builder and wheelwright
Powell Thomas Harcourt Esq., J.P., Drinkstone park
Pullin Mrs., National Schoolmistress
Reader George, shoemaker
Revens George, sexton
Squirrell W., carrier
Sturgeon Charles, farmer, Lower Bucks
Taylor Thomas, farmer, Drinkstone Hall
Wicks Edgar, farmer, Ticehurst Farm
Railway – Elmswell and Thurston
Carrier – W. Squirrell to Bury St. Edmunds Wednesday and Saturday

KELLY'S DIRECTORY for 1900

(population was 396 in 1891)

Introductory information much as in previous directories; includes the fact that Rev. Frederick Edward Horne MA has held the living, which includes 89 acres of glebe and residence, since 1865. The sexton at this date was Wilson Manfield.

Camborne's Charity yielded £34-7s-6d p.a. at this date.

National School (mixed), erected in 1859, for 70 children; average attendance 60; Mrs. Emma Robinson, mistress.

List of landowners:
Hodgson-Roberts Frederick, Drinkstone park

Horne Rev. Frederick Edward M.A., Rectory
Lomax John Chadwick, Drinkstone house
Parker Mrs., Park Corner
Townsend Joseph Edward, Hammond hall
Waller John Anthony, Drinkstone lodge
Commercial –
Barrell Charles, farmer
Bland Charles, shoe maker
Blake John Bennington, shopkeeper, Post Office
Brown Edward William, farmer, Home farm
Churchyard George, carrier (to Bury wednesdays. and saturdays)
Clover Daniel, miller (wind and steam)
Constable Arthur Henry, farmer, Rookery
Cooper George, beer retailer
Halls Charles Louis, grocer and draper
Jewers John, farmer, Whitefield house
Mayes James, farmer
Phillips Hannah (Mrs), dress maker
Nunn William, blacksmith and poors' rate collector
Plumber Henry Robert, carpenter and wheelwright
Reader George, Cherry Tree Public House and shoe maker
Snell Oliver, farmer
Taylor John C., farmer, Ticehurst

KELLY'S DIRECTORY for 1916

Camborne's property (house and 29 acres) let for £30 p.a.

Widow's cottage and land at £4 per annum.

Church land of 5 acres let at £6-6s.

Rector Rev. F. Horne is patron/ incumbent.

Lord of the manor is C. Walter Crassweller.

John Reginald Hargreaves J.P. is living at Drinkstone Park. Population (1911) 377.

Crops – wheat, barley, oats, peas, beans and roots.

Post Office and Telegraph Office – Miss Anna Martha Craske.

School enlarged in 1912. 88 children, Headteacher Mrs. R. Gobbitt.

Carrier – Charles Mothersole (also farmer)
Shirley Brooks, Feoffment House
Commander Clement Cooper Horne, R.N. – The Meade (formerly "Park Corner")
Horne Rev. Francis Herbert and wife – The Lodge
Townsend, Joseph Edward – Hammond's Hall
Wakerley, Rev. John E. – Ticehurst
Webb, Major Duncan – Drinkstone House
Wicks, Edgar – commercial
Bland Bros., blacksmith and implement repairers
Clover, Daniel – miller (wind and oil)
Hale, Hezekiah – Street Farm (farmer)
Halls, Charles Louis – grocer and draper
James, Walter – Cherry Tree Public House
Jewers, John, farmer – Whitefield House and Green Farm
Lambert, Frederick Charles – Rookery Farm

Otterwell, William – farm bailiff to Commander C. C. Horne
Pannell, William – head gardener to Major Webb
Phillips, Hannah (Mrs.) – dressmaker
Reader, George – boot maker
Ridley, Richard – cook, farmer, Home Farm
Sharpe, William – farm bailiff to Rev. J. W. Wakerley
Snell, Oliver – Hill Farm
Sturgeon, Major – beer retailer
Taylor, John C, farmer – Hall Farm
Thompson, Norman – excise officer

KELLY'S DIRECTORY for 1929

Rev. Francis Herbert Horne remains patron and incumbent of All Saints and lives at The Rectory. Rev. Blencowe now lives at The Meade. Rev. Horne has Church land of 5 acres let for £6-6s p.a. plus a yearly rent-charge of 18s, applied to Church repairs.

Main landowners are J.R. Hargreaves esq, J.P. at Drinkstone Park; William Ernest Mann esq,. Major Ernest George Fowler is at Drinkstone House. Mr. Crassweller remains lord of the manor. Population (1921) 397.

A motor omnibus passes through the village on Wednesday for Bury St. Edmunds.

List denotes farms over 150 acres *
Blencowe Rev. Christopher K., M.A. – The Meade
Bruce N. Murray – Ticehurst house*
Gore Francis William B. – The Lodge
Horne Rev. Francis H. – The Rectory
Jewers John – Green Farm
Taylor John Crumpton – Rookery
Townsend Mrs. – Hammond Hall
Bland Bros. – blacksmiths
Bland William John, farmer – Bridge farm
Chandler, Arthur, farm bailiff to J.R. Hargreaves – Home farm
Gibson John Henderson, farmer – Whitefield house*
Hale Hezekiah, farmer – Street farm
Halls Charles Louis, grocer
Last Bros. farmers – Burts farm*
Phillips Hannah (Mrs), dressmaker
Pryke Walter, farm bailiff to Rev. C.K. Blencowe
Reader George, motor car proprietor
Snell Oliver & Son, farmers/owners – Hill farm*
Steggles Walter, Cherry Tree Public House
Taylor John C. farmer – the Rookery
Young William Alfred, shopkeeper

KELLY'S DIRECTORY for 1937

Details of the Church include the fact that the stained glass in the East window dates from 1872, as a memorial to the Rev. W. Horne, "grandfather of the present rector". Also at this date the Church land of 5 acres has been sold, and "the interest is applied to the repairs of the Church". The living "is a rectory, net yearly value £450, including 14 acres of glebe and residence, in the gift of and held since 1913 by Rev. Francis Herbert Horne".

Drinkstone Park mansion is "unoccupied". Major Ernest George Fowler lives at Drinkstone House. C. Walton Crassweller is lord of the manor. Principal landowners are Major J. C. Hargreaves, Hector Elliot Percival Mann esq., Haselden Thompson esq. and Ernest James Mackelden esq.

Sugar-beet is now listed among the "crops". Population in 1931 was 377.

A motor omnibus passes through the village on Wed. and Sat. for Bury St. Edmunds.

Private residents:

Blencowe Rev. Christopher K., MA, The Meade

Campion Mrs. Mary, Ticehurst house

Fowler Major Ernest George, Drinkstone house

Gore Francis William B. The Lodge

Horne Rev. Francis Herbert (rector), Rectory

Jewers John, Green farm

Summers Mrs. Edith E. Hammond hall

Thompson Haselden, Rookery farm

Commercial (farms 150 acres or over marked*) -

Barcock Frederick George, poultry farmer, Garden House farm

Bland Brothers, blacksmiths

Bland Arthur Albert, farmer, Whitefield house*

Bland William John, farmer & haulage contractor, motor tractors for hire, clerk to theParish Council, Bridge & Lodge Farms

Cherry Tree Public House (Walter Steggles)

Clover Daniel, miller (wind and oil)

Craske Anna Martha (Miss), sub-postmistress, Post Office

Drinkstone Stone & Gravel Co. (Herbert Thomas Elmer, manager)

Fabb William Newman, farm bailiff to H. E. P. Mann esq. Hall farm*

Flux Herbert Henry, farm bailiff to E. J. Mackleden esq. Hill farm*

Grimwood Sidney, smallholder

Halls Charles Louis, grocer

Jewers John, farmer, Green farm

Last Bros. Farmers, Burts farm*

Reader Emma J, (Mrs), cycle agent

Renson Bros. farmers, Street farm

Rogers Frank L. smallholder, Yew Tree farm

Thompson Haselden, farmer, Rookery farm

Thurlow Cecil Frank, farmer, Home Farm*

Ticehurst Jersey Farm (Mrs. Mary Campion, proprietress) dairy

Tidswell Fred, boot repairer

Westrup Percy William, farm bailiff to Rev. Christopher K. Blencowe M.A.*

Young William Alfred, shopkeeper

APPENDIX TWO
ATTENDANCE REGISTER OF
DRINKSTONE SCHOOL

THERE ARE 800 names in this register (see p256), of pupils born between 1880 and 1942.

The population was remarkably mobile during this period. Four hundred pupils had attended schools elsewhere, before being enrolled at Drinkstone. At least 320 pupils moved away from the village before completing their education (the actual number is higher but can't be established, since for the first 210 pupils registered, the final column "date and reason for leaving" is usually blank). It's interesting to learn that on 26th September 1904, six children from two families were removed from the School "by Medical Authority", presumably never to return. They were Margaret and Olive Stiff, and Alice, Millie, Herbert and Edward Davey.

More than 180 pupils attended school elsewhere, then moved to Drinkstone, then moved away again while still of school age (50 of these were evacuees during World War II). Some pupils only attended Drinkstone School for a few weeks or months (pupil number 453 was only at the School for nine days!) While most families moved locally (within Suffolk/ East Anglia) locations include London, Yorkshire, Surrey, even Dublin and Paris!

Sometimes it is not clear whether a pupil moved away from the district, or simply transferred to another local school such as Hessett, Woolpit, or Rattlesden, while continuing to reside in Drinkstone. In 1942-3, the School Leaving Age was raised from 14 to 15 years. In the early 1950s Beyton Secondary Modern School opened for older children's education.

Unfortunately, "Home Address" is given simply as "Drinkstone" for the first 553 entries. The record-keeping was not perfect; occasionally a pupil's name was entered more than once, under different numbers. Where "date of birth" or "parent's name" or some other detail, is not entered, this does not mean these facts were unknown. It is likely that many entries were made by hard-pressed teachers (often supply teachers) and the speed of change among pupils on register was tremendous.

It is possible that the phrase "gone home" under the final heading, was in some instances used as a euphemism for "deceased". Where the final column states "left", this usually means the pupil reached school leaving age while at Drinkstone School. Most the dates of registration and leaving are given, but I have omitted these dates so that each entry can be fitted on a single line. I have divided the entries into admissions per year, but this division is not entirely accurate since sometimes (according to given "date of admission") a pupil might attend the School for months, or even years, before his or her name was entered in the Register.

Around the turn of the century, some children seem to have attended from the age of three years!

The entries overleaf are under headings Date of Birth, Name of Child, Name of Parent or Guardian, Home Address, Previous School (if any) and Reason for Leaving.

	Date of Birth	Name of Child	Name of Parent or Guardian	Home Address	Previous School	Reason for Leaving
	PUPILS ADMITTED BETWEEN 1885 and 1893					
1	24/05/1881	Edward Phillips	Edward	Drinkstone	Private	
2	13/01/1883	George Rose	William	Drinkstone	None	
3	19/11/1882	Lily Reader	George	Drinkstone	None	
4	30/04/1882	James Stiff	Nelson	Drinkstone	None	
5	21/09/1881	George King	John	Drinkstone	None	
6	05/02/1881	George Bennet	George	Drinkstone	None	
7	12/03/1882	Alfred Gill	Robert	Drinkstone	None	
8	03/08/1880	Philip Rose	James	Drinkstone	None	
9	31/10/1882	Charles Bland	Cecil	Drinkstone	None	
10	07/08/1883	Albert Rose	James	Drinkstone	None	
11	27/02/1880	Margaret Revens	Samuel	Drinkstone	None	
12	16/05/1881	Minnie Chinnery	William	Drinkstone	Felsham	
13	07/06/1881	Eva Rose	William	Drinkstone	None	
14	09/03/1882	Jessie Cooper	Freeman	Drinkstone	None	
15	26/09/1883	Lily Rose	Elijah	Drinkstone	None	
16	23/09/1883	Gertrude Bennington	Philip	Drinkstone	None	
17	09/04/1883	Daisy Stiff	Harry	Drinkstone	None	
18	15/07/1882	Herbert Squirrel	David	Drinkstone	None	
20	09/06/1880	Ellen Mayes	William	Drinkstone	Rattlesden	
21	30/08/1884	Emma Moore	Charlotte	Drinkstone	None	
22	03/08/1884	Beatrice Gill	Robert	Drinkstone	None	
23	04/11/1884	Harry Stiff	Nelson	Drinkstone	None	
24	03/06/1884	Sidney Young	George	Drinkstone	Buxhall	
25	15/11/1881	Robert Grimwood	Alfred	Drinkstone	Bury St. Edmunds	
26	05/07/1884	Ernest Gowers	James	Drinkstone	None	
27	23/12/1883	Dennis Chinnery	William	Drinkstone	Felsham	
28	20/12/1884	Frank Hazelton	George	Drinkstone	Ixworth	
29	17/09/1882	Mary Rose	George	Drinkstone	None	
30	10/04/1886	Emma Sturgeon	Harry	Drinkstone	Brampton	
31	19/06/1885	Ellen Rose	George	Drinkstone	None	
32	07/07/1885	Mary Rose	James	Drinkstone	None	
33	29/03/1883	Rosalie Revens	Samuel	Drinkstone	None	
34	05/06/1883	Charles Grimwood	Alfred	Drinkstone	None	
35	25/02/1886	Oliver Young	George	Drinkstone	None	
36	15/08/1883	William Bennet	George	Drinkstone	None	
38	13/03/1882	Geoffrey Revens	Samuel	Drinkstone	None	
39	29/03/1884	Frederick Phillips	Edward	Drinkstone	Private	
40	12/12/1885	Walter Mayes	William	Drinkstone	None	
41	17/09/1886	Walter Pryke	Walter	Drinkstone	None	
42	16/02/1886	Oliver Stiff	Harry	Drinkstone	None	
43	22/07/1886	Cecil Hazelton	George	Drinkstone	Ixworth	
44	30/08/1885	Cecil Rose	William	Drinkstone	None	
45	06/11/1886	Arthur Bland	Charles	Drinkstone	None	
46	21/06/1886	Maud Read	George	Drinkstone	None	
47	12/03/1886	Martha Rose	George	Drinkstone	None	
48	05/03/1886	Ellen King	John	Drinkstone	None	
49	04/06/1885	Margaret Nestling	John	Drinkstone	Rattlesden	
50	19/11/1886	Caroline Reader	George	Drinkstone	None	
51	19/11/1886	Agnes Reader	George	Drinkstone	None	
52	16/09/1886	Norah Bennet	George	Drinkstone	None	
53	02/05/1887	Sidney Rose	William	Drinkstone	None	
54	18/05/1888	Bertie Phillips	Edward	Drinkstone	None	
55	17/06/1887	Susan Bennington	Philip	Drinkstone	None	
56	05/06/1887	Christopher Revens	Simon	Drinkstone	None	
57	03/06/1887	Albert Rose	Amos	Drinkstone	None	
58	15/03/1887	Ernest Chinnery	William	Drinkstone	None	
59	16/07/1887	Frederick Nestling	John	Drinkstone	None	
60	12/07/1887	Georgina Rose	George	Drinkstone	None	
61	12/07/1887	Cecil Reader	Walter	Drinkstone	None	
62	01/04/1888	Daniel Stiff	Nelson	Drinkstone	None	

ATTENDANCE REGISTER OF DRINKSTONE SCHOOL

	Date of Birth	Name of Child	Name of Parent or Guardian	Home Address	Previous School	Reason for Leaving
63	12/03/1887	Charles Squirrel	David	Drinkstone	None	
64	02/11/1888	Lapland Revens	Simon	Drinkstone	None	
0	16/07/1888	Gladstone Stiff	Harry	Drinkstone		
66	14/05/1888	Olive Harvey	Alfred	Drinkstone	None	
67	20/07/1889	Emily Allen	Arthur	Drinkstone	None	
68	10/02/1889	Walter Harvey	Walter	Drinkstone	None	
69	03/12/1887	Bessy Rust	Thomas	Drinkstone	None	
70	05/06/1888	Sydney Hazelton	George	Drinkstone	None	
71	25/09/1887	Annie Grimwood	Alfred	Drinkstone	None	
72	21/02/1887	Hilda Cornish	Harry	Drinkstone	None	
73	23/12/1888	Annie Sturgeon	Harry	Drinkstone	Ixworth	
74	28/07/1888	Dorothy Reader	George	Drinkstone	None	
19	25/02/1882	Arthur Rose	James	Drinkstone	None	
75	01/06/1884	Louise Bird	Arthur	Drinkstone	Shimpling	
76	28/12/1884	Ethel Snell	Oliver	Drinkstone	Woolpit	
77	22/08/1886	Sydney Snell	Oliver	Drinkstone	Woolpit	
78	05/07/1888	Ellen Snell	Oliver	Drinkstone	None	
79	05/08/1890	Mildred Harvey	Alfred	Drinkstone	None	
80	11/09/1889	Willy Rust	Thomas	Drinkstone	None	
81	13/08/1889	Rebecca Rose	William	Drinkstone	None	
82	16/08/1889	Hilda Chinnery	William	Drinkstone	None	
83	06/03/1889	Catherine Nutt	Walter	Drinkstone	None	
84	11/05/1890	Frank Reader	Walter	Drinkstone	None	
85	15/10/1890	Alfred Stiff	Nelson	Drinkstone	None	
86	19/04/1888	Rebie Parish	Susan	Drinkstone	None	
87		Emily Allen	Arthur	Drinkstone	None	
PUPILS ADMITTED IN 1895						
88	03/08/1884	Selby G. Robinson	William	Drinkstone	Hessett	
89	08/12/1888	Emma Robinson	William	Drinkstone	Hessett	
90	30/04/1891	Mary E. Robinson	William	Drinkstone	Hessett	
91	15/08/1890	George C. Young	George	Drinkstone	None	
92	20/02/1890	Edward J. Mayes	James	Drinkstone	Norton	
93	17/06/1890	Lizzie Bennett	Archer	Drinkstone	Norton	
94	14/10/1890	Winifred Harvey	Walter	Drinkstone	None	
95	1891	Percifal Revens	Simon	Drinkstone	None	
96	1892	Edward Squirrel	Alfred	Drinkstone	None	
97	07/02/1890	Maude Mayes	Mary	Drinkstone	None	
98	12/01/1890	George R. Mirrington	George	Drinkstone	Rattlesden	
PUPILS ADMITTED IN 1896						
99	10/06/1888	Mabel Rowe	Harry	Drinkstone	Woolpit	
99b.	05/11/1892	Christopher Young	George	Drinkstone	None	
100	12/05/1891	Herbert Rowe	Harry	Drinkstone	Woolpit	
101		Louisa Rowe	Harry	Drinkstone	Woolpit	
102	1892	Albert Rowe	Harry	Drinkstone	Woolpit	
103	16/02/1891	Bertie Halls	Charles	Drinkstone	None	
104	14/04/1892	Alfred Harvey	Alfred	Drinkstone	None	Left
105	23/02/1892	Arthur Pryke	Walter	Drinkstone	None	
106	12/10/1891	Rose Osborne	Kate	Drinkstone	None	
107	16/05/1892	Florence Bennington	Phillip	Drinkstone	None	
108	12/05/1890	Gertrude M. M. Vince	James	Drinkstone	None	
109	04/10/1988	Beatrice Beard	John	Drinkstone	Hessett	
110		George Grimwood	Alfred	Drinkstone	None	
111	12/06/1893	Fred Rowe	Harry	Drinkstone	None	
112	24/02/1893	Oliver J. Mayes	James	Drinkstone	None	
113	17/11/1891	Walter Rose	Amos	Drinkstone	None	
PUPILS ADMITTED IN 1897						
114	12/01/1891	Charles Revens	George	Drinkstone	Cambridge	
115	12/10/1891	Rosalie Osborne	Kate	Drinkstone	Tostock	
116	25/12/1892	May Mower	George	Drinkstone	Oakley	
117	25/03/1887	Ada Hardwicke	William	Drinkstone	Tostock	
118	29/05/1989	William Mower	George	Drinkstone	Oakley	

	Date of Birth	Name of Child	Name of Parent or Guardian	Home Address	Previous School	Reason for Leaving
119	17/07/1892	Bessie Harvey	Walter	Drinkstone	None	
120	05/07/1892	Florence Reader	George	Drinkstone	None	
121	12/02/1893	Margaret Stiff	Nelson	Drinkstone	None	By Med. Authority
122	16/09/1892	Margaret Reader	Walter	Drinkstone	None	
123	24/09/1891	Gladys Hayward	Robert	Drinkstone	None	
124	28/03/1893	Ivy Hayward	Robert	Drinkstone	None	
125	10/05/1884	Sarah Howard	John	Drinkstone	Winsford	
126	19/04/1887	Mary A. Howard	John	Drinkstone	Winsford	
127	03/06/1890	James D. Howard	John	Drinkstone	Winsford	
128	03/09/1886	Alice Mortlock	John	Drinkstone	Stratford	
129	09/1888	Gertrude Mortlock	John	Drinkstone	Stratford	
130	12/02/1893	John Blake	John	Drinkstone	None	Left Village
131	01/1893	Walter Halls	Charles	Drinkstone	None	
132	08/1891	Ruth Artist	-	Drinkstone	Rattlesden	
PUPILS ADMITTED IN 1898						
133	11/05/1894	Frank Harvey	Alfred J.	Drinkstone	None	Age(11/5/08)
134	27/04/1895	William Robinson	William	Drinkstone	None	
135	20/06/1894	Fred Mower	Fred G.	Drinkstone	None	
136	06/1893	Bertie Allerton	James	Drinkstone	None	
137	05/1894	Bertie Grimwood	Alfred	Drinkstone	None	
138	05/1894	Florence Pryke	Walter	Drinkstone	None	
139	10/09/1893	Winifred Reader	George	Drinkstone	None	
140	12/1894	Annie Squirrell	David	Drinkstone	None	
141	02/1895	Miriam Blake	William	Drinkstone	None	Left Village
142	07/09/1890	Ethel Everitt	Joseph	Drinkstone	Brent Ely	
143	20/07/1889	Emily Allen	Arthur	Drinkstone	Berkhampstead	
144	09/1889	Rose Mary Moore	Fred	Drinkstone	Rattlesden	
145	25/09/1892	Lillian Cornish	William	Drinkstone	None	
PUPILS ADMITTED IN 1899						
146	12/11/1890	Stanley Brown	Edward	Drinkstone	Thorndon	
147	20/03/1889	Jack Brown	Edward	Drinkstone	Thorndon	
148	28/11/1883	Kathleen Brown	Edward	Drinkstone	Thorndon	
149	12/03/1890	George G. Cooper	George	Drinkstone	Rattlesden	
150	29/06/1888	Jessie Cooper	George	Drinkstone	Rattlesden	
151	05/09/1886	Nellie G. Robinson	William	Drinkstone	None	
152	27/12/1885	Sidney Brown	Edward	Drinkstone	Thorndon	
153	06/01/1896	Fred Allerton	James	Drinkstone	None	
154	06/01/1896	Olive Stiff	Nelson	Drinkstone	None	
155	1893	Alice Mondew	Freeman	Drinkstone	None	
156	12/1894	Annie Squirrell	David	Drinkstone	None	
157	12/11/1891	Archie Simmonds	Arthur	Drinkstone	Clapham Junction	
158	05/02/1895	Gertrude Brown	George	Drinkstone	None	
159	06/1892	Charles Hawton	William	Drinkstone	Elmswell	
160	28/05/1894	Sydney Mayes	Arthur	Drinkstone	None	
161		Fred Hawton	William	Drinkstone	None	
162	14/09/1894	Ada Halls	Charles	Drinkstone	None	
163	/1896	Lily Harvey	Walter	Drinkstone	None	
164	15/01/1888	Leonard Simmonds	Arthur	Drinkstone	Clapham Junction	
165	15/09/1894	Mary A. Moore	Fred	Drinkstone	None	
166	28/06/1895	Daniel Spink	Charles	Drinkstone	None	
PUPILS ADMITTED IN 1900						
167	28/12/1895	Constance Simmonds	Arthur	Drinkstone	None	
168	12/05/1895	Louie Broadbent	Hartley	Drinkstone	None	
169	22/08/1896	William Pryke	Walter	Drinkstone	None	
170	26/04/1896	William Osborne	Sarah	Drinkstone	None	
171	24/11/1895	Anna E. Phillips	Edward	Drinkstone	None	
172	24/12/1895	Gertrude Browne	George	Drinkstone	None	
173	28/12/1894	Constance Simmonds	Arthur	Drinkstone	None	
174	11/1895	May Halls	Charles	Drinkstone	None	
PUPILS ADMITTED IN 1901						
175	06/01/1896	Olive E. Stiff	Nelson	Drinkstone	None	by Med. Authority

	Date of Birth	Name of Child	Name of Parent or Guardian	Home Address	Previous School	Reason for Leaving
176	12/06/1897	Florence Hunt	George	Drinkstone	None	Left
177	27/05/1896	Daniel Spink	Charles	Drinkstone	None	Left
178	1898	Andrew Blake	John	Drinkstone	None	Left
179	17/11/1896	Stanley Mayes	Arthur	Drinkstone	None	Left
180	01/03/1893	Marcus Rowe	Mary A.	Drinkstone		to Bury St. Edmunds
181	01/08/1896	Lucy J. Nunn	William	Drinkstone	None	Left
182	12/1891	William Lewis	Drinkstone	to Barking		
183	03/1890	Adelaide Fisher	Drinkstone	to Elmswell		

PUPILS ADMITTED IN 1902

	Date of Birth	Name of Child	Name of Parent or Guardian	Home Address	Previous School	Reason for Leaving
184	20/06/1893	Wallace Blake	Harry	Drinkstone		to Newmarket
185	18/11/1894	Annie Blake	Harry	Drinkstone		o Newmarket
186	30/06/1897	Blanche Gallant	Laura	Drinkstone	None	Left
187	02/1896	Olive B. Brabrook	-	Drinkstone		to Bury St. Edmunds
188	05/1897	Maria V. Brabrook	-	Drinkstone		to Bury St. Edmunds
189	06/1896	Louisa Howlett	Francis	Drinkstone Park		to Paris
190	08/1898	Francis Howlett	Francis	Drinkstone Park		to Paris
191	26/07/1891	Sydney Arbon	John	Drinkstone		to Bardwell
192	03/07/1896	James Arbon	John	Drinkstone	Bardwell	Left
193	09/04/1895	Frederick Arbon	John	Drinkstone	Bardwell	Age (14/5/08)
194	25/07/1890	Mabel Davey	Edward	Drinkstone	Woolpit	Left
195	18/04/1892	Alice Davey	Edward	Drinkstone	Woolpit	by Med. Authority
196	06/02/1895	Millie Davey	Edward	Drinkstone	Woolpit	by Med. Authority
197	24/09/1897	Herbert Davey	Edward	Drinkstone	Woolpit	by Med. Authority
198	10/05/1898	Albert E. Bennington	Phillip	Drinkstone	None	Left
199	05/11/1897	Ella Harvey	Walter	Drinkstone	None	Left
200	06/10/1899	Maude Blake	Harry	Drinkstone	None	Left
201	21/09/1897	Nellie Grimwood	Alfred	Drinkstone	None	Left

PUPILS ADMITTED IN 1903

	Date of Birth	Name of Child	Name of Parent or Guardian	Home Address	Previous School	Reason for Leaving
202	18/11/1898	William Grimwood	Alfred	Drinkstone	None	Left
203	10/01/1892	Percy Whent	Henry	Drinkstone	Long Melford	Left
204	25/02/1894	May Whent	Henry	Drinkstone	Long Melford	Left
205	14/04/1898	Reginald Whent	Henry	Drinkstone	Long Melford	Left
206	16/08/1894	Leopold C. Colson	Lewis	Drinkstone	Hartest	Left
207	01/07/1895	Reginald A. Colson	Lewis	Drinkstone	Hartest	Left
208	01/07/1896	Cecil O. Colson	Lewis	Drinkstone	Hartest	Left
209	17/04/1896	Bessie Kemp	-	Drinkstone	Bury St. Edmunds	Left
210		Frances Mason	John	Drinkstone	Woolpit	Left
211		Nellie Markell	-	Drinkstone	Higham	Left Village
212	05/1899	Edward Davey	-	Drinkstone	None	by Medical Authority
213	28/09/1895	Stanley Frost	-	Drinkstone	None	Left
214	09/1898	Lydia Artist	-	Drinkstone	None	Left Village
215	04/10/1898	Ellen E. Pollard	-	Drinkstone	None	Left Village
216	15/07/1897	Florence M. Gill	Robert	Drinkstone	Ipswich	Left
217	05/1899	Lilian M. Clarke	Edgar	Drinkstone	None	Left Village
218	25/01/1890	Bessie S. Blake	John	Drinkstone	None	Left Village
219	14/06/1898	Ruby K. Colson	Lewis	Drinkstone	None	Left
220	20/01/1899	Florence A. Halls	Charles	Drinkstone	None	Left
221	02/1899	Florence K. Taylor	Herbert	Drinkstone	None	Left
222	25/09/1899	Merle-May Harvey	Walter	Drinkstone	None	Left

PUPILS ADMITTED IN 1904

	Date of Birth	Name of Child	Name of Parent or Guardian	Home Address	Previous School	Reason for Leaving
223	29/01/1900	Kathleyn Exhen	William	Drinkstone	None	Left Village
224	18/03/1900	Rebbie A. Squirrel	Alfred	Drinkstone	None	Left
225	1891	Harold Squirrel	Alfred	Drinkstone	None	Left
226	07/09/1898	Herbert Mower	Fred G.	Drinkstone	None	Left Village
227	22/11/1899	Albert W. Mayes	Arthur	Drinkstone	None	Left
228	17/09/1892	Thomas Coleby	Henry	Drinkstone	Wattisfield	Left
229	22/12/1894	Jack Coleby	Henry	Drinkstone	Wattisfield	Left
230	04/01/1894	John E. Goodson	John E.	Drinkstone	Palgrave	Left
231	19/04/1896	Matilda Goodson	John E.	Drinkstone	Palgrave	Left

	Date of Birth	Name of Child	Name of Parent or Guardian	Home Address	Previous School	Reason for Leaving
232	15/10/1898	Leonard G. Goodson	John E	Drinkstone	Palgrave	Left
233	30/01/1898	Jack Eagle	Henry	Drinkstone	Wattisfield	Left Village
234	30/06/1897	Florence Coleby	Henry	Drinkstone	Wattisfield	Left
235	26/08/1894	Dorothy M. G. Rose	Henry	Drinkstone	Rougham	Left Village
236	08/1897	Florence Gill	Robert	Drinkstone	Ipswich	Left
PUPILS ADMITTED IN 1905						
237	27/10/1899	Henry M. Gobbitt	Henry M.	Drinkstone	Norton	Left
238	27/04/1899	Ernest G. Moore	Fred	Drinkstone	None	Left Village
239	22/03/1900	Elsie E. Halls	Charles	Drinkstone	None	Left
240	19/01/1901	Arthur S. Stiff	Nelson	Drinkstone	None	Left
241	24/03/1901	Alfred J. Davey	Edward	Drinkstone	None	Left Village
242	17/11/1900	Geoffrey Bennett	Archie	Drinkstone	None	Left
243	20/04/1901	Harold Squirrel	Alfred	Drinkstone	None	Left
244	13/08/1895	Beatrice Pilbrow	nil	Drinkstone	Felsham	Left
245	17/12/1896	Albert Smith	John	Drinkstone	Felsham	Left
246	08/01/1897	Faith V. Fayers	Arthur	Drinkstone	Felixstowe	Left Village
PUPILS ADMITTED IN 1906						
247	03/06/1898	Lewis H. Coleby	Lewis	Drinkstone	Carlton Colville	Left Village
248	18/05/1900	Clarence Coleby	Lewis	Drinkstone	Carlton Colville	Left Village
249	21/03/1901	Harry Goodson	John E.	Drinkstone	None	Left Village
250	15/10/1896	Cyril Downing	Cyril	Drinkstone	Beyton	Left Village
251	31/12/1897	May Downing	Cyril	Drinkstone	Beyton	Left Village
252	15/05/1901	Lottie M. Grimwood	Alfred	Drinkstone	None	Left
253	31/10/1902	Richard Gobbitt	Henry M.	Drinkstone	None	Transferred - Norton
254	05/07/1901	Mary Halls	Charles	Drinkstone	None	Left
255	06/03/1894	Bertie Brinkley	Edward	Drinkstone	Woolpit	Left
256	14/01/1902	Alfred Wright	William	Drinkstone	Lackford	Left
257	28/09/1898	Stanley J. Frost	Walter	Drinkstone	Hessett	Left
258	16/01/1901	Ernest Frost	Walter	Drinkstone	Hessett	Dead
PUPILS ADMITTED IN 1907						
259	09/11/1895	James Gill	James	Drinkstone	Bury St. Edmunds	Left
260	28/09/1896	Agnes Gill	James	Drinkstone	Bury St. Edmunds	Left
261	31/03/1898	Albert Gill	James	Drinkstone	Bury St. Edmunds	Left
262	13/02/1901	Victoria Gill	James	Drinkstone	Bury St. Edmunds	Left
263	20/03/1903	Avie E. M. Whent	Henry	Drinkstone	None	Left Village
264	17/09/1901	Edith M. Arbon	John	Drinkstone	None	Left Village
265	31/05/1903	Cecil Smith	John	Drinkstone	None	Left Village
266	10/07/1897	Edward Brinkley	Edward	Drinkstone	Woolpit	Left
267	02/01/1903	Fred L. Frost	Walter	Drinkstone	None	Left
268	12/07/1898	Alice Arbon	John	Drinkstone	None	Left
269	15/04/1902	John Bradbrook	John	Drinkstone	None	Left Village
270	08/07/1898	Samuel Mortimer	Happy Samuel	Drinkstone	Ipswich	Left Village
271	17/07/1900	Nelson Mortimer	Happy Samuel	Drinkstone	Ipswich	Left Village
PUPILS ADMITTED IN 1908						
272	04/05/1899	Ivy Burton	Arthur	Drinkstone	Roughton	Left Village
273	26/09/1903	Robert Gill	James	Drinkstone	None	
274	02/03/1903	Lucy Mower	Fred G.	Drinkstone	None	Left Village
275	06/04/1903	Lily Bradbrook	John	Drinkstone	None	Left Village
276	12/06/1903	Gertrude Burton	Arthur	Drinkstone	None	Left Village
277	24/08/1901	Robert Snare	Robert	Drinkstone	London	Left Village
278	31/01/1903	Reginald Snare	Robert	Drinkstone	London	Left Village
279	16/03/1903	Phyllis Mayhew	Ernest	Drinkstone	None	Left Village
280	20/08/1896	Winifred Youngman	William	Drinkstone	London	Left Village
281	09/09/1900	Geoffrey Catchpole	Geoffrey	Drinkstone	Bradfield	Left
282	24/12/1903	Arnold L. M. Mayes	Arthur	Drinkstone	None	Left
283	24/08/1900	Wilfred Barker	John	Drinkstone	Felsham	Left
284	03/08/1901	John Burrows	Ambrose	Drinkstone	Beyton	Left
285		Fred Mayes	Walter	Drinkstone	Great Waldringfield	Left Village
286		John Mayes	Walter	Drinkstone	Great Waldringfield	Left Village
287	24/02/1901	Wilfred Spearen	Henry	Drinkstone	London	Left Village

ATTENDANCE REGISTER OF DRINKSTONE SCHOOL

	Date of Birth	Name of Child	Name of Parent or Guardian	Home Address	Previous School	Reason for Leaving
PUPILS ADMITTED IN 1909						
288	04/01/1904	Kate Sturgeon	Charles	Drinkstone	None	Left Village
289	18/04/1897	Arthur Hunt	Thomas	Drinkstone	Swanton Abbot	Left Village
290	29/06/1901	Robert Hunt	Thomas	Drinkstone	Swanton Abbot	Left Village
291	11/05/1898	E. Winifred Cornish	Walter	Drinkstone	Dalham	Left
292	07/04/1904	John Halls	Charles	Drinkstone	None	Left
293	23/05/1904	Sidney Squirrell	Alfred	Drinkstone	None	Left
294	04/1903	Violet B. Taylor	-	Nedging	Nedging	Left Village
295	31/08/1904	Percy Smith	John	Drinkstone	None	Left
296	31/12/1904	Arthur G. Gardiner	Herbert	Drinkstone	None	Left
297	8 years	Eric R. Rolfe	Fred	Drinkstone	Tostock	Left Village
298	6 years	Kathleen Lambert	(Guardian)	Drinkstone	None	Left Village
299	13/03/1896	Lilian Cornish	Walter	Drinkstone	Thelnetham	Left Village
300	24/09/1905	Walter Gill	James	Drinkstone	None	Left
301	23/11/1904	Brenda Snare	Robert	Drinkstone	None	Left Village
302	03/05/1904	Ernest Whiting	Emily	Drinkstone	Hessett	Left
PUPILS ADMITTED IN 1910						
303	25/12/1898	Herbert S. Stannard	Harry	Drinkstone	Stowmarket	Left Village
304	28/01/1901	Victoria M. Stannard	Harry	Drinkstone	Stowmarket	Left Village
305	14/12/1902	Nora A. Stannard	Harry	Drinkstone	Stowmarket	Left Village
306	06/04/1906	Dorothy V. Gobbitt	Henry	Drinkstone	None	Left
307	18/02/1905	Mervyn C. Bishop	Mary A.	Drinkstone	None	Left
308	31/01/1906	Violet M. Burrows	Ambrose	Drinkstone	None	
309	09/03/1905	Alice L. Sturgeon	Charles	Drinkstone	None	Left Village
310	21/09/1905	Ivy Coleby	Henry	Drinkstone	None	Left Village
311	08/05/1905	Arthur G. Frost	Walter	Drinkstone	None	Left
312	24/01/1905	Bertie G.Rutter	Lewis	Drinkstone	None	Left
313	08/07/1905	Frank R. Pryke	Walter	Drinkstone	None	Left
314	21/12/1905	Arthur Stiff	James	Drinkstone	None	Left
315	21/08/1906	Aubrey Snare	(Guardian R. Mulley)	Drinkstone	None	Left Parish
316	12/07/1898	Alice M. Arbon	John	Drinkstone	None	Left
317	03/04/1899	Agnes M. Brinkley	Edward	Drinkstone	Woolpit	Left
318	16/09/1899	Elsie Hills	Charles	Drinkstone	Ipswich	Left Parish
319	11/05/1898	Winifred Cornish	Walter	Drinkstone	Trumpington	Left
PUPILS ADMITTED IN 1911						
320	21/12/1905	Arthur Stiff	James	Drinkstone	Drinkstone	Left
321	18/11/1905	Agnes M. Arbon	John	Drinkstone	None	Left Parish
322	23/12/1904	Beatrice M. Stannard	Harry	Drinkstone	None	Left Parish
323	01/01/1906	Ernest H. Stannard	Harry	Drinkstone	None	Left Parish
324	20/07/1906	Sidney Grimwood	Alfred	Drinkstone	None	
325	09/09/1906	Charles T. Sturgeon	Charles	Drinkstone	None	Left
326	12/09/1904	William G. Ringer	William J.	Drinkstone	Pakenham	Left Parish
327	06/09/1906	Oliver G. Squirrell	Alfred	Drinkstone	None	Left
328	23/10/1906	Alec P. Mothersole	Charles H. P.	Drinkstone	None	Left Parish
329	13/11/1906	George L. Halls	Charles L.	Drinkstone	None	Left
330	25/10/1906	Muriel M. Burton	Arthur	Drinkstone	Hessett	Left Parish
PUPILS ADMITTED IN 1912						
331	25/02/1907	Reginald A. Mayes	Arthur	Drinkstone	None	
332	17/07/1904	Ernest Bartram	Albert	Drinkstone	Hepworth	Gone Home, Dead
333	04/04/1901	Ernest G. Brinkley	Edward	Woolpit	Woolpit	Left
334	05/08/1905	Ethel M. Cook	Samuel	Drinkstone	Melford	Left, Gone Home
335	09/07/1907	Ellen A. Ringer	William J.	Drinkstone	None	Left Parish
336	19/02/1908	Thomas Burrows	Ambrose	Drinkstone	None	
337	09/08/1906	Alice Wright	Elijah	Drinkstone	Wetheringsett	
338	14/09/1907	Jessie E. Arbon	John	Drinkstone	None	Left Parish
339	17/03/1909	Herbert F. S. Gobbitt	Henry M.	Drinkstone	None	Left
340	23/05/1908	Florence R. Gardiner	Herbert	Drinkstone	None	Left –Removed
341	18/02/1909	John A. Chambers	Alexander J.	Drinkstone	None	Left
342	10/07/1901	May K. Horrex	William	Drinkstone	Norton	Left
343	31/03/1900	Samuel Pike	Samuel	Drinkstone	Barton	Left

	Date of Birth	Name of Child	Name of Parent or Guardian	Home Address	Previous School	Reason for Leaving
344	17/05/1903	Alfred Pike	Samuel	Drinkstone	Barton	Left
345	15/07/1906	Winnie Pike	Samuel	Drinkstone	Barton	Left
346	05/11/1908	Robert Pike	Samuel	Drinkstone	Barton	Left
PUPILS ADMITTED IN 1913						
347	25/04/1901	Florence F. Foreman	John R.	Drinkstone	Great Barton	Left
348	15/06/1907	Mabel L. Foreman	John R.	Drinkstone	Great Barton	Left
349	05/05/1902	Dorothy M. James	Charles W.	Drinkstone	Halstead	Left
350	22/02/1906	Edith M. James	Charles W.	Drinkstone	Halstead	Left
351	15/10/1907	Margaret E. James	Charles W.	Drinkstone	None	Left Parish
352	10/10/1907	Rose A. Bennett	Fred K.	Drinkstone	None	Left Parish
353	07/06/1908	Ruby B. Plummer	Ernest V. A.	Drinkstone	None	Left Parish
354	16/10/1908	Charles S. Barker	Reginald O.	Drinkstone	None	Left Parish
355	20/09/1908	Florence Sturgeon	Charles S.	Drinkstone	None	Left Parish
262	14/02/1901	Victoria G. Gill	James	Drinkstone	Bury St. Edmunds	Left
356	14/05/1902	Horace C. Bartram	Albert	Drinkstone	Fornham St. Martin	Left
357	15/11/1903	Ernest A. Bartram	Albert	Drinkstone	Fornham St. Martin	Dead
358	11/04/1909	Albert Horrex	Harry S.	Drinkstone	None	Left
359	11/02/1910	Frank S. Wright	William	Drinkstone	None	Left
360	11/02/1909	Lily Arbon	John	Drinkstone	None	Left
361	05/10/1908	Fred J. Bartram	Albert	Drinkstone	None	Left
362	24/01/1910	Harry T. Bartram	Albert	Drinkstone	None	Left
363	20/11/1901	Doris K.Wright	(Guardian) Walter	Drinkstone	Ilford	Private School
364	10/05/1906	Philippa M. Crysell	David	Drinkstone	Woolpit	Left Parish
365	05/04/1908	Dorothy M. Crysell	David	Drinkstone	Woolpit	Left Parish
366	02/02/1910	Reginald Barker	Reginald O.	Drinkstone	None	Left Parish
367	07/1906	Frank Shepherd	-	Drinkstone	Bury St. Edmunds	Left
PUPILS ADMITTED IN 1914						
368	12/01/1909	Eunice M. Mothersole	Charles H. P.	Drinkstone	None	
369	13/05/1907	Lily M. Simpson	John H.	Drinkstone	Nowton	
370	06/03/1910	Pearlie J. Plummer	Ernest V. A.	Drinkstone	None	Left Parish
371	28/04/1907	Frank W. Gill	Robert	Drinkstone	Onehouse	Left Parish
372	05/02/1910	Helen G. James	Charles W.	Drinkstone	None	Left
373	02/03/1910	Edith Gill	Robert	Drinkstone	None	Left Parish
374	20/04/1910	Ellen E. Cox	John F.	Drinkstone	None	Left Parish
375	25/06/1911	Stephanie Gobbitt	Henry M.	Drinkstone	None	Ipswich Private
362	24/01/1910	Harry T. Bartram	Albert	Drinkstone	Drinkstone	Left
376	31/12/1909	Eric D. Stiff	James	Drinkstone	None	
366	02/02/1910	Reginald Barker	Reginald O.	Drinkstone	Drinkstone	Left Parish
358	11/04/1909	Albert Horrex	Harry S.	Drinkstone	Drinkstone	Left
PUPILS ADMITTED IN 1915						
377	16/01/1907	Ralph Slade	William	Drinkstone	Stanton	Gone Home
378	15/02/1905	Kathleen R. Southgate	William	Drinkstone	Bramford	Gone Home
379	09/11/1910	Harold C. Sturgeon	Charles T.	Drinkstone	None	Left
380	24/03/1910	Dorothy G. Mayes	Arthur	Drinkstone	None	Left
381	02/06/1910	Beatrice M. Rose	-	Drinkstone	None	Left Parish
382	20/12/1905	Winifred E. Radford	William	Drinkstone	Norton	Left Parish
383	31/10/1902	Richard Gobbitt	Henry M.	Drinkstone	Norton	County School
384	01/07/1911	Florence E. Bennett	Fred	Drinkstone	None	Left Parish
385	19/02/1911	Jack E. Plummer	Ernest	Drinkstone	None	Left Parish
386	02/01/1912	Edward J. Cox	John F.	Drinkstone	None	Left Parish
387	01/03/1905	Ellen Hardy	William	Drinkstone	Sicklesmere	Left
388	04/06/1910	Florence Hardy	William	Drinkstone	Sicklesmere	Left
389	24/05/1907	Victoria M. Minns	Paul	Drinkstone	Halesworth	Left Parish
390	04/02/1906	Horace Gowers	Ernest	Drinkstone	Woolpit	Left Parish
391	27/09/1908	Fred A. Gowers	Ernest	Drinkstone	Woolpit	Left Parish
392	23/05/1911	George G. Gowers	Ernest	Drinkstone	Woolpit	Left Parish
358	11/04/1909	Albert Horrex	Harry S.	Drinkstone	Norton	Left
PUPILS ADMITTED IN 1916						
393	06/08/1903	Hilda E. Brinkley	Edward	Drinkstone	Woolpit	Left
394	13/07/1908	Daisy A. Brinkley	Edward	Drinkstone	Woolpit	Left
395	18/01/1912	Percy W. Lingwood	Mrs. Revens	Drinkstone	None	Left Parish

ATTENDANCE REGISTER OF DRINKSTONE SCHOOL

	Date of Birth	Name of Child	Name of Parent or Guardian	Home Address	Previous School	Reason for Leaving
396	29/06/1912	Florrie Faulkner	Arthur	Drinkstone	None	Left
397	21/01/1912	Dorothy E. Wright	William	Drinkstone	None	Left
398	03/05/1911	Gladys M. Taylor	Charles	Drinkstone	None	Dead
399	12/10/1911	Gertrude Bennett	-	Drinkstone	None	
400	15/09/1903	Claude Dorling	Jessie	Drinkstone	Culford	Left
401	25/03/1912	Ivy E. Mortimer	-	Drinkstone	None	Left Parish
402		Marjorie Allen	-	Drinkstone	Silverton	Left Parish
403	23/07/1911	Olive R. Mothersole	Charles	Drinkstone	None	Left Parish
404	12/06/1913	Kathleen G. James	Charles W.	Drinkstone	None	Left Parish
405	22/09/1911	Phyllis A. Sparkes	Frank	Drinkstone	None	Left Parish
406	24/09/1911	Stephen Barrett	Robert	Drinkstone	None	Left Parish
407		Frederick Gill	Robert	Drinkstone	None	Left Parish
408	25/02/1913	Maud Cox	John	Drinkstone	None	Left Parish
PUPILS ADMITTED IN 1917						
409	24/05/1908	Florence Gardner	Herbert	Drinkstone	Norton	Left Parish
410	11/01/1912	Irene V. Keeble	Walter	Drinkstone	Norton	Left Parish
411	31/12/1904	Arthur G. Gardiner	Herbert	Drinkstone	Norton	Left Parish
412		Walter J. Gardiner	Herbert	Drinkstone	Norton	Left Parish
413		Victor Gardiner	Herbert	Drinkstone	Norton	Left Parish
414	08/12/1912	Vera M. Sturgeon	Charles T.	Drinkstone	None	Left
415	20/05/1912	Ivy M. Spooner	Philip G.	Drinkstone	None	Left Parish
416	02/03/1913	Sidney C. Cox	John	Drinkstone	None	Left Parish
417	24/05/1907	Queenie Minns	Paul	Drinkstone	Halesworth	Left Parish
418	26/01/1913	Henry E. Gardiner	Herbert	Drinkstone	None	Left Parish
419	20/12/1905	Winifred Radford	William	Drinkstone	Drinkstone	Left
420	26/09/1906	Lily A. Sparkes	Montague	Drinkstone	Rattlesden	Left
421	07/06/1908	Ruby B. Plummer	Ernest	Drinkstone	Plumstead	Left Parish
422	19/02/1911	Jack Plummer	Ernest	Drinkstone	Plumstead	Left Parish
423	09/08/1912	Doris Plummer	Ernest	Drinkstone	Plumstead	Left Parish
424	05/03/1906	Oliver Read	Robert	Drinkstone	Barking	Left
PUPILS ADMITTED IN 1918						
425	22/08/1912	Joyce Gobbitt	Henry M.	Drinkstone	None	Left
426	28/02/1913	Bessie A. Seeley	Harry	Drinkstone	None	Left
427	30/04/1913	Geoffrey Keeble	Walter	Drinkstone	None	Left Parish
428	14/05/1913	Ivy E. Mayes	Arthur	Drinkstone	None	
429	10/08/1909	Donald McPhail	Donald	Drinkstone	None	Left
430	02/08/1914	George McPhail	Donald	Drinkstone	None	Left
431	05/03/1910	Malcolm G. Smith	Walter	Drinkstone	Badwell Ash	Left
432	29/11/1905	Violet E. Underwood	Walter	Drinkstone	Stowupland	Left Parish
433	15/04/1908	Sidney Underwood	Walter	Drinkstone	Stowupland	Left Parish
434	24/04/1910	Ivy Underwood	Walter	Drinkstone	Stowupland	Left Parish
435	03/07/1914	Hilda Underwood	Walter	Drinkstone	None	Left Parish
PUPILS ADMITTED IN 1919						
436	28/08/1911	David Rose	George	Drinkstone	Cambridge	Left Parish
437	02/10/1913	Eric Rose	George	Drinkstone	Cambridge	Left Parish
438	11/10/1913	Phyllis M. Dykes	Montague	Drinkstone	None	Left Parish
439	23/03/1914	Kathleen Edwards	William	Drinkstone	None	Left
440	19/08/1912	Fred J. Mothersole	Elijah	Drinkstone	Barrow	Left Parish
441	18/10/1914	Mabel Sturgeon	Charles	Drinkstone	None	Left
442	07/08/1908	Lilian I. Garner	James	Drinkstone	Wattisham	Left Parish
443	02/10/1907	Claude Docking	Alfred	Drinkstone	Exning	Left Parish
444	24/02/1908	Thomas E. Rose	William	Drinkstone	Hull	Left Parish
445	04/09/1909	James W. Rose	William	Drinkstone	Hull	Left Parish
446	02/02/1912	Bessie McPhail	Donald	Drinkstone	London	Left Parish
447	07/08/1914	Florence L. Taylor	Charles	Drinkstone	None	Left Parish
448	02/10/1914	Percy W. Horrex	-	Drinkstone	None	Left
449	14/11/1909	Ronald W. Stephens	-	Drinkstone	Bradfield St. George	Left P.
PUPILS ADMITTED IN 1920						
450	07/04/1909	Ivy Read	Fred G.	Drinkstone	Bury St. Edmunds	Left
451	13/12/1910	Fred A. Bell	Charles	Drinkstone	Herringwell	Left Parish
452	07/01/1913	Roland S. Stacey	Charles	Drinkstone	Herringwell	Left Parish

	Date of Birth	Name of Child	Name of Parent or Guardian	Home Address	Previous School	Reason for Leaving
453	20/03/1913	Edwina Ovington	Edwin	Drinkstone	Hounslow	Left Parish
454	16/12/1914	Charles Read	Ettie Simpson	Drinkstone	None	Left Parish
455	30/04/1916	Eva Wilson	Harry	Drinkstone	None	Left Parish
456	08/04/1916	Harold Read	Fred	Drinkstone	None	Left Parish
457	28/02/1916	Leslie Mills	Edward	Drinkstone	None	Left Parish
458	15/06/1913	Winifred Davey	Alice	Drinkstone	None	Left
459	09/08/1906	Alice Wright	Elijah	Drinkstone	Livermere	Left
460	28/05/1916	Albert Dykes	Montague	Drinkstone	Drinkstone	-
461	04/09/1909	Agatha Miller	George	Drinkstone	Pakenham	Left
462	20/04/1911	Ada Read	Fred	Drinkstone	Bury St. Edmunds	Left Parish
463	14/07/1916	Frances M. James	Charles W.	Drinkstone	None	-
464	16/02/1914	Ruth M. Minns	Richard	Drinkstone	None	Bury R.C. School
465	19/02/1911	George W. Blake	Samuel P.	Drinkstone	Hessett	Left
466	05/03/1914	Harry A. Blake	Samuel P.	Drinkstone	Hessett	Left Parish
467	16/04/1909	Olive M. Blake	Samuel P.	Drinkstone	Hessett	Left Parish
468	13/10/1915	Marjorie H. Edwards	William	Drinkstone	None	Left
469	03/10/1907	Katherine Watling	Arthur	Drinkstone	Grundisburgh	Left
470	28/12/1907	Olive B. Berry	John	Drinkstone	Great Waltham	Left
471	20/09/1910	Winifred M. Berry	John	Drinkstone	Great Waltham	Left Parish
472	11/03/1913	Hilda E. Berry	John	Drinkstone	Great Waltham	Left Parish
473	01/07/1911	Victor A. Gardiner	Herbert	Drinkstone	Saxtead	Left Parish
474	30/10/1915	Lily E. Mayes	Arthur	Drinkstone	None	Left
475	05/11/1915	Violet J. Pryke	Walter	Drinkstone	None	Left
476	16/04/1913	Thomas B. Smith	Albert	Drinkstone	Great Waltham	Left
477	29/11/1914	Albert L. Smith	Albert	Drinkstone	Great Waltham	Left
478	06/03/1908	Victor G. Smith	Albert	Drinkstone	Great Waltham	Left
479	18/01/1915	William Wiles	John E.	Drinkstone	-	Left Parish
480	29/05/1913	Marjorie Wiles	John E.	Drinkstone	-	Left Parish
481	01/12/1915	Myrtle Berry	John F.	Drinkstone	None	Left Parish
PUPILS ADMITTED IN 1921						
482	13/12/1915	John L. Bland	William J.	Drinkstone	None	Left
483	05/05/1914	Dorothy J. Gibson	John H.	Drinkstone	None	Attending Hessett
484	11/06/1915	Ethel M. Gibson	John H.	Drinkstone	None	Attending Hessett
485	18/01/1916	George W. Brown	Albert	Drinkstone	None	Left Parish
486	30/12/1911	Edna M. Wordley	George	Drinkstone	Cavendish	Left Parish
487	13/09/1913	Gladys Hart	T....	Drinkstone	Yoxford	Left Parish
488	24/09/1915	Fred H. Palfrey	Fred G.	Drinkstone	Wetherden	Left Parish
489	27/05/1917	Horace G. Palfrey	Fred G.	Drinkstone	None	Left Parish
490		Doris Allen	-	Drinkstone	None	Left Parish
PUPILS ADMITTED IN 1922						
491	01/01/1917	Doris Sturgeon	Charles	Drinkstone	None	
486	30/12/1911	Edna M. Wordley	George	Drinkstone	Cavendish	Left Parish
492	30/03/1919	Philip W. Rose	Philip	Drinkstone	None	Left
493	07/08/1914	Florence L. Taylor	Charles	Drinkstone	Bacton	Left Parish
494	10/07/1917	Frank N. Blake	Samuel P.	Drinkstone	None	Left Parish
495	07/10/1917	Margaret L. Brinkley	Elizabeth	Drinkstone	None	
496	29/07/1917	Matthew A. Gibson	John H.	Drinkstone	None	Gone to Hessett
497	29/05/1910	May W. Goodson	William	Drinkstone	Hepworth	Left Parish
498	04/07/1912	John T. Foggin	Thomas	Drinkstone	Thurston	Left Parish
499	15/01/1914	Thomas F. Anderson	Arthur	Drinkstone	Hampstead	Left Parish
500	09/04/1912	William H. Anderson	Arthur	Drinkstone	Hampstead	Left Parish
501	03/04/1917	Dorothy Allen	Bertie	Drinkstone	Foxearth	Left
PUPILS ADMITTED IN 1923						
502	27/09/1911	Mary S. Lewis	Lewis	Drinkstone	Shellingford	Left Parish
503	27/04/1913	Stephen A. Lewis	Lewis	Drinkstone	Shellingford	Left Parish
504	07/12/1918	Dorothy M. Smith	Albert W.	Drinkstone	None	Left Parish
505	10/04/1918	May Read	Fred G.	Drinkstone	None	Left Parish
506	20/02/1918	Irene Revens	Nepland E.	Drinkstone	None	Gone to Cockfield
507	30/12/1918	George E. Rose	Philip	Drinkstone	None	Left Parish
508	15/04/1918	Douglas H. Bland	William J.	Drinkstone	None	
509	22/11/1915	Henry J. Minns	Richard	Drinkstone	Beyton	Left Parish

ATTENDANCE REGISTER OF DRINKSTONE SCHOOL

	Date of Birth	Name of Child	Name of Parent or Guardian	Home Address	Previous School	Reason for Leaving
510	21/02/1918	Herbert Minns	Richard	Drinkstone	Beyton	Left Parish
511	25/11/1914	Winifred Godfrey	Ernest	Drinkstone	Norton	Left Parish
512	22/03/1916	John B. Godfrey	Ernest	Drinkstone	Norton	Left Parish
513	21/05/1918	Gordon C. Godfrey	Ernest	Drinkstone	Norton	Left Parish
514	11/11/1918	Victor Sturgeon	Charles	Drinkstone	None	Left Parish
515	02/09/1919	Douglas Godfrey	Ernest	Drinkstone	-	Left Parish
516	29/04/1914	Albert A. Bloomfield	George	Drinkstone	Wetherden	Left Parish
PUPILS ADMITTED IN 1924						
517	29/05/1916	James E. Mitchel	James	Drinkstone	-	Left Parish
518	26/01/1919	William F. Dykes	Montague	Drinkstone	None	Left
519	11/02/1919	Frank H. Allen	Bertie	Drinkstone	None	Gone to Hoddeston
520	17/07/1917	Clement Pierce	William	Drinkstone	Mendlesham	Left Parish
521	25/12/1919	Ellen Blake	Samuel P.	Drinkstone	None	Left Parish
522	14/02/1912	William Mortimer	Herbert	Drinkstone	Rattlesden	to Rattlesden
523	06/04/1914	Arthur Mortimer	Herbert	Drinkstone	Rattlesden	to Rattlesden
524	22/05/1919	Donald Sparkes	Montague	Drinkstone	None	Left
525	10/06/1919	Millicent Revens	Nepland	Drinkstone	None	Gone to Cockfield
526	30/04/1919	Douglas Harvey	Bessie	Drinkstone	None	Left
527	24/11/1914	Joyce A. Gardiner	Herbert	Drinkstone	Saxtead	Left Parish
528	03/10/1919	George Mayes	Arthur	Drinkstone	None	Left
529	02/07/1918	Desmond Moyles	David A.	Drinkstone	Haverhill	Gone to Barrow
530	30/10/1920	Evelyn O. James	Charles	Drinkstone	None	Left age 14
PUPILS ADMITTED 1925						
531	04/01/1920	Rodney C. Steadman	Thomas	Drinkstone	None	Gone to Soham
532	26/12/1919	Gladys D. Prike	Alexander	Drinkstone	None	Left
533	04/04/1920	Albert E. Brinkley	(Guardian) F. Powell	Drinkstone	None	Left
534	08/05/1920	Winifred M. Revens	Percy	Drinkstone	None	Left
535	16/09/1920	Marjorie G. Allen	Bertie	Drinkstone	None	to Hoddeston
536	22/05/1921	Victor Sparkes	Montague	Drinkstone	None	Left
537	11/08/1914	Annie R. Kinsey	Robert	Drinkstone	Tattingstone	Left
538	27/11/1920	Emma F. Kinsey	Robert	Drinkstone	Tattingstone	Left Parish
PUPILS ADMITTED IN 1926						
539	02/01/1921	Helena E. Revens	Nepland	Drinkstone	None	Gone to Cockfield
540	26/05/1921	Percy C. Bloomfield	James W.	Drinkstone	None	Left age 14
541	28/06/1921	James N. K. Rose	Philip W.	Drinkstone	None	Left
542	22/05/1920	Emily C. Mitchell	James	Drinkstone	Horndean	Left Parish
543	13/07/1922	Susan M. Bloomfield	James W.	Drinkstone	None	Left
544	24/06/1921	George Dykes	Montague	Drinkstone	None	Left
545	05/07/1919	Esther K. Nash	Frederick	Drinkstone	Great Baddow	Left Parish
PUPILS ADMITTED IN 1927						
546	24/12/1921	Wilfred N. Bland	William J.	Drinkstone	None	Left age 14
547	09/10/1921	Kathleen N. Revens	Percy	Drinkstone	None	Left age 14
527	24/11/1914	Joyce A. Gardiner	Herbert	Drinkstone	Saxtead	to Saxtead
501	03/04/1917	Dorothy Allen	Bertie	Drinkstone	Burnt Fen	to Hoddeston
548	29/06/1920	Cecil J. Taylor	John C.	Drinkstone	Private Tuition	Left
(Following two boys were boarded out from Stowmarket Home with Mrs. Grimwood)						
549	21/04/1915	Frederick Worledge	(Father dead)	Drinkstone	Rattlesden	Left Parish
550	26/04/1921	Albert R. Bennett	(born London)	Drinkstone	None	Left
551	25/06/1922	Francis G. Brinkley	Edward	Drinkstone	None	Left
552	17/08/1922	Frances V. Horsley	E.	Drinkstone	None	Left
553	29/07/1923	Gladys M. Bloomfield	James W.	Drinkstone	None	Left
(from this point, home addresses in Drinkstone are given in detail)						
554	22/05/1922	Hilda Game	-	Marsh Green	-	Left
555	16/09/1916	Phyllis G. Leach	Herbert	Slugs Hall	Brettenham	Left
556	08/09/1918	Elsie B. Leach	Herbert	Slugs Hall	Brettenham	Left
557	10/01/1921	William G. Leach	Herbert	Slugs Hall	Brettenham	Left Parish
558	04/08/1921	Jack Lord	Herbert	Park Cottages	None	Staying in Ixworth
PUPILS ADMITTED IN 1928						
559	08/10/1914	Ethel Leach	Herbert	Slugs Hall	Brettenham	Left
560	.31/12/1920	Mona Caley	Harry	Slugs Hall	Rattlesden	Left Parish
561	08/1922	Kathleen Caley	Harry	Slugs Hall	Rattlesden	Left Parish

	Date of Birth	Name of Child	Name of Parent or Guardian	Home Address	Previous School	Reason for Leaving
562	22/05/1919	Joyce Caley	Harry	Slugs Hall	Rattlesden	Left Parish
563	06/01/1919	Albert Arbon	Bertie	Church Cottages	Woolpit	Left Parish
564	26/02/1921	Eileen Arbon	Bertie	Church Cottages	Woolpit	Left Parish
565	04/02/1923	Jeoffrey Bennett	Jeoffrey	Shop Corner	None	Left
566	12/09.1923	Alexander Hoy	Joseph	Park Cottages	None	Left Parish
567	06/01/1921	Robert Bielley	James	Meadow Cottage	Hull	to Rattlesden
PUPILS ADMITTED IN 1929						
568	23/08/1920	Thelma M. Clover	Daniel	The Mills	Woolpit	Left
569	29/11/1915	Gladys V. Westley	George	Stone Cottage	Gazeley	Left Parish
570	10/04/1921	Phyllis Robinson	Fredk	Meadow Cottage	Yorkshire	Left age 14
571	27/12/1923	Harry Robinson	Fredk	Meadow Cottage	Yorkshire	Left age 14
572	29/11/1924	John Bloomfield	James W.	Drinkstone	None	Left age 14
573	18/06/1922	Ruby G. Rogers		Yew Tree Farm	Rattlesden	Left
574	22/08/1924	Mary S. Brinkley	Edward	Near Chapel	None	Left Parish
575	20/11/1922	Violet Dennis	Robert	Park Cottages	Elvedon	Left
576	21/03/1923	John A. Leach	Herbert	Cross Street	None	Left
PUPILS ADMITTED IN 1930						
577	01/08/1923	Brian H. Cowing	Thomas	Rolandia	Cockfield	Left
578	26/04/1921	Albert Bennett	(Mrs. Grimwood)	The Green	Rattlesden	Left
579	13/10/1919	Lilian I. Whitton	Mrs. Whitton	Cross Street	Stowmarket	Left
580	09/1925	Jean M. Lord	-	Park Cottages	None	Left Parish
581	13/04/1916	George Whitton	Mrs. Whitton	Cross Street	Stowmarket	Left 14
582	27/12/1921	Dorothy E. Brown	Albert	Park Cottages	Bury St. Edmunds	Left
583	27/03/1925	George Moore	Ernest	Park Cottages	Fornham All Saints	to Ipswich
584	03/06/1919	Barry Cowing	Thomas	School House	Bury St.Edmunds	to Canada
585	22/12/1916	Percy Leech	Albert	Stone House	Whelnetham	Living with Aunt
586	28/03/1918	Horace Leech	Albert	Stone House	Whelnetham	Living with Aunt
587	25/05/1920	Gilbert Leech	Albert	Stone House	Whelnetham	Living with Aunt
588	24/06/1913	Victor Leech	Albert	Stone House	Whelnetham	Living with Aunt
589	06/12/1924	Robert Leech	Albert	Stone House	Whelnetham	Living with Aunt
590	20/04/1924	Albert J. Wright	Charles	Park Cottages	Carlton Rode	Left
PUPILS ADMITTED IN 1931						
591	04/03/1926	John Gibson	-	-	None	Left Parish
592	07/01/1926	Daisy Rogers	-	Yew Tree Farm	None	Left age 14
593	18/03/1926	Phyllis Revens	-	-	None	Left age 14
594	08/05/1926	David J. Bloomfield	William	Cross Street	None	Left age 14
595	11/10/1926	Douglas Williamson	-	-	None	Left
596	17/02/1926	Kenneth Sturgeon	-	Gedding Road	None	Left age 14
597	-	Grace Tolhurst	-	-	-	Left
PUPILS ADMITTED IN 1932						
598	18/02/1926	Ethel Robinson	Frederick	Meadow Cottage	None	Left age 14
599	13/03/1927	James Hovells	-	Rattlesden Road	None	to Rattlesden
600	23/04/1928	Arthur Cornish	Guardian Mrs. Buckle	Church Cott.	None	Left 14
601	15/08/1926	Audrey Fabb	-	Gedding Road	None	Left 14
602	14/08/1928	Raymond Waspe	-	Home Farm	None	Left Parish
603	22/09/1928	Leonard Waspe	-	Home Farm	None	Left Parish
PUPILS ADMITTED IN 1933						
604	14/03/1928	Douglas James	-	Rectory Cottage	None	Left Parish
605	06/12/1927	Joyce Leach	Herbert	Cross Street	None	Left age 14
606	06/07/1928	Denis Bloomfield	James	Cross Street	None	to Ingatestone
607	04/09/1928	Frank Sparkes	Montague	Cross Street	None	Left age 14
608	20/06/1928	James Revens	Percy	-	None	Left age 14
609	26/10/1928	Kathleen Brinkley	Edward	Chapel Street	-	Left
610	30/08/1922	Hilda M. Westrup	William	Mead Cottage	Denham	Left
611	02/08/1927	Henry Westrup	William	Mead Cottage	Denham	Left age 14
612	-	Phyllis Johnson	-	Home Farm	-	-
PUPILS ADMITTED IN 1934						
613	29/11/1928	Gilbert Cross	-	Street Farm	Rattlesden	Left
614	20/08/1929	Ivy Bloomfield	James	Cross Street	None	to Ingatestone
615	09/11/1928	Roland J. Bland	John	Bridge Farm	None	

ATTENDANCE REGISTER OF DRINKSTONE SCHOOL

	Date of Birth	Name of Child	Name of Parent or Guardian	Home Address	Previous School	Reason for Leaving
616	19/08/1929	June Cobbold	Felix	Park Cottages	None	Left
PUPILS ADMITTED IN 1935						
617	26/02/1930	Doreen J. Leach	Herbert	Cross Street	-	Left
618	16/11/1929	Raymond Bland	Arthur	Whitefield House	None	
619	06/07/1930	Peggy L. M. Frost	Fred	Cross Street		
620	22/02/1929	Rowena Grimwood	Reginald	The Park	Little Finborough	Left
PUPILS ADMITTED IN 1936						
621	25/12/1927	Robert Brown	Noel	Rolandia	Rougham	to Rattlesden
622	16/04/1927	William Sparkes	Percy	Park Cotts.	Stratford St. Mary	to Barrow
623	27/11/1928	Cecil Sparkes	Percy	Park Cotts.	Stratford St. Mary	Special School
624	26/06/1926	Audrey Tidswell	Fred	Chapel Lane	Bradford	to Woolpit
625	19/12/1930	Gerald Mayes	Reginald	Stone Cottage	-	Left
626	10/03/1931	Mildred R. Westrup	William	Mead Cottage	-	to Elmswell
627	26/10/1928	Lucy Robinson	Frederick	Meadow Cottage		
628	24/04/1931	Fergus W. Kemp	Alfred	Park Cottages		
PUPILS ADMITTED IN 1937						
629	17/11/1931	Alan M. Robinson	Frederick	Meadow Cottage	None	Deceased
630	10/06/1932	Mary E. Brinkley	(Guardian) Mrs. Buckle	Church Cottages		Left
631	17/08/1926	Beatrice M. Kemp	Frank S.	Park Cottages	Acton	to Sussex
632	04/03/1928	Phyllis M. Kemp	Frank S.	Park Cottages	Acton	to Sussex
633	30/04/1931	Violet E. Kemp	Frank S.	Park Cottages	Acton	to Sussex
PUPILS ADMITTED IN 1938						
634	08/07/1934	William Bloomfield	James	Council Houses	None	Left
635	24/11/1932	Edna Leach	Herbert	Council Houses	None	Left
636	19/12/1932	Marjorie E. Lingwood	William	Chapel Lane	Woolpit	Left
637	15/07/1933	Anthony D. Perkins	Victor J.	Park Cottages	None	to Debenham
PUPILS ADMITTED IN 1939						
638	05/04/1934	Derek Cross	-	Street Farm	None	to Woolpit
639	21/12/1933	Charles F. Robinson	Frederick	Council Houses	-	Left age 15
640	06/10/1934	Vivian James	Mrs. Austin	Marsh Green	-	to Woolpit
641	07/11/1934	Gerald E. Squirrell	Oliver G.	Lodge Cottage	-	to Elmswell
642	12.09.1929	Neville Bland	David	Whitefield House	Southampton	to S'hampton
643	13/04/1928	Frederick Chinery	Mrs. Revens	Chapel Lane	E. Dulwich	Dulwich
644	06/03/1930	Ronald Chinery	Mrs. Revens	Chapel Lane	E. Dulwich	to Dulwich
645	16/12/1934	Raymond Underwood	Stanley	Park Cottages	None	to Rattlesden
646	16/05/1932	Thelma Clover	John	Drinkstone Mills	Colchester	to Colchester
647	28/01/1932	Raymond Frost	-	Drinkstone Hall	Woolpit	to Woolpit
PUPILS ADMITTED IN 1940						
648	22/12/1934	Denis Warren	Mrs. Warren	Rattlesden Road	None	
649	26/12/1934	Derek Westrup	Percy W.	Mead Cottage	None	to Tostock
650	09/1936	Peter Stone	James	Rectory Divisional H.Q.	Ormskirk	to Ormskirk
651	03/08/1935	Fred E. Peach	Harold	The Green	None	to Felsham
652	08/01/1930	Barbara Jones	Frederick	The Rectory	Ormskirk	to Ormskirk
653	09/01/1934	Daphne Clark	Frederick	Home Farm	Felixstowe	to Felixstowe
654	03/06/1936	Peter Thurlow	Cecil	Home Farm	None	to Culford School
655	21/10/1935	Geoffrey Challiner	John	Divisional H.Q. Rectory	H.Q. moved	
656	10/10/1936	Beryl Thomas	Sydney	Divisional H.Q. Rectory	H.Q. moved	
646	16/05/1932	Thelma Clover	John	Drinkstone Mills	Colchester	to Colchester
657	1,934	Gerald Rice	-	Street Farm	Wetherden	to Wetherden
PUPILS ADMITTED IN 1941						
658	27/11/1935	Kenneth Bullet	William	Council Houses	-	Left age 15
659	13/07/1938	Pamela Lingwood	William	Chapel Lane	-	Left
660	26/04/1934	Albert Daltrey	William	School House	Norton	to Norton
661	25/08/1935	Kenneth Daltrey	William	School House	Norton	to Norton
662	06/04/1932	Olive Stott	James	Turtles Cotts. Woolpit Rd.	Stowmarket	to Essex
663	12/09/1936	Veronica M. Kemp	Alfred	Park Cottages	None	

	Date of Birth	Name of Child	Name of Parent or Guardian	Home Address	Previous School	Reason for Leaving
664	30/05/1933	Thomas Greens	Mrs. Buckle	Church Cotts	Bethnal Green	
665	12/12/1936	Joan Robinson	Frederick	Council Houses	None	Left age 15
666	09/09/1931	Donald MacKenzie	Charles	Gedding Road	LCC Party	Dagenham
667	05/02/1934	Edward MacKenzie	Charles	Gedding Road	LCC Party	Dagenham
668	01/08/1931	Joan Harbour	-	Chapel Lane	LCC Party	to Bethnal Green
669	23/09/1930	Florence Hill	William	Chapel Lane Corner	LCC	to Bethnal Green
670	17/06/1932	Irene Hill	William	Chapel Lane Corner	LCC Party	Bethnal Green
671	22/12/1931	Ellen Poulteney	-	Chapel Cotts	LCC Party	returned to London
672	15/08/1935	Marie Poulteney	-	Chapel Cotts	LCC Party	returned to London
673	11/09/1932	Betty Shand	-	2, Council Houses	-	returned Bethnal Green
674	17/08/1932	Joyce Whitmore	Edward	Chapel Lane	LCC Party	to London E2
675	10/05/1934	Gladys Whitmore	Edward	Chapel Lane	LCC Party	to London E2
676	07/09/1935	Shirley Steadman	-	Chapel Cottages	LCC Party	to London E2
677	19/07/1929	David Harbour	-	Whitefield House	-	returned to London
678	01/09/1929	Frederick Whitmore	-	Chapel Lane	LCC Party	to London E2
679	02/05/1933	Stanley Hall	-	Cambourne House	LCC Party	to London E2
680	28/08/1935	Bernard Perkins	-	Meadow Cottages	LCC Party	gone to London
PUPILS ADMITTED IN 1942						
681	29/05/1934	William Ottewell	(Mrs.Smith)	Church Cotts	Birmingham Forest Gate	
682	03/10/1935	Pearl I. Ottewell	(Mrs.Smith)	Church Cotts	Birmingham Forest Gate	
683	01/03/1937	David C. Smith	Victor	Drinkstone	LCC Party	returned to London
684	23/03/1936	Joyce Herron	William	Shop Corner	LCC Party	returned London
655	21/10/1935	Geoffrey Challinor	John	School House	Sonning on Thames	
685	05/03/1937	Michael T. Smith	Thomas	Council Houses	None	Left age 15
686	20/09/1937	Joyce M. Levett	-	Church Cottages	None	
687	02/09/1938	Peter Welham	Maurice	1, Council Houses	Ipswich	to Ipswich
688	05/06/1937	William H. Snell	-	The Cherry Tree	Ipswich	returned Ipswich
689	26/06/1933	Victor M. Smith	Arthur	Bury Road	Chevington	to Cockfield
671	22/12/1931	Ellen Poulteney	-	Chapel Cotts	LCC	returned Bethnal Green
672	15/08/1935	Marie Poulteney	-	Chapel Cotts	LCC	returned Bethnal Green
690	29/03/1933	Eric W. Robinson	William	1 Council Houses	Elmswell	to Elmswell
691	15/01/1935	Doreen Robinson	William	1 Council Houses	Elmswell	to Elmswell
692	21/11/1937	Mary Robinson	William	1 Council Houses	Elmswell	to Elmswell
693	07/07/1931	George A. Grew	John	-	Tostock	returned Bethnal Green
694	20/01/1930	David W. Parker	James	Meadow Cott.	Poplar, London	to London
PUPILS ADMITTED IN 1943						
695	13/02/1935	Donald A. Scates	Arthur	Park Cottages	-	to Wetheringsett
696	22/02/1936	Alfred W. Scates	Arthur	Park Cottages	-	to Wetheringsett
697	25/05/1938	Rosemary Winsall	George	School House	-	to Buckinghamshire
698	07/12/1930	John Graham	John	Post Office Cotts	LCC Dagenham	to Stowmarket
699	31/12/1933	George Doherty	George	Cambourne Farm		to Rattlesden
700	18/05/1937	Mary R.Doherty	George	Cambourne Farm		to Rattlesden
701	21/12/1938	Kathleen Doherty	George	Cambourne Farm		to Rattlesden
702	18/11/1932	William Doherty	George	Cambourne Farm		to Rattlesden
703	23/03/1936	Joyce Heron	William	Shop Corner	LCC	to London
704	09/05/1938	William Heron	William	Shop Corner	LCC	to London
705	29/06/1933	Edith Howard	-	The Bungalow	Ashfield	to Ashfield
706	08/07/1938	Marjorie Underwood	Stanley	Park Cotts	-	to Norfolk
707	22/07/1938	Betty Smith	Thomas	Council Houses		
708	30/06/1938	Gerald Emmett	Frank	Gedding Road		transferred to Rattlesden
PUPILS ADMITTED IN 1944						
709		Josephine Smith	-	Council Houses	Bury St. Edmunds	Left
710	13/08/1938	Robert H. Brown	Albert	Tudor Cottage	-	Left
711	21/09/1938	Dorothy Perkins	-	Shop Corner		returned to Poplar, London
712	20/03/1938	Gordon Maill	Frank			to Sunbury on Thames
713	25/04/1940	Anthony Lingwood	William	Chapel Lane	–	transferred Rattlesden

	Date of Birth	Name of Child	Name of Parent or Guardian	Home Address	Previous School	Reason for Leaving
714	23/10/1931	Helen Newdick	Fred	Gedding Road	Left age 15	
715	23/07/1933	Stephen Newdick	Fred	Gedding Road		
716	03/01/1932	Molly R. Cotton	John	Post Office Cotts		gone to Croydon
717	31/08/1933	John Cotton	John	Post Office Cottages		to Croydon
718	07/02/1938	Michael Cotton	John	Post Office Cottages		to Croydon
719	07/11/1939	Robert Cotton	John	Post Office Cottages		to Croydon
720	16/05/1939	Pauline Squirrel	Oliver	Lodge Cottage		
721	07/09/1935	Shirley Steadman	-	Drinkstone		
722	25/03/1939	John Read	-	Turtle Cottage		
723	03/02/1938	Doreen Blaydon	-	Thompson's Cottages		returned to Wandsworth
724	19/02/1937	John Blaydon	-	Thompson's Cotts		to Wandsworth
725	19/02/1937	Joan Blaydon	-	Thompson's Cotts		to Wandsworth
726	06/11/1933	Leonard Blaydon	-	Thompson's Cotts		to Wandsworth
727	26/08/1936	Terence Pitts	-	Chapel Cottages		returned to Tottenham
728	09/12/1934	Barbara Pitts	-	Chapel Cottages		to Tottenham
729	09/08/1933	Pamela Pitts	-	Chapel Cottages		to Tottenham
730	02/01/1932	Nellie Pitts	-	Chapel Cottages		to Tottenham
731	09/03/1935	George Baldwin	George	Thompson's Cottages		returned to Battersea
732	26/05/1936	Donald Chaplin	-	Bury Road	Dagenham	
733	01/11/1931	Ida Steadman	-	Shop Corner	Battersea	returned to Battersea
734	21/09/1939	Audrey Scates	-	Park Cottages	-	gone to Wetheringsett
735	19/04/1939	Peter Newdick	-	Gedding Road	-	to B.S.E. Grammar School
736	09/05/1939	James Stott	James	Turtle Cottages	-	to Beyton Sec. Modern
PUPILS ADMITTED IN 1945						
737	18/11/1939	Alan Bradley	Herbert	Council Cottages	-	to Beyton Sec. Modern
738	19/11/1935	Kenneth Pollard	Samuel	Church Cottages		gone to Rougham
739	10/09/1939	Kenneth Holloway	David	Chapel Cottages	Botesdale	to London
740	07/12/1937	David Holloway	David	Chapel Cottages	Botesdale	to London
741	31/10/1939	Judy Gray	Guardian Miss Stiff, Norton	Norton	to Norton	
742	19/05/1936	Phylis Rands	-	Park Cottages	Burstall	
743	03/07/1937	Margaret Rands	-	Park Cottages	Burstall	
744	15/11/1939	Sylvia Rands	-	Park Cottages	Burstall	
745	21/05/1940	Philip Donaghy	Philip	The Street	-	to B.S.E. Catholic Sch.
746	09/10/1940	Brian L. Smith	Albert	Turtle Cottages		
747	14/07/1940	Peter J. Cooper	Cecil	Rattlesden Road		
748	04/07/1940	Lilian R. Perkins	-	Shop Corner		
749		Winifred Marshall	-	Church Cottages	Dublin	
750		Shirley Marshall	-	Church Cottages	Dublin	
751	16/08/1932	Jean Price	Charles	-	Barnham	Leaving Age
752	15/10/1934	Brenda Price	Charles	-	Barnham	to Chippenham
753	13/11/1935	Wendy Dunnett	-	-	Norton	to Silver Jubilee Sch. B.S.E.
754	17/11/1935	Evelyn Austin	Charles A.	Meadow Cottage	Norton	to B.S.E.
755	06/02/1937	Brenda Austin	Charles A.	Meadow Cottage	Norton	to B.S.E.
756	01/02/1936	Patricia Austin	Charles A.	Meadow Cottage	Norton	to B.S.E.
757	05/06/1934	June Rice	-	Church Cottages	Woolpit	Left
758	09/07/1940	Petunia Whitton	William	Drinkstone		to Beyton Sec. Mod.
PUPILS ADMITTED IN 1946						
759	09/10/1939	Cyril King	-	Meadow Cottage	-	Left – Woolpit
760	10/04/1941	Kenneth King	-	Meadow Cottage	-	Left – Woolpit
761	27/12/1938	Doreen Boreham	Arthur	Rectory Lodge	Horringer	Beyton Sec. Mod.
762	17/09/1936	Russell Leach	Victor	Chapel Lane	-	to Clopton
763	25/08/1938	Audrey Moss	-	Lodge Cottage	Woodbridge	to Newmarket
764	31/08/1933	John Cotton	John	Church Cottages	Surrey	to Bury St. Eds.

	Date of Birth	Name of Child	Name of Parent or Guardian	Home Address	Previous School	Reason for Leaving
765	07/02/1938	Michael Cotton	John	Church Cottages	Surrey	to Bury St. Eds.
766	07/11/1939	Robert Cotton	John	Church Cottages	Surrey	to Bury St. Eds.
767	07/08/1941	Margaret Bradley	Herbert	1, Council Ho.	-	to Beyton S.Mod.
768	02/09/1942	John G. Pollard	Mrs. Pollard	Church Cotts.	-	to Rougham
769	05/05/1942	Edna Whitton	William	Church Cottages		to Beyton Sec.Mod.
PUPILS ADMITTED IN 1947						
770	24/12/1941	Sheila Sparkes	-	Marsh Green		to Beyton Sec.Mod.
771	19/01/1942	John Donaghy	-	Post Office Cottages		to R.C.School,Bury
772	25/03/1935	Mary Cox	Edward	Hazel Cottage		
773	19/05/1937	Hilda Cox	Edward	Hazel Cottage		
774	19/08/1936	Brian Cocksedge	John	23 Council Ho.	Hessett	Left age 15
775	02/02/1938	Michael Cocksedge	John	23 Council Ho.	Hessett	to Rattlesden
776	25/03/1939	Judith Cocksedge	John	23 Council Ho.	Hessett	Beyton Sec.Mod.
777	13/11/1941	Valerie Cocksedge		23 Council Ho.	Hessett	Beyton Sec.Mod.
778	30/09/1940	Jean Cocksedge	John	23 Council Ho.	Hessett	Beyton Sec.Mod.
779	10/09/1939	Anne K. Sturgeon	Harold	11 Council Ho.	-	Beyton Sec.Mod.
780	07/07/1942	Keith Sturgeon	Horace	21 Council Ho.	Rattlesden	Beyton Sec.Mod.
781	13/01/1943	Dorothy Bradley	-	1 Council Ho.	-	Beyton Sec.Mod.
782	05/07/1943	David Young	Sidney	Grocer's Shop	-	gone to Thurston
783	29/10/1933	Elsie M. Nunn	Frederick	Turtle Cotts	-	Left age 15
784	21/09/1935	Arthur Nunn	Frederick	Turtle Cotts	-	Left age 15
785	28/01/1938	Rosemary Nunn	Frederick	Turtle Cotts	-	Beyton Sec.Mod.
786	03/07/1941	Dorothy Nunn	Frederick	Turtle Cotts	-	Beyton Sec.Mod.
787	30/06/1938	Gerald Emmett	Frank	Gedding Road	Norton	transf. to Rattlesden
788	01/10/1943	Hazel L. Lingwood	-	Chapel Lane	-	Beyton Sec. Mod.
789	25/09/1937	Daphne Shave	-	Park Cottages	-	Left Parish
PUPILS ADMITTED IN 1948						
790	29/11/1933	Michael C.Shave	-	Park Cottages	-	Left age 15
791	22/12/1943	Robert J. Nunn	-	Turtle Cottage	-	Beyton Sec.Mod.
792	25/01/1943	Derek P. Smith	-	9 Council Ho.	-	Beyton Sec. Mod.
793	08/11/1943	Cecily M. Levett	-	12 Council Ho.	-	Beyton Sec.Mod.
794	30/09/1943	Moira E. Donaghy	-	19 Council Ho.	-	to Bury R.C. School
795	30/09/1943	Michael G. Donaghy	-	19 Council Ho.	-	to Bury R.C. School
796	28/04/1944	William H. Mortimer	-	7 Council Ho.	-	left to go home
797	21/06/1943	Anthony P. Mortimer	-	7 Council Ho.	-	left to go home
798	18/04/1938	Yvonne M. Mulley	-	Church Close	-	left for Woolpit
PUPILS ADMITTED IN 1949						
799	17/03/1940	Terence R. Stiff	-	Gedding Corner	-	left to go home
800	06/01/1944	Michael Palmer	Guardian Mrs. Mayes	17 Council Ho.		To Norfolk
801	01/12/1943	Charles Sturgeon	-	11 Chapel Road	-	to Beyton Sec.Mod.
802	02/09/1941	Gillian D. Hurrell	-	The Lodge Cottage	-	gone to Clacton
803	15/09/1944	George R. Whitton	-	13 Council Ho.	-	gone to Beyton
804	01/04/1945	David C. Nunn	-	Turtle Cottages	-	gone to Ixworth

ADMISSION REGISTER for period 1949 – 1986

There was a second Admissions Register in use for these last years of the School, but sadly its whereabouts are unknown. If any reader happens to find it PLEASE deliver it to Suffolk Record Office so it may be re-united with other documents!

Sheila Wright
(Photo by Graham Sessions)

ABOUT THE AUTHOR

SHEILA WRIGHT M.A. (née Jones) was born in 1939. Educated at Wyggeston School in Leicester, Bretton Hall in Yorkshire and the U.E.A. in Norwich, she taught in many village schools (almost half of them Church of England Controlled Schools), first in Hertfordshire, then in Suffolk. She is married to Ron, a music teacher and band master.

Sheila is a Lay Reader in the Church of Egland. Her hobbies include music, drawing and painting, gardening, keeping poultry, escapism in the French countryside, and enjoying the company of her children and twelve grandchildren.

Published by Léonie Press as one of its many titles on the experiences of British homeowners in France:

BON COURAGE, MES AMIS!

Thoughts on restoring a rural ruin
Written and illustrated by
SHEILA WRIGHT

In 1994, primary school teacher Sheila Wright suddenly had the means to buy a house in the Creuse department of France but the amount of her legacy meant that she was looking at "the bottom end of the market". She found herself falling ridiculously in love with a very old stone house which had been abandoned for years and had an alarming 20ft crack up the front.

As she looked round, the smell of damp stone and ancient dust was all-pervading. In the gloom, shadowy alcoves and battered wood frames were barely visible on the rough granite walls. Mysterious bits of string dangled from the immense beams above, and between these beams were dark, narrow boards through which light filtered where rain had rotted them away.

One wall of the room was taken up by a vast fireplace with a huge hearthstone. Up the wide chimney, past various sinister blackened iron hooks, a patch of bright blue sky was visible. The wall separating the adjacent cellar-like room from the adjoining barn had crumbled and fallen, covering the earth floor with tons of loose granite. The jagged top was now only five feet high and over this, the neighbouring cart bay, cow shed and stable were all visible.

From these inauspicious beginnings, Sheila and her family worked hard to create a habitable holiday home full of happiness, music and peace. Along the way she developed a passion for building with stone, constructing two granite staircases herself over a five-year period. French neighbours seeing the Wrights tackle the enormous task fervently wished them *"bon courage"* which could perhaps be loosely translated as "Good luck – you'll need it!"

This book traces the story of the ongoing restoration in a series of chapters giving Sheila's thoughts on many other aspects of Creusoise life and her own experiences in France.

ISBN 1 901253 30 9   184pp, A5, numerous illustrations   Price £8.99
For more information visit www.leoniepress.com